Relational Savoring is truly rev[...] both narrative accounts and research evidence that an explicit focus on positive aspects of relationships can enhance thriving, even for those who have not had a large share of such. Via vivid first-person narratives and a careful review of research—all based on attachment theory—Borelli makes a convincing (and moving) case. Among other features, this book shows that early trauma is not a blueprint for later-life suffering. In fact, despite far too much "doom and gloom" coverage these days on the supposedly permanent effects of early maltreatment, a sensitive focus on interactions that were truly validating can help to turn the tide.

—**Stephen P. Hinshaw, PhD,** Distinguished Professor of Psychology, University of California, Berkeley; author of *Another Kind of Madness: A Journey Through the Stigma and Hope of Mental Illness*

This wise and very readable book offers new and experienced clinicians a fresh, practical, and very useful perspective to overcome blocks in the therapeutic process and promote emotional growth. Jessica Borelli is a gifted clinician and rigorous researcher whose relational savoring approach offers hope, joy, and supportive avenues to self-understanding. Intervention strategies are described clearly, easy to implement, and effective. The book is a pleasure to read. I strongly recommend it as a very valuable professional and personal resource.

—**Alicia F. Lieberman, PhD,** Irving B. Harris Endowed Chair in Infant Mental Health and Professor, Department of Psychiatry and Behavioral Sciences, University of California, San Francisco, and Director, Child Trauma Research Program, San Francisco General Hospital, San Francisco, CA

Jessica Borelli has crafted a brilliant and important book, filled with deep insights into the conceptual underpinnings, clinical applications, and psychosocial benefits of relational savoring. The text is a rich tapestry that blends enlightening case material, foundational attachment theory, compelling research studies, and astute observation in highly creative, intellectually stimulating, and clinically useful ways. I strongly recommend this groundbreaking book to scholars, practitioners, and students alike—for truly there is something invaluable here for everyone.

—**Fred B. Bryant, PhD,** Emeritus Professor of Psychology, Loyola University Chicago, Chicago, IL

In this beautifully written and immensely readable book, Jessica Borelli describes her groundbreaking approach to cultivating positive relational memories and using them to promote healing and integration. Applicable to work in a variety of clinical settings, and with a wide array of populations (adults, children, parents, couples), relational savoring complements a range of other evidence-based approaches to transforming suffering and building lasting, sustaining relationships.

—**Arietta Slade, PhD,** Professor of Clinical Child Psychology, Yale Child Study Center, New Haven, CT

Relational Savoring

Relational Savoring

Using Guided Reflection to Strengthen Relationships
and Improve Outcomes in Therapy

Jessica L. Borelli

 AMERICAN PSYCHOLOGICAL ASSOCIATION

Copyright © 2024 by the American Psychological Association. All rights reserved. Except as permitted under the United States Copyright Act of 1976, no part of this publication may be reproduced or distributed in any form or by any means, including, but not limited to, the process of scanning and digitization, or stored in a database or retrieval system, without the prior written permission of the publisher.

The opinions and statements published are the responsibility of the author, and such opinions and statements do not necessarily represent the policies of the American Psychological Association.

Published by
American Psychological Association
750 First Street, NE
Washington, DC 20002
https://www.apa.org

Order Department
https://www.apa.org/pubs/books
order@apa.org

Typeset in Charter and Interstate by Circle Graphics, Inc., Reisterstown, MD

Printer: Sheridan Books, Chelsea, MI
Cover Designer: Anthony Paular Design, Newbury Park, CA
Cover Art: Photo by Maxim Hopman on Unsplash

Library of Congress Cataloging-in-Publication Data

Names: Borelli, Jessica L., author.
Title: Relational savoring : using guided reflection to strengthen relationships and improve outcomes in therapy / Jessica L. Borelli.
Description: Washington, DC : American Psychological Association, [2024] | Includes bibliographical references and index.
Identifiers: LCCN 2023021064 (print) | LCCN 2023021065 (ebook) | ISBN 9781433840678 (paperback) | ISBN 9781433840685 (ebook)
Subjects: LCSH: Interpersonal relations--Psychological aspects. | Psychotherapy. | BISAC: PSYCHOLOGY / Psychotherapy / Counseling | PSYCHOLOGY / Clinical Psychology
Classification: LCC BF724.3.I58 B66 2023 (print) | LCC BF724.3.I58 (ebook) | DDC 158.2--dc23/eng/20230802
LC record available at https://lccn.loc.gov/2023021064
LC ebook record available at https://lccn.loc.gov/2023021065

https://doi.org/10.1037/0000372-000

Printed in the United States of America

10 9 8 7 6 5 4 3 2 1

*To Dale, Sam, Charlie, and Talia,
who give me endless memories to savor.*

Contents

Acknowledgments ix

1. Overview of Relational Savoring 3

I. THEORETICAL AND EMPIRICAL SUPPORT 15

2. Theoretical Principles Underlying Relational Savoring 17
3. Evidence Base for Relational Savoring 35

II. THE HOW-TO OF RELATIONAL SAVORING 75

4. Phase 1: Memory Selection 77
5. Phase 2: Memory Reflection 105
6. Addressing General Areas of Difficulty and Clinical Techniques to Circumvent Them 145

III. RELATIONAL SAVORING IN CLINICAL CONTEXT 167

7. Tailoring Your Relational Savoring Intervention to Your Individual Client 169
8. Adapting Relational Savoring for Individuals With Specific Mental Health Concerns 195
9. Relational Savoring in Couples and Families 219
10. The Cultural Congruence of Relational Savoring and Partnering With Community Agencies to Heighten It 257

Afterword: Relational Savoring for Therapists 285

References	*291*
Index	*323*
About the Author	*329*

Acknowledgments

This book is the culmination of years of collaborative work: It represents so many people's creativity, energy, and hard work. Dave Sbarra first nurtured my idea and worked to breathe life into it. I am indebted to my colleagues at Pomona College (Pat Smiley, Maggie Kerr, Hannah Rasmussen, Gerin Gaskin, Kathy Buttitta, Sarah Ruiz, Jes Snavely, John Coffey), whose intellectual contributions, hard work, and passion helped move this work from a vision into a reality. Since I moved to UC Irvine 7 years ago, I have worked closely with my community partner, Latino Health Access, to codevelop an intervention that involves relational savoring. Through this partnership, I've learned more than I've taught, in particular from Francisca (Nena) Leal, Rosy DePrado, Gloria Montiel, Nancy Mejia, Patricia Cantero, Gina Torres, and America Bracho, as well as from Nancy Guerra, who guided me through this journey.

Lifelong gratitude to my mentors who set me on my career path: Ann Kring, Joe Campos, Alicia Lieberman, Mary Main, Steve Hinshaw, Phil Cowan, Nancy Suchman, and Linda Mayes. The two anonymous reviewers who provided feedback on the manuscript should be included as coauthors, so helpful was their input.

Bountiful thanks to my editors from APA. Susan Reynolds encouraged me and helped me shape a seedling idea into a book. Further, the text you read here is vastly improved by Beth Hatch's and Joe Albrecht's detail-orientation and patience.

Finally, to the families who have contributed their stories to these pages, thank you. You (and my family) continue to be my greatest teachers. Thanks for letting me listen.

Relational Savoring

1 OVERVIEW OF RELATIONAL SAVORING

Some people already have this magic inside of them—like Jayden, a 16-year-old teenager I have been seeing for several months for depression and anxiety.[1] She's sitting in front of me now. I haven't seen her for a few weeks (she and I had both been traveling during the summer holiday), but now she's snuggled up on my office couch with her legs propped up in front of her, wrapped in a beige Afghan blanket, her fingers twirling the loose ends nervously. She tells me she has been crying on and off throughout the day and she cannot quite put her finger on why. In exploring the feelings that come up for her throughout the day, she stumbles on an explanation that is so poignant it makes me want to cry:

> It's like there is this silent red light that is constantly going off in my brain, all of the time, every minute of every day. It's distracting and irritating, but not painful. It's going off constantly—it's there all of the time, blinking basically anytime. Except when I'm with my mom or my boyfriend. And all of the sudden, when I'm with them, it quiets. It stops completely, and the world around me becomes calm.

---

[1] All case study material in this book is used with client/participant permission or is fictionalized, uses composites, or has been altered by changing names and disguising identifying information for the purpose of preserving client confidentiality.

https://doi.org/10.1037/0000372-001
Relational Savoring: Using Guided Reflection to Strengthen Relationships and Improve Outcomes in Therapy, by J. L. Borelli
Copyright © 2024 by the American Psychological Association. All rights reserved.

My eyes widen and my eyebrows raise as I take in a deep breath and lean forward. "Keep going," I say. "I want to hear more about what this feels like when you see your boyfriend or your mom." Jayden leans forward almost imperceptibly, saying slowly,

> It's almost like I didn't even know that red light was flashing until I'm with them, and then just like that I can feel the difference. It feels so good. It's so much more peaceful without that stupid light flashing in my brain all of the time and distracting me. And with them, it just feels soft and calm and quiet. I can exhale. When I'm sad, I just think about them and how calm and comforted I feel when I'm with them.

Without knowing anything about attachment or relational savoring, Jayden knows it all.

There are many Jaydens out there, people who engage in relational savoring naturally, without prompting. They reach for this strategy instinctively—perhaps they know in their bones that it helps them or maybe they just follow what feels good to them. Then they return to this place in their mind habitually when they are struggling. Like a plant growing toward the light, some people naturally reach for the nourishment that relationships provide when they are hurting. This is the medicine that relational savoring seeks to bottle, the natural healing that many already know about but others cannot access, despite trying their hardest.

Instead, others fumble around in the dark, trying strategy after strategy to improve their mood, reduce their anxiety, and change their relationships, but these strategies are ultimately unsuccessful. Being unsuccessful in changing their situation further convinces the person that they are incapable of changing, which reifies their world beliefs. As a therapist, I come across these clients again and again: clients who travel down the same road themselves, a road that leads nowhere, and clients who want to take the therapist down this road and are difficult to redirect down a different road.

But David was *not* one of those clients, despite what I initially thought. David, a 20-year-old Latino man, had been coming to see me for a month. At his intake session, he told me he wanted help opening up because being so closed off was hurting him in dating relationships. He thought his difficulty opening up might have stemmed from the fact that his father suddenly left when he was 8. However, since this initial conversation in which he shared this information, he was unable (or unwilling?) to speak about anything personal with any kind of depth or emotion—even getting him to provide yes or no answers was like pulling teeth and made me worry I was never going to see him again. If I tried to get him to talk about his feelings or even his likes and dislikes, we entered into a grueling match of the "ask and answer" game, in which we got to see who could sweat it out longer. I kept having to remind myself that it was David's choice to come to therapy in the first place—he hadn't been forced by me or a parent or someone else—to work on some of these things.

I was completely stuck with David, and moments like these left me wondering whether there was a better way to get some traction with my clients. I felt myself wanting to deepen the work, wanting to loosen something that was blocking them from accessing a part of themselves that was walled off somehow. It's as if I knew where I wanted to get, but I just didn't know how to get there. I kept visualizing myself walking down a dark hallway, opening door after door, searching for the door to the room that held these most vulnerable, protected feelings, the ones that David was not ready to feel or express in my presence. Where was that damn door? Did it reside in this painful memory, or could it be in another place? I couldn't seem to find it anywhere, and the harder I worked to find it, the more stuck I became.

But sometimes I am wise enough to listen to the wisdom of my clients, to pay attention to what they teach me, and to be open to receiving their messages. I was still knocking at one of the other doors when David graciously opened the correct door for me, and then walked right in after me. He started talking about something that on the surface seemed completely irrelevant to this whole question of vulnerable, core pain, to the reasons he was held back from being open and honest in his relationships. During one of our sessions, David launched into a story:

> There was a time when I was younger that had surprised me, when I felt something different from the way I normally felt. I had a neighbor during my childhood, this wonderful older woman who lived a couple of doors down—she would welcome me into her home, play music for me, make me snacks, and read books to me. What I remember most is the way she would listen when I talked—so intently, as though every word mattered. She would sit there gripping her cup of tea and hang on each word as though I were someone really important. She remembered things about me—the singers and the baseball players I liked, even the names of the Dragon Ball Z characters I liked to draw, things my mother never learned about me—and suddenly I realized that her house felt more like home than my house. The way she listened to me made me feel known and understood. And safe.

I had to take a deep breath at this moment, and quietly, to not disturb his flow, because this was David—remember, David, the client who wouldn't string two words together let alone a feeling word with a personal pronoun. This person was now sitting here in front of me using words like "understood" and "safe." I was so dumbfounded it took every ounce of self-control I could muster to prevent my jaw from physically dropping down. He continued:

"She seemed to take in every part of me and really see me, and what's more, she not only saw it, but she really appreciated it. And that meant something to me in a deep way." And at that moment, a tear rolled down David's cheek. By this point, gratefully, my therapeutic wits had returned to me, and I was able to meet him where he was, my feelings rising inside of me like an ocean wave. He continued:

> I never forgot that feeling—of being understood and really seen in a way that is naked and also loving at the same time. I never forgot what it felt like because I never got it from either of my parents, and that really, really hurt. The people who should have been looking at me that way, and listening to me that way, wanting to know everything about me and soak me in just like she did so they could love up every part of me—they didn't. They wanted me to be quiet so they could listen to what they wanted to listen to. They wanted me to be who they wanted me to be. But she, she really took me in just as I was.

In that instant, I realized that David had led me to the room where those vulnerable feelings lived (feelings of being cherished, understood, accepted, loved, and seen, as well as feelings of being hurt, rejected, ignored, misunderstood, and judged). I also realized that we could arrive in this room by following these kinds of memories, the kind where we remember being loved, cherished, and protected by an adult who took tender and special care of us. Whereas I had been dead set on looking for these feelings at the end of the hallway of experiences of hurt, rejection, and pain, I now understood that I could arrive at them through a different sort of pathway, and this opened up a whole new world of possibility to me. And just like that, David had shown me a different way of accessing vulnerable feelings.

I decided to use this technique that David had introduced me to with another client, Tanya, wondering if David was onto something that would work for someone other than him. I had been working with Tanya, a 47-year-old biracial woman, for several months on her persistent depression and relationship difficulties. She was divorced and unhappy with her coparenting agreement, felt dissatisfied with various aspects of her work and home life, and struggled with aspects of parenting and dating. Tanya wanted to spend most of her time in therapy talking about her anger and frustration at her ex-husband, particularly regarding the way their marriage had ended, but after several of these conversations in which no new insights were revealed and no behaviors changed, I quickly became convinced that this was a road to nowhere, at least nowhere good. There were only so many times I could hear about the way he packed his bag when he left—the belongings he brought with him and those he didn't—without being able to get to a deeper level of understanding and feelings with her before I was pretty sure we had traversed the same road enough times. So, although the circumstances with Tanya were different, the underlying dynamic—walking the same road and getting nowhere (in other words, repeating problems without touching the emotion underneath)—was similar.

During my next session with Tanya, I decided to gently lead her toward thinking about a positive moment of connectedness. With Tanya, I found this to be a bit more challenging, as her style was a bit different from David's (whereas David had trouble focusing on anything emotional at all, Tanya had trouble disengaging from negative topics). But I found that although Tanya was not able to identify a time when she felt safe or secure anytime around her divorce (in terms of that time of her life), she was able to recall with fondness the way her ex-husband had made her feel at the beginning of their relationship—understood, seen, and special—in a way that was different from how the men she had dated before had made her feel.

At first, I was a bit uneasy discussing this positive aspect of her relationship with her ex, worried it could easily spill over into grief or feelings of loss that I would not be able to contain, especially given the history I had with Tanya of not being able to contain many of her negative emotions. However, she quickly became immersed in describing a time early in their dating relationship when she felt truly seen by him—a time when she was sharing something deeply personal about her feelings regarding her upbringing with him and he listened and asked her questions, not presuming to know or understand where she was coming from but eager to learn from her nonetheless. She described how she felt with him, how this affected her and her development—making her more confident in her relationships and her career. As she was talking, she paused, caught her breath, and said,

> I realize now why I'm so angry at him. He hurt me so much because he made me trust him so deeply. How could someone I trusted so much hurt me so badly? How could he leave me in the dust after he made me love him, and love myself so much?

We paused together and spent time processing a new aspect of her grief and anger. This time, the anger processing felt productive because it was rooted in what she had lost and in the betrayal she felt. This was the first relationship in her life in which she had experienced this kind of respect, love, and safety, and then he had hurt her. By focusing on the experiences of safety she had with her ex, we opened up her feelings of loss.

WHAT IS RELATIONAL SAVORING?

Relational savoring was born out of clinical experience, as so many good ideas are. David led me straight to it. He led me there when the way I was trying to lead him to access his feelings was not working. Thankfully, I was listening to David and willing to follow his lead. Relational savoring is premised on the idea that embedded in most people's daily lives are moments of positive connectedness. These moments can provide significant psychological benefits, yet it is easy to let these positive moments pass us by, especially if they are not consistent with how we view the world and relationships. Bowlby's (1973) attachment theory holds that the quality of early interactions with caregivers shapes the development of people's internal working models of attachment. These internal working models influence how people filter their future interactions through their attention, causing them to view certain information as relevant, important, and consistent with their experiences and other information as irrelevant, unimportant, and inconsistent with their experiences. Relational savoring helps to retrain attention to focus on moments of positive connectedness so we can benefit from the good that already exists in our lives.

Relational savoring is a guided intervention that involves helping the client to become immersed in an experience of positive connection with another person and to deeply attend to the felt emotions, thoughts, and significance associated with these experiences. It involves two phases: (1) a memory selection phase, in which the therapist helps clients identify times when they felt connected to another person; and (2) a memory reflection stage, when the therapist assists the client in deeply reflecting on and making meaning of those memories.

Relational savoring typically lasts between 30 and 40 minutes, and while it can be a standalone intervention (and has been tested in the research laboratory as such), it is more commonly used in clinical practice in conjunction with other interventions. By helping the client notice and expand upon the emotion they experience during moments of positive connection with others, we can make significant alterations in the way clients view themselves and their relationships. As I discuss further in this book, the types of experiences that are ideal for savoring are close, connected experiences occurring within attachment relationships—yet ones that have not been attended to by the client. Engaging in this type of exercise with clients has the potential to change the tone of the conversation and deepen the emotional processing.

Last week, I was working with a client who was describing a series of upsetting events that had happened to her. She is in the midst of dealing with a medical concern and was busily running through a list of anxiety-provoking, distressing, and depressing things that had occurred. As she told me about these events, she was tearing apart a tissue she held in her hands, the discarded pieces falling by the seams of her pants. But embedded in this long list of harrowing events, there was a lovely moment that had unfolded: During a particularly challenging medical appointment, her physician had held her hand, looked her in the eye, and told her that he would be with her every step of the way throughout her illness.

In the retelling of this event, my client gave this experience very little airtime, although she did say it was "nice" and that it made her feel "understood" and "held." But she quickly jetted past this to the retelling of the next anxiety-provoking event. I stopped her midsentence and had her focus on the moment with her physician, really helping her to slow down and deeply process the experience of being in that moment with him: "Let's pause and I want you to try to feel again what it felt like when your physician said those words to you. . . . Where did you feel that in your body? . . . Can you feel it now?" I also encouraged her to examine the meaning and significance of the memory for her. During such a stressful moment in her life, what was it like to be understood and held by her treatment provider? Her hands, which just a moment before were tearing that poor tissue to shreds, fell into her lap, and tears began to fall from her eyes as she exhaled, "I felt like I could finally let go of everything."

RELATIONAL SAVORING: TEACHING ADAPTIVE EMOTION REGULATION

Although here in this book I will be referring to relational savoring as an intervention, it is important to keep in mind that relational savoring is, first and foremost, an emotion regulation strategy that is being co-opted as an intervention. Think back to Jayden, who needed no introduction to the concept because she knew what relational savoring was intuitively. When parents tuck their kids into bed at night and hold on one second longer just because they want to linger in that moment of closeness, they are savoring a moment of connection with their child. When partners close their eyes and bring to mind the time they first met, imagining the way the other person smelled or tasted or felt, they are engaging in relational savoring.

My suspicion is that savoring moments of connection is a natural impulse when we are in a positive or eudemonic emotional state, and that doing so only enhances our positive emotions and feelings of connectedness to the world around us. However, when people get locked into either negative mood states or feelings of disconnect (e.g., social isolation, paranoia, rejection, otherness), they may be more inclined to reach for other cognitive pathways (e.g., rumination, worry) instead of savoring their positive connections.

In addition to these *statelike* differences in people's proclivity to savor relational experiences, there are likely also stable or *traitlike* conditions that render people more or less prone to savor. What this means is that while some people are more likely to engage in relational savoring, others are less likely to use relational savoring as an emotion regulation strategy. Relational savoring may not come naturally to people who have not experienced many positive relational memories, who have a history of attachment insecurity, or who struggle with more negative mood.

My research supports these ideas—I have found that when parents who are lower in attachment security, lower in reflective functioning, and higher in depression (Bond & Borelli, 2017; Borelli et al., 2017; Borelli, Hong, et al., 2022; Burkhart et al., 2017) are asked to engage in a relational savoring task in our laboratory, they do so with less ease—specifically, the narratives that they generate are lower in quality (are less positive in nature, are less rich in connectedness, and contain less specificity). I interpret the findings emerging from my lab to suggest that these same people (those who are lower in attachment security, lower in reflective functioning, and higher in depression) have less practice engaging in relational savoring or that it comes less easily to them.

Conversely, I anticipate that people who are more secure would find it easier to remember memories that involve feeling close and connected to another person or secure in a relationship, likely because the memories are consistent with their internal working model; compared with insecure individuals, they can more readily perceive, integrate into their working model, and recall incidents that fit with their internal working model (e.g., memories that involve closeness and connection, safety and security).

Likewise, people who are higher in reflective functioning are better able to understand others' behavior from the perspective of mental states (thoughts and feelings); this enables a deeper kind of perspective taking and meaning making regarding interpersonal interactions, which can assist people in being able to understand their experiences with greater specificity and depth. Being able to look inside one's own and others' minds in this way helps people to savor relational memories because it imbues memories with greater meaning and significance. Finally, depressed mood can prevent a person from feeling positive emotions, which makes savoring quite difficult.

Further, engaging in relational savoring likely increases all three of these constructs (attachment security, reflective functioning, and positive emotion), such that they are transactionally associated (see Figure 1.1). These tenets are consistent with the theoretical premise underlying the relational savoring model. And although we have studied these connections only in parents, I suspect they are more generalized and that when we conduct more research on other populations, we will find that these findings apply to other people beyond parents.

FIGURE 1.1. Relational Savoring

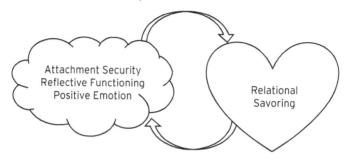

The interesting thing is that although people who are lower in attachment security and reflective functioning might be less equipped to engage in high-quality savoring, they can experience just as positive an effect from savoring. In fact, relational savoring may be most impactful for people who start out with the lowest levels of proficiency in the skill—perhaps these same people with lower attachment security, lower reflective functioning, or higher depressive symptoms. These may be the very people we wish to target with our interventions.

The story is a bit more nuanced than this, as I review in this book, and depends on what type of savoring the person is engaging in (Palmer & Gentzler, 2018), with some studies showing that people with higher attachment insecurity benefit more from savoring interventions, perhaps because they naturally engage in savoring less frequently (Burkhart et al., 2015). The bottom line is there is some evidence that starting at a less skilled place translates into further room to grow (and more room to benefit). And when we work with people through the use of this relational savoring intervention, we are arming them with a skill—an emotion regulation strategy that can be used in many different situations throughout their lives—in the service of improving their emotional and interpersonal well-being.

OVERVIEW OF THE BOOK

I wrote this book for mental health professionals (psychologists, social workers, and therapists), graduate students, and educators. As therapists, so often we are chasing "the problem"—listening to our clients and following their hurt or pain. While following the hurt is undoubtedly important, I argue that *following the healing* is equally critical to helping our clients. I introduce a technique that involves listening for and expanding on the healing that is already present in our clients' lives; these experiences may be overlooked, disregarded, or missed by the client because they are at odds with the client's current state of mind, are fundamentally inconsistent with how the client is usually treated, or seem insufficient to stem the tide of what the client is experiencing. Yet, I believe these experiences of natural healing offer much that is of value; by helping clients slow down and be open to experiencing the feelings that originate in being cared for or from caring for others, we can shift their perspective of themselves, the world, and their place in it. This perspective honors clients' own abilities to heal as well as their own strengths—it acknowledges that clients already have many resources that are embedded within them. These resources might be challenging for clients to identify at first, but they are there, and it is our job to nod in their direction so clients have the benefit of recognizing these hidden gems.

By weaving together case material and research studies into an integrated story, I provide an overview of the rationale and the technique of relational savoring that will leave you with a clear understanding of the intervention. Organized into three main parts, by the end of reading this book, you will understand the theoretical basis underlying relational savoring (Part I) and have a solid grasp of the technical elements of the intervention, including how to anticipate and address areas of potential difficulty when using relational savoring with your clients (Part II). You will also emerge with a sense of how relational savoring can be tailored to fit the needs of different clinical populations and how it can be modified to be consistent with the values of a community organization without losing its defining features (Part III).

As discussed more fully in Part III, while relational savoring shows widespread efficacy in diverse samples, it is consistent with the cultural values of groups that value sharing positive emotions within relationships. For instance, it has shown specific cultural compatibility among Latino/a/x families, which place a strong emphasis on the beneficial role of positive emotion in the context of familial relationships (Borelli, Kerr, et al., 2023). In contrast, relational savoring may not be an intuitive fit or may need to be adapted extensively for cultures that emphasize the distance between people in relationships or cultures that do not value the expression of positive emotion. I argue that taking into account the fit between the values of the intervention and the values of a culture is an important consideration when selecting an intervention approach for each individual client, and additional modifications may need to be made in order for relational savoring to be compatible with cultural groups who conceive of positive emotion from a different stance, particularly in the context of relationships. Finally, the book concludes with a short afterword focusing on using relational savoring to process your own experiences as a therapist.

As the developer of the technique of relational savoring, I will be your guide along this journey, drawing from my experience as a researcher (professor of psychological science, University of California, Irvine) and a practicing psychologist, mixing humor with humility and clinical insight. Although I speak more of my clinical successes than my challenges, I have had my share of challenges. Just like you, I all too frequently puzzle over how best to help my clients. I offer these tools and lessons in the hope that they move all of us a bit further with the recognition that my path is paved with stumbles. Together we will cover significant ground, learn some things that will enhance our clinical practice, and hopefully enjoy ourselves along the way.

This book is chock-full of heart, clinical vignettes, and research. My hope is that it has a little bit of everything, enough to keep people engaged and interested throughout their journey. Before we begin, I want to briefly discuss my approach to using case material, which is omnipresent throughout this book. I have included cases throughout the discussion of almost every clinical issue that emerges in this book to make the discussion more concrete and alive; sometimes this occurs in the context of a summary of a case and sometimes in the context of a transcript of a therapy session. Most of these examples derive from my research studies, though some are from my clinical practice. I am following American Psychological Association (APA) ethical guidelines from their *Ethical Principles of Psychologists and Code of Conduct* regarding the use of case material (APA, 2017) and using a combination of client/participant permission and disguise (and sometimes both).

So your task is to open your mind and be prepared to learn. I would like to invite you into my way of thinking about relationships, clinical work, and emotions. Come into my consulting room, have a seat on the soft couch, grab a cup of your favorite hot beverage in your favorite mug, cozy up with a blanket if you choose, and settle in. Let's dive in, shall we?

PART I
THEORETICAL AND EMPIRICAL SUPPORT

As you have already seen, there is a story behind relational savoring. This story is part personal, part theoretical, and part scientific. In this first part, I strive to blend the personal part of the story with the theory and the research. I hope that as you take in the details of this section, you will find that you experience this as a picture coming into focus. The theory will situate this paradigm within the broader literature, helping to forge connections with other literature and intervention paradigms, and the data and clinical examples provided here will help to ground the image.

In this part, I balance accessible writing with enough context for the information to be meaningful. Readers interested in learning more can access the original research articles, as they undoubtedly provide additional context for this work.

2 THEORETICAL PRINCIPLES UNDERLYING RELATIONAL SAVORING

We begin by discussing the theoretical basis of relational savoring. Although it is true that I first stumbled upon the benefits of focusing on moments of positive connectedness through my direct clinical experience, when I went back to the drawing board to develop the technique, I also looked to theory to guide me.

Of course, there was always theory behind it all. Theory had been breathing wind into the words I was hearing come out of my client's mouth, and unsurprisingly they were the theories I had learned as a trainee and junior psychologist. Like the branches of a tree that had wound its roots deep into the soil, the theories I had learned were deeply entrenched in my thinking, impossible to disentangle from the way I viewed each client and each challenge in front of me. And so, relational savoring has its strongest roots in attachment theory and positive psychology. In this chapter, I take each of those theoretical perspectives in turn and discuss their influence on the development of the model. However, before I discuss relational savoring itself, I want to spend a few minutes discussing savoring in general, which was developed and discussed long before relational savoring and deserves its own time and space.

---

https://doi.org/10.1037/0000372-002
Relational Savoring: Using Guided Reflection to Strengthen Relationships and Improve Outcomes in Therapy, by J. L. Borelli
Copyright © 2024 by the American Psychological Association. All rights reserved.

SAVORING: AN APPROACH TO IMPROVING WELL-BEING

The traditional route of evoking change in psychotherapy has been by targeting or addressing symptoms or negative emotions. The majority of our existing intervention approaches focus on treating symptoms of some kind—for example, there are treatments for depression, eating disorders, and relationship problems. For the most part, these interventions have as their explicit focus the negative cognitions, emotions, and interpersonal experiences that accompany these disorders. It is less common that treatments focus on enhancing functioning, although the past 20 years have witnessed an upsurge of interest in the promotion of well-being through the positive psychology movement (Seligman, 2011). Seligman and others have been careful to distinguish that positive psychology interventions and the promotion of flourishing target not simply the absence of negative in one's life but rather the presence of positive attributes, such as well-being, life satisfaction, and happiness (Keyes, 2016; Ryff & Keyes, 1995).

Savoring can be considered a positive psychology intervention (Bryant et al., 2008) in that it involves the enhancement of positive emotion in the service of improving well-being. Fred Bryant, the originator of the concept of savoring, provided a brilliant theoretical model of savoring in his pioneering book *Savoring: A New Model of Positive Experience* (Bryant & Veroff, 2007). He described savoring as the process of intensifying, prolonging, and appreciating the positive emotions associated with events. Bryant argued that one could savor events that had occurred in the past (such as when one recalls with joy the first time they held their newborn baby [retrospective savoring]), the future (such as when one looks forward to going on a long-awaited trip [anticipatory savoring]), or the present (such as when one closes their eyes and enjoys the taste and smell of their delicious chocolate chip cookie [in-the-moment savoring]; Areni & Black, 2015).

In many ways, I think of savoring as the opposite or the counterpoint to rumination; whereas rumination involves focused, repetitive attention on a negative emotion or memory (Nolen-Hoeksema, 1991; Nolen-Hoeksema et al., 2008), savoring involves focusing one's attention on the details of a positive emotional experience. And just as rumination is associated with a worsening of mood and depression (Conway et al., 2000; Mor & Winquist, 2002), savoring is quite predictably associated with a wide range of positive outcomes. Savoring is considered an emotion regulation strategy by which people extract more positive emotions from their experiences (Fredrickson, 2001). People who go about their daily lives and are naturally more likely to savor are less likely to become depressed and are more likely to experience positive emotions (more frequently and more intense; Bryant, 2003; Carver & Johnson, 2009; Smith & Hollinger-Smith, 2015).

It shouldn't be a surprise that people who spend more time immersing themselves in positive emotions and memories end up with more positive mental health outcomes—after all, we know that positive emotion breeds more positive emotion and well-being—but in many ways, this idea is less convincing than systematic evidence that savoring can also be administered as an intervention, resulting in greater happiness and reduced depression and negative mood (Bryant et al., 2005; Hurley & Kwon, 2013; McMakin et al., 2011; Quoidbach et al., 2009). I say this because it could be that people who are naturally drawn to savoring could be those same people who in general are more optimistic; these people may be more likely to see the joy in life, be able to find the sunny side of a difficult situation, and thus be less prone to mental health challenges. Whereas as therapists, the people we are more likely to encounter in our therapy offices (and more likely to struggle to help) are those people who have trouble finding their way to the upside. So the evidence that savoring interventions can be effective in improving mental health and well-being is more compelling because it demonstrates that experimental exposure to the technique has an impact on people. This is impressive.

I was exposed to the research on savoring when I was completing my clinical internship at UCLA. A colleague (Dana McMakin) who was in my internship cohort had conducted her dissertation on savoring. She was excited about the topic and eager to share her enthusiasm with me and others. When I learned about savoring, I realized that this positive psychology technique shared a great deal with what I had naturally observed my clients gravitating toward as ways of opening up their experience. But from my perspective, savoring as traditionally conceptualized was missing a key component—an attachment focus. Although many people incidentally chose to savor moments shared with others (Bryant & Veroff, 2007), relational savoring includes an explicit focus on memories that are chock-full of attachment content—these memories contain feelings of closeness and connection. Relational savoring privileges the savoring of these experiences of providing or receiving acceptance, protection, support, or adoration to/from an attachment figure (Bowlby, 1973). Let's discuss the rationale for this type of attachment focus now.

ATTACHMENT THEORY: LINKS WITH RELATIONAL SAVORING

Since my introduction to psychology, I was enamored with attachment theory. From the moment I heard Mary Main explain the Adult Attachment Interview (George et al., 1996) in my upper-division psychology course at UC Berkeley,

I knew I had found the theory that resonated most with my understanding of human experience and the connections between people. It made intuitive sense to me that people internalize important messages about who they are, how much they matter, and what their emotions do to themselves and the other important people in their lives, and that these messages become filters through which people view their life experiences. It was at this moment that I fell in love with attachment theory.

From working in Alicia Lieberman's research laboratory, I learned about the importance of feelings of safety and security in the parent–child relationship, and in particular the emotional chaos that ensues when violence, danger, or threat enters that sacred space. My love affair with attachment theory was cemented during my doctoral studies when I benefited from the mentorship of Linda Mayes, Nancy Suchman, and Arietta Slade at Yale University, learning about school-aged children's attachment, emotion, and parental reflective functioning. By the time I earned my PhD, attachment theory was embedded into the folds of my brain, written into the way I saw the world, and impossible to remove from my frame of reference.

The Basics of Attachment Theory and Research

Attachment theory (Bowlby, 1969, 1973) holds that the quality of early interactions with caregivers shapes the development of people's *internal working models* of attachment. These internal working models are cognitive–affective models that describe the nature of close relationships and the self in relationships (Ainsworth & Bell, 1970; Bowlby, 1980). They are heuristics or schemas that provide cognitive shortcuts and help us to navigate the world with greater ease by consolidating our experience and helping us make decisions more quickly.

In John Bowlby's (1969, 1973) conceptualization, experiences of safety, security, acceptance, protection, and autonomy support within these early foundational relationships with attachment figures provide an important foundation for socioemotional health throughout the lifespan (Hughes et al., 2020). These early positive experiences in relationships lead people to internalize a host of important messages about the expression of needs and the self. I will discuss the internalization of attachment experiences (in the form of the internal working model) in greater depth below, but first I want to discuss what attachment looks like in the form of observable human behavior.

Mary Ainsworth studied sensitive responding in mothers, which has since been extended to the behavior of all caregivers. She was an astute observer of human behavior, spending hours upon hours watching mothers caring for children in Baltimore (United States) and Uganda. One of her gifts to the field of attachment was the operationalization of what sensitive responsiveness looks like in a caregiver. Ainsworth argued that sensitivity is comprised of several critical components: attunement (being aware of and keyed into one's child's needs), secure base behavior (acting as an anchor from which the child can explore their environment), and safe haven behavior (acting as a refuge to which the child can retreat should the child experience some sort of threat or distress and require comfort; Ainsworth, 1974; Ainsworth et al., 1974). The Ainsworth method of conceptualizing sensitive responsiveness has led other researchers to consider secure base and safe haven provision to be core components of sensitive responding and key targets of intervention (Powell et al., 2009). These concepts of secure base and safe haven become highly relevant to the relational savoring intervention, so keep them at the top of your mind.

A child who is used to having their expressions of emotional distress responded to in a timely or sensitive manner (safe haven care) internalizes the message that their needs are important and will be addressed; likewise, a child who is used to having their needs for autonomy scaffolded by having their parent by their side (secure base care) internalizes a similar message (Bowlby, 1973; Bretherton, 1992). This type of child develops what Bowlby called *attachment security*, or the felt sense that others will be there for them during times of need (Ainsworth et al., 1978a; Bowlby, 1969, 1980). Children who have secure attachment also internalize important messages about the self—for instance, they learn to expect that they deserve to be loved and treated with respect. Unsurprisingly, children who are parented in this way become adults who seek out supportive relationships later in their lives (Roisman et al., 2005).

On the other hand, children who experience rejection of their emotional or physical needs, children whose needs are inconsistently responded to, or children whose caregivers ignore, neglect, or abuse them (failures of safe haven and/or secure base care) internalize a different sort of message about the world around them and their role in it (Bowlby, 1973, 1988). These children develop a type of *insecure attachment* (*avoidant, ambivalent-resistant,* or *disorganized*; Ainsworth et al., 1978a; Bowlby, 1969, 1980).

Insecure attachment is associated with a set of beliefs that people possess about the impact of their emotions on others and their self-worth. Children with insecure–avoidant attachment have typically had the experience in which their expressions of need have been rejected, neglected, or ignored

(Ainsworth et al., 1978a).[1] These children come to believe that the world is a harsh and unforgiving place; that it is better to hide their feelings than express them, for doing so can alienate the very people they are trying to befriend; and that their emotional and physical needs are unimportant, overwhelming, or upsetting to others (Ainsworth et al., 1978a; van IJzendoorn, 1995). As compared with children with secure attachment, the script they internalize paints a very different picture about themselves, the world, and relationships, leading to a different set of expectations about how to behave and what types of reactions to expect from the world around them (van IJzendoorn, 1995); they may come to believe that they should not have needs, that needs show weakness and vulnerability, and that their needs push others away.

Children with insecure–ambivalent/resistant attachment have received parental care that is inconsistent, making them unsure of what to anticipate; they may have received care that is at times sensitive to their distress, at times intrusive of their exploration, and at times rejecting or ignoring (Cassidy & Berlin, 1994).[2] These children are thought to internalize the message that it is difficult to trust a caregiver to respond, so caregivers must be more closely watched and their own responses to distress must be amplified or exaggerated to be detected (Ainsworth et al., 1978a). They tend to feel that their raw emotions on their own are not sufficient to elicit a response from others, so they must be changed (magnified, distorted) in some way to get the help they need. They internalize negative messages about the self—that they are not enough and their needs are not important—and about others—that others don't really care or cannot be relied on.

A fourth type of attachment was first described by Mary Main and referred to as insecure–disorganized/disoriented attachment. This type of attachment is thought to occur when infants have been exposed to caregiving behavior that is frightening or that contains parental elements of being frightened or overwhelmed. In 1990, Mary Main and Erik Hesse described this behavior as "frightened, threatening, and dissociative," also known as FR behavior. Frightening behavior can include behaviors that are as extreme as abuse or maltreatment, but also less extreme, such as engaging in physical behavior that could appear threatening to a small child—perhaps physically looming over them, widening

---

[1] Later in development (beyond early childhood), this type of attachment is referred to as *dismissing attachment* (within the developmental psychology tradition of attachment research) and *avoidant attachment* (within the social psychology tradition).

[2] Later in development (beyond early childhood), this type of attachment is referred to as *preoccupied attachment* (within the developmental psychology tradition of attachment research) and *anxious attachment* (within the social psychology tradition).

their eyes so the whites are showing, using a haunted type of voice, and stilling or freezing (Abrams et al., 2006). Frightened behavior can include behaviors in which the parents appear deferential to the infant, sexualized toward the infant, or grossly behaviorally disorganized (Abrams et al., 2006).

In 1999, Karlen Lyons-Ruth and colleagues expanded the conceptualization of the parenting behaviors that can contribute to disorganized attachment, arguing that disorganized attachment can also result when parents behave in ways that are extremely insensitive and the communication between the parent and infant is disrupted. In this situation, the parent is repeatedly unable to resolve the child's attachment needs or comfort the child; this pattern of disrupted communication is thought to be disorganizing for the child (Lyons-Ruth et al., 1999).

Mary Main theorized that a child's internalized attachment response to this type of parental care involves experiencing an internal conflict wherein the attachment figure is at once the source of fright and the solution to the fright, resulting in incompatible and competing behavioral responses within the child (Main & Hesse, 1990). This "fright without solution" poses a significant challenge for the child, something that prevents the development of an organized attachment strategy and results in the appearance of contradictory, confusing, or odd behaviors. These behaviors are thought to be the result of underlying fear and confusion on the part of the child (Main & Hesse, 1990).

In sum, attachment theory and research generally support several key principles. These principles were first suggested by Marinus van IJzendoorn (1990), developed and grounded in John Bowlby's and Mary Ainsworth's work, and have since been tested and evaluated in many other studies. The first has been referred to as the *universality hypothesis*. This states that unless not given the opportunity through extreme social deprivation, all infants will form attachments with one or more caregivers. The rare exception to this rule is children with severe neurological impairments. There is very strong support for this hypothesis in Western cultures (Europe, the United States, Australia, Israel) and strong emerging evidence for this in the other cultures that have now been studied (Africa, Asia; Mesman et al., 2016).

The second principle has been referred to as the *normativity hypothesis*. This hypothesis states that the majority of infants will develop a secure attachment pattern in contexts in which health is not threatened (e.g., contexts in which there is no war or famine). This hypothesis also has strong support cross-culturally (Mesman et al., 2016).

The third hypothesis is the *sensitivity hypothesis*, which states that the likelihood that a child will develop a secure attachment depends on the quality of caregiving they have received. In other words, this principle states there is a lawful relationship between the caregiving received and the internal working model that the child develops.

One interesting piece of evidence here comes in the form of a meta-analysis finding that infants show only modest correspondence in their attachment as measured by their response in the Strange Situation Procedure (Ainsworth et al., 1978b) to their mothers and fathers (van IJzendoorn & De Wolff, 1997). The Strange Situation Procedure is an experimental paradigm for use with infants between the ages of 12 and 18 months and their caregivers. The paradigm involves bringing the infant into an unfamiliar laboratory environment with their caregiver initially and then exposing them to a series of separations and reunions from their caregiver. The procedure is videotaped and the infant's behavioral response during the separations and particularly the reunion is used to determine their attachment classification.

This finding that children show only modest correspondence in the way they behave in the Strange Situation Procedure with their mothers and fathers can be interpreted that the infant's behaviorally measured attachment response is person-specific and likely responsive to the individual relationship they have built with each parent. There are less data available speaking to this hypothesis in non-Western countries, but when it has been tested, the data have largely supported this hypothesis (Mesman et al., 2016).

Finally, the *competence hypothesis* states that in most contexts over the long term, secure attachment is associated with the most optimal psychosocial outcomes. The data to support this hypothesis are very clear in Western contexts but still insufficient in non-Western contexts to evaluate its merits (Mesman et al., 2016).

Internalization of Attachment Experiences: The Internal Working Model

As mentioned earlier, internal working models are cognitive–affective models that are constructed based on previous experience within interactions with primary caregivers; they contain important information regarding the nature of close relationships and the self in relationships (Bowlby, 1969, 1973). Internal working models influence how people perceive information regarding their social interactions, causing them to view certain information as relevant, important, and consistent with their experiences and other information as irrelevant, unimportant, and inconsistent with their experiences (Bowlby, 1969, 1973). Bowlby argued that internal working models emerge very early in development. Close interactions with caregivers are filtered through the perceptual and affective schemas held by infants when they are preverbal. Bowlby argued that these internal working models are so powerful because they have such enduring influence but largely exist outside of awareness, primarily because of how they are encoded (preverbally; Bowlby, 1973).

In other words, the internal working model provides a built-in system through which individuals who have had negative early relational experiences perceive their interpersonal worlds as less responsive and supportive—they filter their current interpersonal experiences in light of their prior experiences (Bowlby, 1973). Particularly when we have had negative histories of being cared for, these positive moments become harder to spot because our internal working model tells us they are irrelevant, the exception to the rule, or not informative. Instead, we focus on the moments that are important to remember, according to our internal working model—those moments in which we are slighted, rejected, snubbed, hurt, or attacked by others—those are the ones to hold onto, to process deeply inside and out, to make sure not to miss.

The internal working model of attachment also has implications for the development of mental representations of attachment, which are the cognitive-affective models that people build of their relationships and themselves (Bowlby, 1973, 1980). Children can build a mental representation of their relationship with their mother and a mental representation of their relationship with their father; these representations are thought to help children engage in exploration and manage their distress during separation from caregivers. They also help to guide their specific behavior with each caregiver, allow them to generate predictions about the caregiver's behavior in certain situations, and get their needs met to the greatest extent possible. Representations are thought to start developing in the preschool years and continue developing over time as children's cognitive capacities develop.

There is some dispute in the literature about how attachment representations develop over time. In brief, some scholars argue that children carry individual working models of relationships (or representations) throughout childhood that then merge in adulthood into one integrated model (Furman & Simon, 2004). For instance, Quentin could have a representation of attachment security for his father and avoidance for his mother that could merge into one overall attachment representation in adulthood (security).

In terms of how this process occurs, researchers have suggested that the representation of the attachment figure who has been more involved would be more influential (Bowlby, 1988; Main, 1981). If Quentin has received more caregiving from his father, then his attachment to his father (secure) would be the representation that would take center stage in adulthood. Some of these scholars contend that this generalized attachment representation then applies to all attachment relationships, including adults' relationships with their parents and their relationships with romantic partners (Furman & Simon, 2004). In conceptualizing the growth and development of the cognitive aspect of attachment over time, other scholars argue for more relationship specificity (Grossmann et al., 2005); this is the idea that internal working models and mental representations continue to grow and adapt over time and that different relationships exert different influences on a person's internal working model of attachment (Miljkovitch et al., 2015).

Interestingly, although internal working models are thought to develop based on interactions with individual caregivers during childhood and adolescence, there are actually very high rates of concordance within individuals among their mental representations of attachment in different relationships. In other words, if Quentin is secure in his relationship with his father, he is highly likely to be secure in his relationship with his mother. In contrast, if Quentin is avoidant with one parent, he is likely to be avoidant with the other. In early childhood, the concordance levels are very high (Fox et al., 1991; Monteiro et al., 2008; Veríssimo et al., 2009). Likewise, in middle childhood, a recent review of the literature (Privizzini, 2017) found that the majority of children were concordant in their attachment for attachment figures on the Child Attachment Interview (Shmueli-Goetz et al., 2008), an interview-based assessment for school-aged children.

In adulthood, the evidence is more mixed, depending on how attachment is measured, but there is considerable evidence for a unitary model (concordance) along with evidence for some relationship specificity (Fraley et al., 2011; Furman & Simon, 2004; Furman et al., 2002; Grossmann et al., 2005; Treboux et al., 2004). This reminds me of the argument of *set point* that is used to describe weight (Harris, 1990): the idea that most people have a certain set point that can vary as a function of different factors (environment, diet, exercise). I think of the unitary model in a similar way—that early attachment experiences set a basic framework for the range of responses that people tend to have, but individual relational contexts as well as interventions (like this one) influence where someone falls within that range.

In case it is not already apparent, the internal working model serves as the bridge between early experience and subsequent experiences. The internal working model is thought to be an internalization of the infant's understanding of their experiences with a particular caregiver. These experiences are then internalized, carried forward, and refined and updated by new experiences over time. As I mentioned earlier, the degree to which people carry forward multiple distinct, relationship-specific mental representations or one unitary model of attachment is somewhat disputed in the research literature. What is not disputed is that early attachment experiences influence the development of these mental representations, which in turn influence ways of perceiving oneself, relationships, and the world.

R. Chris Fraley (2002) has framed the debate in the literature in terms of two different perspectives. The *prototype perspective* holds that an individual's attachment representations of early experience are relatively stable and have an enduring influence, whereas the *revisionist perspective* holds that an individual's attachment perspectives of early experience can be modified based on new experiences that the person has, and therefore that they may change over time. Although there have been many longitudinal studies of attachment, this study, published in 2002, which involved a meta-analysis of longitudinal data, was the most sophisticated of its kind in terms of data analytics involved (Fraley, 2002). The study concluded that there was moderate evidence for the prototype perspective. Subsequent studies have largely supported this finding, suggesting moderate stability of attachment (Pinquart et al., 2012) and prediction of continuity or discontinuity by parental sensitivity (Beijersbergen et al., 2012; Opie et al., 2021).

Clinical Application of Attachment Theory

Let me make this more concrete by demonstrating how attachment theory can be useful in understanding a case. Take Jake, a 25-year-old man who experienced severe physical maltreatment from both of his parents as a child. After a series of turbulent and abusive romantic relationships with both men and women, Jake finds himself in a loving romantic relationship with another man, Dave. Dave is gentle, devoted to Jake, and wants to understand him as a person and develop a caring bond with him. Dave spent hours yesterday talking to Jake about Jake's sexual fears within the relationship, telling him he doesn't have to be intimate unless he wants to and feels comfortable and safe. Dave held him and comforted him and said that there is no pressure from him to be sexually intimate—he is fine waiting as long as necessary for Jake to feel safe. However, this morning, when Dave was rushing out of the apartment to go to work, he accidentally grabbed Jake's water bottle instead of his own. Jake spent the morning focusing on how Dave doesn't love him or think about his needs, treats him as though he is an appendage, and is using him.

What's happening here with Jake? He's protectively focusing on the slight from Dave earlier this morning (grabbing his water bottle instead of his own) rather than focusing on the tender, loving care that Dave showed him yesterday, even though Dave's actions and messaging are explicitly communicating to Jake that he is safe and loved and cared for. Because Jake tries to protect himself from hurt by filtering out loving care and instead focusing on slights that reaffirm his history and his feelings about himself, he prevents himself from reaping the benefits of the positive interactions he is having in his life.

As illustrated with the example of Jake, though designed to keep us safe in what Bowlby referred to as the environment of evolutionary adaptiveness (Bowlby, 1969), the problem with the heuristics used by the internal working model is that they can sometimes prevent us from growing toward health. In the case of people who have insecure attachment histories, these heuristics can deprive them of the opportunity to benefit from the positive experiences happening all around them. So two people can experience the same kindness from the grocery store clerk or from their partner, and the person with the secure attachment history may benefit more from that interaction. For the secure person, that positive interaction will not be filtered out as irrelevant information by their internal working model.

In this way, the secure people keep getting richer (so to speak) from their positive experiences while the insecure people persist on their paths of insecurity. In fact, this is just one way in which secure people keep getting richer because secure people are more likely to choose as partners people who are healthier to begin with (Collins & Read, 1990; Kirkpatrick & Davis, 1994; Senchak & Leonard, 1992; Simpson, 1990). Then when they are in relationships, they behave in a way that tends to elicit behavior that is more sensitive and responsive to their needs (Bowlby, 1988). This results in insecure people ending up being triply disadvantaged in their relationships. The fact that there is a high level of continuity in attachment over long periods in part substantiates this (Beijersbergen et al., 2012); although people who were secure in infancy may be on a developmental trajectory in which they continue to be exposed to more optimal life experiences (more enriched relational experiences), one aspect of this stability may be the perceptual lens that people bring to their experiences. It is this aspect that relational savoring seeks to target—the perceptions that people bring to how they view their relationships.

These internal working models, though rooted in early experience, can be updated over time based on subsequent experiences in attachment relationships, although it is thought to be more difficult for the models to shift later in development (Bretherton, 1992; Pearson et al., 1994; Roisman et al., 2002; Waters et al., 2002). We need to find a way to rectify these inequities. Recognizing that the inflexibility of the internal working model prevents people from being able to learn from their more recent positive experiences has led numerous attachment researchers to emphasize the importance of strengthening these experiences of "felt security."

Fortunately, there is evidence to suggest that small manipulations can enhance feelings of security, potentially by tinkering with that internal working model and the way people filter information. For instance, in simple priming studies, or studies in which scientists expose individuals to stimuli (either subliminally or supraliminally) that are intended to evoke a sense of comfort, security, protection, or love, small security inductions can have powerful impacts on their emotions and behavior. Scientists may present participants with words related to attachment security (e.g., love, secure, safe, home), offer participants names of secure attachment figures (e.g., grandmother), or ask participants to recall a memory of a time they felt secure (Carnelley & Rowe, 2007; Gillath et al., 2008; Hudson & Fraley, 2018; J. D. Jones et al., 2022; Mikulincer & Shaver, 2015; Rowe et al., 2020).

According to theories regarding security priming, these stimuli activate mental representations of security, ostensibly by reminding the individual of other people and situations that have made them feel similarly secure (Gillath & Karantzas, 2019; Mikulincer & Shaver, 2007). Security priming has been shown to affect people's mental health (Mikulincer & Shaver, 2007), mood (Mikulincer, Gillath, et al., 2001; Mikulincer, Hirschberger, et al., 2001; Mikulincer & Shaver, 2001; Mikulincer et al., 2003), and ability to cope with trauma (Mikulincer et al., 2006), among other outcomes (Mikulincer & Shaver, 2010, 2015).

In one review of the literature on attachment security priming (Gillath & Karantzas, 2019), the authors concluded that this technique may be especially effective for people who are high in attachment anxiety; these individuals tend to be hyperfocused on threats to their attachment relationships. They reasoned that security priming that is supraliminal may be particularly effective in assisting people high in attachment anxiety to downregulate a hyperactivated attachment system (Gillath & Karantzas, 2019). For our purposes, this body of work is important because it tells us that although the internal working model is a powerful influence on how people interpret their interpersonal environments, it can be manipulated (at least over short periods) through relatively brief interventions.

THE POWER OF POSITIVE EMOTION

Relational savoring is also grounded in a foundational theory within positive psychology that speaks to the central role of positive emotion in human behavior. Fredrickson's (1998, 2005) broaden-and-build framework discusses the role of positive emotion in influencing people's attention, thought, and action patterns. Fredrickson made the argument that being in a negative emotional state can restrict and narrow attention, thought, and action patterns. To illustrate this point, think about how when a client is down or depressed, all they can recall is the other times they have felt the same way. The future looks so bleak and it seems absolutely impossible to change. It is almost as if the person's perceptual field actually narrows such that they cannot see the other possibilities available to them. Part of our job as therapists is to step inside of their perceptual fields and physically push those boundaries further out so they can see the sun poking through.

Fredrickson argued that being in a positive emotional state is the counterpoint to being in a negative emotional state and that whereas negative emotion constricts our abilities to perceive, attend to, think, and feel, positive emotion expands these abilities (Fredrickson et al., 2000). In contrast to negative emotion, positive emotion can enable people to access creative modes of operating that were previously inaccessible to them. Positive emotional states can enable people to become more generative and creative in their thinking and acting (Isen & Daubman, 1984; Isen et al., 1985, 1987, 1991; Isen & Means, 1983) and can inspire people to make all sorts of cognitive connections between ideas that they may not have been able to make when they were in a more neutral or negative emotional state.

Positive emotions are linked to a greater desire to engage in play and exploration, as well as greater dopamine production (Ashby et al., 1999; Cunningham, 1988). Rather than having a specific action tendency, positive emotions help people build psychological resources, such as confidence, optimism, and energy, as a result of these broadened thought–action repertoires. When people are in a positive emotional state, they may engage in behavior that will allow them to build these psychological resources through their actions.

Fredrickson then argued that although negative emotions may confer an evolutionary advantage by helping to promote survival in the moment of threat (i.e., by preparing someone to respond to a predator; Fredrickson, 2001), positive emotions confer a long-term evolutionary advantage by assisting the individual in building resources that could be used later when the person inevitably encounters other threats. This argument is relatively easy to translate into your own life. Imagine yourself when you were last in an elated mood. Do you remember how you felt at the time? Did your mood enable you to believe you could reach new heights or allow you to make connections between ideas you might not have made otherwise? Do you remember coming down from that mood and realizing that you could not, in fact, see three groups of friends in one day as you had ambitiously hoped when you were making plans the night before? I am so much more productive when I am in a happy mood state; I can write more, talk more, clean more, and stay up later. Being in a happy, an excited, or sometimes even an anxious but directed mood state can enable me to reach all kinds of new heights; it gives me tons of energy that allows me to stretch myself beyond my limits and find new limits.

There are many ways to think about how positive emotions affect our overall functioning. First, we could think that just being in a positive emotional state overall has benefits for emotional adjustment. If we surround ourselves with positivity (e.g., spending time around people who express positive emotion, listening to upbeat music, watching movies with positive messages), then this exposure to positivity can rub off on us and alter our perceptions or spur optimism.

But we can go beyond this argument to claim that adopting a positive emotional stance within ourselves—for example, by smiling when you are not feeling that happy or by walking with a skip in your step—also actually improves your mood. In other words, we can argue that behaving as though we are in a positive emotional state can also enhance our overall levels of positive emotion and our well-being. In line with this argument, the facial feedback hypothesis (Darwin, 1872; W. James, 1884) holds that facial muscle activation can influence emotional state, particularly when it is influenced covertly (without the person's awareness). This theory has been investigated extensively empirically, and the results of a meta-analysis support the notion that there is a small but significant association between facial expression and emotional state, which is supportive of the facial feedback hypothesis (Coles et al., 2019).

In addition to allowing people to stretch themselves further, positive emotions can actually undo the physiological effects of negative emotions during or following stressful experiences (Tugade & Fredrickson, 2004), a theory known as the *undoing hypothesis* (Fredrickson & Levenson, 1998; Fredrickson et al., 2000). If you listen to an uplifting song or watch a feel-good movie during or after an upsetting experience (e.g., a breakup, a painful medical procedure), you may notice this principle in action. Your positive emotions are such powerful creatures that they can actually undo the physiological effects of negative emotions or pain.

A now classic study by Barbara Fredrickson and Bob Levenson (1998) tested this idea by exposing participants to two sets of films. In the first set, all participants watched a fear-inducing film. In the second set of films, the participants were randomly assigned to watch one of four different films: films that elicited contentment, amusement, neutrality, or sadness. The participants' cardiovascular activation was monitored while they watched the films. What the researchers found is that those participants who watched the film intended to elicit amusement showed a faster recovery to their baseline levels of cardiovascular activation. They interpreted this as evidence that the positive emotion elicited by the amusement-inducing film hastened the participants' recovery to their baseline physiological state; in other words, it undid their negative emotional state, which in this case, was represented by their cardiovascular arousal.

These effects have wide-ranging applicability and have been replicated in many different contexts. One study (Pressman et al., 2021) conducted by my colleague at UC Irvine, Sarah Pressman, exposed participants to needle injections of a saline solution and randomly assigned them to pose a Duchenne smile (smiling with the eyes as well as the mouth, which is thought to be a more authentic smile; Ekman et al., 1990), a non-Duchenne smile (smiling with only the mouth, thought to be a less authentic smile), a grimace, or a neutral facial expression. This investigative team measured participants' subjective self-reported emotion and pain, as well as their physiological response to the injection (heart rate, an index of cardiovascular reactivity, and electrodermal activation, an index of sympathetic nervous system activation that is thought to provide a window into a person's fear response). They found that participants who were assigned to hold a Duchenne smile or a grimace showed lower self-reported pain responses than the neutral group. Further, the Duchenne smile participants showed significantly lower heart rates than the neutral group. These findings suggest that although both an authentic smile and a grimace were effective in reducing experienced pain, only the authentic smile assisted people in reducing the physiological effects of the injection.

Finally, positive emotions can have interpersonal effects, strengthening bonds between people and generating what Fredrickson termed "upward spirals" (Fredrickson, 2005; Kok & Fredrickson, 2010). When two people experience positive emotion states together—when they laugh together, smile together, or just feel good together—those positive emotions can build on one another and make the bond that the people feel for one another even stronger than it was before. To illustrate this principle, think back to the best times you have had with some of your closest friends or family members. Chances are you may be thinking of times when you were at your utmost silliest over the most inane things (things that if you tried to explain them to someone who was not there, they would not be able to understand why what you were saying was funny and most certainly would not laugh along with you). If those were the times that occurred to you, it is not a coincidence. It's because these bonding times were precisely as they were because the glue of this highly intense positive emotion served to gel your relationship.

DOES POSITIVE EMOTION BYPASS DEFENSIVENESS?

My session with David (Chapter 1) taught me one more thing about the magic of positive emotion and contemplating moments of relationship vitality that is worth mentioning. Talking about moments of relationship wins and positive emotions can be less threatening for many clients than opening up about relationship wounds. My experience has shown me that for many people, positive emotions linked to relationship wins (e.g., pride, closeness, calm, enjoyment) are more accessible, approachable, and ultimately less threatening ways to enter the space of vulnerable emotions than by discussing feelings of pain, abandonment, rejection, loss, and hurt.

And the truth is that these emotions are all connected, so when people access their feelings of being loved, cherished, accepted, and protected, they also access their pain at being overlooked, hurt, rejected, and disrespected. But when they do find their way to these more painful feeling states, they do so with the accompaniment of their positive feelings (loved, cherished, accepted), which helps to buffer the sting of the negative feelings. Sequencing these emotion states makes entering the den of painful feelings more tolerable.

I believe that this strategy of entering the vulnerable feelings chamber through the positive experiences door may be particularly important when we are working with populations that have been historically marginalized or criticized for the way they live their lives or conduct their relationships. Indeed, when clinicians or researchers approach historically marginalized communities with a damage- or deficits-focused perspective, they run the risk of reinforcing the very negative stereotypes we are working to undo (Tuck, 2009). This worrisome dynamic can be further heightened when you, the therapist, are the member of a majority group and your client is the member of a minority group (or when you are a member of a group that has stigmatized or criticized the group to which your client belongs).

Instead, approaching these communities with a strengths-based approach, actively looking for ways to praise and celebrate wins, is a much more affirming stance. By emphasizing a relationship success, you allow your client to be among feelings that help to buoy them, to help them feel more secure and safe, before you ask them to enter into the chamber of more frightening feelings with you. In so doing, you are also allowing them to be witnessed by you as having relationship strengths, as being someone capable of effectively soothing another person (or of receiving loving care from another person), and this in and of itself can be disarming, helping the client relinquish their need to convince the therapist that they have had positive relationship experiences. Thus, an added advantage of this approach is that it may increase clients' openness to discuss difficult relationship experiences after they have had the pleasure of discussing their positive experiences.

I want to comment briefly on how this argument that I am making—that discussing positive moments of connection is a port of entry to vulnerability—fits in with what Brené Brown has argued about vulnerability. Brown has enumerated some of the ways we humans avoid feeling these vulnerable emotional states (B. Brown, 2010a, 2010b, 2012). What my colleagues and I have found is that if a client can embrace joy or gratitude, they can often make significant progress in their emotional journey, finding their way toward other vulnerable emotional states that are worth exploring.

Here is a way to understand how relational savoring works: Beginning to discuss a moment of positive connection with another person may not appear daunting, and it can lead to deeply immersing oneself in feelings of joy, a much more vulnerable experience. In fact, one comment we repeatedly get from people who engage in relational savoring is that they are surprised by how intense the feelings that arise are. I'll talk more about this in Chapter 6, but for now, the relevant point is that the cost of entry into a positive emotional task like relational savoring task is low, while the potential benefits are high.

WRAP-UP

Now I have discussed the two core theories that form the basis for the development of the relational savoring intervention: attachment theory and the broaden-and-build theory within the positive psychology tradition. With the theoretical rationale under our belts, we examine the evidence base for the intervention.

3   EVIDENCE BASE FOR RELATIONAL SAVORING

In this chapter, I review the research studies that provide the evidence base for relational savoring. These are studies that I conducted while at Pomona College (a liberal arts college), where I was on faculty from 2009 to 2016, and at University of California, Irvine (a research university), where I have been on faculty since 2016. These studies represent the work of many others besides myself, including many graduate and undergraduate students, as well as postdoctoral scholars and faculty members. In part due to the fact that I began my career at Pomona College, I designed this intervention to be suitable to be delivered by interveners with lower levels of education (a bachelor's degree or less).

A WORD ON OUR CONTROL CONDITION

Before diving into the specifics of each study, I provide a general background about how my colleagues and I have designed the majority of the studies examining the outcomes of relational savoring. When we set out on this journey, we had the goal of wanting to compare relational savoring to a control condition, but we did not want the control condition to be an inert,

---

https://doi.org/10.1037/0000372-003
Relational Savoring: Using Guided Reflection to Strengthen Relationships and Improve Outcomes in Therapy, by J. L. Borelli
Copyright © 2024 by the American Psychological Association. All rights reserved.

boring, completely neutral control—we wanted to see if relational savoring could actually exert an impact above and beyond something we knew already exerted a positive impact. I mentioned in Chapter 2 that we already knew that savoring itself was a powerful intervention that had effects on emotion, mood, and depression (Bryant et al., 2008; Bryant & Veroff, 2007; Keyes, 2016; Ryff & Keyes, 1995). And we were trying to evaluate whether we could develop an intervention that worked above and beyond the effects of savoring, or an intervention that had effects more specific to the treatment targets—for instance, effects on interpersonal or relational outcomes.

So we created a control condition that we termed *personal savoring*, which involved going through the exact same memory reflection steps as in relational savoring except that the individual was savoring an event that did not involve another person. People in the personal savoring condition savored a range of events and experiences, such as dancing to great music, having a wonderful meal, going on a walk at the beach, getting a promotion at work, finishing a painting, hiking to a waterfall, completing a home renovation, or sewing clothes for the first time by themselves (Borelli, Bond, et al., 2020). The reason we chose personal savoring as our control is that we thought this condition would also activate positive emotion and create some opportunities for meaning making for participants because it involved savoring. We anticipated that participants would increase their positive emotion through savoring personal experiences, but we thought they would not get the relational benefits that participants would obtain from savoring the attachment-based memories that participants in the relational savoring condition would garner.

There are some pros and cons to having chosen such a powerful control condition as personal savoring, which we already know from prior research has positive impacts. The biggest pro is that we are confident that when we find the effects of relational savoring, it means something noteworthy about the impact of the intervention. Further, as intended, we can speak with greater specificity on the effects of relational savoring on key outcomes.

The greatest downside is that in some of our studies (reviewed below), we find that both interventions exert impacts on participants, which is not surprising and makes it difficult to disambiguate impacts. And in many ways, this should not be surprising to us, although it is only in hindsight that I was able to see this. For instance, one of the populations we have worked with has been with mothers of children with autism spectrum disorder (ASD). Our initial rationale in testing relational savoring as an intervention for this population was that children with ASD can have more difficulty showing signs of connection and closeness or can show them in ways that are more subtle or individualized; further, parents of children with ASD experience higher stress levels than parents of neurotypical children (Eisenhower et al., 2005; Hoffman et al., 2009). Yet, parenting sensitivity is nonetheless an important predictor of attachment security in children with ASD (Capps et al., 1994; Koren-Karie et al., 2009), and attachment security in children with ASD is just as important a predictor of beneficial psychosocial outcomes as it is in neurotypical children (Koren-Karie et al., 2009; Rutgers et al., 2007).

Given that relational savoring is an intervention that increases parenting sensitivity in mothers of neurotypical children, we reasoned it made sense to test relational savoring as an intervention in parents of children with ASD. So we conducted two studies in this population, one with mothers of children with ASD in the United States and one with mothers of children with ASD in Singapore. These projects were primarily the work of Dr. Gerin Gaskin (United States) and Dr. Gianluca Esposito (Singapore).

An unanticipated finding of this work was how effective the personal savoring intervention would be: Although in prior studies we typically did find effects of personal savoring, relational savoring most often outperformed personal savoring. But in both of these studies, we found that both personal and relational savoring were effective in increasing certain outcomes, such as positive emotion, and in reducing negative emotion (Gaskin, 2021; Pereira et al., 2021). A clue as to why this might have been the case can be found in some of the qualitative data we obtained from one of the studies (Gaskin, 2021); in Gaskin's U.S.-based study, mothers reported that the personal savoring intervention gave them much-needed time to recharge their own batteries and the permission they needed to focus on themselves. In the words of one of Gaskin's (2021) participants,

> Parents, especially of special needs children, are burdened with guilt because they indulge in something for themselves. It's okay to do so. [Something] as simple as a walk or a drive around town or having coffee can help clear your mind and allow you to "recharge." . . . I think it helps me to become more focused, alert, and attentive towards my family. (p. 88)

Savoring a personal memory provided a different sort of containment and regulation than relational savoring for the mothers in our study, yet one that ultimately had benefits for the mothers themselves and may even have indirect benefits for their relationships. As articulated by another mother who participated in Gaskin's (2021) study, personal savoring provided her with a beneficial respite:

> Time to myself allows me to relax, destress, refocus, think more positively, which I think is important for allowing me to feel as a whole person, my own person, and a more positive-thinking person when I interact with my family. (p. 88)

Another mother explained, "I think it's just as I said before, which is reminding myself it is OK to take time for myself [that is] much needed for my well-being, thus making me a better wife and mother too" (Gaskin, 2021, p. 88).

In contrast to these findings reviewed above, which suggested that personal savoring yields benefits for individual and even interpersonal outcomes in certain contexts, some of our data have suggested that engaging in personal savoring is difficult, unnatural, or impossible for other people or in other contexts. Bryant's early work demonstrated that people gravitate toward savoring experiences that occur in relationships with others (Bryant et al., 2005). If someone were to complete a personal savoring task by savoring a memory of a time they shared with another person, they are no longer engaging in personal savoring.

This blending of the conditions has occurred in at least one of our studies, led by Maggie Kerr, formerly Burkhart, now an assistant professor at University of Wisconsin–Madison (Burkhart et al., 2015), which led us to believe that for some people, savoring memories that did not involve another person is difficult, artificial, unnatural, or difficult, and therefore perhaps not an ideal control task. For example, in Kerr's study, we had several participants completely violate the instructions of the personal savoring task and savor a memory of connectedness with another person for their "personal savoring" condition. We (Burkhart et al., 2015) ended up combining the two conditions (personal and relational savoring) and examining participants' outcomes jointly; while this study provided insights into the impact of savoring overall, it did not yield new information about the unique role of relational savoring. One important note is that this study was conducted online, so participants were following instructions that were given over the computer. Adherence to the personal savoring protocol has been less of an issue in studies in which we have administered the intervention in person.

For many people, there is a natural tendency to introduce relational themes, even when discussing personal positive experiences. We train the personal savoring therapists to help clients stay away from relational themes, but this can be easier said than done. Let's take the following example:

> Um, earlier today I, I had a two hour gap between classes, and um I like this gap because I'm able to kind of, literally do whatever I want at school so today I decided to do a little project for my communication club on Friday we had like a new member appreciation and I set it up all by myself and it was really stressful but as I went on the computer in the computer lab in these two hours um to look at the footage I took that day I was able to really see how like retrospectively how happy everybody was at this thing that I made, so I'm putting together a video with a—a slideshow with pictures and music and everyone's dancing and they're, they're having a lot of fun and um I hadn't thought about,

because I was there that weekend, but I hadn't thought about like what a great impact it was for the new members and for the old staff so to be able to watch those videos and put it together was, was really nice, to see them smile and to realize wow like I did this, I, you know, I made all these people happy for, you know on a weekend night and that was really nice.

In this example, although the content is rich in many ways, her narrative is very fresh, detailed, specific, and highly positive; there is a risk here because there is also a lot of tempting relational content that the therapist will want to steer clear of (e.g., the impact of the video on the new members and old staff, being able to see them smile, and making all of these people happy). These aspects of the memory that we would want to play up if this were a relational savoring intervention are the ones we want to avoid if this is a personal savoring intervention. Instead, we would want to focus on her experience of pride, accomplishment, and flow in the experience of creating something. In this example, the researcher was able to head off this issue by saying the following:

> OK OK good, uhm . . . OK so we're gonna—we'll focus on the first one that you talked about 'cause I think that one's like pretty salient for you um but we really wanna focus on how the event . . . like the personal aspects of the event as opposed to like how it affected other people or how—*OK*—your relationships with other people, so we really want to focus on yourself . . . *OK*?

Nonetheless, the challenges we have had with this control condition do also reveal something important about relational savoring: that savoring relationship experiences is a natural, readily accessible process for many individuals (Bryant et al., 2005). In fact, as I have tried to illustrate, many people have trouble not savoring relationship experiences even when expressly instructed to savor experiences that do not involve other people. When instructed to think of a positive experience we want to revisit in our minds, for many of us, it is quite natural for our minds to turn to an experience that involves close others. This may be particularly true for people from certain cultural backgrounds and with certain relationship histories; however, it is much easier to lead clients down a path they already want to walk down, rather than leading them somewhere that feels foreign or frightening.

Based on this experience, I would like to offer some recommendations for researchers who wish to use a control condition to pair with relational savoring. If you intend to conduct your intervention in person, I think that personal savoring works as a control condition. You need to have highly trained interveners who can work with your participants to help them stay focused on personal experiences, and you should choose outcome measures that focus on relational constructs. Personal savoring also affects positive emotion and well-being, so you will want to ensure you have some outcomes that only relational savoring is likely to affect.

If you will be administering your intervention online or you are working with a new population (that has not previously been tested with relational savoring), I recommend beginning your work with a more neutral control condition. You can use a waitlist control or an attention control task (e.g., reporting on morning routine). I recommend going in this direction because you will have far less control over your participants when you administer the intervention in this format, and participants may have a difficult time focusing on personal experiences.

RELATIONAL SAVORING INTERVENTION WITH PARENTS

The majority of our research on relational savoring has been conducted with parents of young children, as described here.

The Growing Families Study: A Large Online Study With Parents of Young Children

In our first large-scale study (Burkhart et al., 2015), the Growing Families Study, we examined relational savoring as administered over the internet using a single-administration design. The intervention was written out, and participants provided their responses in writing. In this study, we sought to compare relational savoring to personal savoring and a neutral control (recalling one's morning routine).

The procedure for this study is visualized in Figure 3.1. We tested our hypotheses among a sample of 435 parents of toddlers (children 3 years or under). Parents who enrolled in the study completed a baseline assessment, which involved an evaluation of their attachment style (using a self-report measure of attachment), a baseline evaluation of their relationship satisfaction with their child), and baseline assessments of their emotional state. They were randomized to one of three conditions (personal savoring, relational savoring, or neutral control).

After completing the intervention task, they completed a postintervention assessment of their emotional state. Then they completed a stressor task, which involved reading a vignette. The vignette asked them to imagine a scenario in which they leave work late and have to stop at the grocery store on the way home with their child in tow. Their child is crying and whining inconsolably in the grocery store checkout line. Parents were then asked to answer a series of questions regarding the vignette that are designed to make parents focus on

FIGURE 3.1. Procedure for the Growing Families Study

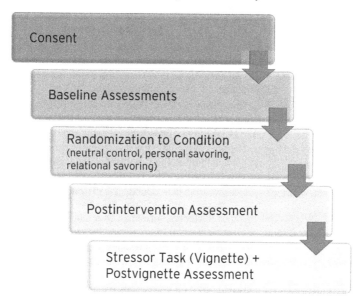

their emotional reaction to the situation ("What are the reason(s) your child is whining and crying?" "How does this make you feel about your child?"). After completing the stressor task, parents once more completed an assessment of relationship satisfaction.

In both the personal and the relational savoring conditions, participants were asked to reflect on memories for at least 2 minutes and were asked a series of questions about their memories, to which they were expected to type responses. Based on a visual scan of our data (see Exhibits 3.1 and 3.2 for examples), we were satisfied that the participants in the relational savoring condition had engaged with the task in the way we had intended. The majority of the participants reported on events that were relational in nature, involved some degree of connectedness, involved some level of attachment content, and involved some level of projection about the significance of the attachment relationship in an enduring way throughout their lives. In the higher quality examples (Exhibit 3.1), participants were really able to connect their experiences to attachment themes, speaking about the strength of the bond they share as parents and children, a bond that will endure forever. In lower-quality examples (Exhibit 3.2), parents were able to discuss positive memories in which they enjoyed their child's company and to write about their positive affection (e.g., love, admiration) for their child.

EXHIBIT 3.1. Excerpt From Relational Savoring Response From Growing Families Study, Higher Quality Example

Prompt	Participant response
Using as much detail as possible, describe what happened.	[Child] and I went to the park. We had a good time going down the slide and swinging on the swing. [Child] seemed to have a good time because she was just laughing and giggling the whole time we were at the park.
What was the air like? What was the weather like?	The air was cool, and there was a little bit of wind also. It was to [sic] cool where it would prevent us from staying to [sic] long. The sun was shining bright.
What time of day did the moment occur?	The time of the day that this even occurred was in the evening time. The sun was still out and it was about 4:30 on a beautiful Tuesday.
What were you wearing?	I was wearing blue ripped up jeans with a black Black Eyed Peas shirt with a saying on it. I had on some high top blue Sketchers. Also I had on a thin black Gap jacket to keep me warm.
What was your child wearing?	[Child] was wearing blue jeans and a red shirt with flowers on it. She had on some white Mary Janes. Also she had on a thin jean jacket to keep her warm.
How did you feel at the time? (excited, proud, calm, relaxed, etc.)	I felt very proud and excited. It felt good to see her enjoying herself at the park. Seeing her smile brings joy to my heart and I love every moment that we spend together.
What thoughts did you have at the time? About your child? About your relationship?	I was happy that she was having a good time and enjoyed being at the park. I thought that we were bonding with each other, having that mother/daughter time. We were having fun spending time together. Even though she is only 6 months and may not remember this moment, I will.
What thoughts are you having now about your child and about your relationship?	I feel that we have a special bond that no one can break. We are always together and no one or nothing can come between that. She is my pride and love and I would do anything to protect her. Our relationship is one of a kind. There is not a greater feeling than being a parent.

Because this was the first study to use an online approach to administer savoring, we wanted to ensure that our two conditions were different using empirical techniques (rather than simply reading through them for content). Accordingly, using a team of trained coders and a manual we had developed for this purpose, we analyzed these typed responses for savoring quality, which allowed us to ascertain the focus of the savoring.

We analyzed these savoring narratives on two variables of interest: the degree to which the narratives were *relational* and the degree to which they were *positive*. Our hope was that in terms of the relational variable, the relational savoring condition would be significantly higher in content than the other

EXHIBIT 3.2. Excerpt From Relational Savoring Response From Growing Families Study, Lower Quality Example

Prompt	Participant response
Using as much detail as possible, describe what happened.	Going to the park with [Child 1] and [Child 2] for the first time. We walked. I brought a toys [sic], a blanket, drinks, and snacks. [Child 1] loved the slide and swings the most. Spent a few hours there.
What was the air like? What was the weather like?	Really nice. [Child] had on a pink jumper and we both got a nice tan! I was able to lay a blanket down in the shade to sit on. It was really perfect park weather.
What time of day did the moment occur?	Early morning to midday. I walked there around 10 with them and didn't get home til after 3!
What were you wearing?	I wore a pair of cut off shorts. They were the most comfortable piece of clothing I had since I gave birth shortly before this day. I also had on a yellow tank top and sneakers.
What was your child wearing?	[Child] wore a bright pink and white jumper her dad picked out for her. She also had on white socks and sneakers.
How did you feel at the time? (excited, proud, calm, relaxed, etc.)	Happy and worried! It was my first outing by myself with my two girls! I didn't know what to expect but I knew [child] needed to play some outside. We both were getting cabin fever after a long hospital stay and delivery of her little sister.
What thoughts did you have at the time? About your child? About your relationship?	I loved her very much and she's a silly girl like me. Watching her go down the slides made me think of the park I use to go to as a kid.
What thoughts are you having now about your child and about your relationship?	I love her and am really happy she is fun, adventurous, silly, and happy! We do so much together! From dancing and singing to cooking to cleaning she is my constant companion.

two conditions, which would not differ. However, our findings revealed that the relational condition was higher in relational content than the other two conditions but that the personal condition was also significantly higher than the neutral condition. Our hope in terms of the positive variable was that the two savoring conditions (relational and personal) would be significantly higher than the neutral condition and that the two savoring conditions would not differ. The analyses regarding the positive scale were in line with our anticipation.

As described above, based on the results of these validity checks, we determined that the personal savoring intervention was not as ideal a control condition as we had hoped because the personal savoring condition contained some relational content; it was not as strongly relational as the relational savoring condition, but it was significantly more relational than the neutral control condition. Therefore, it did not seem justifiable to keep the groups separate for all analyses. We kept the groups separate only while testing for differences between the conditions and then combined the two savoring conditions when testing whether we had any differences in condition that varied as a function of parents' attachment style.

Our analyses examining differences between the conditions revealed that participants in the two savoring conditions increased in self-reported positive emotion as compared with the neutral control and that participants in the two savoring conditions did not differ from one another. Likewise, participants in the two savoring conditions reported lower negative emotion than participants in the control condition, and the participants in the two savoring conditions did not differ from one another. Relational savoring participants showed higher relationship satisfaction following the relationship stressor, which is important given that this is a targeted outcome.

In this study, our sample was large enough to enable us to also examine some interaction effects. We were interested in testing the hypothesis that relational savoring might have larger effects on parents who were more avoidant in their attachment. Although we anticipated that relational savoring would have more benefits for people who are higher in either attachment avoidance or anxiety, this study tested the idea that this brief, single administration of relational savoring would have more of an impact on parents high in attachment avoidance. We argued that people high in avoidance pay less attention to relational experiences (Dozier & Kobak, 1992; Mikulincer & Sheffi, 2000), minimize positive events (Gentzler et al., 2010), and underestimate positive emotions associated with past interpersonal experiences (Gentzler & Kerns, 2006). This evidence led us to believe they would be less likely to independently engage in relational savoring and more likely to benefit from a micro-intervention.

For analyses involving attachment avoidance as a moderator, we combined the personal and relational savoring groups (since the personal savoring group had contained some relational content). We did not find that attachment avoidance moderated the association between savoring and positive emotion, but we did find that it moderated the association between the savoring condition and negative emotion. When parents had low attachment avoidance, savoring did not have an impact on negative emotion, but when parents reported mean or higher levels of avoidance, savoring decreased negative emotion compared to the neutral control condition.

We found a similar pattern when we examined whether attachment avoidance moderated the association between savoring and poststressor relationship satisfaction—the interaction effect was significant, and the pattern that was revealed was that condition was not associated with poststressor relationship satisfaction when attachment avoidance was at mean or lower levels, but when attachment avoidance was high, being assigned to the savoring condition was associated with higher relationship satisfaction than being assigned to the control condition.

Although we had not intended for this to be a longitudinal study, approximately 2 years later, we decided to approach participants in the original sample to see if they would be willing to complete a follow-up assessment. A small percentage of the original sample ($n = 64$) was willing to participate in the follow-up study. We found that among participants reporting high attachment avoidance at baseline, participation in the savoring conditions resulted in higher relationship closeness at follow-up compared to participation in the control condition.

These findings were impressive for the first study of relational savoring that we had conducted among parents, but we were eager to conduct a more in-depth investigation of relational savoring that would improve upon the limitations of this preliminary work. This was the inspiration for the next study that we conducted on relational savoring, which was the most in-depth study to this day.

The PARENT Study: An In-Person Multisession Study

This next study, named the "PARENT Study" (Promoting Attachment and Relational Engagement in Toddlers), was a randomized controlled trial of mothers of toddlers (ages 18–27 months). We chose to focus on mothers because they are more often primary caregivers and because our prior study of parents of all genders had enrolled a minority of fathers (9.4%; Burkhart et al., 2015). Therefore, to reduce statistical noise, we recruited only mothers in this study. This study was important in that it went many steps beyond our initial work on relational savoring; it was a longitudinal study (as opposed to a short-term, cross-sectional study), it involved four in-person administrations of the intervention, and the assessments were much more in depth.

The procedure for this study is depicted in Figure 3.2. Following a baseline assessment, the mothers were randomized to either personal or relational savoring interventions, both of which consisted of four intervention sessions occurring once a week over a 4-week period. In contrast to the Growing Families Study, the intervention sessions in the PARENT Study were conducted in person in mothers' homes in the evening hours, ostensibly (ideally) after their children were asleep. We reasoned that doing the intervention in mothers' homes would help increase engagement for mothers and also would potentially make mothers more likely to use the technique in other aspects of their

FIGURE 3.2. Procedure for the PARENT Study

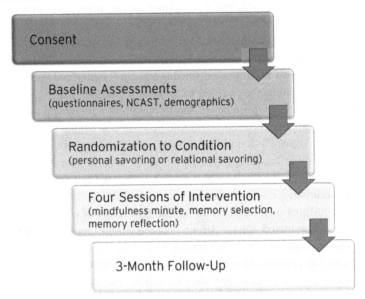

Note. PARENT = Promoting Attachment and Relational Engagement in Toddlers; NCAST = Nursing Child Assessment Satellite Training.

lives. We chose this time based on the idea that for parents of young children, evening hours were quiet times of reflection (relative to daytime hours). We sought to catch mothers at a time when quiet reflection and relaxation were possible to achieve, so they could turn their full attention to the intervention.

The big-picture goals of this study were to move beyond examining immediate postintervention outcomes, which is what we had done in our prior investigations, and also examine longer-term outcomes. We also wanted to assess the fidelity of the delivery of the intervention itself and the quality of the intervention sessions. Finally, we were interested in examining whether the intervention worked equally well or better for Latina as compared to non-Latina mothers.

This latter desire was based on our supposition that the relational savoring intervention is congruent with Latino/a/x cultural values of familism and *simpatía* (Acevedo et al., 2020; Campos & Kim, 2017; Senft et al., 2021). Although not originally designed with the Latino/a/x community in mind, the values underlying the intervention are remarkably consistent with the cultural values that the Latino/a/x community embraces: the values of close relationships and family and the importance of positive emotion expression, particularly in combination with one another. These values are highly privileged within the Latino/a/x community (Holloway et al., 2009), which is evident in a variety of ways, including the way in which Latino/a/x community members discuss their relationships, spend their time, and make major decisions within their lives; family is integral, and there is synergy in the connection between family and positive emotion.

In the words of Abuelita from the movie *Coco*, "Being a part of this family means you are here for this family." In fact, themes like this seem omnipresent in films and books portraying Latino/a/x families. One of Disney's newest movies, *Encanto*, encompasses this notion of family as well within its title. As Abuela states, "We must protect our family, our Encanto." *Encanto* has several meanings, including "to charm," "miracle," and "enchantment." The Madrigal family stands as a pillar to the townspeople of support and positivity—a kind of love and care common in Latino/a/x communities that are reciprocated back to the family at the end of the film. Given this apparent fit of values between the relational savoring intervention and Latino/a/x culture, we were interested in assessing whether this relational savoring intervention worked as well or better for the Latina mothers involved in this investigation.

First, we were interested in examining the fidelity with which the interveners delivered the intervention, as well as the quality of the savoring sessions that ensued. As this was our first in-person administration of relational savoring with parents, evaluating the quality of the sessions was an important first step. In terms of the immediate intervention outcomes, we were interested in examining postsavoring positive emotion and closeness with children, as in our online study. In terms of longer-term outcomes, we examined the following at the 3-month follow-up: whether relational savoring affects parenting behavior (in the form of parenting sensitivity in interactions with the child), parent reflective functioning (the parent's ability to understand that mental states [thoughts and feelings] that motivate behavior), parenting wellness, and intervention uptake (whether parents were still using the intervention; Borelli, Kerr, et al., 2023). These newly added outcomes are critical because they are ones we would expect to be affected by relational savoring but had not been previously examined (Borelli, Smiley, et al., 2020).

Preliminary Outcomes: Fidelity and Quality of Participant Response
First, we found that the intervention achieved a high degree of fidelity despite being delivered by paraprofessionals (undergraduate students, postbaccalaureate students, and graduate students), rather than professionally trained therapists. To assess fidelity, we recorded and coded the savoring sessions using a coding system we had developed in our laboratory.

Our coded data revealed that although therapists in both conditions demonstrated high levels of general rapport-building behaviors (e.g., keeps questions flowing or uses a calm voice), therapists in the relational savoring condition delivered the target behaviors (e.g., asking the participant to think about a time when they felt they were there for their child) more than therapists in the personal savoring condition (e.g., asking the participant to think about a time when they enjoyed something on their own), and vice versa. This adds to the evidence from our earlier internet-based studies that demonstrates that this intervention is highly portable and relatively easy to administer. The interventionists in this study had relatively low levels of experience (in that they were majority undergraduates) and little training in the intervention itself (approximately 4 hours), and this limited amount of experience and training was sufficient to culminate in high-fidelity delivery of the intervention.

Another point worth mentioning is that the participants' responses to the intervention largely mapped onto our hypotheses. Specifically, participants in the relational condition generated narratives that were higher in child focus, higher in secure base/safe haven content, and higher in connectedness with the child, whereas participants in the personal condition generated narratives that were higher in self-focus. These findings suggest that the interventions functioned as we expected (Borelli, Kerr, et al., 2023). Two exceptions to this are that participants in the relational savoring group generated savoring narratives that (a) were more positive and (b) had a higher degree of specificity than participants in the personal savoring group; we had anticipated that these scales would be equivalent across the two intervention conditions.

In terms of the Latina mothers in our sample, our results revealed that they responded to the intervention by discussing their relationships in positive and connected ways. The excerpts from relational savoring sessions included below from Latina mothers in our sample illustrate the emphasis on connectedness and positivity within their relationships (*simpatía*).

> Just like thinking that um my grandpa passed away seven years ago—yeah I think seven or eight years ago and he was a really great cook. And I—I didn't like to cook, I didn't like the kitchen as much but he showed me how to make a pancake so now every time I make pancakes I feel like he's there and I get—and I tell [Child] like oh I remember my grandpa taught me how to make this and I'm happy I can do that for him.
> And I wish I could have learned more stuff 'cause he really cooked a lot. I hope that we remain close as grown-ups, and I would hope that he [Child] sees me as somebody he can be close with, somebody like as a friend and that he would it wouldn't be like negativity [*child fusses*] as he grows up like "oh I did something so now my mom doesn't like me anymore." I always want it to be positive.

[Mother describing recent interaction with child] I was happy and excited that he wanted me. Again, I wasn't expecting to, to, for him to be awake. Uh, so I thought, you know, I was, it always makes me feel good when he's, he wants me. Um, and so I, um, picked him up like I said and, uh, when I started holding him I started to feel calm.

Intervention Outcomes

Now, turning to the outcomes of the intervention, what did we see? Our findings were mostly supportive of the efficacy of the relational savoring intervention: We found that as compared with mothers in the personal savoring condition, mothers in relational savoring reported higher positive emotion (gratitude, pride) and greater closeness to their child immediately following the intervention (Borelli, Kerr, et al., 2023). Further, mothers in the relational savoring condition showed greater sensitivity to their children at follow-up compared with mothers in the personal savoring group.

We also found some effects that were specific to Latina mothers: Among Latina mothers only, relational savoring was associated with higher reflective functioning and intervention uptake at follow-up. The cultural congruence of the relational savoring intervention was indeed important for the Latina mothers; this intervention resonated with the mothers, and the control intervention (the personal savoring condition) was not culturally resonant with these mothers. It was much more like a truly neutral control for the mothers. As stated earlier, we reasoned that the findings underscored the importance of cultural matching of the intervention to the population being served (Borelli, Kerr, et al., 2023) while also highlighting the fact that some interventions do not require a wholesale cultural adaptation to be appealing or effective with minoritized populations.

Finally, relational savoring did not have any impacts on parenting wellness at follow-up; in fact, across the sample as a whole, parents showed significant decreases in parenting wellness from pretreatment to posttreatment. When I say "parenting wellness," I am referring to subjective meaning in the life of parenting (Steger et al., 2006) and subjective happiness in parenting (Lyubomirsky & Lepper, 1999).

Although in some ways the lack of effects on parenting wellness was surprising given that relational savoring had effects at posttreatment on positive emotion, we had two potential explanations for this lack of effects. The first is that the toddler years are challenging ones for many parents, ones that may be difficult to weather with higher levels of parenting wellness. So it may be unsurprising that when transitioning from late infancy to early toddlerhood, we observed decreases in parenting wellness. The second explanation was that the scores at pretreatment were extremely high across the sample (mean score of 6.50 out of 7 on one of the measures), so we reasoned that the decrease could represent a regression to the mean. Either way, we argued that these findings should be followed up in subsequent studies so we can ascertain whether it is a true lack of effect or artifact.

Taken together, we construed these findings as providing evidence of the efficacy of relational savoring in enhancing short- and longer-term relational and individual outcomes when delivered in person in four installments to this population, as well as providing preliminary evidence of cultural congruence for Latinas. The findings were impressive in revealing that a relatively brief intervention administered by paraprofessionals could have enduring impacts over a 3-month period on outcomes such as parenting sensitivity and reflective functioning (Latina mothers only).

In a subsequent analysis of the treatment effects of this PARENT Study trial, we sought to evaluate the mechanisms underlying the links between the savoring condition and reflective functioning at the 3-month follow-up assessment—that is, we wanted to understand *how* reflective functioning was enhanced by participating in relational savoring. This analysis could also be referred to as a statistical mediation.

To do this, we used the savoring session quality coding and examined whether savoring session quality mediated the association between intervention condition and reflective functioning at follow-up. We found that both relational savoring and personal savoring contributed to enhancing reflective functioning though through different means. Specifically, relational savoring had an indirect effect on reflective functioning through higher connectedness and specificity of savoring content. In contrast, personal savoring had an indirect effect on reflective functioning through greater self-focus in savoring content (Borelli, Kazmierski, et al., 2023). We concluded that the ways mothers engaged with savoring—either by reflecting on connections with their children or by appreciating their own growth or happiness—helped to explain why they were able to think more deeply about the thoughts, feelings, and motives of their children.

Community Studies of Relational Savoring With Parents

Finally, we have conducted a larger scale investigation of an adapted relational savoring intervention that was codeveloped in collaboration with a community agency serving low-income Latino/a/x families, Latino Health Access. Latino Health Access uses the promotor(a) model of intervention (Barnett et al., 2018; Elder et al., 2009), which involves employing trained community workers to deploy health interventions to members of the community. This model, which will be discussed in greater detail in Chapter 10, contains strengths in its ability to address linguistic and cultural barriers in treatment delivery (Messias et al., 2013; Rhodes et al., 2007; Tran et al., 2014; Waitzkin et al., 2011). This intervention contained a focus on relational savoring (two of eight sessions are devoted in their entirety to relational savoring) but also contained other foci as well. Further, the entire intervention had been modified from its original form (for example, from how it was delivered in the PARENT Study) as it had been adapted to include feedback from the promotores. Thus, although the intervention was culturally compatible with the values identified by the promotores, it was not as faithful to the theoretical principles as originally developed.

In this study, our research team conceptualized a model of how relational savoring exerts its effects by differentiating between mechanisms of change (attachment security and reflective functioning) and outcomes (depression, anxiety, and externalizing symptoms). Data from 112 mother–child dyads who participated in the intervention groups revealed pre–post improvements in several outcomes of interest. Specifically, within participants in the intervention group, youth under age 14 increased in attachment security from pretreatment to posttreatment and older adolescents (ages 14–17) showed increases in reflective functioning, whereas younger adolescents showed decreases. In terms of intervention outcomes, youth depression, anxiety, and externalizing symptoms decreased, as well as maternal depressive and anxiety symptoms, from pretreatment to posttreatment. Parenting satisfaction also increased (Borelli, Yates, et al., 2021). Further, the promotores reported that the intervention was consistent with their cultural values, and they ended up implementing many of the messages from the program with their own families (Borelli, Cervantes, et al., 2022; Borelli, Russo, et al., 2022).

In interpreting these findings, it is important to note that there is no control group data to compare these findings against and also that the intervention is a broader family resilience program containing two of eight sessions focusing on relational savoring in both mother and youth groups. Thus, of all of the relational savoring studies reviewed here, this represents the least pure form of data, although in some senses the most ecologically valid given that the intervention was delivered by promotores in the field.

An adaptation of relational savoring has also been developed for use with children and their incarcerated parents. This work is led by Margaret Kerr and her team (2022) at the University of Wisconsin–Madison and has involved the creation of an attachment-based intervention called the Enhanced Visits Model (EVM), which is designed to help address common challenges confronting incarcerated parents and their children, as well as to improve the parent–child relationship, attachment security within the child, and parental reflective functioning. EVM involves the combination of in-home video chat via tablet and coaching, delivered via an attachment lens, that is designed to support the child during their visits with the incarcerated parent.

The role of the intervention coaches is to support both the at-home caregiver and the incarcerated parent in using relational savoring as a way to help them understand how their child may be feeling during the video call, as well as to make attachment-based links with their child (e.g., such as the child needing to feel safe or protected or the child missing the parent). The program is in its initial stages of implementation and evaluation, so no results are yet available, but its goal is to enable parents to increase their capacity for reflective functioning by gaining a deeper understanding of the connection between emotions and behaviors within themselves and their child and amplify positive memories that can often be overshadowed by negativity, especially within a high-stress population (such as incarcerated parents).

RELATIONAL SAVORING INTERVENTION WITH PARTNERS

In couple relationships, couples who find ways to capitalize on positive emotions that naturally occur and to upregulate one another's mood states (Costa-Ramalho et al., 2015; Fincham & Beach, 2010; Langston, 1994; Samios & Khatri, 2019) have better relationship outcomes. This includes savoring; research demonstrates that couples who savor more fare better. Specifically, one study, conducted by Susana Costa-Ramalho and colleagues (2015), examined a large sample of adults in committed relationships ($N = 473$), finding that those who engaged in more positive savoring behaviors (counting blessings, feeling relieved, memory building, and less killjoy thinking) reported higher relationship quality and satisfaction.

Another study conducted by Christina Samios and Vidushi Khatri (2019) examined couples and found that for women, savoring more predicted their own and their partner's higher relationship satisfaction, and that for both members of the couple the association between savoring tendency and relationship satisfaction is mediated by positive emotion. This work provides the foundation for the argument that interventions that promote savoring among couples may improve couple- and individual-level well-being.

Interventions that introduce partners to the practice of savoring have also been developed. This work has been less extensive than the relational savoring research conducted within parent–child relationships, but it is worth discussing here. The first study of relational savoring in partner relationships was the Pomona Deployment Study, a longitudinal study of 32 female military spouses whose military partners were all about to undergo a military deployment (their deployments ranged in length, but more than 50% were 9 months or longer); this study was conducted within my laboratory (Borelli et al., 2014). Figure 3.3 presents the procedure for this study. This was actually the first study of relational savoring that was ever conducted, so I consider it to be the birthplace of it all. As a result, the methods used in this study are less well developed than in some of the other investigations.

At the baseline assessment, which occurred 2 weeks before their partners were about to deploy to a war zone, the participants completed assessments of attachment style (avoidance and anxiety) as well as romantic relationship satisfaction. During the deployment (2 weeks postdeparture), the participants completed an assessment over the phone and computer that involved completing three stream-of-consciousness speech tasks in which they spoke in an open-ended fashion about the predetermined topics (the last time they did laundry, the deployment, and their anticipated reunion with their spouse). The reunion stream-of-consciousness recordings were transcribed and later coded for the degree of positivity the nondeploying spouses exhibited, which we operationalized as an index of anticipatory savoring of the upcoming reunion.

For many of these spouses, anticipating a reunion 2 weeks into a 9-month-long deployment is a challenging task; being able to fully immerse oneself in the task of imagining a positive reunion with one's spouse is a vulnerable emotional experience. Those who can allow themselves to experience that positive emotion associated with anticipatory savoring may be protected from

FIGURE 3.3. Procedure for the Pomona Deployment Study

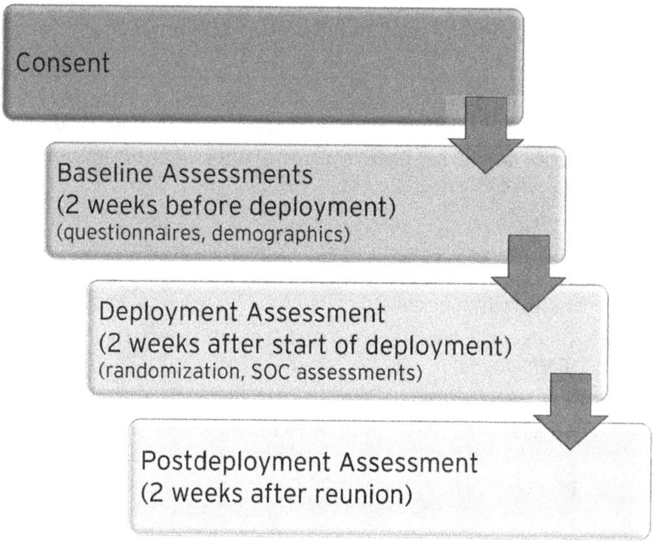

Consent
↓
Baseline Assessments
(2 weeks before deployment)
(questionnaires, demographics)
↓
Deployment Assessment
(2 weeks after start of deployment)
(randomization, SOC assessments)
↓
Postdeployment Assessment
(2 weeks after reunion)

Note. SOC = stream of consciousness.

negative outcomes. We conceptualized this as a measure of nondeploying spouses' ability to engage in savoring during a challenging time (deployment) and reasoned that this would protect their relationships against the stress of the deployment. Indeed, in one analysis of this data set, we found that nondeploying spouses who showed higher positivity during the reunion stream-of-consciousness task were protected from the negative impacts of mental distress on relationship satisfaction (Froidevaux et al., 2023).

Later during this assessment session (after the stream-of-consciousness assessments), we directly tested the hypothesis that relational savoring is protective against risk. Participants were randomly assigned to complete either a relational savoring or a personal savoring task, led by an experimenter. Each task lasted about 10 minutes. During this initial test of relational savoring, we delivered the intervention over the phone, and we encouraged participants to close their eyes if they wanted once we got to the memory reflection stage of the exercise. Further, instead of having participants speak their thoughts aloud, we had them think their thoughts privately in their heads under the assumption that having the thoughts kept private would be more powerful. We did have participants reflect on the experience of savoring. Exhibit 3.3 provides an example of one of these reflections.

In subsequent trials of the intervention, we changed this aspect of the intervention because we thought it might be more effective to say the words aloud. This change was motivated by exposure to the functionalist perspective of emotion, which argues that emotion should be expressed in order for

EXHIBIT 3.3. Excerpt From Relational Savoring Response From Pomona Deployment Study

RESEARCHER:	OK, thank you. Um . . . so in a few sentences, could you tell me about the types of things you were thinking about during this exercise?
PARTICIPANT:	Uh . . . just very positive reminder of when we're together that, um . . . we can overcome anything.
RESEARCHER:	Yeah.
PARTICIPANT:	And when we're—when we're during a rough time, you know, without the kids, without distraction . . . even in the worst of times we're . . . we're [indecipherable].
RESEARCHER:	That's really great, you did *such* a good job with that task. Thank you. [Both laugh.]
PARTICIPANT:	No problem.
RESEARCHER:	So, again, the reason that we're asking you to do this is because we believe that focusing on positive aspects of your relationship, and especially feelings of connectedness while you—with your spouse will help you stay connected to him during his deployment.
PARTICIPANT:	Yeah. I agree.

it to be released. This reasoning holds that saying words aloud and sharing them in an interpersonal context makes an intervention stronger. In this initial study of nondeploying partners, however, participants were asked to think their responses in their minds. Before and after each savoring task, participants rated their emotion using the Self-Assessment Manikin (Bradley & Lang, 1994; Lang, 1980), which measures affective valence, with low scores signifying positive emotion and high scores signifying negative emotion.

Although we did not have a record of thoughts during savoring, we did ask participants at the end of each session a couple of questions about their experience of the savoring exercise, which provided us some insight into their psychological experience of the intervention. We discovered that participants were engaging in the type of psychological process we were hoping to target through our relational savoring intervention. The intervention contributed to a feeling of being psychologically connected, despite being physically separated, to a sense of resilience in the relationship and to the importance of staying connected.

Our focal research question concerned the interaction between participants' baseline attachment avoidance and savoring condition; we reasoned that participants with low levels of attachment avoidance would find the relational savoring task to be beneficial and thus would experience positive emotion, and we anticipated that participants who had high baseline avoidance would find the relational savoring exercise to be difficult and thought it might result in more negative emotion.

This prediction was grounded in the theoretical supposition that people high in avoidance have a deactivating emotion regulation strategy that involves turning one's thoughts and feelings away from attachment-related topics; this ought to be particularly heightened during a time such as military deployment, when one's partner is away and potentially under threat and one's attachment system is activated (Cassidy, 1994; Cassidy & Kobak, 1988). However, as an intervention that turns one's attention toward attachment-related thoughts and feelings, relational savoring disrupts this habitual way of regulating thoughts and feelings vis-à-vis attachment relationships and could result in (at least momentary) dysregulation for individuals who are high in attachment avoidance. Alternatively, people who are low in attachment avoidance, who would not have a deactivating strategy, would hypothetically find the act of turning their attention toward attachment-related thoughts and feelings a welcome activity, one that could bring them a host of positive feelings (such as feelings of closeness).

Our hypotheses in this study were supported; we found an interaction between participants' attachment avoidance and their savoring condition in predicting their postsavoring emotion (after controlling for their presavoring emotion). The pattern we observed was that for participants low in avoidance, those who completed relational savoring reported more positive emotions than those who completed personal savoring; however, for participants high in attachment avoidance, the pattern was reversed, and those who completed relational savoring reported more negative emotions than those who completed personal savoring.

How do I understand the fact that relational savoring resulted in more negative emotion among nondeploying spouses who were high in avoidance when administered during the deployment, especially when the Burkhart et al. (2015) study found that parents low in avoidance benefited the most from relational savoring? One interpretation is that the timing of when relational savoring is administered matters. It may be that providing this intervention to people high in avoidance during an attachment stressor (military deployment) is too disruptive or dysregulating; it may force people high in avoidance to focus on relationships when their modal way of regulating during a relationship stressor is to deactivate the attachment system (to avoid thinking about relationships). So this increase in negative emotion may represent a true perturbation of the system.

Alternatively, it may be that experiencing negative emotion during a deployment is adaptive in terms of the type of emotional processing that occurs over the longer term. Deployments are difficult and can involve some degree of psychological pain and longing. Experiencing negative emotion in the short term could facilitate emotional connection over the long term. In fact, the pattern of means revealed that among the higher avoidance participants, those who experienced more negative emotions in response to the intervention reported feeling more confident about their ability to stay connected to their spouse in response to future separations. These were small, nonsignificant differences, and this was a small sample, so all conclusions should be interpreted cautiously.

My biggest takeaway from these data is that it is too early to tell whether relational savoring is helpful or unhelpful for people high in avoidance when administered during an attachment-related stressor. What I can say with certainty is that when administering this intervention during an attachment-related stressor such as deployment, this intervention may require more clinical acumen and support than we employed in the current study. In this study, as in our other studies, the interveners were undergraduate students, postbaccalaureate students, and graduate students without clinical training. We learned a great deal from conducting this small-scale intervention, including lessons about the importance of collecting more complete data, collecting data from a larger sample, and conducting studies with larger samples when possible. Recruitment was highly challenging with this population, which slowed down the entire study, and therefore we were interested in working with easier-to-access samples in the future.

After the deployment study, we conducted a study on relational savoring that involved partners in long-distance romantic relationships. Participants were given instructions online (in writing) and responded in writing. This study, called the "Partners Apart Study," involved individual members ($N = 533$) of long-distance romantic relationships, defined as romantic relationships lasting at least 6 months in which partners lived 100 or more miles apart (Borelli et al., 2015).

The procedure for the Partners Apart Study is depicted in Figure 3.4. The sample was fairly diverse in terms of race/ethnicity (56% Caucasian, 19% Asian American, 12.5% Hispanic, 6% African American, 5% other, and 1% Native American) and also in terms of reported income (49% reported annual income < U.S. $40,000). The majority of the sample had at least some college education; 40% reported having obtained a bachelor's degree, and 41% reported having earned an associate's degree or fewer years of education. Most of the participants worked outside the home (70%) and did not have children (84%).

In this internet-based study, after completing a baseline assessment in which they reported on their relationship satisfaction with their partner and their baseline emotional state, participants were randomized to one of three conditions (relational savoring, personal savoring, or neutral control [report

FIGURE 3.4. Procedure for the Partners Apart Study

Consent

Baseline Assessments

Randomization to Condition
(neutral control, personal savoring, relational savoring) +
Intervention
(completed online: combined memory selection/reflection)

Postintervention Assessment

Stressor Task (Vignette) +
Postvignette Assessment

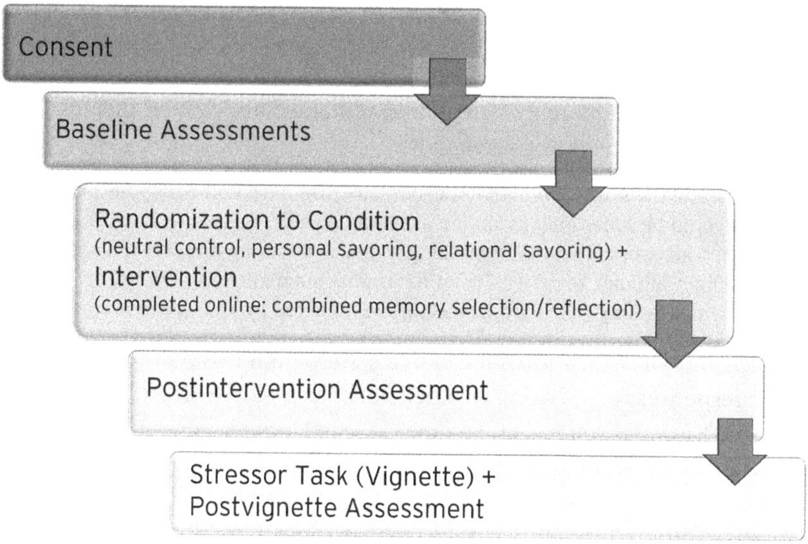

your morning routine]). After completing the experimental manipulation, participants again reported their emotional state.

Next, participants completed a relationship stressor task, developed for the purpose of this study, and then reported on their relationship satisfaction. The relationship stressor task was designed to be stressful given the long-distance context of the relationships of the participants in the study. The task was developed after conducting focus groups with members of long-distance relationships and workshopping ideas for the common stressors within these relationships. We developed the vignette, which was designed to present a situation that was ambiguous but could be interpreted as threatening the integrity of the relationship. Participants were told to imagine that their partners were supposed to call them at a certain time at night after they had returned home from work, but it was now 2 hours past the appointed time and they had not yet called. Participants were asked a series of questions about their reactions to the imagined scenario ("What are the reason(s) your partner has not called? How does this make you feel about your partner?"); our pilot testing of this vignette suggested that the vignette evoked strong reactions from participants.

The outcomes of this study were quite striking. As with the Growing Families Study, in this study, participants had simply been asked to respond in writing to relational savoring prompts that had also been administered in writing. In many ways, we consider this to be a much weaker form of administration of relational savoring than an in-person administration. However, despite this fact, the responses participants provided were highly personal and emotional (see Exhibit 3.4). By and large, the participants engaged with the task in the way we intended. Their responses to the savoring intervention were highly face valid; for the most part, they engaged with the intervention in the way we intended. They generated relational savoring narratives that were personally relevant, were emotionally salient, and contained attachment themes. They responded to the following prompt:

> Think about a positive emotional experience you have had with your partner. This could be something as simple as taking a walk together or laughing over a funny joke, or it could be something as major as taking a vacation or accomplishing a big task together. Try to focus on a single memory of a time when you felt especially cherished, protected, or accepted by your partner.

Participants were then provided with a series of follow-up prompts to guide their responses (e.g., "Using as much detail as possible, describe what happened"; "How did you feel at the time? [excited, proud, calm, relaxed, etc.]").

As evidence of the effectiveness of simple textual prompts, we conducted a linguistic analysis as one way of assessing the degree to which participants engaged with the task. We reasoned that participants in the relational savoring

Evidence Base for Relational Savoring • 59

EXHIBIT 3.4. Excerpt From Relational Savoring Response From Partners Apart Study

Prompt	Participant response
Using as much detail as possible, describe what happened.	When [partner] and I first started dating, we were having conflicts related to his ex. When New Year's Eve came around, it happened to land on her birthday. She threw a big party and said we weren't welcome. So [partner] and I stayed at his place watching the ball drop with his roommate. At halftime, he said he wanted to show me something in his room. Once we got in there, we wrestled a little bit in bed until I was sitting on his lap. He looked me straight in the eye and said, "I've been meaning to say something to you, but I hadn't found the right moment." So I replied with "What is it?". . . "[participant], I love you." My voice caught in my throat as I began to tear up. "[partner], I love you too!" And we kissed and laid there for a few minutes in an tight embrace until we heard that the ball had fallen. I looked into his eyes and I haven't looked away since. The feeling of overwhelming warmth and happiness made me smile from ear to ear for the rest of the night.
What was the air like? What was the weather like?	The air was very dry, and the weather was frigid outsides. It was far below freezing, and there was snow on the ground.
What time of day did the moment occur?	It took place at about midnight PST.
What were you wearing?	I think I was wearing jeans and a t-shirt. I had on Uggs.
What was your partner wearing?	I'm pretty sure that [partner] was wearing jeans and a worn t-shirt, or possibly a sweater.
How did you feel at the time? (excited, proud, calm, relaxed, etc.)	I felt overwhelmingly tingly, giddy, and warm. I couldn't stop smiling. When we went into the room, I thought he was interested in sex, but he caught me completely off guard. When he said he loved me, my heart honestly fluttered, my cheeks flushed, and I smiled wide. I felt like the luckiest girl.
What thoughts did you have at the time? About your partner? About your relationship?	I had strong feelings for [partner] for a while, and apparently when I had a few drinks I would tell him that I loved him, but when this happened I was taken completely by surprise. I had been feeling a little odd to have had such strong feelings for him so fast, and I could tell he had feelings, but nothing had been said. Since early in our relationship, I had been scared that he may not have wanted the relationship [to] last. This moment erased that thought and I haven't looked back since.
What thoughts are you having now about your partner and about your relationship?	[Partner] is my rock. We have gotten through some difficult life obstacles, and our relationship has not wavered. We communicate so well, and we have similar beliefs that it makes being with him effortless.

task ought to use more first-person plural pronouns than participants in the other two conditions if they were engaging in the task as intended. This was the only condition that had an explicit focus on relationships. Focusing on relationships should lead participants to write in a relationally inclusive way, one that involves talking about communal relationships. Greater use of first-person plural pronouns is thought to be an indicator of greater "we-ness," or relational, communal orientation (Rohrbaugh et al., 2008). People are more apt to use *we*, *us*, and *our* language when they are approaching situations as members of a group.

We assessed the frequency of first-person plural and singular pronoun use in participants' responses to the savoring prompts and the control condition (morning routine), and we found that participants in the relational savoring condition used more first-person plural words (e.g., *we*, *us*, and *our*) than participants in the personal savoring condition and in the control condition; the opposite pattern was present for first-person singular pronouns (e.g., *me*, *my*, and *mine*).

We also examined participants' use of positive emotion words and found that as expected, participants in the two savoring conditions used significantly more positive emotion words than participants in the neutral control condition, and that participants in the two savoring conditions did not differ from one another in the frequency of their positive emotion word use. These findings were further validation of the purpose of our personal savoring control condition, which was intended to be a control for the positive emotion aspect of savoring but not intended to evoke a relational focus.

In our hypothesis testing for this Partners Apart Study, we first examined participants' postsavoring emotion, assessing whether there were group differences in positive and negative emotions across the conditions. Here we found that participants in the relational savoring group reported significantly higher positive emotion than participants in the other two comparison conditions (personal savoring and neutral control) after controlling for presavoring positive emotions. We found the reverse pattern for negative emotions, where participants in the relational savoring group reported less negative emotion than participants in either of the other two control conditions after controlling for presavoring negative emotion.

For subsequent analyses of the Partners Apart data set, we grouped the two control conditions (personal savoring and neutral control) together since they did not differ from one another on various indices. Our next goal was to examine whether baseline relationship satisfaction moderated the association between experimental condition (relational savoring and control) and emotion outcomes. In other words, we wanted to examine whether people who had different levels of relationship satisfaction responded differently to the interventions.

Our effects revealed that baseline relationship satisfaction moderated the association between condition and posttask positive emotion but not posttask negative emotion. In the case of posttask positive emotion, it was only when participants began the study with mean or higher relationship satisfaction that relational savoring increased their positive emotion. However, relational savoring resulted in lower negative emotion regardless of participants' relationship satisfaction at baseline.

We also found that these variables (condition, postreflection emotion, and poststressor relationship satisfaction) were linked—such that the way in which people reacted to the savoring or control condition in terms of their emotional response predicted their response to the (implied infidelity) stressor task, which in turn predicted their emotional response to the task. When there was an association between them, it was partially explained by the postreflection task's positive and negative emotions.

Another study of a single-session delivery of savoring compared three conditions, relational savoring, personal savoring, and a mindfulness control condition, all of which were delivered online to adults who were members of romantic relationships for at least 3 months (Wang et al., 2022). This study was conducted by a laboratory from Binghamton University, with lead author Binghuang Wang. The authors hypothesized that as compared with participants in the personal savoring condition, those in the relational savoring condition would have less relationship distress (measured immediately before and immediately after the administration of the intervention), but this hypothesis was not supported. They also tested exploratory hypotheses regarding optimism and positive emotion measured before and after the intervention, finding that optimism did not differ between the two conditions, but participants in the relational savoring condition did report significantly higher positive emotion than participants in the relational savoring condition.

In the remainder of their analyses, they collapsed their two savoring conditions (personal and relational savoring), finding that the link between the intervention condition (savoring conditions vs. mindfulness control) and lower relational distress was explained by indirect effects of positive affect and optimism. Of note is that the authors of this study did include a power analysis and commented that they were slightly underpowered to test their hypotheses; this may have explained why some of their hypotheses were not supported, especially those where the findings were close to statistically significant.

We learned a great deal from the Partners Apart Study and the Growing Families Study. The main strengths of these studies are that they involved large samples and a very small dose of the intervention that was administered in a highly controlled manner (internet administration of written instructions). And yet this dose alone was a strong enough manipulation to affect certain outcomes in the short term.

One very important caveat is that we assessed outcomes only in the short term, at least in the case of the Partners Apart Study (and this is also true for the majority of the Growing Families Study). So, these findings beg the question as to whether people would continue to benefit from this minimal dose if this exercise were repeated over time.

An additional question is whether people would benefit more, or benefit over the longer term, if the dose were stronger. However, in an era when we must be sensitive to the fact that the population's growing mental health needs cannot be met by individual psychotherapy, we must always be on the lookout for scalable solutions. In this sense, relational savoring has promise as an intervention modality that could scale up and be delivered without human input with some evidence of its utility. Of course, as therapists, our interest is typically not in this form of intervention delivery, but we must be mindful of ways to increase access to services beyond the consulting room.

RELATIONAL SAVORING INTERVENTION WITH OLDER ADULTS

Relational savoring has also been tested in a single study with older adults (Borelli, Bond, et al., 2020) in the Reflections Study. At first blush, it might seem unwise to begin a relational savoring intervention with older adults, who are likely to have experienced many relational losses in their lives. However, I would like to argue that older adulthood may be an ideal time to focus on savoring, given the salience of mortality, which may promote a greater appreciation of life overall and a greater desire to look back on memories (Bryant et al., 2011; Kurtz, 2008). Older adulthood is a time for reminiscing, for looking back on life and making meaning of one's experiences. Often older adults do this in the context of valuing their relationships and social connections. And there's even more reason to do this if one is in the position of losing social relationships.

There is also some evidence of the benefits of general savoring (not relational savoring specifically) within older adults, which increases the promise of relational savoring within this population. Indeed, two studies have examined older adults' spontaneous abilities to savor the moment and have found that higher engagement in savoring is associated with greater life satisfaction, greater happiness, lower depressive symptoms, and greater health (Geiger et al., 2017; Smith & Hollinger-Smith, 2015). Further, a handful of studies have examined the impact of a general savoring intervention on older adults and have found that completing a savoring intervention is associated with a host of positive benefits, including reductions in depressive symptoms, increases in happiness, greater life satisfaction, more positive perceptions of aging, greater gratitude, and increases in resilience (Ho et al., 2014; Smith & Bryant, 2019; Smith & Hanni, 2019). The limitations of these studies were that some of them did not include a control group (Smith & Hanni, 2019) or included a no-treatment control group (Smith & Bryant, 2019), and given that they focused on general savoring rather than relational savoring, they do not contribute as directly to the evidence base of relational savoring.

My research group conducted a randomized trial of relational savoring among a small sample ($N = 63$) of older adults between the ages of 60 and 95. The procedure for the Reflections Study is displayed in Figure 3.5. Participants received a single session of either relational or personal savoring delivered in person. Savoring sessions were audio-recorded and preceded by a brief (minute-long) mindfulness exercise. Participants wore a watch that measured their cardiovascular reactivity (heart rate) during the mindfulness exercise and the savoring session. Participants completed the Positive and Negative Affect Schedule (Watson et al., 1988), a self-report measure of emotion, immediately before and after the savoring session, which we used as a measure of positive

FIGURE 3.5. Procedure for the Reflections Study

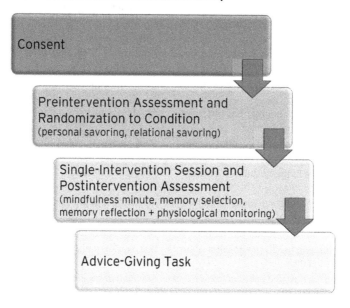

emotion states. Following the savoring session, they completed an advice-giving task, where they responded to the following prompt:

> For our last few minutes together, I'm wondering if you could finish our time giving advice—any life advice that you feel is the most meaningful. You can take as much, or as little, time as you'd like to think about this before responding. We're not looking for anything in particular, and there are no right or wrong answers—just answer with whatever comes to mind after some reflection.

They provided their life advice into an audio recorder. Their responses were then coded for agency and passivity.

The results of the study revealed several interesting conclusions. The first is that older adults were able to engage in relational savoring with high quality. Their responses were connected and engaging. Adults in both conditions were able to discuss a wide range of topics (Exhibit 3.5) and to provide rich savoring narratives in response to the prompts. Participants in the relational savoring group expressed connectedness to their loved ones and valuing of their relationships. In the words of one participant, who savored his experiences with his wife,

> We just feel so fortunate we found each other and to have the life we have together, so we just can't imagine we can't imagine being any other way. We're

EXHIBIT 3.5. Selection of Reflections From Older Adults

RELATIONAL savoring memories	PERSONAL savoring memories
Helping son settle in at school	Graduating college/attending the graduation ceremony
Taking care of/playing with daughter in the backyard	Finishing a painting
Friend offering her support when she was in a tricky situation	Attending a celebration after finishing teaching a class
Being cared for by a friend after receiving difficult news	Cooking a good meal
Rocking her granddaughter back to sleep after she had a nightmare	Creating a business patent
Sister calling participant to comfort/soothe her while she was sick	Receiving an honor at the zoo
Caring for wife in the hospital when she was sick	Hiking to a waterfall
Taking care of his father when he had dementia	Receiving a promotion to be department chair
Friend helping him get up after he fell	Sewing clothes for the first time by herself
Husband driving her to the hospital when she was in labor	Discovering flints while hiking alone
Embracing her husband as he was rocking her	Smelling grass in the morning

both confident in the relationship we have with each other, and uh we just, we just revel in that and we thank god for that every day. So and the fruit of that has been our two children and their families. We just saw, again, how fortunate, so that's where we are.

Another participant savored her experiences with her daughter and expressed valuing in a less emotional but still important way:

RESEARCHER: How will the bond you have together affect your relationship in the future and what other positive things can you imagine happening as a result of your bond to one another?

PARTICIPANT: Well, eh, she's . . . probably . . . the one I'm the closest to because [of] proximity, but also the one daughter that lives fairly close there, [Daughter 2], but she has four children and this daughter doesn't have any and is not married so you know, she just, she has more time to do stuff like this with me. The daughter with four kids doesn't really have the, um, the time to do a lot of these things. And um also [Daughter 1] is, um, she's my executer, for my estate, and um, she probably knows more about me than any of the other kids because um she just asks a lot of questions if she's curious, you know, so she's the one that's always encouraging me to write my memoirs, which I never get around to, um, we've entered a class together at [university] one time, on writing your memoirs. Um, she's um, you know, in an emergency, she's the obvious one that will be called, she's the closest and since she is my executer you know, she'll be the one that's involved—consulting her brothers and sisters of course—but she's the one that'll have the responsibility for that so yeah. We're connected.

This was sometimes challenging for participants, especially when they were recounting extremely difficult circumstances, such as caring for their dying spouses:

RESEARCHER: And I'd like to know what you were thinking when you were taking care of her in that way, in that moment—only in that moment. What about as a result of her being able to experience that care from you? That sounds very powerful—

PARTICIPANT: Well it was. It was powerful, I think. I look on it. She needed me. I was there.

RESEARCHER: Yeah, you were.

PARTICIPANT: And she needed me big time, much bigger than I thought at the—at the moment. Um . . . she felt like she was losing her mind, and . . . she came back . . . into some form of reality.

RESEARCHER: Mhm.

PARTICIPANT: And um . . . then she died.

RESEARCHER: Yeah. It sounds like she was really aware that she needed you and you were aware of her needing you and you were able to fulfill that need for her.

PARTICIPANT: Yeah, it was. . . . It was just our relationship as marriage, in marriage. You know the—if indeed we were sick and we helped each other, and that's I think that's commitment.

RESEARCHER: Yeah. And you showed your commitment.

PARTICIPANT: Yeah.

These types of experiences involving loss were more likely to come up for clients in this study than in our other studies, which is unsurprising given their age, and it posed unique challenges in terms of the clinical intervention strategies required (more on this in Chapter 6).

Our quantitative analyses also revealed an interesting pattern of results. Participants in the personal savoring condition did not increase in their positive affect from before compared with after the savoring session, but participants in the relational savoring session did increase significantly in their positive affect from before compared with after the savoring session. Further, as compared with participants in the personal savoring condition, participants in the relational savoring condition had lower heart rates during savoring after controlling for their heart rate during the mindfulness baseline. Finally, the participants in the relational condition had higher agency and lower passivity in the advice-giving task than participants in the personal savoring task. An example of an advice-giving response coded as having high agency follows:

> If you don't accept and recognize that you have choices constantly, then when the bigger choices come, you're much less likely to realize you do have choices—to turn left or to turn right or to keep straight ahead, so you have to own it. You have to own your ability to make choices. And not let life just make choices for you because if you don't make choices, life will make choices for you. And I firmly believe that some of the best things have happened to me in life is because I just decided to make a choice. I just do not believe that other people should make choices for me—and I believe that no matter what the situation is or what it looks like, I had just as much as challenges as anybody in life. But I, all along, I feel like "OK, this is the situation, what are the choices? What can I do?" (Borelli, Bond, et al., 2020, p. 337)

As a result of this pattern of findings, we concluded that relational savoring had shown initial promise within this sample of older adults and that future research should delve deeper into work with this population.

RELATIONAL SAVORING INTERVENTION WITH CHILDREN

Extremely limited work has examined the intervention with children. We report on the results of one study here (Wang et al., 2021), spearheaded by my former student Binghuang Wang, which examined the impact of a relational savoring intervention among a small sample ($N = 20$) of adolescent males with a mean age of 14.5 years ($SD_{age} = 2.64$) in residential treatment. This study, called the River Stones Study, involved four sessions of either relational or personal savoring with the participants, delivered in weekly doses of in-person sessions within the residential treatment setting. The procedure for this study is depicted in Figure 3.6.

Participants were males who were primarily members of the foster care system or postadoption system and who had psychiatric issues that were preventing them from being in a home environment. All of the participants had been diagnosed with at least one psychiatric diagnosis, including posttraumatic stress disorder, oppositional defiance disorder, and bipolar mood

FIGURE 3.6. Procedure for the River Stones Study

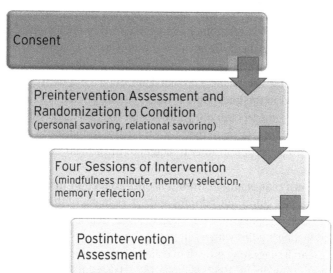

disorder. All participants were receiving psychotropic medication as well as the treatment offered within the residential treatment facility.

At baseline and following the final intervention session, participants reported on their affect using the Positive and Negative Affect Schedule (Watson et al., 1988). They also reported on their attachment style using the Experiences in Close Relationships–Relationships Structures Scale (Fraley et al., 2011). With this questionnaire, they were asked to report on their attachment anxiety regarding an attachment figure with whom they felt close.

Finally, they completed a speech sample task, known as a stream-of-consciousness speech sample, in which we asked them to speak in a stream-of-consciousness fashion into an audio recorder about their relationship with a close caregiver, such as the staff in the residential treatment facility. These speech samples were later transcribed and then analyzed for their use of first-person plural pronouns (e.g., *we*, *us*, and *our*), as in "we really like going to the movies." As described above, more frequent use of *we* pronouns, as opposed to first-person singular pronouns (e.g., *me*, *my*, and *mine*), is thought to reflect a communal focus, one that suggests that the individual views themselves are part of a relational system. This communal focus has been connected in prior work to lower rates of depression in children (Borelli et al., 2018; Sichko et al., 2016) and adults (Rude et al., 2004; Şimşek, 2013; Tackman et al., 2019).

Notably, there was also no attrition in the participant pool, and the participants in the program reported enjoying participating in the program. As this was our first trial with youth, we were also interested in investigating the quality of their responses to the relational savoring intervention. We noticed that their responses were briefer on average than the responses that adults had provided us with in other intervention trials but generally included similar content. Youth were able to respond to the suggestive techniques we include in the intervention, which was one thing we were unsure would occur, without too much difficulty. The example provided in Exhibit 3.6 is fairly typical of how youth responded to the intervention, where the suggestion of the interviewer would be accepted and then the youth would use that suggestion and build upon it to elaborate and share their own thoughts and ideas. In this case, the youth uses this as an opportunity to heighten the attachment content of the narrative.

One pattern that emerged from this data collection that was not unexpected is that the emotional content and the richness of the narratives generated by the participants were noticeably lower than what we had observed when conducting studies with adult participants. This is in line with developmental research suggesting growth in children's narrative capacity throughout development (Freedman, 1987; Kemper, 1984; Peterson & McCabe, 2013) and

EXHIBIT 3.6. Excerpt From River Stones Study

RESEARCHER:	So now I'd like you to think about what you were thinking when you were with [friend]. For example, were you thinking she really cares for me, she really loves me, she really understands me? And what do you think about it now?
PARTICIPANT:	Uh, she really understands me and I believe she still understands me now.
RESEARCHER:	Mhm.
PARTICIPANT:	Cuz she's always like she said whenever I get a friend or girlfriend she will be there to support me and whenever I'm down she's very supportive um and she's very helpful and she's a pacifist so that makes us more alike, too.
RESEARCHER:	Wow, that's really great. How does that make you feel when she says that she will be supportive?
PARTICIPANT:	Um, actually makes me feel like I'm actually very understood and cared for. It's awesome.

also in the capacity to express emotion (Denham & Couchoud, 1990; Denham et al., 1990; Denham, Renwick-DeBardi, & Hewes, 1994; Denham & Zoller, 1991; Denham, Zoller, & Couchoud, 1994; Rawana et al., 2014). However, even when participants were not able to provide rich descriptions of attachment-relevant relationship events or to make clear links between their experiences and emotions, the experience of engaging in the relational savoring intervention still led to the desired outcome.

This participant provides several examples of memories that all seem fairly unemotional and not clearly linked to attachment content. At least, he does not describe them in patently emotional language, nor does he make explicit links to strong attachment content. This is the memory that ends up getting picked by the therapist to be the focus of the savoring reflection:

RESEARCHER: Mhmm.

PARTICIPANT: I remember about three days ago I was really upset and I didn't want to deal with anything at the time.

RESEARCHER: Mhmm.

PARTICIPANT: So, my staff told me I can get out of my room for a little bit and watch a movie.

RESEARCHER: Mhmm.

PARTICIPANT: So, I had a really good time watching this movie. I forgot what it was called. It was called, it was . . . *This Is the End*, I think.

RESEARCHER: Mhmm.

PARTICIPANT: So, I was watching *This Is the End* with these guys and they really cheered me up and afterwards I wasn't angry anymore. So it was like, the staff helped me out, they knew exactly what I needed.

RESEARCHER: Mhmm.

PARTICIPANT: So anyway, yeah.

However, when asked to rate the memory of how close he felt to the staff member, on a scale of 1 to 5, he said 5. The researcher then asked how detailed the memory was, on a scale of 1 to 5, and he said 4. This was the highest rated memory the participant had, and it was the memory that also seemed the most emotionally rich. When the researcher got to the section where they asked the participant to reflect on the thoughts/meaning associated with the experience, the narrative become noticeably more emotional.

RESEARCHER: So, what kind of things were you thinking at that time?

PARTICIPANT: I was thinking that, that they were like kind of trying to calm me down. So, I think they really cared for me and they understood me about what I needed at the moment about what I needed to do, how I felt. Yeah, I felt like they really understand me.

And this richness continued later on in the savoring session:

RESEARCHER: So just letting your mind wander. But keeping it like, in a positive way. [*Silence*] If you could share those feelings that would be really great too.

PARTICIPANT: OK, um I felt like it was really. I felt really tingly like it was like, oh my gosh only one person who actually understands me. Like . . . like . . . there's other people in my life that actually care about me. . . . Like I really need to, like I really just need to shapen up then more people will end up liking me. So yeah it was a lot of things I was thinking about at the moment. Yeah.

And the session ended up with the adolescent commenting on how this technique was helpful and reminded him how reflecting on positive moments can be a helpful emotion regulation strategy.

RESEARCHER: Alright so, lastly if you could tell me in just a few sentences what kinds of things you were thinking about when we were talking about this memory and doing this? Did you feel anything and did you think about anything?

PARTICIPANT: Mhmm.

RESEARCHER: Mhmm.

PARTICIPANT: I was thinking about like, it good to remember some of the positive things when you're feeling upset. And like it was like, I never think about this stuff a lot and then whenever you come.

RESEARCHER: Mhmm.

PARTICIPANT: I think about it.

We also conducted quantitative analyses on these data, but quite frankly, we had low hopes for these analyses given the small sample size, the severity of the difficulties of these clients, and the nature of this intervention (brief, delivered by paraprofessionals). Quite surprisingly, relational savoring participants reported greater decreases in negative emotion compared to participants in the personal savoring condition. In addition, compared to participants in the personal savoring condition, participants in the relational savoring condition also increased significantly more in the first-person plural pronoun use (or "we talk") that they exhibited on their stream-of-consciousness speech tasks they delivered at posttreatment as opposed to the ones they provided at pretreatment. We interpreted this to suggest that they viewed themselves to a greater extent as part of a communal whole, interconnected with others.

We found only a marginally significant effect of condition on attachment anxiety, with participants in the relational condition showing greater decreases than participants in the personal condition. With such a small sample size, we construed these findings as promising evidence that the relational savoring intervention was off to a good start within this population.

OTHER INVESTIGATIONS OF RELATIONAL SAVORING

There have also been innovative applications of relational savoring in other spheres of psychology, including help-seeking and communication.

Help-Seeking Savoring

Help-seeking is important in the context of depression; when people are depressed, they often need additional social supports but have little motivation to seek such supports. Social withdrawal becomes their worst enemy, and they have to fight to engage in healthy behaviors, such as help-seeking, which could result in their getting the support they need.

General savoring has been identified as a means of increasing help-seeking behavior (Siegel & Thomson, 2016; Straszewski & Siegel, 2018, 2020), which is consistent with theorizing that it can activate the caregiving/care-seeking attachment system. For instance, Tasha Straszewski and Jason Siegel (2021) from Claremont Graduate University were interested in exploring whether savoring in general, and relational savoring in particular, could be useful as a public service announcement strategy to help depressed individuals engage in help-seeking behavior.

To test this hypothesis, they designed a study in which participants with at least mild depressive symptoms engaged in one of five writing tasks that varied in self-focus to a control task: vicarious savoring, relational savoring, combination savoring (combination of vicarious and relational savoring), personal savoring, and self-distanced savoring. In vicarious savoring, people are asked to savor a positive experience that occurred to someone else as a way of reducing self-focus. In self-distanced savoring, people are asked to savor as though they were the most positive person they know, which allows people to see more good in an experience than what they may have previously remembered experiencing.

The researchers hypothesized that engaging in a mental reflection task in which self-focus was low would lead to a greater likelihood of help-seeking. Self-focus already tends to be high in conditions like depression, and engaging in reflection tasks that take the focus off of the self might help to disengage attention from the self and motivate the person to seek help from others (D. A. Clark et al., 1999; Straszewski & Siegel, 2018, 2020; Wisco, 2009).

In support of their hypotheses, the researchers found that completing the relational savoring writing task led to higher help-seeking intentions than the other four tasks. Then they built on the results of this initial study and translated this into a public service announcement (PSA) by creating a PSA with relational savoring as its base. Importantly, the PSA was experiential in nature; they asked people to think about a positive experience they shared with someone they cared about and enjoyed spending time with, asking them to visualize the experience and really feel the emotions attached to the experience.

They tested the idea that as compared with exposure to a control PSA (on the importance of decluttering one's life), exposure to the relational savoring PSA would result in greater help-seeking attitudes, intentions, and behaviors. This hypothesis was not supported. In other words, when this relational savoring was translated into a PSA, the desired effects were not obtained. The authors theorized that making additional modifications, such as asking participants to recall an event that occurred within the past week, directing participants to focus more on feelings of security, or having them savor over multiple days, might be more likely to motivate help-seeking behavior.

Communication Savoring

Finally, an investigation has focused on savoring moments of successful or positive communication between people, which the authors refer to as *communication savoring* (Jiao et al., 2021). This could be considered a subtype of relational savoring, in which people are asked to focus on a subtype of a specific type of interaction between two people. As compared with participants in the control task, the participants in the communication-savoring task experienced higher positive and lower levels of negative affect.

WRAP-UP

My colleagues' and my work, as well as that of other researchers, have demonstrated that relational savoring is largely efficacious in improving emotional and relational wellness on the indicators that have been examined. The studies that have been conducted have examined short-term and longer term outcomes and have demonstrated that relational savoring has impacts when administered in various formats (internet, phone, and in-person) and when administered in small doses (single sessions). Although only two studies have examined the longer term impacts of relational savoring, the initial findings are promising and suggest that additional investigation is warranted.

PART II

THE HOW-TO OF RELATIONAL SAVORING

Now that you have a solid grounding in the theory undergirding the technique of relational savoring as well as the evidence base supporting its use, I am excited to share how to introduce it into your practice. Yes, we are now entering the hands-on section of the book, the part where I take off my professor/researcher hat and don my therapist hat. Here I provide hands-on guidance regarding how to engage in the intervention within a therapy session as well as how to address commonly occurring issues that emerge within sessions. To illustrate my points more clearly, I include anonymized transcripts of therapy sessions that showcase the different steps and techniques being used. The purpose of this section is to provide you with the step-by-step knowledge of how to use this technique with clients.

Although I often use the term *partner* to refer to the person about whom the client is reflecting when they are engaging in relational savoring, I would like to note that relational savoring can be used with a variety of relational contexts (e.g., parent–child, partner–partner, child–parent, friend–friend, individual–group, group–group).

4 PHASE 1

Memory Selection

As I explained in Chapter 1, relational savoring is a two-phase process. The first phase in the process is the memory selection phase, and the second phase is the memory reflection phase. In this first phase of the intervention, which is arguably the most important step in the process, the therapist assists the client in identifying a memory to savor. The therapist begins by introducing the client to the purpose of the intervention and helping the client select several memories that could be suitable for savoring and then in Phase 2 moves on to assist the client in proceeding through an invariant series of reflection steps.

In this chapter, I discuss the methods I have used in my research protocols for introducing clients to the purpose of relational savoring, soliciting memories, probing the memories in depth, evaluating them, and ultimately selecting a memory based on predetermined criteria. I discuss how this research-based protocol translates to clinical practice. I introduce the agenda of the therapist during this phase of the process, including what the therapist is prioritizing, how this may vary based on the client's history and presenting problem, and how the therapist may wish to adjust their strategy based on the client's response to the therapist's interventions.

---

https://doi.org/10.1037/0000372-004
Relational Savoring: Using Guided Reflection to Strengthen Relationships and Improve Outcomes in Therapy, by J. L. Borelli
Copyright © 2024 by the American Psychological Association. All rights reserved.

BIRD'S-EYE VIEW

Before getting into the nitty-gritty details of how to administer the intervention, I want to briefly pause and say a word about the general attitude and presence that I advocate therapists adopt when engaging in these exercises with clients. First, I suggest that therapists enter into the exercise with a *calm and reflective* stance. This means that therapists should avoid appearing anxious and should have a slower, gentler pace of speaking, one that conveys all is well in the world. Their posture should be relaxed but engaged, perhaps leaning slightly forward to show interest in the client. The therapist's method of engaging with the client should be one that encourages the client to go deeper with their thinking and feeling, in terms of both the words they use and their vocal tone and posture.

Second, the therapist should approach this exercise with an attitude of *positivity and admiration* toward a fellow traveler. Therapists should be striving to respect the client's inner life and to honor their internal experience. This is a strengths-based intervention, so a central goal is for the therapist to help the client understand their experiences from the perspective of someone who admires them. The therapist should take every opportunity to notice or compliment the client on what they are doing well in their relationships, on the benefits others are receiving from interacting with them and being in relationship with them, and likewise, on the benefits their relationships are bringing to them.

If the client mentions negative relationship behaviors, the therapist should not directly comment on these behaviors unless they pose a direct risk to the client or the client's relationship partner. These can be discussed at a different moment in the session, not during the savoring. The savoring is the moment to celebrate the client's ability to connect, attempt to connect, or desire to connect with another person, and what that means about the client and the relationship they have with this person.

SETTING THE STAGE WITH THE CLIENT: INTRODUCING RELATIONAL SAVORING

Before a therapist begins savoring with a client, I recommend that the therapist provide a rationale for engaging in this type of work with the client and set some expectations for what the work will require from each person. The rationale can take one of several different forms, but it typically includes some statement explaining that because of the client's circumstances (e.g., general busyness, life stress, or mental health concerns), they do not spend time focusing on moments of positive connectedness, which they deserve to do. So the purpose of this exercise is to help carve out time to allow them to focus on these moments of positive connectedness they have in their relationship with their relationship partner (e.g., child, romantic partner). The therapist also expresses that they believe the client has the right to gain the benefit from positive experiences they have had and that this work they are going to do together will help to realize this goal.

The second part of setting the stage involves informing the client of what the work will require from each person. This is the therapist's opportunity to inform the client that entering a state of relaxation and calm will benefit them and that ceding control to the therapist is part of the protocol. This is a reflective exercise in which the therapist will be asking them to generate memories and reflect deeply on them; engaging in the behaviors that promote the greatest reflection will benefit them. Further, articulating the therapist's role can also be helpful. The therapist's approach will be directive. As the therapist guides the client to focus on certain aspects of their memories, the therapist may repeatedly assist them in redirecting their attention back to certain aspects of their memories (e.g., positive emotion). Providing them with a preview of the therapist's behavior will help them to anticipate what this intervention will feel like so they are informed at the outset.

SELECTING MEMORIES

The goal in the memory selection process is to stimulate the client's thinking while also reducing their anxiety in generating memories. Clients have different challenges with this process; some clients immediately think of 10 memories that would fit the bill of what we are looking for with the relational savoring exercise, whereas other clients really struggle to come up with even one. The former is not really a major concern; when clients think of too many memories, the therapist can easily solve this by helping to select the memories that seem most relevant to our framework and asking more questions about these memories in order to identify which memory would be best to savor.

The latter concern, having trouble coming up with memories, is a more significant challenge. The therapist addresses this concern by providing several descriptors to help the client who is struggling to think of any memories. The language we use explicitly targets the types of memories we are seeking: memories of positive connectedness (our so-called low-hanging fruit memories, which are easier for clients to generate but are our second-choice option) and memories with attachment content (which are more difficult for clients to generate but are preferred).

In the sections that follow, I discuss the importance of positive-connectedness memories followed by attachment memories. Below I include excerpts of the treatment manual and italicize the words used that explicitly pull for specific content. Note that the text included in this section is the text we use when helping parents savor their relationships with their children, but it can be easily modified for use with other populations.

POSITIVE CONNECTEDNESS: ... a time where you felt *extremely connected, close,* or *"in-sync"* with your child.

ATTACHMENT CONTENT: ... I am especially interested in hearing about a time when you *found joy in helping your child grow*, or a time when *your child needed you and you were there for him/her*. It may be a time when you felt like you *comforted, soothed, protected, or supported your child*.

In this case, "helping your child grow" pulls for a secure base type of memory, whereas "comforted, soothed, protected, or supported your child" pulls for a safe haven memory. "Child needed you and you were there for him/her" typically pulls for a safe haven memory, but it could also bring to mind a secure base memory if the participant recalls a time when the child needed help trying something new (e.g., taking three steps, going up to the tall slide, or practicing a solo for the choir concert) and was relying on the parent for encouragement or support.

We also include language explicitly designed to reduce the pressure for clients who are wracking their brains to think of a big milestone or achievement but coming up short (e.g., "Feel free to choose something that you felt was a milestone or something simple that happens on a daily basis") as well as for clients who feel pressure to think of several memories ("It doesn't really matter how many you can think of; we're just going to be brainstorming").

SELECTING MEMORIES: THE THERAPIST'S AGENDA

Therapists encourage clients to come up with two to three memories before selecting one to savor. Generating more than one memory allows the therapist some flexibility to be able to perceive the client's range in their experiences and to pick the memory that seems best for savoring. When selecting memories that would be ripe for savoring from the ones a client has generated, therapists follow a decision tree that is based on the content of the memory and the emotional resonance of the memory (Figure 4.1).

In this chapter, I review these considerations in turn: the content of memories and then the emotional resonance of memories. One note as I take you through the considerations that therapists use to guide their selection process is that sometimes when clients discuss their memories, they spontaneously share ample detail about the memories themselves, providing more than enough information for the therapist to use in selecting the memory that is most suitable for savoring. But more often than not, therapists need to ask some follow-up questions regarding the memories, particularly follow-up questions focused on the client's emotional experience of the event (clients tend to be more focused on the details of what happened in the incident described). Asking these questions is an extremely important part of the memory selection process because they allow the therapist to have the information they need to make an informed decision.

Selection Based on Content of Memory

In the memory-selection phase, the first consideration we weigh when evaluating which memory to choose is the content of the memory in terms of what actually occurred in the incident described. The richest memories for savoring are those with the strongest attachment content, so those memories containing secure base or safe haven elements within them are considered to be the highest priority memories for savoring. If these memories are not available or have too high a potential for spoiling (more on this later), then the therapist may choose to select a "positive-connectedness memory."

Let's first review the definitions of these different types of memories. Memories with attachment content are the gold standard memories in relational savoring. There are four different types of memories that we would consider eligible for savoring (Figure 4.2). These four memory types apply to symmetrical relationships, or relationships in which each person has both caregiving and care-receiving roles, such as a romantic relationship, a friend relationship, or a relationship with a coworker. Within symmetrical relationships, savoring across all four domains is possible.

Parent–child relationships are asymmetrical, so the types of savoring within these relationships are different. It does not make sense for a parent to savor times when the child acted as a secure base or a safe haven for them (e.g., a time when a parent was sick and the child took loving care of them). Although this type of experience could occur within the context of a loving relationship in which the roles are preserved for parent and child, this is not

82 • *Relational Savoring*

FIGURE 4.1. Memory Selection Hierarchy

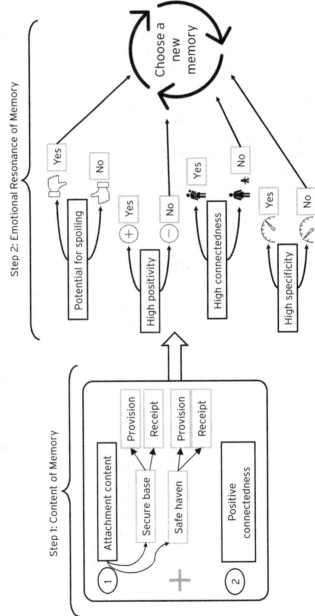

FIGURE 4.2. Types of Attachment-Based Memories

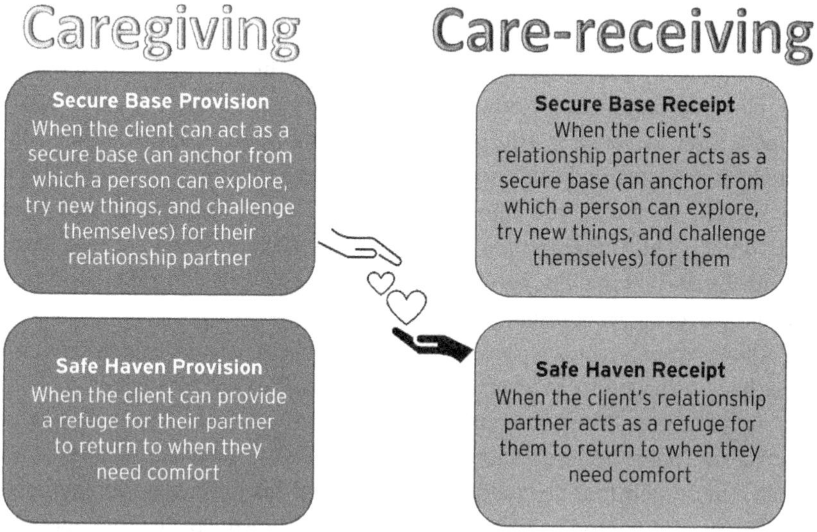

Caregiving

Secure Base Provision
When the client can act as a secure base (an anchor from which a person can explore, try new things, and challenge themselves) for their relationship partner

Safe Haven Provision
When the client can provide a refuge for their partner to return to when they need comfort

Care-receiving

Secure Base Receipt
When the client's relationship partner acts as a secure base (an anchor from which a person can explore, try new things, and challenge themselves) for them

Safe Haven Receipt
When the client's relationship partner acts as a refuge for them to return to when they need comfort

the type of interaction we would want to encourage a parent to savor—it is safer to focus on savoring memories that uphold the parent's role as caregiver and the child's role as care receiver. Within parent–child relationships, I recommend savoring only *secure base provision* and *safe haven provision*.

Let's discuss the four attachment memory types that people can savor in relational savoring (again, within symmetrical relationships). I will begin by discussing *secure base provision* savoring, which involves savoring a time when one acted as a secure base for their relationship partner. For instance, Sally could savor the time when Carlos, her partner, got up with his band in front of a huge crowd at the local beer festival. In his pocket, Carlos kept the lucky penny that Sally had given him before the show to give him that little extra boost of confidence he needed. Here, Sally could savor the confidence she had been able to give to Carlos in his knowing that she was there for him, standing beside him, and supporting him as he pursued his dream. Her reflection could focus on the fact that her belief in him allowed him to push himself further.

Secure-base receipt savoring involves focusing on a time when one received this type of support from another person. The savorer can home in on a time when they felt buoyed or strengthened by the security of their bond with the other person. For instance, Pasco recalls the time when Veronica supported him through a challenging time in his life. Pasco experienced unfair treatment at work as a result of his ethnicity. Veronica helped him develop a plan to address this unfair treatment. Then Pasco went out and enacted the plans they had made, which involved going to the human resources (HR) department at his work and speaking with them about it. It was very difficult for Pasco to do this, as he had always been told by his parents to keep his head down and ignore the negative treatment of others, but Veronica's encouragement had really helped. After he spoke to HR, he felt immeasurably better because they validated his concerns and said they would take steps to address the issue. Then Pasco came back and told Veronica about it, and they celebrated with wine over dinner. This is an example of secure base receipt savoring because Pasco can focus on how having Veronica's support enabled him to take important steps to advocate for himself.

Safe haven provision savoring occurs when a client savors the sensitive care they have provided to another person in response to the person's distress or emotional needs. When Jeremiah learned that a childhood friend died from a drug overdose, he sank to the ground, unable to move. Jeremiah was so broken in despair that he couldn't even reach for his partner or do anything, but Howie came into the room an hour later and instinctively knew how to care for him. He helped him into the bed, pulled up the covers, turned on his favorite sad music, and then climbed in next to him and snuggled him. He stayed with him until he was ready to start talking. Hours later, he made him French toast and strawberries, thinking he might need nourishment. Slowly, the life began to inch back into his body.

Months later, when the rawest pain had subsided, Jeremiah was grateful because when he was in the midst of the deepest agony he had felt in his life, Howie had helped him move the needle ever so slowly from a 100 to a 99 and then to a 98, and so on from there. Looking back, Howie savored all of these aspects of the experience: how he was really there for his partner and how he helped nurse him back from the darkest place of pain. Howie took pride in the patience, steadiness, and bravery it took to stand by his side in that pain. This is an example of *safe haven provision* savoring because Howie is savoring his role in providing safe haven support to Jeremiah.

People can also savor *safe haven receipt*: times when they were soothed by an attachment figure's comfort. Trish could savor the time when she learned her art exhibit had been harshly critiqued in the local paper. She immediately called her best friend, Donna, who drove to where she was (at the local coffee shop) and wrapped her arms around her. Donna sat with her for hours and read and reread the critique's commentary until Trish felt ready to be done looking at it. Then Trish felt like being distracted from her pain, so Donna took her out for beers and to a show at a comedy club. After their night out, Donna slept on Trish's couch and got up and made her breakfast in the morning before leaving to go to work. By the next morning, Trish was still upset about the critic's comments but felt completely enveloped in care and concern from Donna. For years to come, Trish could savor the love and support she felt from her friend when she most needed her, a true example of *safe haven receipt* savoring.

All of these attachment-based memories can be savored and are given equal weight within the therapist's mind as they enter into this memory-selection phase. Any memory with strong attachment content, whether the client is the provider or the receiver, is a strong contender for selection. At this point, we do not know whether clients receive more or fewer benefits from savoring moments of care receipt or provision, so we do not weigh them any differently in terms of the memory-selection process. Thus, attachment content is considered attachment content, and we do not evaluate whether the speaker is the provider or the recipient when making the decision about whether to select the memory.

As I stated previously, the exception to this rule would be if the client is a parent who is savoring a memory with a child and the memory is an example of a child's providing secure base/safe haven care to the parent; this would constitute a role-reversed memory, and we would not want to provide more airtime to this memory. This memory would not fit our definition of a secure attachment memory because a memory in which the roles are reversed does not fulfill our specifications. Likewise, if a child is savoring a memory in which they provided care for their parent (in a way that is role reversed)—for example, a child savoring a time when they took care of their parent because their parent could not wake up after a long night at the bars. This would not be a memory the therapist would want to consider as a candidate ripe for savoring because it is quite likely a role-reversed memory and not a memory of a time in which the child was engaging in appropriate interactions with their caregiver. However, as long as roles are maintained, or in symmetrical relationships (partner–partner relationships or relationships among adults), we do not distinguish between providing and receiving sensitive care.

If a client is unable to generate memories that have explicit attachment content in them (i.e., they do not contain secure base/safe haven themes), then therapists may see if clients can generate what we have termed *lower-hanging fruit memories*, or memories of positive connectedness. When my team and I have written about positive connectedness, we were referring to moments when the client was enjoying being in the physical presence of their partner or enjoying a joint activity with their partner but not experiencing a richer attachment-based engagement with their partner.

Examples of moments of positive connectedness I have seen in my studies include the following: enjoying a quiet moment eating cereal together during the early morning hours, sitting and watching a glorious sunset together at the beach, going on a life-changing vacation together, and holding hands and snuggling on the couch together. Although these are undoubtedly positive moments of closeness and connection within a relationship, moments that deserve to be celebrated (and savored!), they do not at face value contain explicit attachment content and therefore are less privileged in the relational savoring system. Nonetheless, for some clients, these moments of connection are the most powerful memories that are available for them within that relationship. In this case, these moments of positive connectedness may be important memories to pursue for savoring.

Extracting Attachment Themes From Positive Connectedness Memories

If a therapist identifies a memory of positive connectedness, the first step they should take is to try to extract attachment themes from the memory. The reason for this is that quite often there are attachment themes embedded in these positive-connectedness memories that the client has not identified, and the therapist may be able to identify or heighten them.

Let's imagine as an example a mother who describes taking her child to Sesame Place for the first time. When asked to describe what made the whole experience so special, she says, "It was so amazing to get to share this place that I loved so much as a child with my daughter. I got to see her face light up when she met Abby. It was so magical." This is a really good positive-connectedness response—very surface level. If this is as deep as this parent can go with her savoring, savoring this memory might still be a positive experience for her. She might still derive some benefits from reflecting on getting to be the one who shared this magical place with her and the benefits her daughter reaped from this experience. However, if my team and I were working with a therapist to help them get to a deeper level with this mother, I would really want to help this therapist dig in to find a way in which this mother can acknowledge the role she is playing in helping to support her child's growth and development (secure base) or in helping to comfort her child (safe haven). Thus, I would tell the therapist that it was their job to ask some additional questions to get the mom into an attachment state of mind.

- "It sounds like you really enjoyed being able to expose your daughter to something new and exciting, a place that is really special to you. During that experience, did you notice moments when your daughter relied on you, or felt more comfortable because you were there? I bet being there with you was so special for her, too, just as it was so special for you."

- "While you were at Sesame Place, were there things that your daughter did that she wouldn't have been able to do without the confidence of knowing you were there?"
- "Going to a new place like Sesame Place can sometimes be frightening for little ones, especially if they don't have the security of their parent nearby. Were there any moments when you noticed that she really relied on you for comfort or security, or any moments when you thought, 'Oh, she really needs me right now'?"

Chances are, if the therapist asks the mother questions like these, they are going to get her to move to the level of considering her daughter's emotional needs from an attachment point of view. The thing is, attachment needs are operating beneath the surface within people (children and adults) most of the time, but they need to be unearthed to be made visible to the naked eye. Sometimes it is difficult for the untrained observer to perceive them, especially if the individual is not particularly psychologically minded or is not attuned to perceiving the other person in terms of psychological or emotional motivations. Remember how, in Chapter 1, I mentioned that higher savoring quality is associated with higher reflective functioning in parents (Borelli, Hong, et al., 2022)? Those findings are relevant here in that a client with lower reflective capacities—perhaps someone who is not accustomed to perceiving their own actions or those of another person as being caused by thoughts and feelings—may not naturally gravitate toward these types of interpretations.

Take, for example, the memory the mother described above. When I initially spoke with this mother about her memory with her daughter and why the experience was enjoyable, her first descriptions pertained to her daughter's personality; she described her child as lively, "all girl," and "just like her momma" in that she was in love with Sesame Street characters. She was also quick to describe the aspects of the day that made it such a special experience: the weather, the fact that it was just the two of them together, and that Sesame Place had a special exhibit going on related to an anniversary they were celebrating.

However, when I pushed her further with the questions listed above, she was able to go deeper with her reflections, remembering several moments throughout the day that could have been savor-worthy. For instance, she described a moment when her daughter first saw Elmo walk by; she instantly recognized him from a television show she watched at home and started to move toward him, but the mother could tell that as he got closer, her daughter became more frightened of him, and she reached her arm back to hold onto her. The mother stepped forward, holding onto her daughter's hand, and said, "It's okay, he's not going to hurt you; he just looks bigger in real life." And she recalled vividly how her daughter put one foot in front of the other, her body turned sideways as she looked back and forth between Elmo and her mother, still clinging to her mother with one hand and reaching the other out to touch Elmo's hand. When her daughter reached him, she squealed, "Elmo!" And turned back toward her mother with delight. Her mother recalled this memory with pride and warmth.

This memory contains great richness and depth for savoring. Although the mother does not mention much emotional content in her recalling of the memory, her memory is extremely detailed, which is the hallmark of a wonderful memory to savor (remember how I discussed in Chapter 3 the connection between memory specificity and savoring outcomes?). Having a highly detailed memory gives the therapist so many footholds to work with: It tells the therapist that the memory paints a vivid tapestry in the client's mind, that the sensory details are fresh, which quite likely also means that the emotional aspects of the experience will also be easier to access.

This mother's memory about her child's interaction with Elmo would fall squarely into the secure base provision category in that the mother was providing support for her child to try something she would not have been able to try without the security of knowing her mother was there. She would have been too frightened without the safety and security of her mother's presence. However, having her mother there allowed her to reach further, extend into that zone of discomfort, and pursue a goal she wanted to pursue: reaching Elmo.

So this is the experience the therapist would want to zero in on with the mother. If you as the therapist know where you want to take the client, you can take them there with this exercise. The client may not recognize where you are going, but you will, and that is all that is needed. So in this scenario, let's imagine that after learning about this contextual information from the mother, I replied in this way, with the goal of heightening the mother's awareness of the attachment content embedded within the memory:

> Wow, that is such a lovely experience that you had with her. It's so apparent to me how much she trusts you. And how much she looks to you for guidance when she is feeling unsteady or scared, or when she wants to go after something but isn't sure it is safe to do so. I can really tell from the way you described that, especially with that level of detail, that she was looking to you, her rock, for guidance in that moment about whether she was safe. And what's so important is that you gave her that guidance that she needed. She was looking to you for support, and you were right there for her. She held onto you every step of the way, and she was able to get what she wanted, to reach Elmo. And then she was so proud of her accomplishments and wanted to share those feelings with you! You must have been so elated to get to join in that moment with her! This really tells me a great deal about your relationship.

Notice how in the comments I made to her, I am trying to heighten her awareness by pointing out in several different ways the following things: (a) Her child had an attachment/emotional need, (b) she was looking to her parent to get this need met, (c) the parent was there to meet her need, (d) the resolution of the child's need led to shared positive emotions between parent and child, and (e) this interaction means something very significant about their relationship (that the child trusts the parent and looks to the parent for guidance when she feels unsteady). Using my comments, I take this specific incident and make it into a general statement about the relationship, effectively inflating the significance of the memory. So this memory signifies not only that one positive interaction occurred between the dyad but also that this dyad is capable of strong, positive, trusting, loving, supportive interactions.

Because this client did not get to this place on her own (without significant prompting from the therapist), I would also recommend that the therapist engage in additional prompting to remind the client about the attachment content immediately prior to entering into the next phase of the savoring intervention, the memory reflection stage. So in this instance, I said the following immediately prior to entering the memory reflection stage:

> I recognize that the trip to Sesame Place was kind of a big event—the whole day contained so many positive moments and a lot of them were really special to you. You could probably fill a scrapbook with all of the different things that were special about that day! Because this is a big memory with so many different parts, it is going to help us if we focus in on one smaller portion of this larger memory. As we move into this next part of the exercise and focus in on this memory, I want you to really zoom in on this moment you had when she tried to reach Elmo and you were there to support her. I'm focusing on that moment because it's a time when you being there gave her the confidence to feel safe enough to try something new.

By restating the desired focus at this critical juncture, the therapist helps the client remember the goal of the memory reflection task. You may notice that the therapist has become very directive here, helping the client pay attention to certain parts of the memory. It is worth mentioning at this point that sometimes the therapist must devote a great deal of time and effort to helping the client develop positive-connectedness memories into attachment memories. It is important to do this in a way that avoids shaming the client's initial point of focus in the memory. Instead, I recommend adopting a strengths-based approach and praising the client for the fact that the memory is chock-full of positivity, all while underscoring that there are good reasons to home in on this aspect of the memory.

Some clients require even less prompting than this; they may require only a small nudge in the direction we want them to go in. These may be people who are highly eager to please, such that when they hear the words *in sync* or *connected to* in the script, they jump at that and stop listening to the other words we say. This might be an example where a small redirection is all it takes to set a client down a path we would like them to go. Let's listen in on this mother's first relational savoring session with her therapist, in which she describes a lovely moment of being together and enjoying positive connectedness with her daughter:

CLIENT: OK, um we went to the beach this weekend. . . . Um and splashed in the waves, that was fun. Um, we sat together after I'd been gone for a few hours today and read books. That was really sweet. Um . . . trying to think of one to, we um it was when [participant's husband] was training in [city] a few we—like about a month ago. She and I just went down and like explored [city] and found a park and played and had a picnic and tea party. That was a really fun day.

THERAPIST: Mm, OK.

CLIENT: Um more?

THERAPIST: Um not necessarily, let me ask you some questions about 'em. Um so of with those is there one where you feel like you—you were able to kind of like support her or be there for her whether that's like she needed you or she was exploring and you helped her discover something or you really felt like um you connected because you were providing something for her?

CLIENT: Yeah, we'll go with the beach.

THERAPIST: OK, OK.

CLIENT: Yeah.

THERAPIST: So tell me a little bit more about that.

CLIENT: So we went to the beach um and she helped me pick a spot for us to sit down. We did the whole sunblock, and explained you know why we wear sunblock [*interviewer laughs*] even though it's not her favorite thing [*interviewer laughs*] and then she wanted to go put her toes in the water, which really means I hold her while I put my toes in the water [*interviewer laughs*]. Yeah. And so um just kind of the process of like talking about what the ocean does and watching the waves and just holding her and kind of being in sync and laughing and you know . . .

THERAPIST: OK, yeah.

CLIENT: Just all the fun um and then you know pushing her a little bit to explore and to try something new um and seeing how even though her instinct is to cling to me to . . . to try to give her a little bit of space to um you kn—you know i—in a supported safe way um do something that might feel a little scary to her but will ultimately be a fun thing.

THERAPIST: Sure, sure.

CLIENT: And so her getting to feel like you know she could run back and forth in the waves without being in my arms necessarily.

THERAPIST: OK, OK, so I think—let's, we'll just move forward with that one.

So in this example, the client's memory is ready-made for relational savoring, and the therapist needs to do very little to prepare it for the memory reflection stage.

SUBJECTIVE EXPERIENCE OF THE MEMORY: LISTENING FOR EMOTIONAL RESONANCE

In memory selection, the second consideration we make pertains to the emotional quality of the memory, or what I refer to as *emotional resonance*. These dimensions are depicted in Figure 4.1. When it comes to considerations of emotional resonance, there are three affirmative criteria (the degree of positivity of the memory, the degree of felt connectedness, the degree of specificity), or criteria that ideally a client's chosen memory will fulfill, and one negative criterion (potential for spoiling), or criteria that the memory will avoid fulfilling. Let's discuss these in turn.

I will begin by discussing the affirmative emotional resonance criteria. The first of these is *connectedness*. Connectedness refers to the degree to which the client is emotionally connected to the other person in the memory: How close to the other person do you think they felt at the time this experience was occurring? How close do you think they feel now? High levels of closeness are important unless your stated goal of conducting the intervention is to enhance closeness with someone with whom the participant does not have high levels of closeness.

The second affirmative criterion is *positivity*. Positivity refers to the degree of positive emotion the person experiences regarding the memory. The nature of the positive emotion can vary; as stated in the instructions for the intervention, the client can feel high-arousal emotions such as intense joy, excitement, and giddiness, or they can experience low-arousal emotions such as calm, peace, and connection.

To assess the connectedness and positivity aspects of emotional resonance, we use both participant input and researcher/therapist judgment. When we are administering relational savoring in a research context, we will typically ask participants to rate each of their memories on two scales. For instance, we ask them the following question: How close and connected do you feel to the people in this memory when you think about it now, and how do you feel emotionally when you think about this memory?

We present our participants with a rating scale known as the Self-Assessment Manikin (Bradley & Lang, 1994), a 1–5 pictorial system that displays androgynous computerized characters ranging from one that appears sad on one end of the scale and another that appears happy on the other end of the scale. When using relational savoring in a clinical setting, the therapist may wish to modify this process to be more conversational but may still want to ask the client for their input regarding their felt experience of connection to each memory. We use these participant-reported scores as convergent information in addition to the researcher's own judgment of how connected the participant feels to the memory and how rich the positive emotion is that the participant experiences when reliving the memory experience.

Typically, therapists have a felt sense of how connected and emotional an experience was for their clients. Their perspective on this may diverge from that of their clients, which is why I recommend also asking the client, but it is also important for the therapist to tune into what their own impression is of these qualities. Do they perceptibly change when they are discussing these memories? Do they appear transported to a different time and place? Do they get a wistful, far-off look in their eyes or a smile on their faces? Because the therapist will ask for several memories, they can also compare across memories and use the client's behavior as their own baseline.

The third affirmative criterion is *specificity*. We are also assessing (through clinical judgment) the degree of specificity of the memory, which enables us to judge the vividness of the participant's recollection of the memory. How many details is the client sharing? How present versus absent does the client seem when discussing the memory? Could the client paint a picture of the scene if asked to? Could you (as the therapist) place yourself in the scene based on the details provided?

Specificity is an important feature of memories because it allows us to tell how close to the surface the memory is for the participant. And if you remember one of the conclusions from Chapter 3, specificity was important in predicting treatment outcome; it turned out to be one of the main mechanisms of action in predicting higher reflective functioning in our large randomized study of mothers of young children (Borelli, Kazmierski, et al., 2023). We need the memories to be relatively fresh in terms of level of detail because we are going to need the participant to be able to access their emotional experience, and we use the degree of specificity of the memory as a heuristic for being able to assess how easy it will be for the participant to access the emotional content associated with the memory.

There are occasions when the participant's judgment of how close/positive they feel when recalling the memory conflict with the researcher's judgment of the way the participant seems to feel. There are also occasions when the participant reports feeling very close and/or high levels of positive emotion but the researcher perceives things differently. In both circumstances I train researchers and therapists to follow their clinical judgment and select the memory that they deem to be the most suitable for savoring even when it conflicts with the participant's ratings. Although generally speaking I consider people to be the experts of their own experience, in this circumstance, I trust that the researchers/therapists are more highly trained in the nuances of relational savoring than the participants and thus have a better ear for what type of memory should be selected over others.

Finally, we are also assessing a negative, nonaffirmative quality in the form of the memory's potential for *spoiling*. I have touched upon this issue at various points throughout the chapter, but I will delve more fully into it here. In Chapter 6, I provide some strategies for how to address client spoiling at various points during the intervention. *Spoiling* is the term my colleagues and I use to describe the process that occurs when participants seem to have an internal magnet toward negative emotion that pulls at them and prevents them from being able to focus productively on the savoring at hand. An example would be Alice, who is savoring a time when she and her wife, Marta, were on the beach, holding hands and sharing their love with one another. Then, suddenly, this makes Alice think about how few years she is likely to have left with Marta, whom she fears will be taken from her at a young age. This devolves into Alice discussing her fear of being alone in old age and having nobody to talk to or be with, and nobody to share growing old with, as well as her discussing all of the regrets she has in her relationship with Marta.

When discussing spoiling, it is important to distinguish this type of emotional process from the productive expression and exploration of negative emotion that we often see in relational savoring interventions. Although the explicit focus of relational savoring is on positive emotionality, this does not mean that negative emotion does not have a place in this intervention.

Quite the contrary: We often find that focusing on negative emotion paves the way for deeper, more productive and meaningful engagement with vulnerable positive emotion. Further, the best memories to savor are often memories that are preceded by some sort of challenge, which inevitably involves negative emotion. Being able to talk about and experience the negative emotion associated with these memories is a crucial part of fully engaging with the intervention.

However, there are also times when people seem to be led astray by negative emotions, particularly emotions such as guilt or anxiety/fear, and sometimes anger, in a way that feels like a runaway train. This type of emotional experiencing during the savoring does not seem like productive emotional processing. Rather, in my view, it has the ruminative quality that Les Greenberg, the developer of emotion-focused therapy, would identify in someone who is stuck in a secondary emotional state (Greenberg, 2015). It serves to distract from the central purpose of the intervention, which is the processing of vulnerable positive emotions related to connections with others.

When wondering whether a client who is experiencing a negative emotion is doing so productively (in which case, this is likely to lead to a deepening of the savoring) or unproductively (in which case, this is likely to lead to spoiling), the therapist may wish to ask themselves the following questions: Does this emotional processing have a forward-moving quality, or is it circular in nature? Does the processing seem to be taking us to a deeper, more vulnerable state, or is the processing leading you to the same level of vulnerability? Is the client introducing new themes and ideas or returning to old ones? Does the client seem deeply in touch with highly resonant emotion, or does the client seem to be experiencing a superficial level of emotional vulnerability? These questions are all quite similar; indeed, they are different ways of phrasing the same question.

In developing his theory of change in psychotherapy (and emotion-focused therapy specifically), Greenberg and his colleague developed the Levels of Emotional Processing Scale (Pascual-Leone & Greenberg, 2007), and when I learned of this coding system, I thought it would be the perfect coding scheme to ascertain whether a particular memory has a high potential for spoiling. However, we would need to do so in post hoc analyses of intervention sessions in order to identify behavioral markers that are readily identifiable by the therapist as they are conducting the session.

The therapist has to make these decisions about which memories to select in the moment, so in the end, it comes down to clinical judgment and training. It also comes down to the therapist's confidence in handling spoiling should it occur—more on that in Chapter 6 when I discuss strategies for addressing spoiling in the moment.

PROVIDING A RATIONALE TO THE CLIENT

When it comes to the final stage of choosing a memory to use in the memory reflection stage, the therapist will often make the ultimate call as to which memory is most suitable. I recommend that the therapist provide an explanation to the client as to why they are recommending that the client focus on that specific memory. The explanation should always be worded in the affirmative direction so the client ends up feeling complimented and as though they came up with a host of wonderful memories and the therapist only gets to choose one.

We would never want the client to feel shamed in any way, as though any of their memories are less than desirable. And yet the therapist should actually be in charge and be the one selecting the memory that is going to take the client where the therapist wants them to go in terms of the savoring goals, so finding a way to provide the client with a rationale regarding why the chosen memory has been chosen must be artful. Here are some ways my team and I have come up with for therapists to recommend the selection of certain memories:

- "It sounds like the first memory is really salient in your mind. Let's focus on that one for today."

- "Since the second memory was more recent, we'll go with that one today."

- "It sounds like you have already spent some time processing this memory, so let's go with the other one today."

- "That memory involving the movie theater was so vivid and impactful—I want to give you a chance to revisit that one today."

In my view, the substance of the rationale does not matter as much as the fact that the client has been provided with a rationale, that the rationale makes sense in light of what the client has shared, that the rationale is affirming of the client's success with the task and the beauty of the memories they provided, and that it seamlessly paves the way for the therapist to choose the memory they think is the ripest for savoring.

One thought that may come to mind is whether it is important for the therapist to stay consistent in the rationale they provide across sessions (if the therapist is doing a multisession relational savoring intervention); this has not been our experience. In our studies of relational savoring, we have changed the rationale based on the memories presented, and this has never come up as a cause for concern among participants in our studies or people in our clinical practice, so we do not have a reason to think it is problematic.

96 • *Relational Savoring*

WRAP-UP

To put all of this together, Table 4.1 provides a transcript of a memory selection from a savoring session from one of our studies and describes the decision-making process of the therapist conducting the intervention. I will note that this is a more challenging relational savoring session; I share this as an example because it provides ample opportunities to witness the different strategies of the therapist as well as the decision-making points.

TABLE 4.1. Memory Selection Process

	Relational savoring session	Analysis/interpretation
THERAPIST:	Uh parents often tell us that they don't have much time to focus on positive experiences that they've had with their children because they're just really busy, they don't have time to stop and reflect.	Rationale for introducing relational savoring provided
CLIENT:	Sure.	
THERAPIST:	So for the next few minutes, I am going to help you come up with a memory of a time when you felt extremely connected, close, or "in sync" uh with your child.	Positive-connectedness language
CLIENT:	OK.	
THERAPIST:	I'm sorry. Your child's name is?	This is not ideal (therapist should remember child's name)–this session was done in a research context, but still, not ideal for building rapport.
CLIENT:	[Child 1].	
THERAPIST:	[Child 1]. That's right. So uh we're especially interested in hearing about a time when you found joy in helping [Child 1] grow, or a time when she really needed you and you were there for her. Uh it may be a time when you felt like you comforted, soothed, protected, or supported her. OK. Um feel free to choose something that you felt was [*cough*] a milestone or something simple that happens in everyday life.	Secure base/safe haven language
CLIENT:	OK.	
THERAPIST:	Um.	

TABLE 4.1. Memory Selection Process (*Continued*)

Relational savoring session	Analysis/interpretation
CLIENT: So is it supposed to be joyful though?	
THERAPIST: Yes. Definitely something positive.	
CLIENT: OK.	
THERAPIST: That's filled with you know, happy, joy . . .	
CLIENT: OK, alright.	
THERAPIST: . . . pleasant emotion.	Initially this client comes up with a memory that involves some negativity (injury or illness). This might have been an appropriate memory to consider if the mother had experienced positive emotion related to being there for her child. But she says explicitly that it was not joyful so the therapist does not probe further.
CLIENT: So I took her to the doctor's yesterday [*cough*] and I definitely comforted her, but that was not joyful.	
THERAPIST: Right.	
CLIENT: OK alright. Let's think.	
THERAPIST: So we'll just brainstorm with you . . .	
CLIENT: OK.	
THERAPIST: and I'll help you decide . . .	
CLIENT: OK.	
THERAPIST: . . . which one we'll do.	
CLIENT: OK.	
THERAPIST: So sometimes people can think of one . . .	Interviewer normalizes the difficulty client may be having in coming up with memories.
CLIENT: OK.	
THERAPIST: . . . or many; either is fine um we'll just kind of um think out loud and pick one that works.	
CLIENT: OK.	
THERAPIST: Um if you can, just think for a second and tell us out loud if you have a memory like that.	
CLIENT: Um I thought of her birthday party. That I just threw for her and her brother a few weeks ago.	Client provides example that is about an event that was fun (positive connectedness)—surface level, descriptive, not emotional or relational.
THERAPIST: OK.	
CLIENT: That was really fun. For her, I think.	
THERAPIST: OK. And uh during this birthday party um maybe if you could think of a specific moment about it. Uh how connected did you feel, like is there a time during the birthday party when you felt very connected to [Child 1]?	Therapist directs mother to focus on feelings of connectedness because mother did not explicitly mention these.

(*continues*)

TABLE 4.1. Memory Selection Process (*Continued*)

Relational savoring session	Analysis/interpretation
CLIENT: Oh I remember we were like all singing happy birthday to her.	Client again answers with a behavioral descriptor; not elaborated (why does mother feel connected to her?). Therapist could have done a better job asking questions at this juncture to draw the mother out, rather than asking these research-based numerical questions.
THERAPIST: OK. And how connected did you feel to her at that moment?	
CLIENT: Very connected.	
THERAPIST: And uh you said this was a couple weeks ago.	
CLIENT: Yeah, it was uh [Date 1] um or something.	
THERAPIST: How detailed would you say your memory was?	
CLIENT: Oh very. I'd say very detailed.	
THERAPIST: OK. And um is there a specific moment that you can think of at that birthday party where you felt you know you were really doing something special for her, like you felt connected, that she was there uh you were there for her?	Therapist again directs client's attention to feelings of connectedness. Then therapist asks about specific moment in which mother felt really connected to her or really there for her.
CLIENT: Um, the whole thing. I feel like.	Client provides general answer and then reverts back to talking about the details of the day.
THERAPIST: Uh huh.	
CLIENT: I think. Singing happy birthday was really fun, I know that was a real moment. Um. Nothing else super significant about the day, it was just a really fun day, all the friends were there, all the family was there, she was dressed really cute. I dressed her up like Cinderella.	
THERAPIST: So it sounds like that time when you were singing happy birthday kinda stands out.	
CLIENT: Yeah.	
THERAPIST: So I'm wondering if during that time you recall feeling any uh particular emotions?	Therapist directs client to her emotional experience in order to deepen access to emotions.
CLIENT: Yeah I just feel really grateful that I have two children, [Age 1] and [Age 2], and they're healthy and you know we have a home and family and friends . . .	Client is able to acknowledge more vulnerable emotions—gratitude.
THERAPIST: Uh huh.	

TABLE 4.1. Memory Selection Process (*Continued*)

	Relational savoring session	Analysis/interpretation
CLIENT:	. . . and can have this big party. And really grateful like wow this is my life, this is great.	
THERAPIST:	OK. Great. So it sounds like that was a, it was a nice moment with your daughter. Mhm. Um So let's uh brainstorm a few other memories too . . .	Therapist is satisfied, having arrived at a more vulnerable emotion with this memory. Then therapist moves on to identify if there are other memories that the mother has.
CLIENT:	OK.	
THERAPIST:	. . . and then we'll pick one and go deeper into it. So if you can just think, take a second to see if there's anything else of a time when you felt really connected or close to [Child 1]. Or a time when you felt like you were doing something special for her, or she was relying on you.	
CLIENT:	It's hard because I mean I usually—is it OK? I usually have both kids with me. Mhm, I'm very rarely with just one kid.	Client has difficulty focusing on only one child—this may reveal that her mental representation of the child is not unique/individualized to that child.
THERAPIST:	Yeah, uh yeah If they're both there that's fine, as long as you uh, you know, maybe there is a particular part of that memory that was you thinking of [Child 1] specifically and you felt like there was.	Therapist gives client tip to focus in on one child. Therapist asks client to focus on one specific instance.
CLIENT:	Uh let's see . . . I mean it's pretty mundane, we drive to school every day or grocery shopping, and you know she's usually the one who likes to um, she'll request songs . . .	Mother mentions that life is mundane. Memory is focused on child's behavior but not on the interaction between parent and child.
THERAPIST:	Mhm.	
CLIENT:	. . . to listen to. And it's real fun, we just kind of sing along . . .	
THERAPIST:	Mhm.	
CLIENT:	and she's really cute. She'll dance around. Usually my son's really grumpy so it's more enjoyable to be with him, I mean with her.	
THERAPIST:	To her.	
CLIENT:	She'll interact and have fun.	

(*continues*)

TABLE 4.1. Memory Selection Process (*Continued*)

Relational savoring session	Analysis/interpretation
THERAPIST: Yeah.	
CLIENT: Sometimes he is, but . . .	
THERAPIST: So was there a particular uh specific time that you're thinking of, or maybe you thought to yourself, Um I'm really enjoying.	
CLIENT: Yeah there was a couple of days ago when there was this one song, that she likes to listen to and she was like singing along to it. You know, I just thought, ugh, she's so cute and adorable. You know she just loves music, she loves to dance to music, play music, that's just her thing.	
THERAPIST: Uh huh.	
CLIENT: So I thought that was just really sweet.	
THERAPIST: Right.	
THERAPIST: And um during that time where [Child 1] was singing in the car, and you thought it was really special how connected did you feel at time, to her, to [Child 1]?	Therapist assesses to see what level of connectedness is present in the memory. Here therapist does not ask as many questions about how the mother felt during this time. Questions such as these might have revealed more about the experience. However, the therapist might have sensed (from the mother's vocal tone or posture) that the memory was not as emotionally resonant as the first one. It also seems less detailed (even though the mother says it is detailed).
CLIENT: Fairly connected. I mean she's in the back seat, in the car seat. But you know. I kind of feel like even if it's a 15-minute drive every day it's still a nice little time with my kids. You know the screens and you know we're just there in the car and I you know, can interact with them and yeah.	
THERAPIST: And um if you can think back to that specific time when she was singing and you were enjoying it, how detailed would you say your memory is of that event?	

Phase 1: Memory Selection • 101

TABLE 4.1. Memory Selection Process (*Continued*)

	Relational savoring session	Analysis/interpretation
CLIENT:	Detailed.	
THERAPIST:	Pretty detailed?	
CLIENT:	Yeah.	
THERAPIST:	OK great we have two memories. Let's just do one more, and we'll pick one.	
CLIENT:	OK.	
THERAPIST:	If you could try to think one more time of something where you felt you know, you were, you were there for [Child 1] or that she was coming to you when she needed you and you felt you were able to provide her for something? Something um where there was a real close connection.	
CLIENT:	So much of every day is just mundane. It's just getting through the day.	
THERAPIST:	Right. [*Laughs.*]	
CLIENT:	Um. Oh . . . OK she got a haircut the other day.	
THERAPIST:	Uh huh.	
CLIENT:	I took both kids to get their haircuts.	
THERAPIST:	Uh huh.	
CLIENT:	She was really good, she wasn't scared of the haircut. And I was like, wow, she's such a big girl. So I was proud of her.	Mother states emotion that she felt during the haircut without prompting.
THERAPIST:	Oh OK. That's great. So um. This was a few days ago you said?	
CLIENT:	This was uh Friday.	
THERAPIST:	Oh OK. So it sounds like um during that time you felt, you said proud of her?	
THERAPIST:	Mhm.	
CLIENT:	That she was growing up, getting her hair cut.	
THERAPIST:	Mhm. Mhm.	
CLIENT:	Right. Yeah. Not screaming her head off . . .	The use of "not screaming her head off" brings up a negative image, as though mother is comparing child to a negative reference point. Could be potential for spoiling.

(*continues*)

TABLE 4.1. Memory Selection Process (*Continued*)

Relational savoring session	Analysis/interpretation
THERAPIST: Right.	
CLIENT: . . . that kind of thing.	
THERAPIST: Was there a particular moment when you might have had that thought, like oh wow she's really grown up?	Therapist redirects back to positive.
CLIENT: Yeah there was another kid actually having an absolute fit, my son used to have a fit and I was thinking wow, this is her second haircut and she's just totally fine, and you know that's [Child 1]. She's easy.	Here is the negative reference point—mother is thinking about son's behavior. This could be potential for spoiling if this memory reminds mother of son's negative behavior.
THERAPIST: Uh huh.	
CLIENT: She's the easier kid. Well so far.	
THERAPIST: Uh huh. And did you feel like maybe you in that moment that maybe you felt, like because of you and what you've done maybe that she's grown up and she's . . .	
CLIENT: I don't know, I honestly feel like that's just who they are. They're just born with their own personalities. And [*laughs*] . . .	Her feelings are not about connection but rather about child's characteristics. This memory may not be a good one because the parent may be too focused on the child's fixed characteristics (not open to mentalizing about these qualities of the child).
THERAPIST: . . . but you were proud of . . .	
CLIENT: Yeah.	
THERAPIST: . . . of how she . . .	
CLIENT: Yeah.	
THERAPIST: turned out.	
CLIENT: Well I was just happy for her, that she's not like, having a complete fit and flipping out. You know.	Here again, the mother's framing her daughter's behavior in terms of a negative reference point.
THERAPIST: Uh huh. Right.	
CLIENT: That she can just sit there and talking back with the haircutter person. Yeah.	
THERAPIST: Uh huh. OK. Great. So I'll ask you the same questions about that memory. How connected did you feel at that time?	

TABLE 4.1. Memory Selection Process (*Continued*)

Relational savoring session	Analysis/interpretation
CLIENT: Fairly connected. Yeah. Well I had two kids getting haircuts at the same time so I was going back and forth between the two of them.	This does not seem very connected. Her answer ends up focusing on divided attention, which does not seem connected.
THERAPIST: OK. How detailed is your memory of that event?	
CLIENT: Detailed. Yeah.	
THERAPIST: OK. So let's see we have the birthday party and um the song in the car, and uh [*page flipping*] the haircut. So I think it sounds like the birthday party event, your uh, it sounds like you had a special uh moment there, and that you were able to give her a nice birthday . . .	Therapist chooses the first memory because it was the most connected overall; it had the highest degree of detail and the lowest potential for spoiling. Therapist provides a rationale to the client for why they chose the memory they chose. The rationale is affirming in nature (compliments the mother's memory and the mother's action) and simultaneously provides a clear direction for which memory to savor. In support of therapist's decision, mother affirms the "connectedness" feelings and says, "Yeah, connected to everything."
CLIENT: Yeah.	
THERAPIST: . . . and that she's growing up and that was a positive moment . . .	
CLIENT: For sure.	
THERAPIST: . . . where you felt connected to . . . [Child 1]. So let's go ahead.	
CLIENT: Yeah. Connected to everything.	
THERAPIST: Everything.	
CLIENT: Yeah yeah.	
THERAPIST: Well that's fantastic.	
CLIENT: Yeah.	
THERAPIST: So let's go into that a little bit deeper. OK so, let's make sure I'm doing this right [*page flipping*] . . .	Therapist next commences memory reflection stage.
CLIENT: Do you need more light? Is that, I've got overheads.	

This example illustrates the complexity of extracting a suitable memory and helping to massage the memory so it is savor-ready. With the understanding that this was a complex case, it is important to keep in mind that sometimes it can be a winding path to guide a client toward a memory that is likely to have the highest potential for high-quality savoring. The most important thing to do is keep in mind the general principles of seeking to find a memory that has high attachment content (secure base/safe haven/connectedness) and high-quality emotional resonance (high positivity/connectedness/specificity and low potential for spoiling). Just as there is no such thing as a perfect relationship, there is no such thing as a perfect relationship memory, so the best strategy is to make peace with the messiness and to have faith that by using these guiding principles and knowing where you want to take the client, you will be able to guide them there. Now we will move on to the memory reflection stage!

5 PHASE 2

Memory Reflection

In this second phase of the intervention, the therapist has selected a memory for the client to savor. The therapist guides the client through a series of five reflection steps to help the client deepen their emotional experience related to that memory. I believe that the internal working model of attachment can shift through this process (Bowlby, 1973) and that these shifts occur when a client takes a risk and has a novel emotional experience, resulting in growth.

In this chapter, I describe the five-step process the therapist follows to pursue this goal, including the rationale and best practices for each step in this process. I then present the methods I have used in my research studies as well as in my clinical practice to pursue these steps, using case material to help support these goals. The majority of my descriptions and text come from studies of work with parents, so the words you will see focus on the parent's relationship with the child, but keep in mind that we use a nearly identical manual with respect to other relationships. Figure 5.1 presents the steps of the memory reflection process.

Before I begin describing the manualized memory reflection steps, I want to first describe the brief introduction the therapist provides to the process of memory reflection.

---

https://doi.org/10.1037/0000372-005
Relational Savoring: Using Guided Reflection to Strengthen Relationships and Improve Outcomes in Therapy, by J. L. Borelli
Copyright © 2024 by the American Psychological Association. All rights reserved.

FIGURE 5.1. Five Steps of Memory Reflection

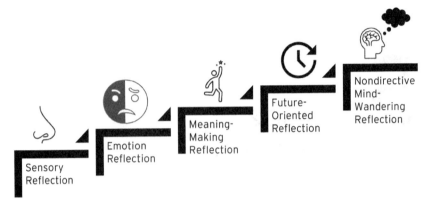

THE THERAPIST'S INTRODUCTION TO MEMORY REFLECTION

In essence, this amounts to the therapist saying something like, "Now that we've walked down memory lane together, seen all of these wonderful memories you have with [person], and chosen a memory together, I would like you to sit back and relax, to really settle in. I will guide you through this process." When we have conducted studies in my research laboratory, we are much more formal in what we ask the therapists to say, but I always give the therapists the guidance to make sure they are using words that fit their own vocabulary, feel natural (and not scripted), and can roll off their tongues with the flow of their own diction. The actual script that we provide to therapists is as follows:

> What's going to happen now is that I'd like for you to sit comfortably and relax. I'm going to have you really focus on this memory for the next 10 minutes. I'll ask you to focus on specific parts of the memory at different times and the feelings you had during this special moment with your child. You can feel free to relax and close your eyes if that will help you focus.

A couple of points are important to emphasize here. First, we explicitly tell clients that we are going to ask them to focus on different parts of the memory at different times. Making a statement to this effect has both a practical purpose and a clinical purpose. The practical purpose is that it involves giving clients a preview of the format of the intervention, which may be different than other forms or modalities of therapy they have received in the past, including from that same therapist. This portion of the intervention is highly therapist directed and involves drilling into small details of the remembered experience. It involves zooming the memory camera in and out flexibly, so the client needs to be prepared and ready to do that. The second purpose is a clinical one: By giving the client a heads-up that this is going to be the approach taken, the therapist has some clinical license to be more directive in their approach. By saying this explicitly, the therapist is less likely to be perceived as rude, dominant, or aggressive. This can be an important move in very established therapeutic relationships, especially if this type of approach is quite different from the therapist's typical therapeutic style, and it can also be important in newly developing therapeutic relationships when the alliance is more vulnerable to each and every therapeutic move the therapist makes (Horvath & Luborsky, 1993).

The next point I would like to underscore is that we give clients permission to close their eyes during the reflection task. Some people feel more comfortable reflecting on memories and emotional states when their eyes are closed. It can allow this memory reflection experience to feel more personal (and less interpersonal)—less as if they are performing or talking to a stranger and more as if they are alone with their memories. This is especially important as we are asking people to dive into doing deep emotional work the first time we meet them (Glenberg et al., 1998; Perfect et al., 2011; Vredeveldt et al., 2012). Not everyone closes their eyes, but we like to provide it as an option to clients in case this feels more comfortable for them.

Next, we move on to say,

> Now I'm going to ask you some questions, and I'll pause a bit in between so you have a chance to reflect on your feelings. For each question, I will give a few examples of things you may want to think about as you focus on this memory, but when you respond, don't feel the need to answer each and every question. As you reflect on your feelings during that special moment with your child, please speak those feelings out loud. And if you run out of things to say, don't worry about it and just keep thinking about the experience until I ask you another question. If you notice that your mind wanders to unrelated or negative thoughts, just gently bring it back to the positive aspects of this event. Does this sound OK? Do you have any questions?

In providing this portion of the instructions, the most important components are laying the groundwork that the therapist is going to provide example questions or statements to use as guideposts but that the client should not feel limited to respond to only those prompts and/or should not feel they have to respond to all of the prompts. The goal of these reflection steps is to create a climate in which the therapist provides sufficient support and guidance for the client so they can be scaffolded toward generating a savoring narrative, but not so much scaffolding so they are held back or constrained in their savoring narrative. By previewing this with the client before beginning the memory reflection, it's more likely the client will respond in the desired fashion to the prompts.

It is important to preempt the situation where a client does not have enough to say to fill the allotted time. When we conduct relational savoring intervention studies, we allow each reflection step to last a certain amount of predetermined time to increase the likelihood that the client is reflecting on that aspect of the memory for some time. This can create some anxiety on the part of clients who are less talkative, so normalizing the fact that some clients do not talk for the entire time and it is OK to use the last part of the time reflecting internally can be helpful.

If you are working with a client who follows this pattern, it can be helpful to reiterate this feedback once you have begun the memory reflection steps. In the clinical office, however, greater flexibility would likely be desired, and you may wish to move on to the next reflection step once the person has stopped talking. However, I would encourage you to ensure they are taking their time answering the questions and, if you feel they are rushing, to assist them in easing in more to the reflective process, as moving too quickly through the reflective process will circumvent the whole purpose of the exercise.

Finally, I always recommend making a statement about negative or unrelated thoughts. We have adopted nonjudgmental language that is similar to what is used in many mindfulness and acceptance-based interventions (Baer et al., 2006; K. W. Brown & Ryan, 2003; Kabat-Zinn & Hanh, 2009) regarding thoughts that are unrelated to the intervention. I recommend that therapists comment about clients noticing those thoughts and then nonjudgmentally bring those thoughts back to the task at hand.

In interventions in which we are working with community members (and not psychotherapy clients), such as what the text above was drawn from, we do not use words like "nonjudgmental" because these are words that many community members may not be familiar with or socialized to understand. However, if you are working with clients for whom these words are familiar, you may wish to use them. The hope is that statements like this preempt a process that can make savoring difficult, a process in which the client gets caught up in a cycle of having a negative/tangential thought or feeling, becomes judgmental about having had that thought or feeling, and then allows the self-judgment to distract them from the task of savoring. By acknowledging that these types of thoughts are expected or inevitable and that they do not detract from or derail the task, the therapist can preempt a judgmental or self-critical process from interrupting the savoring session.

After the therapist provides this explanation, the therapist and client are ready to begin the memory reflection stage of the savoring process.

STEP 1: SENSORY REFLECTION

The first step in this guided reflection is the *sensory reflection* step. In this step, the therapist leads the client through a series of prompts/questions that encourage the client to really "set the scene" about the memory. The prompts/questions are designed to help the client paint the picture and visually place themselves back in the memory, to bring to mind as many possible details as possible, and ideally to generate details that involve the senses and the body.

The manual that we have used in our relational savoring studies with parents includes the following words:

> I'd like you to relax and begin focusing on the time when _____ with _____ [person's name]. First, I want you to notice and remember the details of the event. What was the weather like that day? What time of day did the event occur? What did _____ [person's name] look like or what were they wearing? Do you remember what you were wearing? What kinds of sounds could you hear? What kinds of things could you see?

Here it is important to remember what I mentioned above about the client not being asked to answer each question/prompt we have asked them. Rather, the goal of providing specific questions/prompts to the client is to help the client generate specific topics of discussion. If the therapist simply says, "I want you to notice and remember all of the details of the event" and stops at that, some clients might find that to be sufficient prompting to paint the whole picture of the scene where the memory took place, but others may say a few words or sentences about the memory and then be unable to continue. By providing a tantalizing list of different possibilities of what the client could focus on and encouraging them not to focus on any particular detail, we provide many possibilities and encourage maximal flexibility.

Next, I provide an example of this section of a savoring narrative where Nancy, mother of Theo, a toddler, is savoring a time when she and her child made eye contact in the locker room:

NANCY: Okay, so, it was um, 9:30 or 9:45. Um, so class was over. And, um we decided, like I decided to take him actually to the girl's locker room, because the family locker room there's boys in it. So, um, or there's fathers so I didn't want to like get naked in front of fathers. So, we did that and then um, after I finished giving Theo a shower. Um, it was my turn and so I, I dressed him up and I'm still like in my bathing suit, I'm still wet. I dressed him up and I got out some snacks and I said "you know sit here, just sit here, and I'm gonna go take a shower," like I'm trying to like, let him know mommy's taking a shower.

110 • *Relational Savoring*

RESEARCHER: Mhm.

NANCY: And then he's like "OK," so he's like "OK" and um, so I'm taking a shower and he's really quiet and so, I have a, I have a little, um, have a peek through the curtain and then he just looking at me and so we're looking at each other and I'm like I'm looking at you, I'm right here, I'm right here and we're just talking kinda like eye contact talking or I'm just talking and Theo is just like looking at me. You know, he's just sitting there very quietly and very still and being you know really good about it.

RESEARCHER: It's really great.

NANCY: Yeah.

RESEARCHER: Do you remember any of the kinda what was going on around you?

NANCY: Um, . . . there's, there's probably, so there's probably, I think there was um, a couple more people taking showers also, um 'cause they had several classes there for people of all ages, but none, none, nobody really bothered us and um, it was, nobody was in our row, I don't think. And it was particularly quiet and um, yeah. I think it was just the two of us really maybe 'cause there's, um, there's like two rows and so on our row of showers, there was no one there. And then I think there was a couple people in the other row of showers. And then when, and then it was nice because it was nice and warm inside, it wasn't very cold, and then I just thought taking my shower, you know, I thought maybe I wouldn't be able to wash my hair but I was able to do that, you know, got out of there, I was able to dry up, you know, while him just like right there, sitting.

RESEARCHER: That's really great.

NANCY: Yeah.

RESEARCHER: That must have been really nice; it was reassuring.

NANCY: Yeah, it was. Yeah.

In this example, Nancy engages readily with the task and dives deeply and quickly into talking about the details of the memory. It is easy to picture the scene she is describing. In the beginning of her narrative, Nancy focuses more on describing the people around her and the commotion rather than the sensory details, but that may be because it was a rather busy, bustling type of situation (lots of people milling about the shower), but toward the end of the description, she talks about the sensory details, describing the temperature, for instance.

The therapist prompts her once to get her to focus on the scene around her, likely because the mother had begun describing the details of the memory again (the interaction between her and her child), rather than focusing on the sensory aspects, which is the aim of this step of the memory reflection). From reading this example, one can see how Nancy did not touch on many of the questions asked but still provided a full description of the scene in which the memory takes place. As a result, it is possible for an outsider to listen to this description and place themselves in the scene, so the client has accomplished their goal, even if they have not ticked all of the boxes.

In this next example of an older adult from our study of 60- to 95-year-olds, the client, Michelle, starts out by providing ample sensory details regarding the ambient environment but does not provide many details regarding the other person (her daughter, Sarah), so the therapist encourages her to provide some information about that person:

MICHELLE: Okay. The um let's see the um, the smells, the ocean. Salt, salt air. It was a lovely day, temperature was 77, something like that. Um, the sounds, I remember specifically, oh, when we walked past the pools lots and lots of children, so those were sounds I remember there. And then we were sitting outside and I remember, um, a crow that was very noisy and he'd-he'd fly away and then he'd come back and then he'd fly away and then he'd come back and there was a pigeon walking—we were on high stools and he walked underneath of us. Um the things I saw were, maybe I said this already, the ocean. Um, they were in a very nice condo, I remember commenting on the furniture and the carpet and it looked so new. Um, what else, can I think of something else . . .

RESEARCHER: Um, do you remember what you were wearing, and what Sarah was wearing? Or how she looked?

MICHELLE: Oh, mhm, she was wearing some um, black sweatpants and a blue and black blouse, and I was wearing um, a um, I was wearing white pants, and then a um, light blue, um T-shirt and a, a um light blue shirt.

In this next example, a mother, Kim, provides more sensory details up front along with some details about the interaction between herself and her child, Thomas:

KIM: K, um, we were in the middle of the, like, the kiddie pool. Um, and, uh, I had to kind of kneel in that area. And Thomas probably could touch the floor if he really wanted to. I think it's just, um, I can tell he gets very anxious when I try to get him to kind of say, like, "OK, look, look, it's not that far down." 'Cause I think he gets very, um, I can, I can, I can sense his anxiety 'cause he tenses up whenever I try to say, "Look you can stand here!" Because yes, he probably could stand, he's just going to go underwater a little bit. Um, he doesn't like that feeling nothing below him.

RESEARCHER: Mhm.

KIM: Um, so he was holding on tightly to me. And, um, it was, um, pretty warm day. Uh, our class starts at, um, 10 o'clock [*laughs*], which you think it would be kind of cold, but it's actually kind of warm during that time. The sun was out. And we could hear a lot of other children, um, in the pool splashing, playing with, um, there are other, there's a lot of different swim classes going on at the same time. And he's wearing his little rash guard and his, um, swim trunks. And I'm in my, um, black bathing suit. And, um, I'm holding on to him. Just telling it's OK, Thomas, or, I'm sorry. His instructor is telling us, uh, you know, bob him back and forth, do a little bounce, do a little bounce. And she said OK, "Go lower. One, two . . ." And then you take them down. And so I, I, you know, we're getting him used to it, and he's, he's kind, "ahh, ahh" 'cause he could feel the water. And I said, "Okay, one . . . two . . ." and I hesitated and I dunked him under. But right after, when he came up, he was just stunned.

RESEARCHER: Mhm.

KIM: And he just [*coughing*]. And so I, you know, when he started to cry, I, I held him close to me, and I said, "Oh, it's OK, baby. It's OK. You're OK. Momma would not let anything bad happen to you." I said, "I'm here."

RESEARCHER: Mhm.

KIM: I said, "I would not let anything bad happen to you." He started crying a little bit right after, but then he kinda calmed down when I started to reassure him that he was fine and I was not going to let him get dunked or stay under water.

In this example of Kim speaking about Thomas in the swimming pool, the therapist did not have to do any prompting but rather just indicated the fact that they were tracking the client's statements. At the end of this last statement, the therapist moved on to the next section of the reflection task.

In this next example, which comes from our study of adolescent males in residential treatment, the client, Sylvestre, responded question by question. He begins his response by responding to only the last question asked, so the interviewer responds by asking a series of additional questions (which actually involves repeating the questions that have previously been asked) to encourage the adolescent to engage in the exercise.

Although this is not ideal in that it does not facilitate the client becoming immersed in the memory-recall experience in the way that is intended, it is better than having the client provide brief, one-word or one-sentence answers. We can also hope that in interventions in which the client will be exposed to savoring on multiple occasions, they will come to internalize the idea that it is supposed to be not an ask-and-answer dynamic but rather a dynamic in which the therapist proposes a series of ideas for reflection and then the client reflects for a while using the prompts as a guide. However, in the case of Sylvestre, this is the third session, so it seems unlikely that this is a case of lack of exposure to the intervention context:

RESEARCHER: Alright, OK um. I'd like you to relax, begin focusing on the time when your staff member really took care of you um, by um taking your time and watching movie together. So first, um I want you to notice and remember the details of the event? So, what was the air like that day?

SYLVESTRE: Cold, about 60, 70 degrees.

RESEARCHER: Mhmm and what was the weather like?

SYLVESTRE: It was dark it was maybe like 12 so it was maybe like outside?

RESEARCHER: And um, you said it happened around 12 o'clock like midnightish?

SYLVESTRE: Mhmm.

RESEARCHER: And what did the staff look like?

SYLVESTRE: One of them had a beard, he was White. He was wearing a Cookie Monster shirt on. Ha ha.

RESEARCHER: [*Laughs.*]

SYLVESTRE: And also uh, white jeans.

RESEARCHER: Mhm.

SYLVESTRE: And then there was another staff. He, he I'm not sure what race you could consider Chinese. Um, he was wearing black jeans and a blue shirt. I'm not sure what shoes he was wearing but yeah.

RESEARCHER: What kind of smell was in the air?

SYLVESTRE: Froot Loops. Yeah, Froot Loops sort of.

RESEARCHER: And what kind of sounds could you hear.

SYLVESTRE: I could hear the movie going on and I could hear kids playing video games in the other room. I could also hear the microwave going and people talking around the TV.

RESEARCHER: What kind of things did you see?

SYLVESTRE: In the movie?

RESEARCHER: Yeah in the movie but maybe other things too.

SYLVESTRE: Um, I saw . . . I saw uh. In the movie, I saw a guy and then they were laughing right next to each other but then they got sucked into a black hole. It's pretty much all I remembered.

RESEARCHER: Mhmm.

SYLVESTRE: And then, they ended up in this whole different dimension and I don't even know where they were. Everything was pink and like marshmallows and stuff.

RESEARCHER: And were you in like a room? And what did that kind of look like? It, kind of a cozy room or . . .?

SYLVESTRE: Yeah, I was sitting on a leather. I'm not sure if it was leather or not but it was like cushioned.

RESEARCHER: Mhmm.

SYLVESTRE: And um, there was like. Like I was sitting with like two pillows and like a blanket.

RESEARCHER: Mhmm.

SYLVESTRE: We were all sitting there watching a movie. It was like the windows were opened all the way. The light was off. It was like, two people on either side of me so it was like cool at that time. So, yeah we all watched the movie.

Finally, in this last example, which comes from our study of adults aged 60 to 95, the participant, George, provides a detailed description of the memory itself and, in so doing, shares sensory details (warm, hospital gown, early in the morning). The end result is a very vivid scene that emerges of the memory itself.

> So we'd stay the night in a hotel there um before [*mumbles*]. And we got to the hospital early in the morning, early and they were ready for us which is good. And I had no fear of what was going to happen, but uh my wife and my daughter were both with me. So I had no fear even though it was quite dangerous, I was out for 7 hours. Midway coming back from the procedure, umm, my daughter and my wife were right next to the bed. I was in a hospital gown of course and uh, yeah the bed covering was sort of close to me. I felt warm and I felt uh confident and they were there looking at me, both of them were looking right at my face and just uh, wonderful sweet looks. And uh, then I began to discover what had happened and what the doctors had said and realizing the true significance of what had happened. Those are my feelings and uh they they actually reached out and touched me, just touched my arm. So, meaningful to me. Anyway. So when you're going under something like that, you never know that truth of what's going to happen and so there was some relief but it, you know, just uh, I didn't feel really good at [that] point.

In sum, the purpose of the sensory reflection step is to assist the client in immersing themselves back in the experience. Ideally, the client will be able to reenvision or paint a picture of the details of the scene. It is less important that they hit upon every sensory detail and more important that they become immersed in the retelling of the experience, providing a vivid account of what occurred. Clients will vary in terms of how much support and what kind of support they require in this step of the memory reflection.

STEP 2: EMOTION REFLECTION

The second step of the reflection process is the *emotion reflection* step. The explicit focus of this step is to assist clients in identifying, experiencing, and expressing the feelings they were having during the memory. By *identifying*, I mean I intend for the clients to attach words and bodily sensations to the emotional experience. By *experiencing*, I mean I would like clients to reactivate those emotions in the moment. We accomplish this by asking clients to describe their sensory experience, to connect their sensory experience and visceral states to their felt emotion, and to try to embody the emotional experience in the moment. Finally, by *expressing*, I mean I would like clients to share these emotions in the savoring session with the therapist—the premise here is that in expressing these emotions, they will experience themselves in the eyes of the other, affirming person, who can witness and validate their emotional experience (Borelli, Smiley, et al., 2020).

By engaging in this process, I hope the client will be able to deepen their emotional experience as well. The manual we have used in our relational savoring studies with parents involves the following words:

> Now I'd like you to notice how you felt at this time. What kinds of things were you feeling in your body? Were you feeling happy and excited, or were you deeply calm and relaxed? Think about where in your body you felt these emotions and try to feel them now.

I want to mention a couple of things about the emotions chosen for this prompt. The first is something I mentioned in Chapter 4. Positive emotions can be both high in arousal (happy and excited) or low in arousal (calm and relaxed)—either is suitable for savoring. Different people prefer to savor different types of emotional experiences. One study has examined the difference in savoring high- versus low-arousal memories among adults with higher depressive symptoms, finding that savoring higher arousal memories uniquely increased help-seeking behaviors (Straszewski & Seigel, 2020). We have not examined which types of emotional experiences yield better results in relational savoring, but my default assumption is to allow clients to gravitate toward the emotional experiences that pull them most strongly. This may also be a factor you can tailor to your specific client and their needs—for instance, clients with depression may benefit from savoring higher arousal memories, whereas clients who are anxious may benefit from savoring lower arousal memories.

The second point is about the emotional depth of these words. The words we use are fairly superficial in terms of their emotional depth (happy and excited, calm and relaxed). We envision this as the starting place, but through the act of relational savoring, we try to get clients to a deeper emotional place. So we attempt to move clients from more general, nonspecific, or superficial feeling states (e.g., good, happy, upset, joy) to more specific, attachment-related states (e.g., It sounds like you really enjoyed spending time with her; can you say what about it you enjoyed?). The therapist may also engage in conjecturing, asking questions such as, "Was it a feeling of taking care of her that made it feel so special?" Or, "It seems like you were really there to support her when she needed you, or at least that's how it seems to me. Do you notice that too? And does that make you feel proud? Or close to her?"

Here is an example of a parent, Gina, engaging in this part of the savoring intervention:

RESEARCHER: So now I'd like you to notice how you felt at the time. What kinds of things were you feeling in your body? Were you feeling happy and excited, or were you deeply calm and relaxed?

GINA: I think it was more—I was really happy and excited because I was—I remember I wanted to get home and tell my husband "this is what the teacher said!" you know, um, even like yesterday, I told [name] "you don't understand how incredibly happy I feel for Jose." I think he's, like, accomplished so much, and you know, in these few days. Imagine being in a classroom and you don't understand a single thing.

RESEARCHER: Mhm.

GINA: You know, you're trying to figure it out, um, and you're only two. And so, um, that—and just that bursting of joy. I think, like, I mean, my—[child] gets compliments—had gotten compliments a lot. "Oh he's such a focused child," "he's such a big boy," "he's such a happy boy," yadda yadda yadda. And, every time it's like "oh yeah, thanks! You know, that's great." Um, but just that compliment from the teacher was—cause she was so happy too—was, like, I was just, you know, really, really excited and happy for him and just joyful. Joyful, yeah.

RESEARCHER: Can you think about where in your body you were feeling the joy?

GINA: It was, like, right here in the—in, like, chest area. I—I just—I just think—remember, it was like, that one moment when picked him up it was like that "throom"——

RESEARCHER: Mhm.

GINA: feeling and I was just like, you know, when—when people say bursting with joy I think I know what they mean now.

RESEARCHER: Mm.

GINA: It's that bursting with joy. And, um, I don't know if I'll ever feel it again, but it was just that bursting with joy.

RESEARCHER: I'm sure you will. [*Laughs*] OK.

This example is really poignant because Gina's description is so vivid and visceral—when she gets to the point of describing her feeling of "bursting with joy," as a reader or listener, one can feel their chest burst a bit alongside her. It is easy to imagine that Gina is actually feeling those "bursting with joy" feelings again in the moment as she is describing this memory because this is how vivid her description is. This is the holy grail, so to speak, of what you want to target in this step of the intervention. If you get a person to become so immersed in a feeling that you really feel they are reexperiencing their feelings in the moment, you have achieved your goal. And if you are feeling their feelings alongside them, all the better.

Let's look at one more example of a client, Imani, who becomes fully immersed in the retelling and reexperiencing of her emotions during this section of the intervention, to get a really solid feel for what this looks like. When reading this excerpt, also pay attention to the care and level of detail that the therapist uses when describing the client's emotional state in the prompting—the therapist provides the perfect softball pitch, so to speak, so the client can hit the ball out of the park:

THERAPIST: I'd like you to think about where in your body you felt these emotions. At first the happiness, and later the calm and as you were holding him, and then the bond that you felt, um, just one at a time. Where in your body you felt them, and if you can, try to feel them right now.

IMANI: Um, I feel like the happiness that I felt, it was just kind of warm—my face—and [*laughs*] like I, I know I smiled at him when I saw him.

THERAPIST: Mhm.

IMANI: And he was just, like I said, he's like full eyes were big [*laughs*]. And so I smiled and I knew that when I was happy and excited to see him and 'cause I could feel it in my face. Um, when I was calm and starting to calm down, I actually could feel it kind of throughout my body. Um, sometimes I do tense up and, um, it takes me some time to kind of just relax and so I could just kind of all over. And, um, when I feel the closeness for the bond to him, I feel it like right here.

THERAPIST: Mhm.

IMANI: Like in my heart. That's when I feel, like, close to him.

And hit it she does! It's as if Imani has painted a beautiful picture of her emotions, one that is complete with sensory details (temperature muscle tension), emotion descriptors, and physical location—therapists could not have done this better themselves.

This step of the intervention is integral to its success, but it needs to involve deep exploration of feelings to help the client engage in a new emotional experience. Thus, I am going to take you through several more examples of people who respond to this prompt in different ways to help you see the diversity of ways in which people respond to enhance your preparedness to respond to client's needs. This next dialogue provides a more complex example wherein the client's response offers the therapist various potential directions. It is helpful for the therapist to have a clear idea of where they are headed before beginning.

RESEARCHER: Mhm. OK, and so now I'd like you to notice how you felt when you were holding [child], just calming him down and reassuring him. What kinds of things were you feeling in your body? Were you feeling happy and excited? Or were you deeply calm and relaxed? Think about where in your body you felt these emotions, and try to feel them right now.

WEI: Okay, calm and relaxed. Um, 'cause I wanted, I felt like if I was kinda excited and happy, he would've probably freaked out [*laughs*].

RESEARCHER: Mhm.

WEI: So, very calm and, um, just trying to give that calmness to him so that he feels OK [*chuckles*].

RESEARCHER: Mhm.

WEI: And calm down 'cause again, I didn't want him to start freaking out. And, um, and I felt it, you know, in my chest, in my heart area. And, um, in my breathing 'cause I was, you know, I stayed very calm [*chuckles*].

RESEARCHER: Mhm.

WEI: I didn't, um, try to excite him 'cause I knew he was already kind of, like I said, excited. He knew that this was happening, and he wasn't very happy to be at the doctor's office. Um, so when I reassured him I made sure that I was breathing very calmly, very steady. And, uh, you know, I wasn't laughing at him or making fun of him 'cause I know that, um, I don't want him to think that, that, yeah, it was a direct relation that I was making fun of him for, you know, feeling like that he didn't

> like being at the doctor's office. But I reassured him and, like I said, like I felt it in my heart, and I felt it in my lungs when I was, you know, calming him and breathing and reassuring him.

RESEARCHER: All right. Sounds like you really, uh, create a safe space for him.

In this previous example, Wei goes in the direction of making a distinction between calm and relaxed on the one hand and happy and excited on the other. This distinction is a bit of a distraction from the meat of the intervention; it could take Wei to an intellectual place rather than helping her experience and express her feelings by putting herself back into the situation when she experienced this connection with her child. On the other hand, having clarity on her emotional experience might help her identify what the experience was, which could help her engage in the subsequent steps of emotional processing (experiencing and expressing). The therapist must decide whether the exploration is facilitating Wei's ultimate emotional processing or detracting from it. In the end, the most important task for the therapist is to redirect the client back to their internal emotional experience, particularly the positive parts of their emotional experience, and the positive impact they were having on their child.

Some clients have difficulty talking about emotions. When explicitly directed to do so during this step of the reflection stage, they may instead resume talking about the details of the event rather than focusing on the emotions. This can occur in response to this prompt in particular, especially for people for whom discussing emotions is difficult. The therapist needs to pay particular attention to what the client is saying in order to notice whether the person is truly focusing on emotion or whether they have lapsed into describing the details of the event again. Sometimes the details can be very vivid and can even feel emotional without explicitly containing emotional content. In this case, it is important to keep in mind that the client may not even be aware that they are not explicitly discussing their emotional experience; this is particularly true if they are experiencing their emotion while they are speaking.

This next dialogue is a good example of the point I am illustrating. The client, Maya, is providing a lot of details but not really getting into the emotional content of the memory, so the therapist needs to redirect her back to focusing on the emotional content:

RESEARCHER: Now I'd like you to stop and notice how you felt at this time you were rocking Jonah. Uhm hm. And telling him that you loved him and him telling you that back. What kinds of things were you feeling in your body? Were you feeling happy and

Phase 2: Memory Reflection • 121

excited, or were you deeply calm and relaxed? Think about where in your body, in your body you felt these emotions and try to feel them now.

MAYA: Uhm [*sigh*], I was probably feeling, I felt, I think I felt more rushed than anything, uhm, because honestly I think that day, I just wanted to put him down, but most of the time, he's a really heavy baby, uhm, and most of the time, like I said I was really tired, but most of the time, when I put him down, it's our time of rocking, I don't feel like he's heavy, you know, I feel like, I only get this small chance, you know, small window of his life that I can, what I call slow dance with him. Uhm, he's not gonna want to slow dance with me when he's 16, 17, so, uhm, I tried to do it as long as I can, and most of the time, he's very light. Uhm, he doesn't feel as heavy as when I'm, you know, doing other things with him and he wants to get picked up. Uhm, so, that night, prob—, you know, I think I felt rushed but, I also felt calm, and a sense of uhm, accomplishment, I guess 'cause I was able to have him say I love you back, uhm, you know, and I think, I'm pretty sure he knows what that means, because whenever he says it, he was like "squeeze me a little bit tighter." So, yeah, I think that was it but you know some nights it's a good night. Some nights are more rushed and mechanical and sometimes he just, some nights he's just really tired, and you know, I know it and so it's, it's not even rocking it's just here, just go to sleep. Yeah.

RESEARCHER: Can you think of a place in your body when you were feeling these things?

MAYA: Uhm, you know what I felt it, my place, it would be like from my knees to my feet.

RESEARCHER: Uhm.

MAYA: Because I'm standing there and you have to be pretty solid on your feet because uhm, you can't wobble or you can't because if you wobble, they feel, they feel that they're gonna fall too, and that excites them more, and makes them not wanna sleep more. And so, you have to have like some type of strength right, so, uhm, again, you know, you're, you're feeling light. I guess strong on my feet to be able to hold him and be able to lean over him, put him down because even with Micah [other child], if I accidentally put them down too, uhm, fast, they can get nervous and then they start crying and then they don't want to sleep. So, uhm, it's more like I was feeling more stronger from my knees, like you're locking your knees and you're just like back and forth, swaying back and forth. So, when he says, you know, I love you back, you feel that strength, I guess, more, you know holding him. And also uhm, my cheeks would, when he—hold me right here on my shoulder, I would always lean my cheeks next to his and we would snuggle kinda together like that. Yeah.

RESEARCHER: It's a nice feeling.

MAYA: Yeah.

In this previous example, Maya verges on discussing some emotional topics—for instance, she says, "I felt more rushed" and "I just wanted to put him down more than anything," both of which speak to her emotional state (nervousness, fatigue), but these are not particularly positive or connected emotional states. She also mentioned that she "felt calm . . . and a sense of uhm, accomplishment," but she keeps getting distracted by other details, such as how heavy her baby was, or how tired she was, so the therapist needs to redirect her by asking her how she was feeling in her body.

Again, in cases such as this, clients may not be aware that they are not explicitly discussing their emotional experience, especially if they are experiencing emotion while speaking. Therefore, being gentle and using words that do not call them out when suggesting they look inward and explicitly discuss their emotional state is of the utmost importance. In this instance, the therapist also could have directed her to focus more on her internal state by commenting directly on the feelings she was endorsing, for example, by saying something like, "Tell me more about how you were feeling in that moment when you were so calm" or "I can really hear the feeling of accomplishment in your voice—it's such a powerful feeling, isn't it?"

It can be a very helpful strategy to point clients right to the exact moment you want them to focus on, especially when working with a memory that is multifaceted, is emotionally complex, or has a number of different elements to it. The assumption we have is that in heightening this aspect of the memory, the therapist will activate the feelings of having that attachment need be met and get the largest mileage in terms of affecting the internal working model. So the therapist directs the client to focus on not only the memory itself but also the exact moment when the attachment need was activated and met right at the beginning of this prompt:

RESEARCHER: I'm curious, like, how you felt at that time, like when you got to the door and she was gonna sit with you and kinda wait with you? Um, what kind of things were you feeling in your body? Like were you feeling giddy and excited, or were you deeply calm and relaxed? Think about where in your body you felt those emotions——

KAMAL (*interrupting*): Where, when I was at the hospital or when I came home?

RESEARCHER: When you came home and you were in this safe, secure space with her.

KAMAL (*interrupting*): I was, I, I think um, it's very vivid, I, I remember walking through the door, and feeling this incredible feeling of, oh my god I did it, and um, uh, you know, I got to the hospital [*laughing*] we got home I walked through the door, I was, you know, I was still, basically still standing, and I remember just feeling very um, you know, just proud of myself, that uh, I had the strength to go through that situation. And I didn't um, but I felt very safe with Raya there. I mean I felt like I could just be myself, like I, I could let go and not feel like I had to take care of her.

RESEARCHER: Yeah.

KAMAL: Cuz see, my personality is, a very high need to care [*emphatically*] for [*laughs*], so to allow myself to be cared for is, was and I, I ju—, I knew I had to just let go and just, um, like I didn't, I didn't have to prove to her that, you know, I could be independent and I, right? For that moment in time, not that I had to be, dependent, but I needed her help.

In this example, Kamal responds to the therapist's directive, providing an answer. Further, Kamal acknowledges that allowing himself to be cared for in this way is difficult and involves taking a risk but that it means he did not need to prove he is independent; he could just need his daughter, Raya's, help and that could be OK. This kind of closing the loop is a therapeutic win when it happens spontaneously in this way—as in, when the client leads the way there themselves, without being directed there by the therapist. Kamal is making the connection that he felt safe experiencing something new and different in this situation that they do not normally feel comfortable experiencing, and the therapist is there to witness and validate this experience. This marks the changing of the internal working model.

In this next example, the therapist uses the technique of pointing a laser beam toward the exact point where they want the client to focus their attention. This memory involves a medical situation that Mario, the client, went through, and the therapist wants Mario specifically to focus on one moment within the memory, ideally the moment when he felt most taken care of by his adult daughter.

RESEARCHER: Now I'd like you to notice how you felt at this time, specifically when you first tried to walk and your daughter was there. What kinds of things were you feeling in your body? For example, were you feeling maybe giddy and excited or were you calm and relaxed? Think about where in your body you felt these emotions and try to feel them now as you describe them.

MARIO: Well I was actually trying not to be emotional because I wanted to focus on moving my feet [*chuckles*] and uhh you know, despite the fact that the nurses get your belt, one hand on the belt, I wasn't sure that if I slipped [*chuckles*] that was gonna be enough, so I was really focusing entirely on moving my feet. And I would have to say that I was satisfied that I hadn't fallen down yet, but uh, that didn't mean I was, you know, able to just run around, sing and laugh and pay attention to something else. All they task me with at that point wouldn't have been possible.

In this example, the approach of pointing the laser beam at the moment of attachment connection still results in Mario answering by saying, "I was . . . trying not to be emotional." In other words, Mario avoids answering the question. The therapist could have followed up by saying something like the following:

> I know you said you were trying not to feel. It makes sense that it might be hard to even acknowledge the feelings you would have in that moment. It can be hard to rely on people at these times when we really need them. And yet, it seems like it was such a powerful moment in your life and in your relationship with your daughter. What was it like for you to have her by your side at that time when you really needed her?

This type of response acknowledges the difficulty in expressing feelings, validates that having feelings during vulnerable times is challenging to do, and then once again upholds this idea that having the daughter be there during that time was significant. This way of acknowledging, validating, and reframing the question may still result in difficulty responding with emotion, but then the therapist will have asked the question twice and can feel pretty confident they probably will not get a different answer.

In sum, the goal of this emotion reflection step is to encourage the client to identify, experience, and express the feelings associated with the memory. Ideally, the therapist is working to move the client to a deeper level of emotional understanding and expression than where they began. This is accomplished by helping them slow down, as well as by asking them questions that help to expand on their understanding of their experience. With clients who are more experientially avoidant, this step can be more challenging and require greater care.

STEP 3: MEANING-MAKING REFLECTION

Step 3 in the reflection process involves helping clients derive significance or meaning from the memory they are savoring. We accomplish this goal by asking people to focus on the thoughts they are having as they reflect on the memory. When we do this, we are looking for a specific type of thought—we are going after thoughts that have relational or attachment content in them, seeking to heighten those types of cognitions in the service of increasing the relational significance of the memory and the emotions attached to it. When we use the relational savoring intervention with parents, we say these words to parents in this section of the intervention protocol:

> Now I'd like you to reflect on what you were thinking when _____ [point to the specific moment in the memory when the attachment content was highest]. For example, were you thinking, "_____ [child's name] really needs me at this moment," "_____ [child's name] feels really close to me," "I feel so close to _____ [child's name] at this moment," or "I feel comfortable being _____'s [child's name] parent"? And what do you think about it now?

If you think a client might be having different types of thoughts that are not included in this prompt, I recommend modifying the prompt to include those thoughts. The more tailored this prompt can be to the situation your client is savoring and the thoughts your client might be having, the better. Your client will likely correct you if the thoughts you have suggested do not describe their experience, and as I describe below, this is a desired outcome. However, the intervention may better support their reflective process if the exemplar thoughts you suggest better map onto their experience. Using the exact words or ideas of this intervention is not what is important; what is important is that you follow the steps and direct clients to focus on their emotional experience and then direct them to make meaning of that experience.

How do clients respond to this step of the intervention? Let's begin by looking at an example of a client who responds to the prompt in a fairly straightforward way, but also in a way that is not very elaborated. This client, Mai-Lin, answers the prompt, but that is all the client does.

RESEARCHER: So now I'd like you to begin thinking about what you were thinking when you were holding Yun and trying to reassure him. For example, were you thinking, "Yun really needs me at this moment"? "Yun feels really close to me"? or "I feel so close to Yun"? Or "I'm comfortable being Yun's parent"? And what do you think about it now?

MAI-LIN: Um, at the moment, I felt that he really needed me. Like, he really, really needed me. Um, and, um, I was definitely comfortable being his parent. And I did feel close to him 'cause I knew that he needed, he needed his momma. Um, looking at it now, I am trying to think what Yun would be thinking.

Mai-Lin's response is completely satisfactory, but it is not overwhelming in its complexity or depth. Mai-Lin is responding to all parts of the prompt, so in this sense, Mai-Lin has completed the task at hand, but one is not blown away by the richness of the response provided. Some clients only provide responses with this level of depth, so the therapist should be satisfied with this type of response. However, other clients may be able to progress to a deeper level with their processing. Let's look at another exchange to see an example of a client, Amir, who moves beyond the level of processing offered by the therapist and offers their own depth and interpretation of the prompt. (Note: This is an older adult client who is savoring a memory of when their grandparent gingerly pulled out their tooth, which was hurting them.)

RESEARCHER: Now I'd like you to think about what you were thinking when your grandmother, uh, did this for you I guess. Were you thinking—"She really cares for me, she really loves me, she really understands me"? And what do you think about it now, looking back?

AMIR: She knew what was good for me. And and, that's the first thing that comes to mind. *In that yes, she was taking care of me but it was because she understood what I needed and was taking care of me.*

In this example, I have italicized what I see as the key moments in the passage in terms of Amir's meaning making. This is where Amir moves beyond what was offered by the therapist and makes it their own. The next client

I am going to show you does this to an even greater extent. Meet Nova, mother of 2-year-old Yarom:

RESEARCHER: So now, I'd like you to think about what you were thinking when you first hugged Yarom when you heard this news. For example, were you thinking, "Yarom really needs me at this moment"? "Yarom feels really close to me"? or "I'm really proud and comfortable being Yarom's parent"? And what do you think about it now?

NOVA: I think it was *more mm* [smacks lips], probably *"I'm really proud that I was Yarom's parent."* And, I was really just—I think when he hugged me also, like, we had, like, *this really deep connection* 'cause it's like we were *trying to get to a goal together and we—we met that goal.*

RESEARCHER: Mhm.

NOVA: You know, and he's—he just turned two,

RESEARCHER: Mhm.

NOVA: And so it's like I don't even know if he understands but I feel like in some ways he does understand, but it's like when you're doing a project together with someone and um it—it's been taking months and you can't seem to solve this one problem and *finally just—this one day you just solve it and it's like "wow."*

RESEARCHER: It's a breakthrough.

NOVA: It's like a breakthrough, yeah. And I think um him and I—*when I hugged him, like, he realized that, you know, that was the breakthrough.* Granted, I dropped him off today, he still tugged on me, he still cried. But, once I left, he was fine. No, um, he was full of smiles. The teacher said he didn't cry, so yeah. I think he still, like, um I still—I still think he doesn't want to—he has that, like, apprehension when he's at that school, when he starts, when he goes in the beginning, but towards the end he's fine.

RESEARCHER: Mm. Mhm.

Nova listens to the suggested thoughts and ideas that the therapist has provided and says "it's more like" and then offers a different thought that she was having about the experience. This kind of autonomy in characterizing the experience is desired because it shows that Nova is perceiving and interpreting the experience through her own lens rather than the lens that was provided to her. The therapist then builds on this interpretation that Nova has offered, suggesting a frame that fits what Nova has described (the word *breakthrough*).

In this next example, the client, Sara, accepts the thoughts the therapist has suggested and then builds on them by suggesting her own thoughts and ideas, not in a way that contradicts what the therapist offers but simply in a way that adds to what the therapist has suggested.

RESEARCHER: So now I'd like you to think about what you were thinking about when you were working on numbers with Gabriela. Mhm. Um, for example, were you thinking, "[child] really needs me in this moment"? "She's really close to me. I feel really close to her"? Um, "I feel comfortable being Gabriela's parent"? And what do you think about it now?

SARA: Um, I feel all of those things I felt being very connected to her. And like we were so in sync 'cause obviously she was filling in all the blanks and I was helping her along the ways. And we were perfectly in sync.

RESEARCHER: Mhm.

SARA: And I also felt like happy 'cause I know like, how [Ricardo, child's father]'s working on it too. You know, we've always been on the same page, like parenting-wise.

RESEARCHER: Mhm.

SARA: And just know, even though we're separated, we're still—we care about her more than anything in the world.

RESEARCHER: Mhm.

SARA: So he's working on it too which is awesome.

RESEARCHER: Mhm.

SARA: And this is perfect.

RESEARCHER: Great. Awesome.

This example brings to mind the broaden-and-build theory of emotion (Fredrickson, 2005)—for Sara, one positively valenced thought (*being so in sync*) leads to another thought (*that Ricardo, Gabriela's father is also working on it*), which leads to another thought (*that Sara and Ricardo have always been on the same page, parenting-wise*), which leads to another thought (*that even though they're separated, they care about their child more than anything in the world*). The client has suddenly created a whole string of positive thoughts and emotions that connect to one another and layer on top of one another, and now the memory has projections to so many different facets of the client's life. Not only is it about a moment of connection with her child or a moment in which she provided for her child, but also it is about this wonderful network of experiences in which she and her child's father are working together to show their child how much they love her.

The memory says something about relationships and life and love that is bigger than the moment itself. When the client is able to make connections in this way, the power of the punch is much greater because the client is gaining the benefit of not only the memory itself but also a memory that has projections into many other areas of the client's life. Picture a tree that has roots that project very deep into the soil; in this exercise, we are trying to help clients reach within themselves very deeply into their root systems, because if they can reach that far, then the benefits of the exercise will eventually affect the entire system rather than having a more local benefit.

Finally, I am going to review an example of this section of the intervention as conducted with two children. These sessions were conducted with children and adolescents within our study of males in residential treatment, most of whom were selected from a foster care/postadoption population, so their level of relational deprivation was significant. The purpose of reviewing these examples is to provide some context into what this section of the intervention looks like with children/adolescents, and also what it looks like with clients who have far more adverse histories.

The first response is briefer but responsive to the prompt. The client, Brandon, is able to express his perspective about the other people in the situation and himself, and to share the impact of others on himself.

RESEARCHER: Yeah, it's totally fine. So we'd like you to know, uh to think about what you were thinking back then. So were you thinking that Aaron really cares about me and really understands me. And he really loves me. So we would just like to know what you were thinking back then?

BRANDON: I honestly think that, that Aaron is really there for me, like he knew, he knew everything about me even though I've been here for six months. It was like he knew exactly what I needed and exactly what I wanted. [*Inaudible.*]. So, yeah like, he was there for me, he understands me.

RESEARCHER: And now, what do you think about him now? Has it changed?

BRANDON: I still think he's a cool guy yeah.

This is no small feat for an adolescent male, let alone an adolescent male with significant adversity. I will call it a win. The client is savoring a positive experience he had with a staff member at the facility, and the thoughts the client expresses are consistent with attachment themes.

The second example presents a more challenging case, one in which the therapist really has to chase the client, Kai, to get them to discuss thoughts that are relevant to the memory under discussion, which involves the client's grandmother taking them out to eat:

RESEARCHER: Alright. So now let's think about what you were thinking when you were with Grandma. So, for instance, um, were you thinking she really cares for you, she really loves you, she really understands you, and what else were you sort of thinking in that moment?

KAI: Um, I guess when I was with her, um, I don't really really think that, "Oh, Grammy's so cute. To talk with me or eat with me, she must really care about me." Like, none of that, but, I just think I . . . I don't know how to say that, just um, I just think [*inaudible*]. It was good.

RESEARCHER: Mhm.

KAI: I guess that's what, I guess that's what it all picking up.

RESEARCHER: I see.

KAI: Yeah.

RESEARCHER: So you, were you feeling something for your caregiver, like your grandma? That time at all, or . . .?

KAI: Yeah yeah yeah, I was thinkin' like, thankful . . .

RESEARCHER: Mhm.

KAI: at that time.

RESEARCHER: Yeah can you, can you like tell me a little bit more about that?

KAI: Um, I guess it was [*inaudible*]—like, I said thank you and stuff, talked about it. Not talked about it, but talked. So yeah that was, that was, thinking about what we were talking about, but I don't remember what we were talking about though.

RESEARCHER:	Let's see. Um, hmm, do remember, can you try to remember, maybe what you were saying? You said you don't remember it but maybe like try to think about it. Or maybe like other things that you maybe are thankful, like, that she came.
KAI:	I don't remember much of anything that we were saying. Honestly I just can't recall anything.
RESEARCHER:	Mhm. Do you remember, like, what else you were thankful for? Except for like [*cough*] coming out and . . . eating food?
KAI:	Um, just thankful for her being there, I guess. *Um, I've never really spent a whole night thinkin' about what I'm thankful for.*
RESEARCHER:	Mhm, yeah, yeah. Alright. I can understand that it's different and hard to think about things you haven't thought about before. Um, do you, and what do you think about it now, um, looking back sort of?
KAI:	Mm, I guess it was a fun dinner.
RESEARCHER:	Can you tell me a little bit more?
KAI:	Like, I don't really know what to say, it's, we went out, had some, I mean, burgers, talked, went home . . . I guess, I said thank you for the dinner, and I ate. And that's basically it. That's the dinner. On Sunday—on Saturday night.
RESEARCHER:	Okay. Alright. Um, do you have anything else to say, or . . .?
KAI:	No, not really.

In this excerpt of their relational savoring session, it is easy to perceive Kai's avoidance of the attachment-related themes, but the therapist continues to redirect Kai toward the topic at hand. The therapist does not get very far with Kai, but the therapist's persistence is admirable, and the therapist gets further through trying than they would have without trying. In the italicized section, Kai indicates that he has not spent much time thinking about what he is grateful for. Indeed, this does feel like unexplored terrain for this adolescent. One benefit of the therapist placing so much emphasis on this topic is that Kai will emerge having thought more about the topic and having felt this topic is worthy of exploration and attention.

In sum, the purpose of this step in the reflection process is to assist clients in deriving significance or meaning from the memory they are savoring. Therapists are specifically interested in helping clients derive attachment-based or relational meaning from these experiences—they wish to draw clients' attention toward these themes. As with other steps, variability exists in clients' readiness to engage in this type of processing, but there are strategies to help clients who struggle with this step.

STEP 4: FUTURE-ORIENTED REFLECTION

The fourth step of the intervention is a future-oriented reflection. The goal of this step is to help our clients take the sensory details, emotional experience, and meaning they have just derived from Steps 1, 2, and 3, respectively, and extend their impact. Specifically, we want clients not to see this memory as an isolated incident, a one-time occurrence, but rather to perceive what has happened in their relationship as something that has tremendous significance for this specific relationship and for their lives as a whole.

When I think about this step of the intervention, I now think about the movie *Inside Out* and the notion of core memories (although we began doing this work before this movie was produced). The concept of core memories is used in the film to explain how key moments in people's lives have an outsized influence on their personality and life course; each character has these core memories that are stored in their brains that to some extent define them and are associated with certain emotional states (e.g., joy, disgust, anger). I like to think that with relational savoring, we are trying to strengthen the power of these memories and increase the likelihood that they are going to vie for attention as core memories—by explicitly helping participants see the importance of the memories, their connection to their future, we are trying to encourage them to draw lines between these experiences and their own and their relationship partner's lives.

What follows are the words we use to guide the clients through this section of the intervention:

> Now I'd like you to turn your focus to the future. Focus on how close you felt to _____ [person's name] at that time. How will the bond that you have together affect your relationship in the future? What positive things can you imagine happening as a result of your bond to one another?

In this section, as in other sections of the intervention, the more specific the therapist can be about the aspects of the memory that are most salient and that connect most to the attachment-relevant content, the better. So in this script, we have written "how close you felt to [person's name]," but if the client was more specific in their description of their feelings toward the other person (e.g., they felt "deeply connected" or "at one with" or "soulmates with"), it would be even better to tailor this statement more specifically to the words the client used.

Using the exact verbiage the client has used will make the statement more personal and meaningful to the client, so it would behoove therapists to tailor the intervention to the individual client. The key elements of this section of the intervention help the client focus on how the memory they have just savored, and specifically the positive-connectedness aspect of the memory, will affect (a) the relationship they have with this person and (b) other aspects of their lives, including, but not limited to, personal aspects of their lives and personal aspects of the other individual's life.

In this section of the reflection, clients bring up a variety of different topics. For instance, they mention that the relationship will continue to be strong and enduring, that the relationship will help the individual be confident throughout their lives (secure base theme; commonly arises when parents savor experiences with their children), that the relationship will help them know that others will always be there for them (safe haven theme), and that the relationship will help them pursue things that are hard to pursue (secure base theme). Other topics that emerge are that the self has value or worth and that relationships are an important part of life worth investing in.

It is important to note that sometimes these topics are introduced as guesses about what will happen as a result of these experiences (e.g., *I think they will mean that . . .*) and sometimes they are introduced as wishes (e.g., *I hope they will lead to . . .*). Sometimes clients will comment on how they would like to change their behavior in the future as a result of what they have learned or some insights they have gleaned as a result of engaging in this reflective practice.

Let's look at some example responses to this prompt to get a feeling for how different people respond to this section of the intervention. The first example illustrates the way in which a client, Debbie, responds when she expresses that engaging in the savoring exercise has prompted her to want to change the way she lives her life (in this case, the way she interacts with her child):

RESEARCHER: Okay, lastly, uh, is there anything else you'd like to say about this memory or do you have any takeaways from engaging in this reflection process?

DEBBIE: And, um, like I said because of that, I think my takeaway is that it's really making me think about how I interact with him. . . . Um, so instead of him constantly hearing this no, no, no and, like I said, it makes me think about . . . consciously making sure that I be more positive in my interactions with him.

Here is a response from our study of older adults. Speaking about a relationship with a friend, this client, Galen, responds by saying that he thinks the closeness and connection achieved with the friend have helped him learn lessons about the value of certain qualities within relationships that have caused him to change the way he interacts in future relationships for the better:

RESEARCHER: Now, I'd like you to turn your focus to the future. Focus on how it felt to receive care from Julie—how will the bond that you have with your friend affect your life in the future? What positive things can you imagine happening as a result of the friendship that you had with her?

GALEN: Well I think uh probably helps . . . in our, my current relationship, my marriage, in that uh . . . uh when my um first wife died, I didn't realize that we were, we didn't discuss things as much as I wished I had. There were things that um I didn't or I realized that I didn't tell her I loved her enough. Or I didn't— I didn't pay the attention to her that I should have during. So I have regrets there. But, in the relationship I have with Julie, I had learned how important uh it was to um be very honest and open with uh our relationship. So as I'm, as I'm progressing with Martha, this time, my current wife.

Galen's reaction to this question shows that his relationship with Julie showed him the importance of being open and honest, which he has taken into his relationship with his current wife, Martha. To maximize the power of this memory, the therapist could build on this message, driving home the point that Galen feeling safe enough to be open and honest with Julie, particularly during such a vulnerable time in his life, means he is capable of sharing these parts of himself with others, which is a real source of strength for him.

In this next example, the parent, Juana, provides a mix of beliefs and hopes regarding how this memory has implications for the future.

RESEARCHER: Now I'd like you to turn your focus to the future. Focus on how close you felt to [child] at that time. How will the bond you have together affect your relationship in the future? And what positive things can you imagine happening as a result of your bond to one another?

JUANA: Well I hope that she knows that I'm always gonna be there for her. I'm not gonna let her fall. I'm not gonna, you know, but I'm also like not gonna do everything for her, like I want her to learn and grow on her own with me just providing, you know, the steps

	and um the care for her, but um. . . . Sorry I thought I heard her um. . . .
RESEARCHER:	Oh yeah [*laughter*].
JUANA:	Uh anyways uh, but I—I do hope that she—she knows that I'm always gonna be there for her and I'm not gonna let her get into harm's way to fall and—and all that.
RESEARCHER:	Definitely.

Let's transition now to talking about challenges that can occur in response to this prompt. The goal of introducing this prompt is to allow the magic of the current memory to expand into something that goes beyond the present. We want the memory to project forward; we want to magnify its impact on the clients we are working with. However, when therapists make this move, it can be met with a range of reactions from clients.

Sometimes clients respond to this prompt with anxiety or concern. Below is an example of a parent, Luna, responding to this prompt by expressing the wish that the closeness she has with her daughter, Isabella, will continue into the future. Her anxiety is not explicitly stated but can be found between the lines:

RESEARCHER:	So now I'd like you to turn your focus to the future. So focus on how close you felt to Isabella at that time how will the bond you have together affect your relationship in the future what positive things can you imagine happening as a result of your bond to one another?
LUNA:	Um hopefully in the future I will be able to comfort her like I do now. Like I'm telling her it's OK like every time she gets emotional that I'll be there for her. Like she can talk to me or anything so she can tell me what's going on especially like when she's a child and she does end up getting sick I want her to open up and tell me. So that I know what's going on with her. So hopefully that'll be stronger like have a stronger relationship on understanding her.

In this example with Luna, this question may have brought up some anxiety about whether Luna will be able to meet Isabella's needs in the future. I am inferring this based on the fact that Luna answers this question by talking about what she is doing to meet Isabella's needs for the first section of the response and then ends by stating what she hopes for the future, that they will have a stronger relationship.

In a case like this where the therapist senses that the question may have activated some anxiety, the therapist may wish to remind the client that the memory they have shared already shows that they are providing the other person (in this case, the child) with a sense of security that will carry them forward. For instance, the therapist can say something like, "Actually, I have already seen an example of you giving your daughter everything she needs—it sounds like she really trusts you. Trust like that doesn't develop overnight. It's built on thousands of moments she's had with you where you've been there for her. So I know she has that history with you and it is this that she will carry forward with her."

Let us look at another example of a mother, Tessa, discussing her relationship with her child, Arlo. This example has a different feel to it:

RESEARCHER: Focus on how close you felt to Arlo at the time. How will the bond you have together affect your relationship in the future? And what positive things can you imagine happening as a result of your bond to one another?

TESSA: Um, I hope that he'll take risks, you know, in life. I think it's always scary because we always want to cling to what's comfortable, you know. We always want to stay in the shallow end or not you know go in the deep end, not jump in. And I don't want his fears to inhibit him, you know, I mean—it sounds kind of crazy. I don't want him to go crazy and be an extremist. But on the other hand, I don't him to be so, um, kind of crippled by fear that he doesn't take a risk, and doesn't do anything in life. *And so I hope that he knows that he has me as a support system.* That when things are scary and maybe he's not comfortable doing some things, that you know *at least mom will be there to, you know, hold him or hold his hand or, you know, get him through that scary part.* 'Cause you know, it's just all part of life. It's all part of growing and, you know, there's always that unknown factor. There's always the, you know, what if or this is scary. 'Cause we *don't know what's underneath us, we don't know where the pool ends.*

RESEARCHER: Mhm.

TESSA: How deep it is. So, um, *I kinda hope that he, you know, takes that trust. That he knows that I'm there even when he's going to take a risk.*

RESEARCHER: Mhm.

TESSA: *That I will help him.*

RESEARCHER: Mhm, that's really great that you're able to stay attuned to him and how he's feeling.

TESSA: I try [*laughs*].

RESEARCHER: [*Chuckles*]

TESSA: There's times that I'm, like, I have no clue what's going on with him [*laughs*].

RESEARCHER: [*Laughs.*]

TESSA: Especially, like I said, these last, uh, just this week before turning two and turning two, I'm like, what is happening.

RESEARCHER: [*Chuckles*]

TESSA: 'Cause there's some things that he does that we're like, it's just bizarre.

RESEARCHER: Mhm.

TESSA: So, we try, I try at least to kind of gauge what's coming from him. Is it anxiety? Is it, you know, is he just excited? What is going on? But, yes, lately it hasn't been quite so easy [*laughs*].

RESEARCHER: [*Chuckles*] I mean, from what you've told me, it sounds like you've really been able to create a safe space. [*I try.*] Where he's able to really feel comforted and supported.

TESSA: I try, I try, yeah definitely.

RESEARCHER: Mhm.

TESSA: Definitely.

RESEARCHER: Great.

TESSA: [*Chuckles*]

In this example, Tessa becomes much more abstract about the influence of this experience on Arlo and talks about how she hopes Arlo will be able to experience trust with her. Tessa is very lyrical and articulate in how she speaks about this experience, especially her hopes regarding his emotional experience, but she is unable to remain confident in her assessment of the situation (the future impact of experiences like this). Instead, her anxiety begins to creep in a bit, and she is unable to hold onto the positive, confident stance, even though the therapist affirms her in this place (e.g., "It's so great that you're able to stay attuned to him and how he is feeling"). Tessa then makes a statement that reveals her anxiety: "There's times that I'm, like, I have no clue what's going on with him." And she's off in the place of talking about and likely feeling her worries and anxiety. Importantly, the therapist is able to bring her back to a calmer, more confident and grounded place by reaffirming that they see that Tessa has provided Arlo with a secure foundation.

Another challenge that can emerge is that the client might discuss part of the answer to the question without answering the whole question. In this next example, the client, Alicia, had responded to the prompt by answering how the experience might have affected her child, Max, but did not comment on how it would affect their relationship or herself. So the therapist asked a follow-up question to more specifically inquire about the impact of the connection they have together on their relationship:

RESEARCHER: How will the bond you have together affect your relationship?

ALICIA: I hope that he feels close to me, um, even when he gets older. And, and I know adolescence is the time when they're trying to kind of find their own, and they try to be independent. And I want him to know that he doesn't have to need me in the same way, but that we're still close, that I still love him the same way. That even though, you know, he's probably going to not want to be, you know, cuddling with his momma when he's, um, a teenager [*chuckles*]. Uh, and I get that, but that, you know, um, he'll still remain close to me in other ways, in ways that he, you know, feels comfortable being close to me. Um, and that hopefully even beyond that into adulthood, that we'll at least still have a close relationship when he's an adult and on his own. . . . And, um, even though there may be distance I hope that there's, again, he still feels that there's a bond or a closeness to me, you know, and not something that I am hoping, that's what I look forward to in the future.

Once the intervener explicitly directs the mother to discuss the impact of the memory on the relationship, she is able to do so in an open, vulnerable, and seemingly honest way. She just needed that extra nudging to go there. Alicia talks about some of her thoughts about Max becoming an adolescent and adult, losing the need to be cuddly and close and hoping that he will still be comfortable having some kind of closeness with her. This description is hopeful and positive, without much anxiety or fear about a potential loss of closeness.

One thing that is interesting to note about all of the examples I provided here is that the clients were quick to focus on what the memory meant for the relationship and/or the other person in the relationship, but few of them focused on what the experience meant for themselves as individuals. If you are specifically interested in exploring this with your client and your client does not provide a response that addresses this part of the prompt, you can always follow up this general prompt with a more specific prompt (e.g., "What does this experience mean for you personally?" or "What does this experience say about you?"). Adding a question like this will help to direct your client's attention back to the self and the relevance of this experience for them as a person. This may be especially helpful for clients who diminish their importance in the relationship, such as clients who have low self-worth, are depressed, or struggle with attachment insecurity.

In sum, this step in the reflective process is intended to help clients zoom out in their focus and allow them to expand the significance of the memory they have savored—from it being one moment in time to it having an impact across many years. Although most clients perceive this as a welcome step in the memory reflection process, some find it challenging. Being prepared to handle the challenges that will arise is the best strategy for addressing them.

STEP 5: NONDIRECTIVE MIND-WANDERING REFLECTION

The final part of the savoring intervention is a nondirective mind-wandering reflection. This is included in the intervention as a last step because often at the end of this reflective task, clients have more to say about some aspect of the memory and we want to give them a platform in which to talk about it. The goal behind this step is quite simple—it is just to open up the floor for them to say anything and everything that comes to mind about this memory. As with the general savoring intervention, the underlying goal is to keep them focused on the positive, connected parts of the memory (and away from the negative, anxious, guilty internal magnet, to be discussed in Chapter 6). Here are the words we use for this part of the manual for our intervention studies:

> For the last part of this reflection, please let your mind wander in any way you'd like related to this event. You may want to think about things I have asked you to think about earlier or you may want to think about how this memory is related to your other relationships and your life. It's normal for your mind to wander to other topics or feelings—if you notice that your mind has wandered, just gently bring it back to the positive aspects of this event. Let your mind wander in any way you'd like, but try to keep focused on the positive, personal parts of this memory.

After the client has finished speaking for this portion of the reflection, the therapist says to the client, "Lastly, is there anything else you would like to say about this memory or do you have any takeaways from engaging in this reflection process?"

The responses to this section of the intervention vary quite a bit (by design), but oftentimes clients express a valuing of the connection and relationship with the person in the memory. Clients also express sadness or fear about losing that connection (growing up, growing apart). They will also share how valuable the exercise of engaging in the savoring itself can be in their lives.

The stance of the therapist is important in this reflection step. Similar to prior steps, the stance I suggest is one of an admiring fellow traveler, someone who is also embedded in their own social relationships. Even when the client expresses fear of losing a connection, the therapist can empathize that it can be so challenging to love someone so much that it causes fear of losing them.

This first client, Fatima, speaks of the benefit of the relationship with her child in her life in terms of the impact of these interactions on her mood:

FATIMA: I think all I have to say is that, just that moment in time in like just, it—I had a—my day started off really bad and so to end it off like that and . . .

RESEARCHER: Mhm.

FATIMA: It just made everything else just go away like, and so I mean any time like I'm with her and I do stuff with her it's—it's if I'm having a bad day like she definitely like makes the day better and makes my day great.

RESEARCHER: That's awesome.

FATIMA: So yeah.

RESEARCHER: Mhm. Yeah, I bet you make her day too.

FATIMA: Yeah, I hope so [laughter].

RESEARCHER: Lastly, is there anything else you'd like to say about this memory or do you have any takeaways from engaging in this reflection process?

FATIMA: Uh. No, just that, it's just the fact that it, . . . just made my day a whole lot better [laughter] or my week or yeah. So far my week a whole lot better.

Note that the therapist also took the opportunity to underscore the positive impact that Fatima has on the child. This excerpt illustrates how Fatima is taking the opportunity to really relish in the joy of the connection, acknowledging how the child brightens up her life. The therapist's role is to witness this joy, acknowledge and reflect it back, and augment it when possible.

In this next example, the mother, Luhua, is talking about her connection with her toddler-aged child and how it makes her think about moments of future connectedness with him. Specifically, she is imagining dancing with him at his wedding during the mother–son dance, thinking about how this moment will hold some special significance for her. She's making a connection between her interactions with her son now and how he will treat women later in life.

LUHUA: Uhm hm, uhm, I think about like slow dancing with him. I think it's really nice. Uhm, and what's really sad but also gratifying is, you know, when he gets older and I'll get to slow dance with him at his wedding, you know, with mother and son dance and I think that'll be the time where I feel like, I'm, I, I've succeeded. You know, and I just wanna raise a really good son, you know, I don't want him to. I want him to be a gentleman, uhm, and I'm hoping the way he treats me is the ways he'll treat other women. Yeah, and not be a douchebag [*laugh*]. Uhm, yeah. Yeah.

RESEARCHER: Yeah it's a really cool thing to want for your son.

LUHUA: Yeah like I mean I do it with Milo now too, you know, he goes to sleep and he'll still put a shoulder on me and we'll slow dance too. Uhm, yeah. Yeah. Yeah.

RESEARCHER: OK. Lastly, is there anything else you would like to say about this memory or do you have any takeaways from engaging in this reflection process?

LUHUA: Uhm, maybe I should rock him a little bit more, or slow dance a little bit more or I'm thinking maybe I should do story time more . . . yeah, I feel like uhm, I should, we should create more quality time together. You know maybe he needs that more, but who knows? Yeah.

RESEARCHER: Uhm hm. OK, OK.

In the session above, the therapist does not comment on Luhua's suggestion that she should be doing more with her son. The therapist just sidesteps this issue. The relational savoring approach does not involve making behavioral suggestions to clients, so perhaps the therapist was unsure how to respond to Luhua's own suggestion that she do more in her parenting. However, an intervention that would have been consistent with the relational savoring approach (and that could have augmented the existing intervention that the therapist was enacting) would have been the following statement by the therapist:

> What I notice here, and what I really admire, is how you are already creating so many opportunities for connection between you and your son. And here you are looking for even more chances to connect with him. It's so wonderful that you are giving him so many chances to feel safe with you.

In other words, the therapist could have made a statement that simultaneously affirmed what Luhua was already doing to support a connection with Milo, praising her for the efforts she was making and the success she was having in supporting and upholding that relationship. In so doing, the therapist is sending a message that being connected is important and investing in the relationship is important, but they are sending that message by saying "what you are already doing, and already doing so well, is really important," rather than saying, "I agree that you need to do better at this thing," which is what the client might have heard if the therapist had simply said, "Yes, I agree that you need to do more activities that nurture your child" or something similar.

If this were a situation where the therapist does not think the client is being sufficiently nurturing or sensitive toward the relationship partner and it would feel inauthentic to make a statement to this effect, the therapist could instead say something to the effect of,

> What you are doing here is so important—thinking about the relationship and how you want to invest in it—it can be really painful to scrutinize our own behavior in relationships, and here you are, doing just that, all because you care so much about this relationship and how to improve it.

Finally, let us look at a reflection in which the client talks very explicitly about the importance of appreciating the moment. Here the client, Angela, speaks about the benefits of being able to reflect, which one is not able to do when "caught in the moment":

> Um, I like, like I said, I think I said before, you know, being able to kind of reflect upon it. 'Cause a lot of things, you know, life happens so fast. And, um, I think I said before, you know, when you're caught in the moment, you really don't, sometimes, really think about some of the things that you do and why you do them. And, um, I really like that, um, I've been able to really kind of just think about, um, you know, my interactions with him and how I, uh, you know, um, kind of approach him sometimes. You know, 'cause I mean it's, sometimes it is difficult [*chuckles*]. Um, but also, I like that I can think about the positive things that we get to do together.

In sum, the aim of this final step of the reflection process is to provide clients with the space to explore their thoughts and feelings. The therapist's job is to step back a bit and allow the client to step forward (in terms of the directive stance). The client should be able to free-associate related to what reflecting on the memory has brought up for them, with the therapist there as a supportive presence should the client need them.

WRAP-UP

When clients reach the end of this reflection process, they are typically in a vastly different emotional place from when they started the exercise—calmer, more peaceful, more connected, and often experiencing more positive emotion than before. Our experimental data support this conclusion, revealing increases in positive emotion and decreases in negative emotion. In addition, administering this intervention is also delightful, as listening to people's positive memories is typically an uplifting experience. We often conclude by asking them how they are feeling as a way of checking in after the exercise and also of figuring out whether any feelings have emerged for them during the exercise that would be important to explore. This is also an appropriate time for the therapist to express appreciation to the client for sharing their thoughts and feelings.

I want to finish this chapter by highlighting the characteristics that describe the most effective relational savoring interveners. Those who implement this technique with the most aplomb tend to have the following qualities: (a) They praise the client frequently for the qualities they notice them exhibiting or describing, and in so doing, they align themselves with the client's perspective and strengthen the client's confidence; (b) they worry less about following the verbatim manual and focus more on following the guiding principles of the intervention (e.g., go deeper with positive emotion, help clients identify moments of positive connectedness with others and recognize the benefits of these connections in the short and long term for themselves and for others); (c) they find ways to remind clients again and again of the specific moment they want the client to focus on—memories are multilayered and complex, so it behooves the client to have multiple opportunities to be oriented to specific topics, feelings, or interactions as focal points, and for these reminders to come at pivotal moments in the intervention (right when the reflection prompts are delivered or in the middle of reflections if the client is getting off track); (d) they exude acceptance of clients and their emotional experience and behavior in relationships; and (e) they savor alongside their clients, experiencing mutual delight in the memories with their clients. This mutual appreciation is palpable by the client and is expressed frequently by the therapist ("How fortunate you are that you got to have these experiences," "I'm so grateful I was able to learn about this from you"). This parallel process enhances the intensity of the savoring experience.

6
ADDRESSING GENERAL AREAS OF DIFFICULTY AND CLINICAL TECHNIQUES TO CIRCUMVENT THEM

In this chapter, I focus on three areas of difficulty that have occurred most commonly in my work with this technique. In Chapters 4 and 5, I provided some examples in which there were some challenges, but the examples were relatively mild and the therapist's attempts to address them were relatively successful. And for the most part, relational savoring tends to work fairly well with the populations we have worked with thus far, at least in terms of how the sessions proceed and whether clients are able to identify memories and proceed through the reflection steps. However, it does also happen that clients encounter more significant difficulties in engaging in the savoring process. When difficulties do occur, the difficulties that clients stumble onto tend to be fairly predictable.

In the current chapter, I review the most commonly occurring difficulties and discuss when they occur as well as provide some potential solutions for how to address them in the moment when they transpire. Once again, I rely heavily on case material to illustrate the points I am making. My hope in providing this information is that in reviewing it, you will be more prepared to address issues of client resistance and/or difficulty engaging with more challenging clinical issues when they arise.

---

https://doi.org/10.1037/0000372-006
Relational Savoring: Using Guided Reflection to Strengthen Relationships and Improve Outcomes in Therapy, by J. L. Borelli
Copyright © 2024 by the American Psychological Association. All rights reserved.

The three most commonly occurring issues are difficulty accessing memories, difficulty engaging in elaborative emotional processing, and difficulty handling negative emotions when they arise in the session (spoiling). Let us take these up in turn.

DIFFICULTY ACCESSING MEMORIES

One issue that can make savoring difficult right off the bat is when a client has difficulty accessing memories at all or when they have difficulty accessing rich relational content from their memories. This means that the setup for the savoring is going to be quite weak, which is going to lead to savoring that is going to be fairly unproductive. Several strategies can be used to assist with the difficulty recalling memories or difficulty recalling relationally rich memories, and we will review these strategies now (see Figure 6.1). Some of them may sound a bit familiar, as we touched on a few of them in Chapter 4 when we discussed general strategies for engaging in memory selection.

The first strategy is to normalize the client's difficulty in remembering things; the therapist may wish to make comments such as the following: "It's extremely common to struggle a bit in coming up with memories—this isn't something we do every day, so it's like a muscle we aren't used to exercising."

FIGURE 6.1. Steps for Addressing Difficulty in Accessing Memories

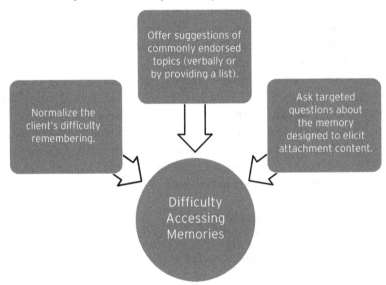

The therapist can also say something to help remove any sense of time pressure that the client might be feeling: "We aren't under any time restrictions, so you can take as much time as you need. Really just settle in and let yourself and your memory relax."

The therapist can assist the client by making some suggestions of things that other clients have suggested or that commonly come up for people, but in doing so, the therapist should preface them by saying something that further reduces the pressure:

> Sometimes it helps to have some suggestions, so these may or may not apply to you, but if it's OK with you, I'm just going to throw some ideas out there to see if it helps to spark some ideas for you. Feel free to pick up on anything I say or cut me off at any time. Again, these may not at all be relevant, but I'll just suggest them in case they are.

If the therapist suggests options, they should make sure to suggest not only big milestone events (e.g., helping a partner overcome a phobia, being there for a child during a major medical challenge) but also small, daily events to help jog a client's memory for the types of things that clients often miss in their daily interactions (e.g., kissing a partner goodbye before work in the morning, exchanging a knowing/meaningful glance with a coworker during a work meeting, sending a thoughtful text to a friend, giving a hug to a child after a hard day). It's helpful for the therapist to keep a running list of 20 to 50 potential ideas that could apply to the population the client belongs to (e.g., parent, partner, caregiving, child) that they could draw from and share with a client.

Again, when offering suggestions, it is extremely helpful to normalize, normalize, normalize difficulty with memory and the difficulty in coming up with examples. Even saying things like the following can be helpful:

> I do this exercise with people frequently, and it's very common to struggle to come up with examples. In fact, that is exactly why it's useful to work on this together—because it is so challenging to come up with these memories, but they can be helpful to think about.

It may help to even keep a written list of commonly endorsed memories lying around the office or laboratory—I would not recommend providing this to the client right away, but this could be helpful to give to the client once they demonstrate they are struggling in coming up with a memory. Much like the provision of a feelings chart, the provision of a list of commonly endorsed attachment memories helps to prime the mind a bit and helps the individual identify experiences they might have had but might not categorize or readily recognize as fitting the descriptors we are looking for.

Once the client has generated some candidate memories, there can be additional problems, such as the memories themselves not containing sufficient relational/attachment content. This step requires some degree of coaching to help clients perceive the attachment content within their memories. After all, most clients are not trained in attachment theory and do not readily perceive the attachment content within their memories. So, that's where the therapist comes in, ready to help the client read the tea leaves from their memories. The therapist *can* perceive this attachment/relational content, as they have the benefit of many years of training and/or having read this book (see what I just did there?). The therapist is well equipped to identify the needle in the haystack, to perceive the attachment content from within the memory, and to highlight it for the client.

I recommend the therapist follow a series of steps within the memory selection phase to cultivate or foster awareness of the attachment content within these memories ("that moment when you held him and helped him calm his fear" = safe haven; "the time when she was able to challenge herself to take a risk, knowing you were there for her" = secure base). The first step is to ask additional questions of the client to glean more information about the memory. This task serves the dual function of both informing the therapist of additional information they can use to build up their mental model of what attachment content the memory contains and also highlighting this same attachment content within the mind of the client.

As you may remember, one of the mechanisms of change of this intervention is enhancing awareness of sensitive behavior—drawing clients' attention to the sensitive behavior they are exhibiting or receiving is one way of accomplishing this goal. You likely want to angle these questions slightly differently if you anticipate that the memory has a secure base slant to it versus a safe haven slant versus a connectedness slant, as I explore in greater detail in the sections that follow.

Questions to Ask When the Memory Is About Connectedness

As previously stated, our higher order goal is for these memories to have a secure base or safe haven focus (as opposed to a connectedness focus), but if a client begins with a connectedness focus, you can start there and attempt to deepen their experience through questions. Sometimes the answers to the questions will lead to the jumping-off point for secure base/safe haven memories. Here I provide the questions I recommend asking *when the client or participant offers a memory of positive connection whose attachment themes are not explicit*; I provide them here in the format we would ask them of a parent but can easily be modified for another relationship context (e.g., couple, friend, parent).

> It sounds like you really enjoyed this moment of closeness you had together. During this experience, were you enjoying anything in particular, such as the tenderness of snuggling with her? Was it about giving your child a safe harbor, someplace warm and nurturing where she can retreat to and always feel comfortable and calm? Or getting to share that experience with her, such as showing her something you enjoyed for the first time? Or were you thinking about the specialness of getting to share that experience with your child? It's such a privilege to be able to share something you have witnessed with someone else and to watch as they experience it too!

For instance, if a client answers the question about "giving your child a safe harbor, someplace warm and nurturing where they can retreat to and always feel comfortable and calm" in the affirmative, then they are providing tantalizing information that leads you in the direction of a safe haven type of response. You can build on their response, asking them additional questions about their role in protecting their child (what are they protecting them from, how do they feel when they provide their child with protection and nurturance, and how does their child react and feel when they are given this protection?), and then you would use this explicit safe haven focus of the memory going forward into the memory reflection portion of the savoring exercise.

Likewise, if a client answers the question about "getting to share that experience with her, or showing her something you enjoyed for the first time" in the affirmative, you can ask them to describe this in greater depth. This type of experience—exposing someone to something new—can be a *secure base* type of experience. It is one person leading another person into new territory and sharing a new experience with them, acting as an anchor for them. Especially if the other person experiences some degree of trepidation or uncertainty in taking the steps to explore the new experience, then you have the makings of a secure base experience. And you can route them in that direction.

Questions to Ask When the Memory Is About a Secure Base

If a client has provided a response that is richer than a positive-connectedness response, one that falls into a secure base type of memory (one where the individual acted as an anchor for another person, providing support that allowed them to achieve their goal, or was provided this type of support by another person), then the therapist can lean into asking questions designed to heighten the secure base content of the memory. Likewise, if the client's responses initially routed them down the path of a connectedness response but then follow-up probing made the therapist think their memory followed more of a secure base profile, the therapist may wish to follow up with a series of questions designed to heighten the secure base content. The probes I recommend for heightening secure base content are as follows, framed in the format we would ask them for a couple context:

> It sounds like you really enjoyed being able to expose [partner] to something new or exciting. During that experience, did you notice moments when your partner relied on you, or felt more comfortable because you were there? Were there things that he/she did that he/she wouldn't have been able to do without the confidence of knowing you were there?

Questions to Ask When the Memory Is About a Safe Haven

If a client has provided a response that is richer than a positive-connectedness response, such as one that would be considered a safe haven type response (a time when they provided nurturance and care for their partner when they needed this type of support, or a time when their partner provided them with this kind of support during their time of need), but the memory salience needs to be heightened, then the therapist can move on to asking the safe haven questions. Alternatively, if the client's responses initially routed them down the path of a connectedness response, but then follow-up probing made the therapist think their memory followed more of a safe haven profile, the therapist may wish to follow up with a series of questions designed to heighten the safe haven content. The probes I recommend for heightening safe haven content are as follows:

> It seems like it really made you feel good to be able to provide comfort for her during that time—that it made you feel really useful to be in that role, to really be the one who could help her. It's a pretty special and important position to play in someone's life, and it's such a unique opportunity to be able to serve in it.

After having asked these questions and gotten the client's responses, the therapist will wish to make use of the client's responses in subsequent sections of the intervention. The fact that the client had difficulty accessing the attachment-based aspects of the memory to begin with suggests that the client has a vulnerability factor for subsequent memory processing. Specifically, this suggests that the client is more likely to struggle to keep the attachment or connectedness aspect of the memory at the fore and thus that the client will need a more active therapist throughout the memory reflection portion of the intervention. This means the therapist should be ready to prompt the client throughout the intervention with several key phrases (generated by the client) that will help jog the client's memory of the salient aspects of the memory.

It is always helpful to take notes while conducting an intervention session to have a solid grasp of the wording that clients use to describe their experiences. Then the therapist can use these exact words back with the client to help the client hold onto the significance of their memories. I recommend using the exact words the client used at the beginning of each step of the memory reflection to help cue clients to focus on the exact moment of the memory that the therapist wants the client to focus on.

DIFFICULTY ENGAGING IN ELABORATIVE EMOTIONAL PROCESSING

A second central difficulty that can occur with this intervention is difficulty in assisting clients in engaging in elaborative emotional processing. Said differently, it can be difficult to help clients become reflective about their experiences, and it is incredibly important for clients to adopt a reflective, inward-looking stance when completing this intervention. If clients are having difficulty adopting this stance, the intervention can be difficult to complete and far less effective. Further, when the intervention involves a client who is not reflective, it can make the therapist feel incompetent or inert. In addressing this challenge, I will review several different strategies: promoting a reflective environment in the therapy room, reducing client anxiety, and scaffolding the elaborative emotional processing.

Promoting a Reflective Environment

So let's talk about techniques we can use to address this issue. The first technique involves promoting a reflective environment in the therapy room. I recommend doing this by cultivating a sense of calm and peacefulness among the client and therapist. A state of calm helps to create a climate in which the client can be more introspective, which is of the utmost importance for this intervention. When we deliver the intervention in a research setting, we always begin by doing a minute of mindfulness practice. The goal of this minute is to help the client slow their breathing and relax their bodies so they are not operating in a fast-paced, anxious state but are calmer and able to process their experiences more deeply and internally. I recommend doing the same in clinical practice, especially with clients who might need more help slowing down in order to augment the reflective process.

When training therapists in delivering relational savoring, I encourage them to complete the mindfulness minute alongside the clients because I think it helps therapists slow down their minds and bodies alongside the clients.

I often need this myself before engaging with a client—I am a fast-paced, somewhat anxiously wired person who needs to slow down my thinking and my body a bit before I sit across from someone, and I think it is good practice to train oneself to get into the mode of slowing down before a clinical encounter.

I also find that clients who have a difficult time slowing down and opening up tend to make therapists want to speed through an intervention protocol; they make them feel anxious, and the natural tendency is to move faster to get through this painful experience. However, the opposite approach is often most helpful with these clients. Slowing down more, taking more deep breaths, and easing into the approach more with these clients is a better approach. Many times these clients take more time to process what the therapist is asking or saying, and giving them more time to answer can help them feel less anxious, as if there is no time pressure to respond within a certain window.

In addition to the use of mindfulness, you may wish to attend to your physical space to ensure it conveys calm. What are the ambient sounds in the environment? What can the client see? Modifying your environment in the direction of promoting calm, even in small ways, can go a long way.

Reducing Client Anxiety

With clients that struggle with engaging in elaborative processing, anxiety can be a significant barrier. Reducing anxiety may not be sufficient to address the problem, but it may be necessary in order to begin to address the issue. Here, the anxiety might present in different ways, such as difficulty stating what feelings are, talking about the facts of an event (e.g., first we did this; then we did this) instead of talking about feelings, or difficulty remembering details of an emotionally salient experience.

As with the first challenge I discussed (difficulty generating memories), normalizing the difficulty that the client is having can go a long way in terms of addressing the difficulty (Figure 6.2). Making explicit statements that address any difficulties the client is having in this domain as being normal, typical, or expected can be helpful. Likewise, it is useful to convey complete acceptance of their stance. No matter what they say, you as the therapist must convey an accepting, positive attitude, affirming them for the way they are approaching the intervention and praising them for what they have shared. You will be working as diligently as you can to increase their engagement and help them feel comfortable opening up while at the same time you must reward them and compliment them for every morsel of engagement that they give in this task. Then, after the session is over, the therapist can seek support

FIGURE 6.2. Steps for Addressing Difficulty in Engaging in Elaborative Emotional Processing

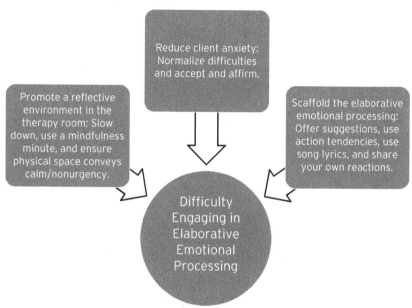

and supervision or consultation from others regarding the difficulty involved in trying to engage a client who is extremely difficult to engage because, let's face it, this is really challenging!

Scaffolding Elaborative Emotional Processing

It can also be helpful to scaffold the client's conversation about emotions. The therapist can introduce this as a narrative that is co-created, that they can build together. They can offer to help the client figure out how they were feeling at the time, saying things like, "It can be really difficult to identify our feelings in situations, but maybe if we put our heads together about this, we will be able to come up with something that feels right." Then the therapist should be ready to provide ample examples, which the client can reject at will. The therapist can provide examples of feelings that the client might have experienced in response to a particular memory. "Might you have felt joy or happiness? Did you feel understood? Some people say that they feel a sense of being seen by the other person or held. Or did you even feel relief?" At this juncture, providing a feeling chart or list of feelings that clients often endorse could be a useful device to scaffold a conversation about feelings.

To further help a client who is struggling to put feelings into words, therapists can also ask clients to describe their feelings as though they are an action tendency ("Did it make you want to come out of your shell and explore more of the world?"), to put their feelings to song lyrics, or to think about their feelings in terms of movements or gestures. If a client is able to put their feelings into words but the words are fairly surface level and the client has difficulty going beyond this, the therapist can share what the words the client has shared make them think of:

> Joy and delight—I hear lots of that in what you said, and I also hear something that speaks to a sense of the importance of your role in their lives. That you give them something really important that only you can give them, and perhaps you get a sense of pride and meaning from that.

In this way, the therapist is scaffolding the client's ability to identify and express certain emotional states. If the client cannot independently identify these emotional states, perhaps when the therapist suggests them, they will perceive them as well, allowing the client to identify them in the future.

DIFFICULTY HANDLING NEGATIVE EMOTIONS IN THE SESSION (SPOILING)

The third challenge that emerges commonly in relational savoring is when clients have difficulty managing their negative emotions in session, which I refer to as spoiling. I briefly touched on this topic earlier in the book (see Chapter 4), but I would like to discuss this more thoroughly here. When people think about relational savoring, they tend to think that clients exclusively experience and express positive emotions (pride, joy, gratitude, positively tinged feelings of closeness), but the reality is that the majority of memories that are savored involved some degree of negative emotion. One reason for this is that many memories that are savor-worthy involve some kind of challenge or struggle that has been overcome; this challenge then sets the stage for a meaningful interaction in which the connection between two people can grow.

Many of our most meaningful experiences of connection occur against the backdrop of some kind of pain or challenge. If you think about some of your most meaningful experiences of emotional connection to another person, do they involve some experience of challenge, difficulty, or pain? Most of mine certainly do. When I think of times that people were really there for me in a meaningful way, or times that I was there for others in a meaningful way, nearly all of them involve some degree of difficulty, even if the difficulty was relatively minor (e.g., a child getting hurt and my being there to comfort them, me helping someone who was fearful achieve a goal they so badly wanted) though some involve major challenges (e.g., helping a friend overcome a significant loss or medical challenge). To some extent this speaks to the nature of the types of attachment-related experiences we are looking for with this intervention; these experiences that activate the attachment system all involve some degree of emotional or physical pain. To contextualize this idea, I look to the words of Brené Brown (2010a), who describes the difficulty of holding onto positive emotion because we often imagine life without it at the same time:

> Most of us have experienced being on the edge of joy only to be overcome by vulnerability and thrown into fear. Until we can tolerate vulnerability and transform it into gratitude, intense feelings of love will often bring up the fear of loss.... These are anxious and fearful times, both of which breed scarcity. We're afraid to lose what we love the most, and we hate that there are no guarantees. We think not being grateful and not feeling joy will make it hurt less. We think if we can beat vulnerability to the punch by imagining loss, we'll suffer less. We're wrong. There is one guarantee: If we're not practicing gratitude and allowing ourselves to know joy, we are missing out on the two things that will actually sustain us during the inevitable hard times. (p. 59)

This perspective of Brown's is important to hold onto as well—that we cannot prepare ourselves for the inevitability of the pain and loss by tamping down our happiness, which is ostensibly a reason we go to this place of converting to a negative, worry-centered place. Instead, we might want to center ourselves in this notion that only through being grounded in gratitude and joy will we be able to weather the more difficult times. It is important for the therapist to feel grounded and confident in this stance when working with clients who have a negative internal magnet because this will help the therapist convey this energy to the client.

So relational savoring is not allergic to the expression of emotional pain; what we want to see alongside this emotional pain is love, support, and comfort of another person, either the self (if the person is savoring the provision of care) or the other (if the person is savoring the receipt of care). And the central focus of the act of savoring should be not on the painful part of the memory but rather on the fact that when there was pain, someone was there to bear witness to that pain to help heal it and to encourage the person to persist toward their goals despite the presence of the pain.

However, because the discussion of negative emotions and negative experiences is part and parcel of relational savoring, there are various places where clients can get stuck on the road to savoring. Specifically, they can become immersed in the retelling of the negative aspects of the difficult experience or they can become drawn to the negative emotions associated with an experience. The narrative can have a ruminating type of quality, instead of progressing in a linear, forward-moving fashion toward the goal of deeply processing the meaning and significance of the positive connection with the other person.

There are various strategies to address this type of internal draw toward negative emotion that many clients exhibit (Figure 6.3). The first is to understand at your core that this is completely natural; negative emotional experiences are very absorbing, and it is difficult to disengage one's attention from these experiences in the first place. What we are asking clients to do is a tall order, and it may be difficult or impossible for some clients to accomplish this goal. Understanding that this may be challenging is an important stance for the therapist to embrace.

If a client becomes very absorbed in the details of describing a negative emotional experience in the memory selection stage, one effective strategy to circumvent this from becoming a larger issue in the memory reflection stage is to select a different memory. Absorption in the details of a memory, particularly when describing one's negative emotional experience or when discussing details in a way that paints a vivid, lifelike picture of the event, may indicate that the individual is deeply immersed in the experience to an extent that they will be unable to effectively psychologically separate themselves from the experience and savor it.

This degree of psychological absorption is similar to what people exhibit when they have been traumatized by an experience, and we would not expect people who are in the midst of a trauma response to be able to separate themselves from their experiences to the point where they could savor the positive aspects of it. In fact, when psychologists discuss the notion of posttraumatic growth—the process of growing psychologically after enduring painful, challenging, or grueling psychological circumstances (Calhoun & Tedeschi, 1999, 2001)—they are careful to argue that this cannot occur in the midst of the psychological processing of the trauma itself. The growth does not happen as a result of the trauma (Tedeschi & Calhoun, 2004). In other words, it cannot happen when the person is actively caught up in the horror, fear, sadness, or grief of the trauma—it has to come after the initial intensity has passed, when the individual is able to get to the point of making sense of the experience. The rebuilding of their lives after the initial trauma has remitted from its hold is what is experienced as growth (Tedeschi & Calhoun, 2004).

Likewise, we cannot expect our clients to be able to find the diamond in the rough, so to speak, and focus only on that diamond when the rest of the memory is so painfully rough. Selecting a memory that in the memory selection stage seems less preoccupying is going to be a safer bet; if the client is

Addressing General Areas of Difficulty and Clinical Techniques to Circumvent Them • 157

FIGURE 6.3. Steps for Addressing Difficulty Handling Negative Emotions in Session (Spoiling)

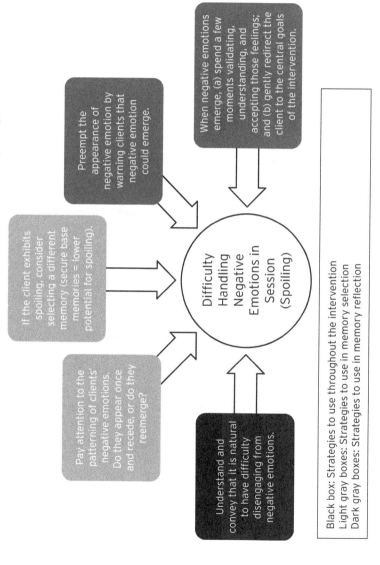

Black box: Strategies to use throughout the intervention
Light gray boxes: Strategies to use in memory selection
Dark gray boxes: Strategies to use in memory reflection

able to discuss the memory with a higher level of coherence (e.g., with some detail but not a highly absorbing level of detail, one that indicates they are still aware of their audience), they are more likely to experience higher-quality savoring in the memory reflection stage.

In making this recommendation, I am in part drawing on Mary Main and colleagues' conceptualization of narrative coherence on the Adult Attachment Interview (George et al., 1996; Main, 1991; Main et al., 2008), an interview that prompts people to describe their early childhood relationships with their caregivers. This interview is now an extremely well-established framework for analyzing narrative.

The developer of the interview, Mary Main, argued that people who can speak clearly, collaboratively, and concisely, thereby generating a narrative that is believable and able to be understood by a naive listener, are more likely to be secure in their attachment. She grounded her conceptualization of narrative coherence in Gricean maxims of linguistic discourse (Main, 2000), which emphasize the importance of speaking with relevance, keeping responses the appropriate length, responding to the prompts at hand, and speaking in a way that conforms to speech standards.

But this framework can be extended more broadly than as a predictor of attachment security—Joe Allen and Erin Miga (2010) have argued that narrative coherence, measuring using the Main framework, could represent a way of measuring emotion regulation. From this perspective, people who speak more coherently are likely to be more regulated in the moment when they are speaking, and thus may be more able to get some psychological distance from their memories to the point where they can reflect on them, which might be necessary for savoring. Too high a degree of psychological immersion, particularly immersion in negative emotions, may be too difficult a state from which to disentangle a client so they can be supported through the savoring process.

This finding also has parallels to two other research traditions: Jamie Pennebaker's work on verbal immediacy measures the degree of connectedness people exhibit to the experiences they describe as measured through a linguistic variable (Pennebaker et al., 2003; Pennebaker & Stone, 2003). Pennebaker and his colleagues have argued that higher levels of verbal immediacy suggest that the individual is highly connected to their experiences to the point that they may be quite psychologically immersed in them (and may not be able to psychologically remove themselves from them; Pennebaker et al., 2003; Pennebaker & Stone, 2003). For instance, following the 9/11 attacks, online posts were initially high in immediacy and then dropped off over time, suggestive of reductions in psychological immersion (Mehl & Pennebaker, 2003).

Similarly, Ozlem Ayduk's and Ethan Kross's more recent work on psychological distancing holds that to make sense of an experience, one has to have some degree of distance from said experience (Ayduk & Kross, 2010; Kross & Ayduk, 2011). Ayduk operationalizes psychological distancing differently than Main or Pennebaker, but to a certain degree, the notion is quite similar; the individual has to have a certain degree of separation from the experience being perceived or narrated to be able to work with or question the perspective. Ayduk argued that a decentered or distanced perspective is necessary for individuals to be able to change their perspectives on their experiences (Ayduk & Kross, 2010; Kross & Ayduk, 2011).

In sum, when an individual is psychologically absorbed in an experience, it may be difficult to draw them out of that experience and orient them toward a new way of perceiving their experience. Thus, trying to do so through sheer will may be a waste of effort or may require alternate techniques.

OK, so back to relational savoring and my recommendations for preventing or addressing spoiling. The first, as you might remember, is to choose the target memory carefully. If the client speaks with detail and richness about the aspects of the memory that involve negative emotion (distress, pain) but is unable to speak with the same level of detail and richness about the pleasurable aspects of the memory, this is not a good memory to select.

Similarly, if telling the memory follows a circular pattern wherein the client begins by talking about the negative part of the memory, then discusses the positive part, and then returns to the negative part (or worse yet, if the client makes several of these loops that involve a return to the negative), this may be a danger sign. It is much more encouraging to observe a pattern in which the client is able to discuss the negative part of the memory, then put that part of the memory to bed, so to speak, and then fully embrace the positive part of the memory.

Of course, this is what we as therapists will help the client with during the reflection part of the intervention, but the selection part of the task is where you as therapist have the opportunity to do some assessment and discover which memories may be ripest for savoring and which ones have some danger to them. The ones that repeatedly pull the client back to the negative emotion signify that the negative emotional gravitational pull is very strong; such memories may not be ideal because you are going to have to contend with this gravitational pull throughout the savoring exercise.

In addition to paying attention to the amount of negativity and the temporal ordering of the negativity present in the initial memory selection, you may also wish to pay attention to the way in which the client frames the negativity of the memory. Dan McAdams has studied people's production of spoken and written narrative and has discussed what he refers to as *redemption sequences* (McAdams et al., 1997, 2001). He argued that when people describe difficult personally meaningful life events in certain ways—specifically, in ways in which the individual "transforms or redeems bad scenes into good outcomes" (McAdams et al., 2001, p. 475) as opposed to simply describing or discussing them without deriving this level of meaning or positivity—these people are more likely to report higher well-being and better mental health.

A second piece of advice that pertains to the memory selection phase is the following: If the client has an internal negative magnet (i.e., they are prone to go toward the negative and this is a challenge that presents itself repeatedly throughout the savoring sessions), you may wish to prioritize memories that contain secure base or connectedness content over safe haven content. Of all of the memories, safe haven memories are the ones that are most likely to contain negative emotional content, because they are typically preceded by a negative emotional state (i.e., what leads the careseeker to need a safe haven often involves negative emotion).

Negative emotion can also come up in the memory reflection section of the task, but it is more common for negative emotion to present itself in this initial place within the memory itself. Thus, especially in the context in which you are completing savoring sessions multiple times with a client, if you have had the opportunity to observe that a particular client is particularly prone to spoiling or negative emotionality, you may wish to prioritize other types of memories over safe haven ones in order to reduce the likelihood that negative emotions will become difficult to handle within the context of the savoring reflection. For instance, that client may fare better with secure base memories or even connectedness memories rather than safe haven memories.

Once you have selected a memory, there are also important ways to address the expression of negative emotion within the savoring session. As discussed earlier, negative emotion is expected and understandable within this context, so it is important to adopt an understanding, validating, empathic stance toward the appearance of negative (in addition to positive) emotional states. The first important step to take within the intervention is to attempt to preempt the appearance of negative emotion by warning clients that this could become an issue. We typically recommend saying something like the following immediately before the beginning of the memory reflection stage of the intervention:

> I want to mention that it can be difficult to focus on the positive aspects of memories, especially when life is full of so many challenges, but precisely

because life is full of so many challenges, it is important to give yourself a break from the stresses and difficulties you face and create a space to focus on good feelings. So with your permission, I am going to help you do that—if I notice you veering into a stressful or negative place, I will help bring you back to a place where you are appreciating the positive aspects of this wonderful memory you just shared with me. Because you really do deserve to have this time and deserve to get this benefit from this experience. Does that sound OK to you?

Notice the language I used at the beginning of this statement—"when life is full of so many challenges"—this language can be modified for whatever population you are working with. For instance, if you are working with a client who is struggling with an eating disorder, you can say something to the effect of, "It can be difficult to focus on the positive aspects of memories, especially when in the midst of dealing with something as difficult as an eating disorder" or "especially in the midst of dealing with something so challenging." You can alter the words there to fit your client's situation so that the statement is tailored to their specific circumstances. The sentiment should remain the same though: We get that it is challenging to focus on positive things when life is hard.

Making a statement like this accomplishes three important goals: First, it alerts the client that negative emotions may arise in the context of the memory reflection and that this is natural and normal, and second, that if they do, the therapist is going to redirect them back to the positive aspects of the memory. The third goal that this accomplishes is that it gives the therapist permission to go ahead and redirect without feeling rude or insensitive to the client's experiences later on—after all, this is what was previously agreed upon and is central to the goal of the intervention, promoting the client's positive emotional experiences. By making a statement like this early on, the therapist has hopefully laid the groundwork so they feel comfortable being more directive with the client and the client feels more comfortable receiving this direction.

Even if forewarned, a client might still become negative during the memory reflection. If this occurs, the therapist should respond as they would normally during a therapeutic encounter, by accepting and validating these feelings. For instance, the therapist can make statements such as the following: "Of course you have those feelings; of course you are angry/sad/upset (speaking directly to whatever the client's feeling states are). Anyone in your position would feel that way. You have every right to be incensed by that."

Whenever negative feelings arise, the therapist should spend a few minutes with the client, validating, understanding, and accepting those feelings. If the therapist moves on too quickly, they risk alienating the client, making them feel rejected by the therapist, or making them feel as if their feelings are not important. After the therapist has spent a few minutes exploring, accepting and validating their feelings, however, the therapist can feel free to move back to the central goal of the intervention, which is to focus on the positive aspects of the experience. In so doing, the optimal way of redirecting the client is to remind them that precisely because of the difficulties they have had, they deserve to be able to carve out a moment and/or a space to focus on the beautiful, positive, special moments of the experience they had, and that the therapist's role is to help them do just that. The exact words said by the therapist should be tailored to the experiences that have been shared by the client, but I provide this as a sample response that a therapist could give in the process of delicately redirecting the client back to the task at hand:

> I completely understand and hear that you have these feelings of shame and loss, and I don't mean to at all diminish the importance or significance of those feelings. At the same time, I want to create some space for the positive feelings that you also really deserve to experience, especially given how much pain and shame and loss you had to endure. So with your permission, I'm going to help us turn back to the positive part of this experience, the part where you were feeling really appreciated and really valued for the positive contribution you made to this person's life. Is that all right with you? Do you feel ready to move back to that focus? Can you remember how you felt about that part of the experience? I can help you zoom in on that part of it if you would like.

In this excerpt, the therapist used the words "shame" and "loss" to describe the client's experience; here, it is desirable to be as specific as possible to what the therapist believes the client's emotional experience to be (and ideally, what the client has articulated previously). At the end of this prompt, the therapist asks several times if the client is ready to move back to this new direction but does so with a forward motion and confidence that conveys this is the appropriate direction to go with the intervention.

It has almost never happened (in all of the studies we have done) that clients have said they have not been ready to move on with the focus of the intervention, so powerful is this prompting. This does not mean clients are truly ready to move on—many of them are not ready to move on. Many of them need more time spent lingering in the negative emotion and processing their feelings of grief and loss, and we can tell this because they continue to struggle with bouts of negative emotion coming up throughout their savoring.

When we have delivered this intervention as part of a manualized protocol through research studies, we do not deviate from the protocol, so we continue with the protocol and hope the clients will be able to benefit some from the intervention, even if we are moving them forward prematurely.

However, in clinical practice, if you sense that your client truly is not ready to move forward, you could make the decision not to do so and instead to spend time focusing on the negative emotions (sadness, grief, loss, shame, anger, anxiety) that the exercise has brought up. I discuss this more in Chapter 7.

Before we move on, let's look at one other way this might come up in the context of a savoring session and how the therapist could address this issue seamlessly, particularly if the therapist decides they do not want to address the issue head-on. Once again, therapists should be on the lookout for spoiling to occur, particularly when a client is savoring an event that occurred adjacent to a difficult life event. Especially when clients discuss difficult topics, they may answer a reflection question by diving into something negative; they could describe the details of a negative event, sometimes the same event they have already described in Step 1 of the reflection (sensory reflection) or another event, or they could begin talking about negative emotions they are having or have had in reaction to the initial inciting event or another event.

In the following example, initially the client, Marc, is savoring his relationship and connection with a close friend, Tania, who has really been there for him throughout the process of grieving his wife's death. He starts out by discussing one particular incident in which his friend was there for him (they are talking on the phone) and then, in response to this prompt, mentions another pivotal moment, which occurs immediately after his wife dies. So instead of responding to the meaning-making prompt, he begins talking about another time when the friend was there for him:

THERAPIST: OK. Now, I'd like you to think about what you were thinking when you were talking to your friend on the phone. For example, were you thinking she really cares for me? Or she really loves me? Or she really understands me? And what do you think about it now?

MARC: We were very good friends. Um uh and had been for probably 20 years. And uh I—I would say I loved her, but she was married. That's—that's not uh wrong to love somebody. But understanding their other responsibilities. So there were there were no uh I mean our relationship was str-strictly from the emotional side. And just and talking. She was the—during this year—eight months—she was probably somebody I turned to many times. Or she was there when I mean, my wife died. She just happened to—my wife was in the hospice at the house. I was the hospice provider. And, or caretaker, whatever. And my wife died and she showed up [*slight chuckle*], showed up from work. I had already been retired. And she uh she just stayed in the car, uh but we talked. Uh the hospice people, the uh yeah hospice people had already come and had taken my wife. Or it wasn't the hospice, but uh can't forget what they were. [Hospice] people had taken her already. So I was in the midst of uh so our—that kind of relationship and she knew me quite well. We salsa-danced together for years as couples. And um I don't know what she said. I just remember my side. But I know that that wasn't a long discussion, but I continued on then. But I'm pretty sure it was on the way to counseling.

THERAPIST: I'm so glad you had this kind of connection with her—that she was able to be there for you at this time. It sounds like she was really there for you throughout this whole grieving process. It wasn't only this one time, it was so many times that she was there for you. I'm wondering what you thought about her being there for you throughout the process, or even what you think about it now—what does it mean to you that she was really there for you in this really important way? What does it tell you about you as a person? Or about her? Or about life?

Notice how the therapist allowed Marc to finish his thoughts on this topic. From a clinical standpoint, it would not have been wise to prevent Marc from finishing his thought, even though what he is saying is not responsive to the meaning-making prompt. This is because Marc is speaking about a topic that is deeply emotional and therefore incredibly difficult to interrupt. And because Marc moves on himself to talk about the connection with Tania, there is no need to intervene and move him on with a prompt. It is much better for Marc to move himself there than for the therapist to move him there.

Instead, the intervention that the therapist makes is following up by expressing gratitude for the kind of connection Marc had with Tania. The therapist makes several statements that underscore this connection to really drive that point home and to move Marc to the place of really focusing on the connection (and away from focusing on the loss). The therapist chooses not to focus on the loss at all but to focus their comments on the connection between Marc and Tania. And then the therapist moves on to ask more questions about what this means to Marc that Tania was really there for him, questions that are designed to get him to focus more deeply on this moment.

In sum, the therapist should follow the steps outlined above, which entail validating (the client's negative emotion) and redirecting the client back toward the positive, unless the therapist perceives that it is not clinically indicated to move the client on so quickly, as is the case in the above example. In that latter case, the therapist can choose to allow the client to pass through the information they are providing, as well as the feelings they are experiencing, and then focus on the topics that are most relevant to the savoring portion of the intervention in their response. This more indirect approach is indicated in cases in which the client is discussing a highly sensitive situation.

A WORD ON GENERAL RESISTANCE TO RELATIONAL SAVORING

Before closing, it is important to discuss what happens when none of the strategies I have outlined in this chapter work. Therapists who use this intervention may encounter clients who do not seem to be responsive to any of the interventions outlined above. If you have tried all of the interventions I have suggested and none of them seem to be working, there may be good reasons for this. If you get the feeling that the client is being purposely resistant to engaging in the exercise, it may be wise to step back and discuss the client's feelings about the savoring (rather than continuing to try to engage in it, as doing so may not be productive). Perhaps they have the sense that you are forcing them to feel something they do not want to feel or think about something in a way they don't want to. The best approach may be to pause and assess with the client what about the intervention is not working for them. Does it feel artificial? Does it seem to miss the mark in terms of addressing their real issues? Or do they in general not feel deserving of focusing on positive moments in their lives?

Discussing this topic could lead to useful conversations where you could hear their perspective on the approach and you could also describe your perspective regarding the justification for relational savoring again—you are not trying to make them think or feel a certain way; rather, you want them to believe they have the right to benefit from certain experiences they have had, particularly in light of other extremely difficult ones they have endured, and you would like to help guide them to that place. It doesn't negate in any way the pain they have suffered—you still hold that in mind—but you want to carve out a little space for them to experience some respite from the pain as well. It may well be that you end up in the same place, agreeing with them that this is not the best approach for them, but it ought to open up a fruitful discussion with plenty of material for therapeutic fodder.

WRAP-UP

The suggestions provided here offer a framework for ways to circumvent some of the challenges that emerge in using relational savoring with clients. My colleagues and I have found these tools to be effective in preventing these challenges from occurring in the first place or addressing these challenges once they have emerged.

PART III
RELATIONAL SAVORING IN CLINICAL CONTEXT

In this last section, I move fully into the clinical context. By "clinical context," I mean that I am going to set the research aside and more fully embrace my identity as a therapist in the service of providing enough information to advance clinical work. In other words, I am giving myself permission to think creatively about the intervention and the ways it can be applied clinically as an extension of the research my team and I have done. This also means I will be extrapolating a bit beyond the confines of the research studies we have conducted. Also, because I will be moving away from the research, I will rely more on clinical cases, which are used here with the permission of the clients and also through the use of disguise.

Here I focus on specific populations in the context of relational savoring, as well as ways to think about adapting relational savoring within the context of specific clinical contexts. I will focus on relational savoring as it might be useful in addressing individual mental health concerns, as well as relational savoring in the context of couple and family therapy. The topics discussed in this section of the book are not meant to be exhaustive but rather meant to provide a sampling of how relational savoring can be tailored for specific populations while retaining its core features, as well as how relational savoring is uniquely congruent with the cultural values of certain groups (e.g., Latino/a/x culture).

7
TAILORING YOUR RELATIONAL SAVORING INTERVENTION TO YOUR INDIVIDUAL CLIENT

In this chapter, I'm going to address how you would go about actually using the relational savoring intervention in practice with your client. Here I am going to ask us to put down the research manual and look up to focus on the client sitting in front of you. I want to consider how using this intervention might work in a clinical setting, such as in a private practice, an intensive outpatient program, or a psychiatric hospital.

DIFFERENCES BETWEEN RESEARCH STUDIES AND CLINICAL PRACTICE

First, I am going to spend a few moments talking about the differences between working clinically in research contexts and working in clinical contexts. Relational savoring is a manualized treatment, like many others in our field. In research, we stick to the treatment protocols because we want to be

https://doi.org/10.1037/0000372-007
Relational Savoring: Using Guided Reflection to Strengthen Relationships and Improve Outcomes in Therapy, by J. L. Borelli
Copyright © 2024 by the American Psychological Association. All rights reserved.

able to assess their impact on our outcomes of interest (behavior, emotion, or attitude change) in a community or clinical population without regard to the particular psychological needs of the participant/client. Standardization is very important in research because it allows us to know that we are testing the intervention that we have developed.

When used clinically, however, we would want to take these three perspectives into account: (a) using the intervention flexibly as client needs arise, (b) tailoring its use to accommodate the special knowledge you have of your client, and (c) considering how to integrate relational savoring into a broader treatment plan that may or may not include other treatment goals. I will discuss these in turn.

Using the Intervention Flexibly as Client Needs Arise

Manualized interventions are wonderful tools that can provide direction to trained therapists. Having a theoretical framework and a manual to guide your approach is like having a map when you are trying to navigate to a place you have never been. Without it, we would make lots of wrong turns and the client would be along for the ride.

However, if you are like most therapists, you are not likely to take a manual off the shelf and use it as is; if I were to hand you the manual for relational savoring, you wouldn't take the manual and read it to your client (or even memorize and deliver it to your client) verbatim. This would not be very effective therapy. You are much more likely to digest the manual, understand its principles, and apply them in a way that makes sense to you and fits your therapeutic style. Just as with many other forms of therapy, even the forms of therapy with the strongest evidence, many therapists who are trained in the skills use them and apply them flexibly.

For example, I love Phil Kendall's Coping Cat treatment for anxiety (Beidas et al., 2008; Kendall & Hedtke, 2006a, 2006b). I find it to be an accessible and fun way of engaging children in a basic cognitive behavior protocol for treating anxiety. But when I administer it, I often administer it with breaks in between sessions to address additional needs the client has or to elaborate on what the treatment manual has brought up for the client. Hopefully, Kendall wouldn't be offended by hearing this—no offense to him or his work because I truly am a huge fan of the intervention program. It is just that when I am administering it in my practice, I prefer to do so with some flexibility built in so that when my little client comes in having been bullied the day before, I can take time to talk to the client about that experience.

I may pull from the principles we have already talked about (e.g., talking about the toolbox we have created, if we have gotten that far within the treatment), but I will be moving off of the manual to focus on the client's issue. I am guessing that most of the therapists reading this book are similar to me and prefer to engage with interventions in a flexible way, one that embraces the spirit of the intervention but also honors the needs of the individual client.

Tailoring the Intervention's Use to Accommodate the Special Knowledge You Have of Your Client

One benefit of working with a therapist over a longer term is that the therapist can tailor the intervention to meet the client's unique characteristics and needs. Applying a manual flexibly is a client-centered approach to using a manualized treatment. As your client's therapist, you know your client better than the manual does. This is because you likely have a relationship with your client in which you know them very well, understand the intricacies of their lives and experiences, and have a sense of where you want them to go.

Clients differ in their sensitivities and in the strategies that are likely to be most successful in reaching them. As their therapist, you are in the best position to know the most effective approach to working with your client. In contrast, the manual is, well, a manual, which is a one-size-fits-all approach that by its very nature, cannot acknowledge or embrace the uniqueness of your client. This is not the fault of the manual; manuals are designed to be general enough to fit most clients, but not specific enough to address the idiosyncrasies of your particular client. This is where the art of therapy comes in and why it is essential for the therapist to know how to flexibly apply the manual to the particular client. It's up to you to bring this personal touch to the intervention.

Let's make this more concrete by considering an example that applies well to the memory selection phase of relational savoring. For instance, if your client is the type of person who does not like to engage in affectionate touch—for example, they find this intrusive or off-putting—then this part of the intervention would not make sense for your client. Using any words in the intervention manual that refer to physical touch would make your client think that you don't know them well or have not been listening to them; these are undesirable outcomes and ones we would like to avoid.

If you as a therapist were to come in and use the manual as it is written without regard for what you know about your client, you would definitely risk alienating them. Conversely, when we administer the intervention within a research setting, we have just met the client, and when we are doing the intervention, we are applying solely this intervention and no other intervention. So under these conditions, we do not know whether the clients do or do not like physical touch, or what kind of relationship they have with their relationship partner (child, romantic partner, etc.).

We may have done a brief assessment beforehand to assess the quality of their relationships, such as conducting the Parent Development Interview (Aber et al., 1985; Slade et al., 2003) or the Adult Attachment Interview (George et al., 1996). We may also have provided them with some self-report measures of relationship quality (parenting satisfaction: Kansas Parenting Scale (D. E. James et al., 1985); marital satisfaction: Kansas Marital Scale (Nichols et al., 1983), or attachment style (Experiences in Close Relationships–Revised; Fraley et al., 2000), but these measures may or may not provide this level of detail about preferences for contact and connection within relationships. They certainly do not do so to the same degree as having an ongoing therapeutic relationship with a client. Thus, it's both a benefit and a bit of a liability that you have this added knowledge about your client; you are able to better tailor the intervention to your client, but you must use the knowledge you have about your client to personalize the intervention or risk alienating them.

Considering How to Integrate Relational Savoring Into a Broader Treatment Plan

Third, as your client's therapist, you must work collaboratively with them to develop a treatment plan to address their presenting problems and reasons for seeking therapy. Relational savoring improves emotional and relational well-being. These are not the most common reasons people seek therapy. Among couples seeking therapy, problems with communication and lack of emotional affection are the most commonly cited difficulties (Doss et al., 2004). Among adults seeking therapy, depression and anxiety are the most common problems (Parker-Pope et al., 2021), and among youth seeking therapy, the most common issues are anxiety, depression, ADHD, and trauma-related disorders (Cullinan, 2018).

Relational savoring is theorized to have downstream impacts on mental health (Borelli, Smiley, et al., 2020), and pre–post results from a group therapy intervention program in which relational savoring played a prominent role demonstrated reductions in internalizing symptoms (depression and anxiety) in mothers and youth (Borelli, Yates, et al., 2021). Yet, the evidence for this approach in reducing mental health symptoms is thin. As a clinician, you likely want to choose evidence-based treatments for the primary difficulty your client is facing, often depression or anxiety, and as an ancillary approach, incorporate relational savoring, for which there is less research support.

If your primary focus in therapy is on reducing psychological symptoms, you may wish to adopt an approach with a strong evidence base, such as behavioral activation for depression (Lejuez et al., 2011), cognitive therapy for depression (Muñoz et al., 2000), or mindfulness-based cognitive therapy (Segal et al., 2018). Although relational savoring per se has not been examined for its efficacy with depression or anxiety, it is worth mentioning that other interventions that bear similarity to savoring may help increase the evidence base for using savoring indirectly.

The most rigorous of these trials was conducted by Michelle Craske and her group. Craske recently developed a treatment that focuses on the enhancement of positive affect (and the reduction of anhedonia, as a key symptom shared across depression and anxiety (Craske et al., 2016). This 15-session treatment focuses on scheduling pleasant events (seven sessions), attending to the positive (three sessions), and cultivating the positive (four sessions), plus one session of relapse prevention.

The last substantive module, *cultivating the positive*, bears the greatest similarity to the relational savoring intervention. Craske describes this module as consisting of experiential exercises "designed to cultivate and savor positive experiences." This module focuses on the mental act of giving, the physical act of giving, the mental act of wishing good to self and others, and generating a sense of gratefulness. Each of these practices is boosted by savoring positive emotions.

This treatment, referred to as positive affect treatment, was recently tested in a two-site randomized controlled trial at outpatient centers (Craske et al., 2019) of adults with anxiety and depression, with findings revealing that the positive affect treatment was superior to a negative affect treatment on positive affect, negative affect, depression, anxiety, stress, and suicidal ideation. Similarly, a small study of a savoring-based intervention revealed reductions in depressed mood of college students (McMakin et al., 2011). Likewise, a preliminary evaluation of a 10-session positive activity intervention (Amplification of Positive Activity; C. T. Taylor et al., 2017) revealed that as compared with a waitlist control, the intervention enhanced social connectedness (C. T. Taylor et al., 2020), and the study found that increases in positive affect predicted increases in social connectedness. This is a smaller sample study, but it involved treatment-seeking adults with clinically significant anxiety or depression, so it's relevant for our discussion.

In sum, relational savoring itself has not been evaluated as a treatment for clinical samples, so it should not be used as a first-line treatment for these disorders, but the evidence for other, similar treatments is growing, which can be used to increase the support for using relational savoring alongside other evidence-based treatments.

Further, given the importance of goal consensus and collaboration between therapists and clients (Tryon & Winograd, 2011), it is important to use an approach that on its face addresses the issue the client is presenting. So if a client comes in looking for help addressing their depression, even if you as the therapist feel it is their lack of connectedness to people around them that is driving their depression, you probably would not want to go after that with your intervention approach without providing the client with a treatment plan that helps the client understand why you would focus on lack of connectedness. Otherwise, you could risk losing the client through therapy dropout or reduction in motivation; they might feel as if their therapist does not understand what they need or want or does not see them as they want to be seen.

It is crucial to ensure that clients and therapists collaborate on defining the goals of therapy (Tryon & Winograd, 2011) and potentially also the path toward achieving those goals, although the therapist typically has a larger role than the client in identifying the best approach to reach those goals. All of this is Therapy Skills 101, but it bears mentioning here when we are considering how to best integrate this type of intervention into clinical practice.

That being said, it may be consistent with your treatment plan and therapy goals to integrate relational savoring into your overall treatment approach with your client. Just because savoring is not the only approach you will use with your client does not mean it cannot be part of what you do with your clients.

So for these three reasons—that you might like to use the intervention flexibly, you know your client better than the manual does, and you may be using this relational savoring intervention in combination with other interventions—it makes sense to have a different stance when it comes to using relational savoring as a clinical tool versus using it as a research tool. So, now that we have discussed these basics, let's dive into talking about how it *does* make sense to use this intervention in the clinical/consulting room, shall we?

THE WHEN AND HOW OF USING RELATIONAL SAVORING WITH YOUR CLIENTS

In this section of the chapter, I am going to dive into helping you consider when you might wish to use relational savoring and how you might go about doing that. Let's start with the *when*. As I said above, you want to consider which clients are appropriate for using relational savoring and at what time it might be appropriate to use the intervention. In Figure 7.1, I provide some suggestions for when it might be clinically indicated to use relational savoring as a first- and second-line treatment. In this context, when I say "first line,"

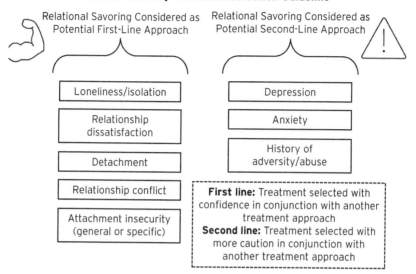

FIGURE 7.1. Relational Savoring Treatment Selection Guideline

I mean that relational savoring would be an excellent choice to augment an existing treatment approach.

So let us take for an example the issue of attachment insecurity. Let's imagine a couple who are going through therapy because of relationship difficulties and attachment insecurity; the therapist working with them decides to adopt an emotionally focused therapy (EFT) approach (Johnson, 2019). EFT typically lasts between eight and 20 sessions. Although the second stage of EFT involves helping the couple bond and reconnect, the therapist may feel that individual members of the couple would benefit from engaging in some additional work to boost their ability to notice moments of positive connection as they occur and appreciate them after the fact.

Further, as we know, relational savoring enhances positive emotion and relationship satisfaction, as well as providing a low-pressure way of articulating emotional needs. The therapist may wish to have members of the couple engage in relational savoring—individually, conjointly, or individually and then conjointly—in order to enhance these skills. This may be particularly warranted if one or both members of the couple are showing difficulty being emotionally vulnerable in their interactions with their partner, or if one or both members of the couple seem to have difficulty noticing positive moments in their interactions with one another. My apologies to Sue Johnson if she takes offense at me for suggesting this, but perhaps pausing in the sessions of EFT to insert a few sessions of relational savoring could help the couple boost their ability to be more positively engaged with one another, more present, and more grateful for the emotional connection they have with one another. Buoyed by this enhanced connection, the therapist could then resume the EFT-based work.

I have also indicated a second column of conditions where relational savoring might be useful but the evidence base is less strong. Here I would recommend using it always in conjunction with another evidence-based treatment and while carefully monitoring its impact. I mentioned earlier that we have used relational savoring with people with histories of abuse but not with people who were explicitly in treatment for that reason. Likewise, we have used relational savoring with people with clinically significant depression and anxiety, but these were not treatment-seeking populations; this was in the context of research studies that were evaluating a prevention program.

For this reason, I recommend more caution when working with individuals with clinically significant concerns. For instance, one may wish to check in more frequently with the client to monitor the impact of the relational savoring, even using mood and anxiety questionnaires to evaluate the impact. I would also recommend checking in with the client following the relational savoring sessions to ensure they did not have an emotional backlash in response to the savoring (such as an increase in longing or loneliness following the savoring). However, as described above, the recently emerging evidence for positive affect interventions, such as Craske's intervention, is highly encouraging and certainly adds to the enthusiasm for this program, particularly for people with comorbid mood/anxiety and relationship concerns.

Now let's move to the *how*. Because you already know about your client, you have the benefit of being able to steer your client much more adeptly than the manual we have written specifies. For instance, you may wish to skip the memory selection phase entirely because you have already heard enough from your client(s) to know what you want them to savor. Perhaps in telling you about something else, they have already relayed a memory that is so ripe for savoring you just can't wait to have them dive into that memory reflection. If so, then there is no need to engage in the memory selection stage of the process; rather, you can provide them with the rationale for why you are asking them to engage in the savoring and then jump right to the reflection task. You can offer them an explanation that looks something like this:

> If it's OK with you, I'd like us to try something now that is designed to help enhance your positive emotion and your feelings of closeness to your [partner/child/etc.]. As you know, I think that if we can enhance your positive emotion and feelings of closeness to your [partner/child/etc.], this might go a long way in helping to improve some of the things you have been dealing with [feeling

dissatisfied with the relationship, feeling disconnected, depression, etc.]. The premise of this exercise is that we all have moments of connectedness within our lives, but these moments can pass us by unnoticed because there are so many other attention-grabbing things in our lives. We are naturally drawn to focus on frightening or stressful things, or depressing and upsetting things, and the purpose of this exercise is going to be to help you focus on a positive moment of connection so you can get the full benefit that the moment contains. If it's OK with you, I'll lead you through this exercise and help you focus on things and help you reflect on a particular memory.

You can and should also use your clinical superpowers to tailor this message more precisely to the needs, sensitivities, and individual preferences of your specific client. For example, if you have a client who has experienced a great deal of adversity in their lives, you might also insert a statement about how this kind of work is even more important for people who have had difficult childhoods or difficult early life experiences; their early experiences tell them it is more important to pay attention to the interactions they have in which there is a potential for rejection, neglect, abuse, or harm, for part of them believes that paying attention to this aspect of their interactions will protect them. However, this hypervigilant stance toward viewing the world actually deprives them of reaping the benefits of their positive interactions, and if anyone deserves to get those benefits, it is them.

I have also worked with clients who experience the world as a very hostile and unfriendly place; these clients would react quite negatively if I were to make a statement like, "We all have moments of connectedness within our lives." Some of these clients feel they are different than other people, that they do not have moments like these, or as many of these moments as others do. If I were to make a statement like this with this type of client, I would risk making my client feel I had not been listening to the fact that they do not walk through the world in the same way as others do; they experience things in fundamentally different ways because they feel the world does not react to them in the same way as it does to others. So for this type of client, I would change the message to something like the following:

> I know you do not have the benefit of having many of these moments [of positive connectedness], and in fact, this is something that is really painful for you and something we are working together to change. And I can understand why that would be so painful: It leaves you feeling really alone and separate from the rest of the world. Precisely because of that fact, I want to focus on the positive experiences you do have, infrequent and minor though they may be, to make sure you get the maximum benefit from them. You deserve that—you deserve to really soak up all of the richness and goodness from these experiences that are present in them.

Perhaps your client feels they already spend a lot of time focusing on positive memories, but from your perspective, they do not focus on them in the way you think is most helpful (i.e., focusing on experiences that emphasize superficial moments of connectedness rather than ones rich with attachment content, or focusing on them in a way that typically veers toward the negative [e.g., guilt, anxiety, resentment]). In this case, you may wish to steer them toward the exercise in a different way. For example, you might say something like the following:

> I recognize that you actually spend a lot of time thinking about positive moments in your life and you're fortunate to have a lot of these really wonderful moments of connection, which is a great place to be starting from. What I want to work on together, and what my role with you will be, is to help you focus on certain parts of the memories that I think are really significant and that might not get as much attention as they deserve.

You may wish to deliver this rationale and introduction to the exercise more as a dialogue than as a monologue, depending on your style of relating with your client. And speaking of, depending on the degree to which you normally use a directive approach with your client, you may wish to preface to your client that you will be a bit more directive when going through this relational savoring exercise. As traditionally delivered, relational savoring is pretty directive (therapist led), and if you wish to deliver it in a way that is more adherent to this means of delivery, then you might want to give your client a preview of that. To accomplish that, you could say something like the following: "As we go through this exercise, you may notice that I am leading you a bit more than I usually do. This technique involves more of me showing you where to go."

Even with existing clients whom you know extremely well, you may still need to do memory reflection with them. I have needed to do this with clients who infrequently speak of positive moments of connectedness with me. Alternatively, sometimes when I bring a memory back up that a client has previously discussed, the memory no longer holds any positive emotional resonance for the client. This may be because this is how the client's memory works—it is extremely difficult for the client to hold onto the positive emotion associated with memories (maybe all memories, or maybe just interpersonal memories)—or because the memory is not positive unless they are the ones to bring it up and it occurs to them to feel positive about the memory. But either way, the result is that once-positive memories no longer seem positive when I bring them up.

If I find this to be true, my strategy is to quickly drop this approach and move to doing more of a true memory selection. But the memory selection might look a bit different than when conducted in a research setting, and this is also because the therapist can draw on their knowledge and experience with the client to guide the conversation. For instance, they can ask questions based on what they know to be the client's typical way of engaging with the world, and they can praise the client for ways of being or relating that the client values about themselves. For instance, if you have a client who has previously told you how much effort they put into getting to know others' interests, you can make comments to this effect in the memory selection phase:

> This memory really helps me see how you spent a lot of time learning about the things that were important to him, and perhaps this was a way for you to show that you cared about him. This is a really good example of you putting a lot of effort into your relationships, and I bet that he felt that interest that you were showing for him. When someone makes such a concerted effort to get to know you, it communicates that you are important and valued, and you gave him that.

In other words, you can use the memory sharing that occurs in this part of the intervention as an opportunity to build on the narrative that the client has provided you with and a way to show the client that you have been building up a mental model of who they are. In addition to this, you should be using this memory selection as an opportunity to further the goals of the relational savoring intervention, which include coming up with a memory that is highly positive, is specific, has strong attachment content, and has low potential for spoiling.

When you arrive at the memory reflection portion of the intervention (whether you go straight there or precede it with memory selection), in contrast to the way in which we do the intervention in research studies, when working with your clients in clinical practice, you may wish to use your knowledge and the flexibility you have in clinical practice to push the boundaries further. For instance, if you know your client is particularly visually oriented, as opposed to being grounded in their auditory senses, you may wish to focus more on this aspect of the first reflection step, knowing this will appeal to them more, make more sense to them, and naturally ground them in the experience. Knowing that the actual goal of the first step of the reflection is to ground them back in their experience, help them recall the sensory details of the experience; it makes sense to help them bring to mind those sensory details that are most vivid to them.

I am not a visually oriented person; I can almost never remember what someone was wearing (myself or the other person), but I can usually remember what I could hear around me (auditory), what the person felt like (touch), and definitely what I felt like emotionally at the time. So for me, if I was asked to recall what I could see in the room I was sitting in or what the other person looked like or was wearing, I might get a bit lost in a cognitive, nonemotional kind of state where I would be focusing really hard on trying to remember something that I did not encode initially. This is not the goal of the intervention—trying to help people bring to mind things that they did not encode or only barely encoded.

The goal of this step of the intervention is really to help them place themselves back in the memory so they can more aptly activate the emotions (Step 2) and meaning/cognitions (Step 3) in subsequent steps. So anything that takes them away from their bodily/remembered experience and puts them in a more cognitive stance is counter to the goals of the intervention. These are the types of sophisticated therapeutic maneuvers that no therapist can be expected to know about a client the first or second time they meet them; however, these may be qualities that you are well acquainted with about your clients.

This is just one example of how you may wish to tailor your delivery of the memory reflection portion of the intervention. There are too many other ways to possibly describe here, but the general principles that should be followed are (a) identifying where your client's strengths are, (b) using those to guide the intervention in terms of its delivery, and then (c) focusing your intervention on the client's targeted areas for growth. In other words, capitalize on your client's strengths in ways that will allow the intervention to be absorbed to the greatest degree.

The tip I provided above about playing to your client's sensory preferences is an example of the way in which you would consider your client's strengths in terms of mode of delivery. Further, you will also want to identify the specific relational or emotional areas in which the client needs to grow and try to guide the client in this way as well. Your case conceptualization likely involves a deeper understanding of your client's issues than that they feel lonely or socially isolated, that they feel dissatisfied with their relationships, or that they have lots of conflict in their relationships. Quite likely, if you have been working with your client for some time, your case conceptualization might look more like the following example:

> The client has a difficult time allowing people to get close to them because they are afraid of being vulnerable around others. This difficulty may be related to experiences they have had earlier in their life (childhood, early romantic life) and has manifested in extreme difficulty showing up for others. In order to block against this fear, they react to their own and others' vulnerability with hostility and anger. They have a host of beliefs about how it is important to be strong in the face of life's difficulties and how emotions make a person weak. This results in their partner feeling let down by their lack of responsiveness; their partner is also often made to feel as if they are the problem (they are

too anxious, too hysterical, too emotional). And sometimes the partner does get highly emotional (angry, upset), typically when they feel they can't get the response they need from their partner, or when they feel their partner is denying their feelings or reality. On the other hand, the client feels frustrated because they feel they are giving everything they have to give.

So yes, this is much more in-depth, much more nuanced, than a simple descriptor, and because you as a skilled therapist can come up with a detailed case conceptualization of the client's relational challenges, you can target your relational savoring intervention much more precisely to address these needs. I have provided some sample ways in which you might consider targeting your intervention on clients' specific relational needs in Table 7.1, but you may be able to generate even more sophisticated ideas for how to go about engaging in this process. In moving deeper with the intervention and tailoring it to your client's specific needs, I would encourage you to ground yourself in the core principles of the intervention and then focus on your client's treatment goals.

TABLE 7.1. Relational Savoring Treatment Selection Guideline

Relational target	Therapeutic techniques
Client struggles to accept and respond effectively to the emotional needs of others (becomes defensive, angry)	Identifying times when client successfully responded to partner's needs; processing client's feelings about these experiences and also encouraging client to notice/discuss the partner's reaction
	Identifying times when others successfully responded to client's needs; processing client's feelings about these experiences of having needs and having them responded to
Client feels that nobody is there for them (feels lonely, feels let down by others)	Focusing on savoring times when client's needs were met by others, minor though they may be, as examples of times when they felt supported by others; using these memories to fortify the client and help the client feel that others can be reliable, interested in them, and supportive
Client feels unsafe in relationships (secondary to history of abuse)	Focusing on times when client was made to feel secure and safe, when boundaries were honored, with or by another person
	Identifying times they had treated another person in such a way to make them feel safe and secure, honoring their boundaries

USING RELATIONAL SAVORING TO PURSUE YOUR THERAPEUTIC GOALS IN A MORE TARGETED WAY

Another advantage that you as a therapist have, as opposed to a researcher working with a participant in a research study, is that you know exactly what your therapeutic target is and you can go after it with relational savoring in a more targeted way. So for instance, if you are trying to enhance the client's feelings of emotional security in order to reduce their anxiety, you can really hone your intervention to maximize the likelihood that you will hit your target. I will revisit this topic again in Chapter 8 in terms of the way in which a therapist may wish to use relational savoring to address specific psychological symptoms.

Rather than describe this in a hypothetical way, I am going to provide an example of the way a therapist used relational savoring to work this way with a client. The client was an 11-year-old boy who was suffering from obsessive–compulsive disorder that was quite impairing. The therapist was working with the client using a cognitive behavior therapy approach, exposure plus response prevention (Piacentini et al., 2007), using a manual developed by John Piacentini and colleagues. However, she wanted to augment this work with some relational savoring, which she was also trained in. The therapist's goal in using relational savoring was to heighten the client's memories of feeling safe in relationships with others; the idea is that this would be an antidote to feelings of anxiety and fear (in relationships and in general).

Unsurprisingly, the child, whom we will call Liam, discussed a time when he was frightened. He talked about his close friend helping him; they were rock climbing in a nearby region and his friend (Tara), with whom he feels very close, helped guide him in how to put his feet in the right places. In this passage, I italicized what I see to be the most relevant sections for his treatment:

THERAPIST: Yeah so why don't we think about that one. Can you, uhm, you said it was in [place] so, uhm—and on some rocks right? So can you describe the scene a little bit? Like, where was Tara, where were you, and what color were the rocks, and—

LIAM: Alright.

THERAPIST: What did the air feel like?

LIAM: Uh, well, so it was this, so I was [*inaudible*], so you have to climb really high up—

THERAPIST: Mhm.

LIAM: And it was like—so it was kinda all these boulders like crashed down and you can just like jump rocks and rocks—

THERAPIST:	Ohh.
LIAM:	And you get higher each time—
THERAPIST:	Yeah.
LIAM:	And it got really high and there was this pathway were my brother and Tara's brother and like one other person were like climbing really far—
THERAPIST:	Mhm.
LIAM:	And we were like, "we can do that" so then—but there was a wall and it was like . . . like really steep. It was like this [*shows with hands*].
THERAPIST:	Mhm.
LIAM:	And there were some places were like, were in or like rocks that you could like step on your feet—
THERAPIST:	Mhm.
LIAM:	And uh I got really scared 'cause like "what if I fall" or like "what if I like—like die." Yeah, so I got really scared and then Tara was like "Well if you put your foot there [*inaudible*]" and uhm then she did it and she was like "You can really do it" and then once I did it I'm like, "I did it!"
THERAPIST:	Yeah.
LIAM:	*She helped me out so much because if you panic it doesn't help.*
THERAPIST:	Yeah.
LIAM:	So it helped me out a lot because . . .
THERAPIST:	She showed you where to put your foot?
LIAM:	Yeah and like—
THERAPIST:	She did it.
LIAM:	*And encouraged me so I wouldn't like fall and die.*
THERAPIST:	Yeah.
LIAM:	Yeah.
THERAPIST:	Yeah 'cause you were—so tell me about that, you were like really scared inside.

LIAM:	Yeah.
THERAPIST:	Yeah.
LIAM:	The color of the rocks was like reddish and like yellow like—
THERAPIST:	OK.
LIAM:	Red, yellow, and gray and there was like some little like—like little grass plants on there, inside the hole growing.
THERAPIST:	Oh yeah, OK.
LIAM:	The sun was very hot—
THERAPIST:	Yeah.
LIAM:	So I wore sunscreen.
THERAPIST:	Yeah.
LIAM:	Uhm, and from there this like—you're like up here and then you can see the campsite from here—
THERAPIST:	Mhm.
LIAM:	And uhm there's also really nice shady place over at this other rock next to really close by—
THERAPIST:	Mhm.
LIAM:	So I usually read there.
THERAPIST:	Oh, OK.
LIAM:	Yeah, it was really fun.
THERAPIST:	OK, when you weren't climbing you'd read over there.
LIAM:	Yeah.
THERAPIST:	So with—with the climbing you were, were you like uhm a third of the way up or half the way up when you started to feel scared or like way near the top or?
LIAM:	I mean we weren't like all the way really far but we were like halfway.
THERAPIST:	Halfway.

LIAM:	And I started being really scared but the thing is once we got up there there was a little cave and it was really shady and it was so nice in there so it was kind of worth it.
THERAPIST:	Yeah.
LIAM:	Yeah.
THERAPIST:	So when you were scared did you actually say to Tara, "I'm scared." Or did you say, "help me," or?
LIAM:	I was kind of like uhm, "I'm like really scared I don't think I can do this cause—"
THERAPIST:	Ahh.
LIAM:	I'm kind of like, I'm like just like, it's like—it's like I do diving so sometimes when you dive and your body just resents you and it's just like "Don't do that."
THERAPIST:	Yeah.
LIAM:	And that was kind of what was happening—
THERAPIST:	That was a feeling—
LIAM:	And it was like my body was like not working—
THERAPIST:	My chest was tight so all the way through here it was like "stop."
LIAM:	Yeah.
THERAPIST:	Like "stop, I don't want to go anymore."
LIAM:	Yeah.
THERAPIST:	Yeah.
LIAM:	And uh—
THERAPIST:	So how did you show her that you needed her help?
LIAM:	Uhm well I said I'm probably—'cause she was already inside by then and I'm like, "I'm really scared, can you help me? Like, what if I can't? I'm just going to go back down 'cause I'm really like really scared."
THERAPIST:	Mhm.

LIAM:	And I'm like—she's like, *"It's OK just like—you're fine, I did it. Like, you can do it. Just put your foot right there and grab on to the rock, like, there so you don't fall off and I promise you you're gonna like make it."* So that—she really like encouraged me—
THERAPIST:	Yeah.
LIAM:	And then uh then the next thing I did, I did it and I didn't fall and I was safe.
THERAPIST:	Yeah.
LIAM:	*It was actually really fun, yeah.*
THERAPIST:	Did you have good shoes for climbing?
LIAM:	What?
THERAPIST:	Did you have good shoes for climbing?
LIAM:	No, I had like, these.
THERAPIST:	Oh, OK.
LIAM:	The shoes I'm wearing right now are like running shoes, they were not good.
THERAPIST:	Not great for climbing.
LIAM:	But I think I do have another pair of like hiking shoes but that's another story.
THERAPIST:	Yeah.
LIAM:	But, yeah.
THERAPIST:	So she encouraged you by saying "I did it."
LIAM:	Yeah.
THERAPIST:	"And you can do it too."
LIAM:	Yeah and the thing was she had kind of the shoes I had so I was like—
THERAPIST:	Oh OK.
LIAM:	If she did it then I can do it—
THERAPIST:	You think you can do it yeah. Was it the—do you think it was her words or the tone of her voice or the fact that she had done it? What was—what was most encouraging?

LIAM:	Uh, it was kind of just—it her talking to me uh—
THERAPIST:	Yeah.
LIAM:	She—she did it and was not getting hurt and, uh, and like what I get to do at the end.
THERAPIST:	Yeah.
LIAM:	And like, it was a really nice area and you can just like chill in the shade and uhm and then like the next time I went up there I wasn't really—
THERAPIST:	Mmm.
LIAM:	Scared again so—
THERAPIST:	Yeah.
LIAM:	I did it last time, I can do it again.
THERAPIST:	Right.
LIAM:	But—
THERAPIST:	But she helped you see the—the goal, like how far you could get, and how nice it was up there, and how good it would feel—
LIAM:	Yeah.
THERAPIST:	To accomplish that. And do you think it made you feel like you could rely on her in the future? Or like she could give you more good feelings about your friendship with her?
LIAM:	Yeah, uh definitely because like also she's older than me so—
THERAPIST:	Mmm.
LIAM:	Uh, like I think like she's older than me so, uhm, so I mean she's like probably gonna be—*she usually when I was scared she probably does it first or like—or usually, but sometimes, I will go first so yeah.*
THERAPIST:	OK, so because she's older she often does something before you and shows you.
LIAM:	Yeah but, I mean not all the time—
THERAPIST:	Yeah.

LIAM: Because sometimes she's like terrified and then I go and then 'cause like the other day uh we were gonna—actually yesterday, we were going in the pool and it was really cold and—and—and then, uh, and then I was at the pool and like, and like at the pool, wait no—yeah so she went to the pool first right—

THERAPIST: Mhm.

LIAM: But she was like terrified and I'm like I'll jump in and then—and then—and then when I actually jumped in the water it was freezing—

THERAPIST: Yeah.

LIAM: But I'm like I can do it so then she was like standing there like, "Stop, like no I don't wanna move."

THERAPIST: [*Laughs.*]

LIAM: And I was like, "it's actually—you gotta just move and once that it's not that cold." And then, uhm, uh, and then after a little bit I'm just kinda like "you might" and then I splashed her only because—

THERAPIST: OK.

LIAM: Only because, uh, she literally froze like that for like twenty minutes.

THERAPIST: OK, she was just standing there. You were trying to get her to get used to the water.

LIAM: Yeah and—and then after that we just went to the water.

THERAPIST: Yeah, OK.

LIAM: But, I think some other time, uh, I think—I can't really recall, I mean I don't like—I didn't—I don't really remember any experiences where like—I mean do I? I feel like—I know, I know sometimes I went first—first and like first but uh I think . . . yeah but there was sometimes I did go first and—

THERAPIST: Yeah.

LIAM: And honestly but I don't really care who goes first sometimes and—

THERAPIST: Yeah, yeah.

LIAM: Because it's like I don't really care 'cause we're just friends.

THERAPIST: That's right, that's kind of how friends are, yeah.

LIAM: Yeah.

THERAPIST: So she helps you sometimes and you help her sometimes.

LIAM: Yeah and any—that's kind of what friends have to do—

THERAPIST: Yeah.

LIAM: Because you want to help your friend—

THERAPIST: Yeah, exactly.

LIAM: And I think, I think she's probably my closest friend than any of my—*she's probably the closest friend I have because I like tell her everything and*—

THERAPIST: Mhm.

LIAM: So I think we—I think she, I kind of have a better friend.

THERAPIST: Hmm.

LIAM: It's really nice. Honestly, I don't really—*even if she's three years older than me I don't really care how old she is, I just want to be friends.*

These excerpts of this savoring session illustrate a boy who was able to derive comfort from his friend during a time of fear (secure base receipt savoring) and to use that encouragement to overcome his fear and do something that scared him. Further, this moment of connection made their relationship stronger.

Going forward, the therapist used this memory as a way of enhancing the client's feelings of emotional security during times when he felt frightened. For example, in his obsessive–compulsive disorder treatment, the client and therapist worked on helping him reduce compulsions and confront obsessive thoughts—this increased his feelings of fear and anxiety in the short term, although the ultimate goal was to reduce his anxiety.

The boy also experienced some separation anxiety and had difficulty sleeping apart from his parents, which was also a focus of the treatment. The therapist directed him to focus on the feelings he experienced during this moment with his friend and to try to recreate that feeling of emotional security and safety during times when he is experiencing intense anxiety, such as when he is alone in his bed, separated from his parents. The therapist's goal was to use this type of emotional activation as a means of self-soothing during times of anxiety in order to help him regulate and manage his distress. This exercise may have served as a means of mentally representing a feeling of emotional security vis-à-vis a memory when he lacked a feeling of safety in other ways. The therapist also considered creating a physical reminder of the memory that he can place near his bed (e.g., a picture from the outing) to remind him of the way he felt supported by his friend. From reviewing this excerpt, it is also apparent how flexibly the intervention can be used. It is clear the therapist used the intervention to guide her work, but she used a principle-guided approach as opposed to a manual-guided approach.

The point of presenting this case example was to illustrate how one can use relational savoring as a specific tool to work in a targeted way toward a treatment goal; in this case, the goal was reducing anxiety through enhancing emotional security. The therapist accomplished this by first engaging in the relational savoring task and then using the savoring as a cue later in the therapy to help the client regulate his emotions.

USING RELATIONAL SAVORING BETWEEN SESSIONS

Another advantage of using relational savoring with your clients is that after you have worked with them in-session with the technique, you can ask them to implement the strategy in between sessions. You can do this by having them recall and savor moments of positive connectedness before they go to bed each night, by having them journal about moments of connection they have had, or by simply asking them to notice these moments of connectedness so you can discuss them together during your next session.

My colleagues and I have developed a few methods of prompting people to savor at particular points during their day, and I use these methods to augment my clinical work. For instance, I have created short handouts that describe the steps of relational savoring that I provide to people when I give workshops, and sometimes I will also give these to clients to help remind them of the steps of memory reflection. These handouts have also been distributed without therapy by Kaiser Permanente and in other nonprofit organizations, so they can be used in that way as well. If you are working with parents, a helpful resource is a journal created by Rishma Walji called *The Connected Parent Journal*, which has a section on relational savoring (Walji, 2022).

My colleagues and I also recently developed an app-based platform to deliver relational savoring, called mSavorUs, which we just finished testing in a pilot study (the results of which are not yet published). The sneak peek of the findings is that, overall, the participants (who were college students) liked the platform and the intervention but did not like the delivery; in this study, we were testing a means of delivering just-in-time interventions when participants were likely to be experiencing loneliness. However, this meant that participants were prompted to use the app while they were going about their business during their day, which was inconvenient for them. However, their feedback regarding the intervention itself was positive. In terms of using this in a clinical context, I would argue that it would be more beneficial to use the app after having worked through the intervention in person with your clients so they understand the goals of the practice before using it independently. Therapists interested in providing access to the app to their clients can contact me through email and I can provide you with login details.

In addition, in some of our studies, we have chosen to deliver relational savoring close to bedtime based on the assumption that near bedtime is a time not only when there is more space for reflection but also when anxiety and worries can set in (Harvey, 2002). If we conceptualize relational savoring as an emotion regulation strategy that runs counter to rumination or worry, then engaging in this type of emotion regulation at a time when one is prone to engage in rumination or worry could be protective. In assigning homework, I always try not to let the perfect be the enemy of the good, so I remind myself that the ultimate goal is to help people activate these memory networks more frequently and experience the emotions associated with these memories. Of course, the deeper they can dive into these memories, the better, but it is important to remember that the more frequently people access these memories at all, the better, so any accessing is a positive thing that will strengthen the memory networks.

When assigning homework, I recommend asking how the homework went and how the client felt while completing the homework and after completing it. Inquiring about homework is one way of following up with clients about their experience; this also helps to convey the importance of the assigned task. Further, asking these questions about the homework will reveal important information about what the experience was like for the client that can guide your work with them. This is also an important time to reinforce how talking and thinking about positive moments can enhance mood and relationship satisfaction.

RELATIONAL SAVORING "LIGHT"

Before I begin this section in which I give you my blessing to run with this intervention as you see fit, I want to clearly state that I believe you will get the biggest bang for your buck if you adhere as closely as you can to the intervention I have developed, all while being sensitive to the individual needs of your client. I say this because I know the most about this intervention as developed—it has been carefully studied. I do not know what the benefits are of relational savoring "light." However, I strongly believe in a glass half full mentality. Now, let me leave this aside for a minute.

This is the section of this book that no intervention developer ever wants to write or think about. But here I am, writing it, because if anything, I am a realist, someone who embraces the principle of "better something than nothing." In other words, having spent a great deal of my career refining the ins and outs of this intervention, obsessing over the nuances and details, I'm still about to tell you that my best guess is that using any part of it is perhaps better than using nothing at all. I cannot tell you that with certainty, because I have not studied that empirically (though perhaps I should), but my gut says that encouraging our clients to focus in some way—maybe in any way—on their moments of positive connectedness might be better than not doing it at all.

So, if you are someone who is going to walk away and take only one thing from this book, maybe this is it: that having an orientation toward finding these moments and going deeper with them can positively affect your clients. Exactly what *deeper* means, I will leave up to you to decide. I have already told you how I define *deeper* and what I recommend in terms of memory reflection and processing. So my greatest recommendation for you would be to not consider the positive memories to be irrelevant, unimportant, or uninteresting. There is so much of interest and value in these little gems, and I challenge you to find it.

In preparation for writing this book, I took a poll of some of the therapists who have been exposed to relational savoring over the years, by hearing me talk about it, working on a research study that involved it, or reading some articles on it. I was interested in finding out how learning about this intervention had affected their practice, if at all. (Keep in mind that this is not a controlled study because I did not assess them before and after learning about relational savoring. In fact, this is a very poor informal investigation, not a study at all.)

The questions I asked them included whether they still used relational savoring with their clients, which types of clients they used it with, and how they used it—as well as all of the ways they used it. I broke this down into whether they administered relational savoring in its full-blown glory by (a) taking them through all of the steps (33%), (b) asking clients to think of moments of interpersonal connection and go through some but not all of the steps (67%), (c) asking clients to think of interpersonal connection but not go through all of the steps (78%), (d) asking clients to notice moments of positive interpersonal connection in their daily lives (67%), and (e) asking clients to notice moments of positive interpersonal connection with their therapist (33%). I also asked them what types of clients they used the technique with, and they said they used it with adults in individual therapy (89%), couples in joint sessions (44%), couples in separate sessions (33%), children in individual therapy (22%), and families within family therapy (33%).

I provide this data because I think it is helpful for us to have a realistic sense of what practicing therapists who have been exposed to the concept of relational savoring do with the knowledge they have: Some of them implement it with true fidelity in their practice (33%), but most of them take bits and pieces of it and apply it as they find it useful throughout their sessions. And this is why I am a realist about this; I recognize that therapists are creative, intelligent people who like to take the tools they have been taught and apply them intelligently to the specific person they are working with. My goal is to arm you with enough knowledge regarding the theory and ideas behind the technique that you can do just that. Take all of the knowledge you have gleaned, combine it with your own wisdom (from your many years of learning and practice) and your understanding of your specific client, and make your own decision about the best way to implement the intervention. Now go forth and be great!

WRAP-UP

In this chapter, I focused on taking this intervention, which was developed in the confines of a research laboratory, and helped you make it yours—or, more accurately, yours and your clients'. Once you have internalized the key tenets of the intervention, you can use it in the way you think makes the most sense for you and your client. This is where the scientist and the artist meet in the therapist—using the science in the way that flows most appropriately and fits within the interaction you are having with your client. It is an art (though perhaps something we can study with scientific methods). In my mind, this is akin to a theater director spending months teaching a student the technical aspects of a scene—making sure the student has mastered every precise aspect of blocking, rhythm, pitch, and tone. And then once the student has mastered all of these aspects of the scene, the teacher encourages them to let go of the nitty-gritty—to stop focusing on the steps, the timing, and the lines—and instead to focus their mind on how the character feels and to pour themselves out into the scene. The actor is supposed to make it theirs. In essence, the time has come for you to make this intervention yours.

8
ADAPTING RELATIONAL SAVORING FOR INDIVIDUALS WITH SPECIFIC MENTAL HEALTH CONCERNS

Adapting an intervention initially developed for use with community (i.e., nonclinical samples) to use with clinical samples requires careful consideration. The intervention must be intentionally adjusted to the unique needs of the population, with attention given to the framing of the intervention, who will deliver the intervention, and what type of support the clients receiving the intervention will need in order to obtain its benefits. Lack of attention to these details risks alienating the clients by delivering an intervention that fails to address their needs or, worse, violates them.

In my work, I have used this intervention with various populations with different mental health concerns, and each time I have started out working with a new population, I have become aware that it is extremely important to think carefully about the way in which the intervention must be adjusted for that population. These adjustments can be made in the context of research studies, the conclusions of which can be passed down to therapists, but therapists may also wish to take the central tenets of the intervention and modify it to clinical populations without an explicit evidence base in existence for that specific population. Note that if there were evidence that the intervention was

https://doi.org/10.1037/0000372-008
Relational Savoring: Using Guided Reflection to Strengthen Relationships and Improve Outcomes in Therapy, by J. L. Borelli
Copyright © 2024 by the American Psychological Association. All rights reserved.

contraindicated for a specific population, then it would not be wise to use it in that population, but the state of the current research literature is that there have not been enough studies with enough different clinical populations for us to ascertain whether it is efficacious in different clinical groups.

In this chapter, I discuss the general conclusions that have emerged from my research on relational savoring within populations at risk for mental health concerns. I offer some ways of thinking about the potential for using relational savoring within the context of working with clients at risk for psychopathology. I then discuss the specific conclusions that have emerged from the different populations with whom my team and I have worked. Note that the focus of this chapter is on working with clients in an individual therapy context, whereas in the next chapter, I focus on using relational savoring in a couples and family therapy context.

GENERAL TAKEAWAYS

Before diving into some lessons learned from working with specific clinical groups, I would like to pause to speak a bit about general takeaways from working with clinical populations, as opposed to working with community samples (non-treatment-seeking individuals) or individuals without psychopathology. Some of the lessons I describe will apply to the couples and families that seek therapy, as well as individuals who seek therapy for their own mental health concerns, so this is important to keep in mind as you digest the information.

Lesson 1: In General, Staying Focused on Positive Emotion Is More Challenging With Clinical Populations

In general, people with mental disorders have higher levels of distress and negative emotions than people without mental disorders, as well as lower levels of positive emotionality (Carl et al., 2013). If you think of some of the classic mental disorders, such as anxiety (Amstadter, 2008; D. C. Clark & Fawcett, 1987; Hofmann et al., 2012; Prenoveau et al., 2010; Srivastava et al., 2003), depression (Atherton et al., 2015; D. C. Clark & Fawcett, 1987; L. A. Clark & Watson, 1991; Gorwood, 2022; Hofmann et al., 2012; Prenoveau et al., 2010), obsessive–compulsive disorder (Abramovitch et al., 2014; Macy et al., 2013; Yap et al., 2018), personality disorders (Bland et al., 2004; Marissen et al., 2012; Verona et al., 2012), posttraumatic stress disorder (Frewen et al., 2012; Hopper et al., 2008; Kashdan et al., 2006; Litz et al., 2000; McLean & Foa, 2017; Schick et al., 2020), and schizophrenia (Blanchard et al., 1998;

Burbridge & Barch, 2007; Cho et al., 2017; Watson & Naragon-Gainey 2010), they are characterized by heightened levels of negative emotionality, as well as difficulty experiencing or expressing positive pleasure or joy (anhedonia). This basic fact that people with psychopathology have more negative emotion and/or less positive emotion to begin with makes it more challenging to do the work of savoring. If a client has a presentation in which either negative emotion predominates or positive emotion is scarce or difficult to activate, engaging in savoring is a challenge. However, it is likely more strongly indicated.

In fact, there may be a reciprocal relationship between low positive emotion (or low traitlike propensity for savoring) and psychopathology (Bryant, 2021), such that deficits in traitlike propensity for savoring increase the risk for the worsening of psychopathology (Raes et al., 2012; Raval et al., 2019). And when people increase their positive emotion through interventions, they also experience reductions in negative affectivity, such as depression (C. T. Taylor et al., 2017). The studies reviewed above pertained to general savoring (not relational savoring specifically), but in the realm of relational savoring, we found that people with higher depression produced lower quality relational savoring narratives (Borelli, Hong, et al., 2022).

Although this link between psychopathology and difficulty savoring may be discouraging, another way to look at this is that these individuals have further to go in terms of the benefits they can obtain from the act of engaging in savoring. If one of the goals of savoring is to improve one's emotional state (i.e., increase positive emotion and/or reduce negative emotion), then people who start out with few difficulties in terms of their mood and emotions have less to gain from this intervention, at least from the perspective of improving their emotional state, whereas individuals who struggle more in this domain can gain more.

However, the lack of positive emotion and/or relatively higher levels of negative emotion can make savoring more challenging for reasons I have articulated earlier in this book. It may mean that these individuals will have fewer memories at the ready that have positive emotional content in them, or that the memories, once recalled, will be difficult to sustain in their positivity. If positive emotion is more elusive, either because of anhedonia or because of the intrusion of negative emotion, then sustaining positive emotion during savoring may be more difficult and require the therapist to be more actively involved in the process.

Lesson 2: Clinical Populations Have Fewer Positive Relational Memories to Savor

Relatedly, people with mental disorders may be less likely to have positive interpersonal memories to draw upon for savoring than people who are not experiencing mental health difficulties. There are several potential reasons for this discrepancy. One is that people with mental health disorders may actually have fewer positive interpersonal experiences that occur in their daily lives. Mental health difficulties are associated with impairment in interpersonal behavior (Hartmann et al., 2010; Puschner et al., 2005; Salzer et al., 2011), including difficulty establishing and sustaining satisfying long-term relationships, as well as more conflict in interpersonal relationships (Braithwaite & Holt-Lunstad, 2017; Connolly et al., 2014; Whitton et al., 2013), and this can make it more difficult to have positive interactions to draw upon.

Further, difficulties with mood can also contribute to interactions that do not feel as satisfying, even if outside observers might perceive them to be as positive as those of people without mental health disorders (Assaad, 2016; Assaad & Lemay, 2018; Blais, 2020; Forgas et al., 1984; Schuster et al., 1990). For instance, if an individual is feeling down or depressed and has a positively valenced interaction with a colleague or friend, the interaction may not be perceived as positively in the moment or may not be imbued with as much relational significance.

Finally, even if the individual initially perceives the interaction positively (i.e., during the minutes or hours following the interaction), if they are contending with higher levels of emotional negativity, it may be difficult for them to hold onto that interaction in a positive way; the positivity and salience of that interaction may recede over time, especially if it is not congruent with their mood state or their internal working model of attachment. This is the primary motivation for doing the intervention in the first place, to enhance the salience of this type of memory and help the individual hold onto these memories so they become more salient and more strongly integrated into their identity and working model of relationships and themselves.

These factors mean that once again, the therapist may need to put in greater effort in order to retrieve memories from the client initially and then to ensure that the memories have sufficient relational content and positivity attached to them once activated.

Lesson 3: Clinical Populations Have More Life Stressors

To add insult to injury, people with mental health difficulties deal with more life stressors than those without, adding an additional layer of complexity to intervention delivery. They are more likely to deal with financial hardships (Padgett, 2007; Spivak et al., 2019; Uutela, 2010; Wilton, 2004), food insecurity (Heflin & Ziliak, 2008; A. D. Jones, 2017; Mangurian et al., 2013; Pourmotabbed et al., 2020), divorce (Breslau et al., 2011; Frank & Gertler, 1991; Kessler et al., 1998), legal difficulties (Osher & Thompson, 2020; Teplin, 1984), exposure to abuse and domestic violence (Howard et al., 2010; Ludermir et al., 2008), and exposure to racism and discrimination (Berry et al., 2021; Okazaki, 2009; Williams & Williams-Morris, 2000).

In addition to all of these difficulties, people with mental health disorders face stigma regarding their mental health issues (Ahmedani, 2011; Bharadwaj et al., 2017; Corrigan et al., 2014), which in and of itself can exact a significant toll (Rüsch et al., 2005; Sharac et al., 2010; Sickel et al., 2014). As if dealing with mental health concerns were not difficult enough, people with mental health concerns have additional burdens to bear.

What does this mean for this particular intervention? As therapists, we need to be sensitive to the fact that our clients who are contending with mental health difficulties are likely dealing with not only those difficulties but also potentially an array of other difficulties that come alongside their mental health problems. These additional difficulties can pile up on one another and make it difficult to focus on the psychological or emotional issues that we as therapists may want them to address.

Before working to engage a therapeutic target (for example, by doing a relational savoring exercise), we may need to ensure that our clients have the emotional bandwidth to do so. The intervention itself should relieve some stress and negative emotion, but we also must acknowledge that there may be some stressors or situations where the difficulties are too large to put aside. For example, if a client is in the middle of a legal difficulty, they may be unable to place this aside and be able to focus on a moment of safety and security in their relationship. This is similar to the idea I presented previously that clients cannot be fully immersed in a traumatic experience to savor effectively—they need some distance from the trauma to focus on the positive aspects of an experience.

The same can be said for clients who are in a state of chronic stress: If their stress levels are too high, they may not be able to pause and reflect in the way we are looking for. In this circumstance, it may behoove the therapist to pause and work on problem solving for the most pressing stressor or crisis situation. Once that situation has been handled or resolved (if that is possible), or the client has had some space to process the situation (if it is a situation where resolution is not possible), then the therapist may be able to return to the task of relational savoring.

Just as with the greater experience of negative emotion, the relatively higher exposure to additional life stressors means there may be more room for psychological experiences such as posttraumatic growth (Calhoun & Tedeschi, 2001; Tedeschi & Calhoun, 2004). Clients who have had greater adversity can also come back from this adversity and use it to make meaning from their experiences and deepen their understanding of their lives. So this doesn't necessarily have to be a net negative (in other words, something that will make the experience more challenging overall); when a client has had more negative life circumstances, their difficulties can give them a greater perspective on what really matters in their lives.

THE USE OF RELATIONAL SAVORING IN INDIVIDUAL INTERVENTIONS FOR INDIVIDUALS WITH MENTAL HEALTH CONCERNS

Relational savoring could be a useful component to an individual intervention program for clients dealing with a wide variety of mental health issues. As I discussed in Chapter 7, as with any other intervention, in developing a treatment plan for a client, it is most important to identify what their need is and then identify a treatment that addresses that need. In this chapter, I focus more on this concept in terms of its relevance for psychopathology specifically.

Thinking about the areas that relational savoring targets (emotion, connectedness to others, and disrupted sense of safety), there are several mental health conditions where these aspects of people's experience are disrupted. For instance, people with depression and persistent complex bereavement disorder suffer from disturbances in mood/emotion (Katzman & Papouchis, 2022; Park et al., 2019; Rottenberg et al., 2002) that could be targeted via relational savoring. There is a link between depression and social isolation. In older adults, the link is more robust for subjective than objective measures of social isolation (H. O. Taylor et al., 2018). In young adults, the link is stronger with loneliness than with social isolation (Matthews et al., 2016). In persistent complex bereavement disorder, social isolation can also be a risk factor for the onset or worsening of these conditions (De Stefano et al., 2021; Nakajima et al., 2012). Relational savoring could target social connectedness for these populations.

People with anxiety struggle with emotion dysregulation (Cannon & Weems, 2006; L. A. Clark & Watson, 1991; Suveg et al., 2010) and a disrupted sense of safety (Brosschot et al., 2016; Woody & Rachman, 1994). People with substance use disorders suffer from emotion regulation deficits (Cheetham et al., 2010; Di Pierro et al., 2015; Gold et al., 2020) and also difficulties with social connectedness (Choi & Smith, 2013; Copeland et al., 2018). Finally, people with personality disorders experience difficulties in emotion regulation, social connectedness, and safety (Chu, 1994; Herr et al., 2013; Holm & Severinsson, 2011; Katsakou & Pistrang, 2018; Liebke et al., 2018; Ooi et al., 2020; Salsman & Linehan, 2012).

In sum, there are many different mental health conditions that fall into this intersection of emotion, social connectedness, and safety, and this means that clients with a wide variety of concerns may benefit from this intervention.

The next step in selecting this intervention is to consider how relational savoring can be adapted to fit the treatment goals you have for your client. In the sections that follow, I describe the conclusions that emerged from working with three different populations as well as how my team and I modified the intervention to meet the population's needs. As the therapist, you might want to consider modifying one or more of the following: (a) the rationale you provide the client (personalizing this to their treatment goals), (b) the memory selection (specifically targeting memories that will achieve your treatment goals), and (c) the memory reflection (working to highlight certain aspects of the memory to underscore the points you want your client to focus on).

As an example of how you could tailor the savoring to your treatment goals, in the case of a client who is grieving, the therapist could frame the savoring to focus on memories of the person who has died if their goal is to heighten the client's feelings of closeness to what they have lost. Alternatively, if the client's chief complaint is feeling disconnected from the living, the therapist could shape the savoring to focus on memories with people in their daily lives. By repeating this exercise, the client may slowly experience an increase in feelings of closeness and positive emotion associated with specific relationships. They may also experience a reduction in feelings of loneliness, disconnection from others, and grief.

Clients who have posttraumatic stress disorder might be able to benefit from engaging in relational savoring to reestablish a sense of safety. Focusing on safety as experienced in relationships can build on existing strengths to heighten feelings of safety and security in the here and now. For instance, a client with a history of intimate partner violence could savor a time when they felt safe with their current partner in order to combat their feelings of violation and danger within intimate relationships.

This type of work can complement a trauma-focused cognitive behavior therapy approach (McDonagh et al., 2005) in which the client builds a trauma narrative; this work explicitly focuses on reliving the negative, terrifying aspects of the traumatic event. In this way, relational savoring can provide an antidote or complement to other forms of therapy, focusing on enhancing the memory network for experiences that contradict the traumatic experience (those in which the client feels safe, protected, and nurtured).

These are just two examples of how a therapist could adapt relational savoring to account for the client's specific mental health concerns, but in mentioning these examples my intention is not to single these out but rather to elucidate a process through which therapists can engage to more precisely target their client's symptoms.

Although I have examined relational savoring in the context of only a few forms of mental health concerns, I suspect it has relevance for many others. The next sections provide three examples of specific populations my research team and I have worked with to illustrate how relational savoring might be adapted for specific populations: parents of children with special needs, adults with eating disorders, and young adults at risk for schizophrenia spectrum disorders.

PARENTS OF CHILDREN WITH SPECIAL NEEDS

In this section, I discuss the adaptations the therapist may want to consider when working with parents of special needs children. At the outset, I would like to make it clear that although this adaptation focuses on parents, the work my colleagues and I have conducted with this population is intended to be administered in an individual therapy framework. This is in contrast to the focus of Chapter 9, where I will tackle relational savoring as it applies to relational systems, such as couples and families.

The target of the intervention is the parent of the special needs child. This is based on the assumption that parents of children with special needs face a unique set of challenges. These parents may have a very strong desire to connect with their children, but they also have additional difficulties in their relationship with their children. There are undoubtedly differences in every family and every parent–child relationship, including those with a special needs child. Yet, the relationship between a parent and a special needs child is somewhat atypical in that the child has a different way of perceiving information and relating to the world around them, one that may or may not be shared by the parent but is not typically shared by the broader world surrounding the child. These distinctions in information processing can (but don't have to) separate parents of special needs children from parents of typically developing children. Parents who feel separated from other parents can feel isolated, alienated from other parents, and even incompetent in their roles as parents.

As a case in point, parents of children with autism spectrum disorder (ASD) experience higher levels of stress (Phetrasuwan & Shandor Miles, 2009) and struggle with their feelings of competence in the parenting role; this is understandable given the challenges they experience as parents (Mohammadi et al., 2018, 2019). Given these additional challenges that parents of children with ASD face, exposing these parents to an intervention that seeks to explicitly promote parents' awareness of the positive impact they have on their children's lives is indicated.

We have conducted a couple of studies among parents of autistic children (Gaskin, 2021; Pereira et al., 2021); in this population, parents yearn for connection with their children. They may also struggle with feelings of rejection because how they may want to connect with their children may be quite different from how their child wishes to connect with them (Grey et al., 2021). As the parents tries to find a way to be in sync with their child (Dallos et al., 2022), these feelings of rejection and also frustration may rise. This dynamic can also create pain within the child, who may feel alone and alienated from and by their parent and environment.

And yet, for autistic children, developing a secure attachment with their caregiver is a strong predictor of psychosocial outcomes, including psychopathology, although limited work has been conducted on this topic (Rutgers et al., 2004; Teague et al., 2017, 2020). This means it is important for parents to find a way to be there for their children—to demonstrate consistency and responsiveness to their children's needs in ways that their children perceive as responsive (not necessarily the way that the parent perceives to be responsive).

The goal of conducting savoring with this population is to help them recognize the powerful and important role that they have in meeting their child's needs, even if it is not always easy to identify or recognize. Through engaging in relational savoring, we hope to help the parents feel pride in the moments when they have been able to meet their child's needs, even if those needs are expressed or acknowledged in subtle or nonintuitive ways.

As a therapist, and especially if one is a therapist who does not have children or does not have a special needs child, it is important to remember that to a certain extent, we all experience this in different ways in our relationships. We experience this when we realize that the people we interact with perceive the world in different ways than we do. We also experience this when we realize that the way in which we want to be treated differs from the way others want to be treated.

In some senses, this is akin to Gary Chapman's now canonical concept of five love languages (Chapman, 1992), the concept that each of us has a certain way we wish to be loved, and this may differ from those around us, but we all carry with us implicit assumptions that others are like us and wish to be treated like us. What is required to love and be loved is to appreciate that others do not share our implicit assumptions about love. Instead, we must have conversations that allow us to unearth others' preferences about love and share our own, and then love others as they wish to be loved. With respect to children with special needs or children with ASD, the situation may be slightly more extreme than this example because the way in which a parent wishes to provide love (e.g., by hugging the child) may actually offend or upset the child, which in turn can feel quite rejecting to the parent.

We have conducted studies with parents of children with ASD three times, twice delivering relational savoring in an online format (over the internet) and once delivering it in person. Even when delivering relational savoring online, which arguably is more challenging because there is not a live therapist there to help guide the parent's responses to the intervention, the parents often still have the desired response. For instance, when asked what their takeaways are about doing the intervention, parents respond by saying that thinking about the positive aspects of their memories is a welcome break from their typical thought patterns and that getting in this positive reflective mode helps them feel closer to their child and more relaxed. Let's hear Meg's response to the intervention:

> Doing this activity of focusing on the positive moments with my child breaks my typically negative thought pattern and makes me feel calmer, more relaxed, and less pressured. It enables me to change from my fear of a dismal future and be open to other possibilities.

And here is Janai's response to the intervention:

> It was nice to focus only on the positive aspects of the memory. I often go straight to what didn't go well or something along those lines rather than focusing only on the positive and it was a nice diversion for me. Made me feel closer to Ranya thinking about all the details.

Parents completing the online version of relational savoring for this population will also respond by saying that it provides opportunities to help them consider more optimal ways of responding to their children. Leilani, a mother in one of our studies, shares her reflection:

> This reflection process is wonderful for parents of ASD children. In most cases, we do not have time for self-care and positive reflection. This activity also helps us process what happens and how to respond better to our child. It puts us in a better mental state.

When we conducted the intervention in person, as we did in one of our studies, the responses we obtained were more elaborated. This likely occurred for a number of reasons: One of them is that parents spoke their responses rather than writing them (as they did in the online study), which freed them up to be more verbose and allowed their thoughts to come out faster. The second is that the therapist was there to scaffold and support their savoring and reflective practice, which ought to have resulted in richer savoring narratives.

One observation we had from conducting this study was that parents in the study tended to savor developmental milestones that their children had reached. It makes sense that these might be more likely to be savored among this population than among parents of neurotypical children, as it is more challenging for children with ASD to achieve these milestones (and thus, there is more to celebrate when they do). Especially when the developmental milestones pertain to social/interpersonal skills, these may be ripe for savoring. The excerpt I am going to show you now comes from Sofía, who was savoring the first time her child, Luca, said the word "mommy," as she answers the feeling reflection prompt:

SOFÍA: OK. I feel, I felt very happy, like excited happy, that's why I was tearing.

THERAPIST: Mm hm.

SOFÍA: 'Cause I was like, wow, my daughter is saying my name. Not my name, but saying *Mommy* and ran to me.

THERAPIST: Mm hm.

SOFÍA: So like I can feel like my heartbeat was like faster,

THERAPIST: Mm hm.

SOFÍA: 'Cause I was so excited.

THERAPIST: Yeah.

SOFÍA: And um, I don't know any other words to describe, but I was like extremely happy and surprised.

THERAPIST: Mm hm.

SOFÍA: Surprised too because I didn't expect this to happen.

THERAPIST: Mm hm.

SOFÍA: And I think the first thing I went to the car I sent my husband, message, I was like Luca said *Mommy* today and ran to me! [*Both laugh.*] You know I shared this information with him.

THERAPIST: Yeah.

SOFÍA: And then yeah I was just very happy, and um, yeah happy. Happy, excited, surprised, thankful.

THERAPIST: Yeah.

SOFÍA: Thankful yeah, yeah.

THERAPIST: Yeah yeah.

SOFÍA: [Laughs.]

THERAPIST: So you kind of said like your heart beating it feels like you kind of felt that mainly in your chest?

SOFÍA: Yeah.

THERAPIST: Yeah, yeah.

SOFÍA: I can feel 'cause the moment I bend down and I looked at her eyes, her eye contact is very good.

THERAPIST: Mm hm.

SOFÍA: 'Cause normally she has poor eye contact.

THERAPIST: Mm hm.

SOFÍA: But when she wants to make eye contact with you it very strong.

THERAPIST: Yeah.

SOFÍA: So I cherish every time she tries to make eye contact with me, mm hm, I'll make it fun and you know just try to cherish those moments.

This mother's narrative is teeming with pride and enthusiasm; her feelings are infectious, and even just reading it brings a smile to my face. She is so immersed in the positive emotion that the therapist barely has to do anything to promote this engagement, so fresh and resonant are her feelings. This positive connection is extremely important because parenting children with ASD can also be extremely challenging and can cause a great deal of stress (Davis & Carter, 2008; Hoffman et al., 2009; Phetrasuwan & Shandor Miles, 2009), so holding onto those positive moments and making the most of them may be even more important for these parents than for parents of neurotypical children.

Another theme that emerged in the narratives of mothers of children with ASD is a deep sense of meaning and a different type of meaning than that which emerges from the narratives of parents of neurotypical children. We heard parents discuss how their experiences parenting their children, difficult as they were, taught them something important about their lives, and sometimes about their purpose in the world, that was extremely instructive to them and helped to guide them along their path.

This reminds us that sometimes what can emerge from challenging life experiences is a renewed sense of purpose, a reason to give back to the world and to others. This is not news to people who have studied reactions to trauma; the literature on posttraumatic growth is devoted to understanding how people react positively in the face of difficult life events, making meaning from them and developing new purpose (Calhoun & Tedeschi, 2001). Interestingly, it is encouraging and moving that we observe some of those themes in the narratives of people who have struggled more. Here is an example of a mother, Barbara, completing relational savoring and exhibiting this type of pattern:

BARBARA: I mean definitely us continuing to you know make it together, I feel like we are always just we have each other um . . . I definitely feel like he's my saving grace um not that I was like doing bad before him but it's hard but it also is like having a purpose you know so I feel like um . . . our bond is important for both of us for both of our sake you know what I mean . . . and even though he's like my biggest difficulty in life he's also like my biggest motivation. So I know that as long as it's hard with him but as long as like each time I kind of pass a rough spot you know that motivates me to keep going and I just I feel like I have purpose like my life has completely changed like it's not what I thought it was going to be at all but sometimes I'm OK with that. You know? It's like this is what it is now and maybe this is what I was meant to be doing anyways you know? Because even in my career you know, my career goals have changed from what I want to do.

THERAPIST: OK, so there's been a lot of change.

BARBARA: I would love to like open up a day care for children like him, you know?

THERAPIST: Aw wow.

BARBARA: Because there-there's a need, there's a very big need.

THERAPIST: Yeah absolutely.

BARBARA: And that is something I never would have thought of before I had him.

In sum, different topics emerge from these parents' savoring than we observe among parents of neurotypical children. Although savoring may seem more challenging with this population, the rewards may also be greater. The themes that emerge when these parents savor experiences with their children are powerful and borne of their journey.

ADULTS WITH EATING DISORDERS

Eating disorders are notoriously difficult to treat and pose a significant public health threat: Estimates suggest that a large number of clients fail to respond to current treatments (Eddy et al., 2017; Monteleone et al., 2022). Further, 50% of clients with anorexia nervosa relapse 12 months following weight restoration (Frostad et al., 2022). These factors indicate the need for more efficacious treatments, ones that target underlying vulnerability factors, such as social connectedness and emotion regulation challenges (Grisset & Norvell, 1992; Lavender et al., 2014; Limbert, 2010; Linville et al., 2012; Peters & Fallon, 1994; Tiller et al., 1997). Attachment insecurity likely plays an important role in the development of eating disorders, with estimates suggesting between 70% and 100% of people with eating disorders are insecure in their attachment (Tasca et al., 2011). These factors combined suggest that in addition to other forms of treatment (e.g., cognitive behavior treatment, family systems treatment), individuals receiving intensive treatment for eating disorders might benefit from an adjunctive attachment-based intervention such as relational savoring that targets relational and affective concerns.

In collaboration with a national residential treatment facility (Center for Discovery), my team and I have also been conducting a study of relational savoring among adults with eating disorders for the past several years. With this study, as all the participants were adults, we offered them the opportunity to savor a moment in which they either provided or received care to/from another individual (secure base receipt/provision and safe haven receipt/provision savoring). The control condition in this study is personal savoring. The study has been slow moving and was interrupted by COVID-19, which prompted us to transition to a Zoom delivery platform. This study was very experimental in that I had never before conducted a savoring study with this population.

Data collection for this study is ongoing, so our findings are preliminary, but I am sharing them in the service of informing clinical care. In many ways, similar lessons that emerged from prior trials of relational savoring emerged from this study. First off, savoring had an overall positive impact in terms of the reports of the clients who experienced it. They reported that becoming more aware of their positive experiences was an overall benefit for them. First, we will hear from Lisette:

LISETTE: I just think it's cool to be aware of like the positive moments and like that's definitely something I've tried to implement being here.

THERAPIST: Mhm.

LISETTE: I mean I had a really rough week but like I could still pick out something you know and like before I wasn't able to do that. So it's cool being aware of like the positives and allowing myself to like go there.

As we have seen with other populations, within this population, relational savoring brought about strong themes of interpersonal connectedness, enhancing feelings of being cherished, loved, accepted, and close to others. The activation of these feelings is crucial within this population in particular, given the links between poor-quality relationships, absence of social connectedness, loneliness, and longing for closeness. For instance, this client, Ariella, reports feeling deeply loved and understood:

ARIELLA: I feel very, I felt very loved . . . this sense of course she's always been there.

THERAPIST: Mhm.

ARIELLA: She's always loved me. It just kind of reaffirms an affirmation of that right. Um yeah. And I'm always feeling very very grateful and blessed to have her.

THERAPIST: And what do you think about it now?

ARIELLA: I am actually feeling very grateful for talking to you now and not realizing that so many of those memories—I tend to focus on negative memories.

THERAPIST: Mhm.

ARIELLA: That's exactly probably the reason for this study and I'm now I am realizing how much gratitude it's bringing to me which I would think and then would help with my recovery. . . . Um and I guess my sister and I just kind of like get each other. Like we mm don't really have to like—I don't know. Talk.

THERAPIST: Mhm.

ARIELLA: Like I don't know catch up. We just—I don't know so it's very—I'm always calm around her and j—can just totally be myself. Hm. And be goofy and um yeah! So I just—I'm probably like the most comfortable with her.

THERAPIST: Mhm.

ARIELLA: And I just can—I don't know—be myself [*super quiet*].

Notably, Ariella expresses a great deal of gratitude for having had these experiences and this relationship, as well as the recognition that this exercise (relational savoring) might exist because of the gratitude she was experiencing as a result of having engaged in this practice.

Some clients commented on the emotions they felt in their bodies as a result of their connections with others, underscoring the broader point that relationships are regulating. Chandra says the following:

> And then once she got there and like I gave her a big hug and um everything. It was just kind of like calming 'cause she's just—I don't know. Just always kind of calms me down and I just feel really content when she's around.

This next client, Paulina, comments on the feelings of care that she experienced from her brother and then moves to the point of feeling pride as a result of the fact that she has this relationship, a relationship where someone cares enough to stand up for her in this way:

PAULINA: I could definitely feel that he really cared for me um and I was also I was like strangely proud, you know?

THERAPIST: Mhm.

PAULINA: That I had a brother that would like do anything to protect me.

THERAPIST: Mhm.

PAULINA: You know, that he would like literally like push this guy out of the way with his body like [laughs].

THERAPIST: Mhm.

PAULINA: Um so yeah I—I was really proud and I felt honored you know um that someone would like care enough to like do that.

THERAPIST: Mhm.

Some clients were able to gain some clarity on certain relationship situations that may be somewhat difficult for them to understand, or about which they have mixed or complicated emotions. For instance, clients may feel a mix of love/acceptance and rejection based on the behavior that the person exhibits or the fact that the person's behavior is inconsistent across contexts. In this study, we saw evidence of the clients working through their feelings related to and the meaning regarding these interactions during the savoring sessions, even though focusing on mixed emotions is not an explicit part of the intervention. It is as if focusing on the feelings of being loved and cared for helps the client to reconcile some of the difficult feelings they have regarding other experiences (such as feeling overlooked or rejected at times). Here is Juliette's perspective:

JULIETTE: But yeah, I just remember just like feeling so loved and cared for, like genuinely. I felt like my daddy loves me . . .

THERAPIST: What do you think of it now?

JULIETTE: I think it's good to remind myself that he does love me. Even if he doesn't always show it the way that I think he should or the way that I normally would understand love.

In terms of eating disorders specifically, the relational savoring exercise offered the clients an opportunity to not think about the topics that often preoccupy their thoughts and feelings—for instance, negative thoughts about their bodies, their disorder, or food (Ben-Tovim et al., 1989; Davidson & Wright, 2002; Ralph-Nearman et al., 2019). Some clients, like Kris, commented on this aspect of the intervention, stating that the intervention gave them a breather from focusing on eating- or body-related topics:

KRIS: Well because for a moment I wasn't even thinking about myself necessarily like I wasn't even thinking about my body or food.

THERAPIST: Mhm.

KRIS: Like I normally am. I was just thinking about how much I loved her.

Further, some clients experienced a growth in insight about their psychological symptoms during the savoring exercise. This client, Camille, found that focusing on the memory she savored made her feel safe, and she reflected that her eating disorder came from not having had enough of that feeling:

> I think it confirms what I think about like eating disorders and any disorder, and it's like—it just comes from a place of scarcity. . . . So, because it's um, because eating disorders it's about creating safety. Yeah, it's a like a safety net of when you feel unsafe in the world and so I think like that memory makes me feel safe.

Next, this client, Riley, experienced love in the relationship she is savoring, which in turn gives her the confidence to feel that she can manage the recovery process, armed with the confidence of this relationship:

RILEY: And um I felt such love for her for being so kind.

THERAPIST: Mhm.

RILEY: And um it made me feel like "I can do this." Um that I've got a good chance at recovery.

THERAPIST: Mhm.

RILEY: Um that I'm not alone.

This previous excerpt ties back to the sense of purpose we saw in the narratives of parents of children with ASD, where reflecting on moments of positive connection helps to increase the resolve that the clients have to pursue a goal, push through a problem, or help others. This final excerpt helps to drive this point home; here, the client, Daria, is focusing on her motivation to help others in her situation avoid the same struggle:

DARIA: Just taking the experience maybe and like helping other models like not get into like eating disorder um situations.

THERAPIST: Mhm.

DARIA: Regarding modeling, because I know that's a common misconception. However I do know that it exists a lot in um the modeling world.

Focusing on moments of positive connectedness can be quite powerful; it helps people come in contact with their strongest self, or the strongest parts of themselves, the part that wants to fight for what is right and for the way that the world should be.

YOUNG ADULTS AT GREATER RISK FOR SCHIZOPHRENIA SPECTRUM DISORDERS: INDIVIDUALS WITH HIGH LEVELS OF SOCIAL ANHEDONIA

Although on its face, risk for schizophrenia spectrum disorders might seem like a dramatically different clinical terrain from the two mental health concerns previously discussed, all of these conditions share a common risk for social disconnectedness. Schizophrenia spectrum disorders have a significant public health toll and are devastating for the individuals who experience them. Although the overall incidence of disease in the general population is low (McGrath, 2006; Sartorius et al., 1986), the rates of developing schizophrenia are significantly elevated among people with social anhedonia; one study (Kwapil et al., 2009) found that 24% of college students high in social anhedonia were ultimately diagnosed with a schizophrenia spectrum disorder within the next 10 years. Therefore, identifying interventions that can reduce risk is of the utmost importance; specifically, the development of interventions that prevent the conversion of social anhedonia into a more severe schizophrenia spectrum disorder is extremely important.

Whereas schizophrenia spectrum disorders were once considered to have a rapid onset, now the field has begun to adopt a developmental approach to the understanding of this class of disorders, looking for risk factors and underlying endophenotypes that can portend difficulties for individuals in the future (Broome et al., 2005). One of these underlying risk factors that has emerged in the literature is social anhedonia, which occurs when people have lower motivation to engage in social interactions and experience reduced pleasure when they do (Kwapil, 1998; Kwapil et al., 2008). In addition to this reduced need and motivation to engage, people with social anhedonia also experience what Thomas Kwapil and colleagues have termed a deficient need to belong (Kwapil et al., 2008, 2009; Silvia & Kwapil, 2011). People with social anhedonia report higher positive emotion and lower negative emotion when alone than when with other people (Kwapil et al., 2009).

Social anhedonia is different from social anxiety in that people with social anxiety do have a need to belong and worry about what others think of them; in contrast, people with social anhedonia feel less self-conscious in social interactions than people with social anxiety (L. H. Brown et al., 2007). Consistent with its conceptualization as a risk factor for psychosis, social anhedonia is a symptom of schizophrenia and schizotypy, and the strongest predictor of schizophrenia spectrum disorders (Gooding et al., 2005; Horan et al., 2011; Kwapil, 1998; Kwapil et al., 2008; Meehl, 2017). Importantly, social anhedonia is actually a transdiagnostic risk factor, as it is elevated among people with not only schizophrenia and related disorders but also ASD, eating disorders, and depression (Barkus & Badcock, 2019). As such, social anhedonia is an important target of interventions, as reducing social anhedonia holds promise in preventing not only psychosis spectrum/schizophrenia spectrum disorders but also a whole range of disorders.

This work has been conducted in collaboration with Dr. Elizabeth Martin, associate professor of psychological science at UC Irvine, and Jocelyn Lai, graduate student at UC Irvine. The central premise of our work is that relational savoring might be a useful intervention for people with social anhedonia. As a general rule, individuals with high social anhedonia find social interactions to be less rewarding and less motivating (Kwapil, 1998; Kwapil et al., 2008). We know that individuals with social anhedonia are at risk for poorer response to treatment and poorer prognosis (Ahmed et al., 2016; McCarthy et al., 2018; Tarbox-Berry et al., 2018); thus, we reasoned that finding ways to heighten people's social engagement and taking steps to reduce their social anhedonia might be helpful in reducing their risk for psychosis spectrum/schizophrenia spectrum disorders.

As a result, we have been conducting a study examining the efficacy of relational savoring with college students at high risk for psychosis (by virtue of being high in social anhedonia) for the past 4 years. This study has been slow going due to the difficulty of recruiting participants who meet clinical criteria for this study as well as disruptions from the COVID-19 pandemic. However, I am excited to share some of our preliminary findings here.

In general, with this population we found that the relational savoring intervention was a bit more difficult to complete, perhaps because the topic was less familiar to the population with whom we were working. The participants would sometimes act as though the questions we were asking did not make sense—as in, the very requests seemed off base (why would someone want to spend time thinking about positive interactions they had with others?). The memory selection phase sometimes involved the generation of memories that would not be suitable for this type of memory reflection task, so the therapists were left with only one memory that would work for the reflection task.

This information was helpful to receive because it can inform the way we develop the intervention in the future. For instance, perhaps we need to include a rationale or introductory statement to the intervention that will make more sense to this population. Providing a justification for why we are conducting an intervention that makes sense to the population we are working with is important in increasing buy-in. These findings led me to believe that prior to our next study with this population, it may be important to conduct focus groups with people with clinically significant levels of social anhedonia to better understand what justification or rationale would motivate them to reflect on their relationships. In the context of a research study, the financial compensation can sometimes provide ample motivation to complete tasks, but for this intervention to translate into a task that could work well for clients in the community, it is important for us to enhance our rationale. Another idea would be to add a brief module of motivational interviewing prior to engaging in relational savoring, something that helps to heighten clients' motivation to increase their positive engagement in and enjoyment of interpersonal interactions. These ideas are testable within the laboratory or clinical practice with clients who struggle with social anhedonia.

Another difficulty that emerged was that clients sometimes spent a great deal of time discussing the sensory or other details of the experience and very little time focusing on the relational aspects of the experience. This should be unsurprising given the difficulties of individuals high in social anhedonia. But given these difficulties in enjoying social relationships and interactions, it is still a triumph when we notice these clients embracing their memories of positive interactions with others with joy. Here is an example from Phil:

THERAPIST: Um so looking back at these various details of the event, I would like for you to notice how you felt at this time. What were you feeling at the time?

PHIL: I felt um some sort of excitement because, as I said, we hadn't seen each other in a long time and umm, it was like . . . yeah, just like excitement and happy.

THERAPIST: Nice, OK, so that sounds wonderful and recalling this enjoyable memory, now I would like for you to think about what you were thinking at the time the event, so, for example, were you thinking, "I feel close to these people or I'm having a great time"?

PHIL: Umm yeah definitely. Um, I, I distinctly remember how like, since they were my middle school friends and like it's been a, since we didn't go to school together for high school, I—I remember thinking how like, even though we've been apart for like. For our schools, we still like are like, pretty close together and I didn't feel like a sense of awkwardness when we're talking, even though we've been like apart.

THERAPIST: Yeah well, it's so nice that you're able to like, still connect with them, and you know. OK, uhm.

And every once in a while, we had the experience of conducting a session in which we hit the jackpot—that is, we created a situation in which the client would discuss an experience in which they discovered a relationship connection they were surprised to have found (or one they were surprised was as positive or enjoyable as it was). And this, in essence, is exactly what we were striving to do with our intervention: help these individuals discover hidden gems within their relationships. We wanted to help them discover that moments of connection could be more enjoyable than they originally anticipated, or they could be less effortful than they anticipated, or that when looking back on it, they found they carried more meaning or weight after all. Let me share an example of one of these sessions with you; here is Sergio's narrative:

THERAPIST: So I want you to really focus on these moments when you were with your friend and what made a difference for you. Um, and when—and the moments that you were really in sync in how you felt at those times. So during this memory did you notice any moments when you felt especially connected to-to her?

SERGIO: Umm . . . I felt um [*laughs*] we went—when we were on the um hippo trip, on the boat um, she sat next to me and she asked me if I wanted one day to go visit her. And then, she asked her kind of like, um I guess supervisor or the person that came with her, the adult, and she asked her if like, it was possible for her—for me to stay at her place because I guess, I think they were related or something like that or they were really really close so, I really felt that—mhm—she really did want me—she didn't—she really did want me as her friend because she even invited me to like, go visit her one day.

THERAPIST: OK, cool. Um and were there things that you wouldn't have been able to do without the confidence of knowing that your friend was there?

SERGIO: Umm. Um, during the project part of like the experience um, I'm not really a person who likes to um, like, talk in a public setting

216 • *Relational Savoring*

I get like, nervous. So, she was telling me how like—mhm—when she talks in public, she likes to not focus on like the people, but focus kind of on her hands and what she's doing because she feels like talking with your hands is a way to um, allow—allow your audience to know that you're like, that you're interested in the topic and that you're not kind of just blabbing. So, I think without that I would have not like been able to um, present with my group because, I was the only person in the group who spoke German, so and our audience was partly Ger-um they partly spoke German. So um, with that I was able to, get through it yeah.

THERAPIST: OK, nice! Do you have any thoughts now about this interaction?

SERGIO: Umm. I just think about the day and like um, about how like what if I was in her group? Like wha-what kind of difference would that wo—that would have made yeah.

In closing, I want to share that one of our participants, Mira, shared with us a message that is an important take-home point:

THERAPIST: Yeah so like if there's anything you'd like to say about the memory, or do you have like you know any takeaways after reflecting about it.

MIRA: I mean like umm, as you said in the beginning of how like it—it it may be hard sometimes to like recall back on like positive memories. I definitely feel that. And so, like during this like when I was thinking about it, I realized how like. How much I kind of like miss umm being with them and, like having fun.

This reflection that the process of looking back on positive memories can be difficult at first but in the end feels worth it may reveal an important insight about people at greater risk for schizophrenia spectrum disorders (by virtue of having high levels of social anhedonia) or about people in general: that sometimes it can be intimidating to engage in this process of reflection for many different reasons, but often when we do so, we find that what awaits us on the other side was worth pushing through the resistance for.

WRAP-UP

The central goal of this chapter was to provide insight into how my colleagues and I have used and adapted relational savoring for use with different clinical populations. These clinical populations differ in important ways but also have many commonalities in the way the clinician approaches working with them. By illustrating this process across three different clinical contexts, I sought to provide you with enough examples of adapting the intervention based on presenting problem that it becomes possible to envision engaging in this process in multiple different contexts. This is the ultimate goal I am building toward: being able to adapt this intervention to work with the individual sitting in front of you, your client. Next, we will turn to examining how we approach the situation when your client is a relational system.

9 RELATIONAL SAVORING IN COUPLES AND FAMILIES

When we say *relational* savoring, what do we mean? *Relational* can refer to any relationship that people choose to savor, but for many people, the relationships they want to savor are the relationships with their family members: relationships with partners, parents, and children. Unsurprisingly, this is where the majority of my research has been focused—on parents savoring their relationships with their children and partners savoring their relationships with one another. But of course there are other relationships out there to savor; people can savor relationships with roommates, neighbors, friends, mothers-in-law, professors, grocery store clerks, ministers, and therapists—the list goes on and on.

From a practice-oriented perspective, we may also wish to direct our clients to savor particular relationships with people with whom they are struggling in order to improve their connection with a person. For instance, let's imagine a father, Adam, who is seeking therapy for help with his relationship with his son, Harper. In this context, it is less likely that we would direct Adam to savor his relationship with his neighbors or grocery store clerks in order to improve his relationship with Harper, but we might wish to have

---

https://doi.org/10.1037/0000372-009
Relational Savoring: Using Guided Reflection to Strengthen Relationships and Improve Outcomes in Therapy, by J. L. Borelli
Copyright © 2024 by the American Psychological Association. All rights reserved.

Adam savor his relationships (any relationship) to improve his overall well-being or general feelings of security in relationships generally.

The theoretical model underpinning relational savoring holds that savoring any relationship that contains an element of attachment security in it (even if it is just the memory itself that contains some security) ought to strengthen one's overall mental representation of attachment security (Borelli, Smiley, et al., 2020). The researcher in me must mention that we have not extensively tested the assumption that relational savoring enhances attachment security (Wang et al., 2021). We do have support that relational savoring enhances relationship satisfaction and feelings of closeness, but our evidence that it increases attachment security is less developed. It is also unknown whether savoring a memory of an experience within the targeted relationship is a better route to strengthening one's sense of security within that relationship than savoring a memory outside of that relationship (i.e., if my goal is to strengthen the relationship between Partner A and Partner B, is it better to have Partner A savor a memory with Partner B or with someone who is not Partner B?).

Going back to this same father–son dyad, Adam and Harper, who's to say we would focus on Adam? Perhaps it would make more sense to start with Harper and to have him engage in the savoring. How do we know where to start? How do we know where to begin when working with families and couples? The purpose of this chapter is to provide a guiding framework for approaching relational savoring in working with relational systems. Because many of the issues discussed in this chapter pertain to both couples and families, I combine the discussion of these issues into one chapter, but when there are separate decision-making processes for different circumstances (as a function of family configurations), I signal this to be the case.

RELATIONAL SAVORING WITH SYSTEMS

As the therapist begins this kind of work with a family or couple client, the first set of questions to ask oneself is: (a) Who is the client? and (b) What is the therapeutic goal in this situation?

First, as many therapists ask themselves when working with families or couples, the therapist must ask themselves, who is the client? More specifically, who within this dyad, triad, or family needs to have their sense of security within the relationship strengthened? Whom do we identify as the target client? When working with multimember family systems (e.g., parent–child, partners, two parents and a child), the answer to this question may vary dramatically.

To begin to answer this question, let's start with the simplest example of a dyad: two adult partners. In this partnership, it could be the case that one member of the dyad needs a relationship security/closeness boost while the other does not (their sense of security within the relationship is thriving), or more commonly, it could be the case that both members of the relationship are struggling in terms of their sense of security. Figure 9.1 depicts these different relationship configurations. A true systems-oriented therapist would say that regardless of who is carrying the insecurity, the "client" is the system (the couple or the family, whoever is presenting for therapy). Similarly, regardless of who the couple or family identifies as the client, the therapist would identify the client as being the system. Having a solid case conceptualization regarding who carries the insecurity and why is important because it has implications for how the therapist directs their intervention.

It is also helpful to identify early in the work what the client is insecure about. Is the client insecure about the partner not caring about them or not desiring them? Are they feeling neglected by the partner? Or is the client feeling as if they have not been useful within the relationship, as if they do not have a role or a place within the relationship? Does that client have free-floating insecurity without known origin? I mention these different options because they may point toward the utility of focusing more on different types of savoring. Specifically, if the client is feeling insecure regarding the partner not paying attention to them or not caring about them, then savoring that focuses on the receipt of care (care-receiving savoring) may be most strongly indicated, as it may enhance the feelings of security that the client has in their feelings of being wanted, needed, appreciated, cherished, and loved by the partner.

FIGURE 9.1. Relationship Configurations That Inform Treatment Planning

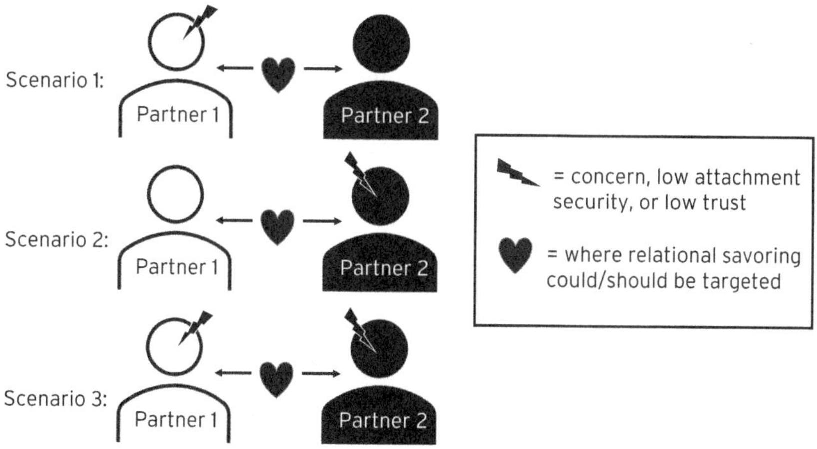

On the other hand, if the client is feeling the type of insecurity that stems from not being able to provide for the partner, not being able to give the partner what the partner wants, or not having been able to comfort the partner in the way that feels good to the partner, then using savoring that focuses on the provision of care might make the most sense (caregiving savoring). This type of savoring may enhance the client's feelings of being important, being useful, and having a crucial and irreplaceable caregiving role in the partner's life.

If the client has a sense of insecurity and is unable to place why they feel insecure, using all of the different forms of relational savoring may be helpful. This could function as an assessment tool (helping the therapist see what types of savoring are more challenging for the client, which could reveal areas where the client's insecurity is higher) and also as an intervention tool.

In Scenario 1, Partner 1 alone is struggling with their sense of security and trust in the relationship and could use a boost to this, whereas Partner 2 is feeling confident and secure in the security of the relationship. Scenario 2 is very similar to Scenario 1 except the person who holds the insecurity is reversed. In these two circumstances, the therapist can target their relational savoring focused on the insecure partner alone, target their relational savoring toward the other partner alone, or target relational savoring toward both partners. Let's consider the merits of all of these approaches.

First, let's consider the merits of targeting the relational savoring toward the insecure partner alone.[1] One benefit of focusing on the insecure person alone is that this individual will get a lot of dedicated focus within the therapy sessions, which might be indicated since they are the one who is overtly suffering at the current moment. The intervention could focus on helping them savor moments when their partner was there for them and successfully met their needs, which may reactivate memories of times when they felt secure in the relationship. Alternatively, if the therapist is not able to access memories with content that is as deep (in terms of its attachment focus), the savoring could focus on the pleasantness of being connected to the other person during a time when it felt safe to do so. As described previously, the savoring might focus on moments when they effectively met their partner's needs (if the situation has indicated that this is the most optimal approach for addressing the client's difficulties).

The therapist may also wish to have the other partner in Scenarios 1 and 2, whom I will refer to as the *unaffected partner*, engage in savoring. This savoring

---

[1]Note that I am using the term *insecure partner* as shorthand for ease of communication, but I do not mean to convey that this person is insecure in general; rather, I mean that this person is currently in an insecure frame of mind, which is the focus of the intervention the therapist seeks to make.

can be conducted in the presence of the insecure partner or without the insecure partner present. Either way, the goal should be to eventually introduce the material that has been generated or revealed during the savoring with the unaffected partner to the insecure partner.

The decision about whether to conduct the savoring "live" (i.e., with the insecure partner present) is a bit of a judgment call. The judgment call may depend on (a) the therapist's assessment of the current status of the relationship and also (b) the ability of the unaffected partner to generate memories that are going to be beneficial for the insecure partner to absorb/witness in an unfiltered, unprocessed way.

The first topic (current status of the relationship) pertains to whether the relationship can withstand the "rockiness" of the unaffected partner engaging in relational savoring in front of the insecure partner. I say "rockiness" because there is an unknown present in the process of engaging in the memory selection and memory reflection, and in some relationships that are particularly vulnerable or turbulent, or in some situations in which one partner is in a particularly insecure or vulnerable place, it may not be ideal to conduct the relational savoring in front of the insecure partner at first. It may instead make more sense to do some relational savoring work alone with the unaffected partner and then come back together again once the initial work has been done—that is, the therapist has done some initial sessions and generated some memories and reflected on those memories; then the unaffected partner or the therapist can share those memories with the insecure partner in a way that is more likely to evoke the type of response that is desired from the insecure client. At this juncture, the therapist can help the insecure client process their reaction to the experience.

Alternatively, if the insecure partner is more robust (i.e., less vulnerable) or the climate in the relationship is stronger, then the therapist may wish to conduct the relational savoring with the unaffected partner in front of the insecure partner. Doing so would expose the insecure partner to a wider range of positive memories—they would be able to hear their partner describe many different experiences with them—and also have a front-row seat to the raw, unfiltered emotional experience their partner has when they first access these memories and describe them, as opposed to the way they would describe them after they have accessed them and processed them once with the therapist. There is something really special about getting to hear someone access memories for the first time, and getting to be privy to that would be a really privileged experience for the insecure partner. So if the therapist believes that the insecure partner can handle this experience, this might be the way to go!

The second factor to consider in terms of making the decision about whether to conduct relational savoring "live" (*with both partners present*) or to do it behind closed doors with the unaffected partner *first* is the ability of the unaffected partner to select memories that are going to be beneficial for the insecure partner to absorb/witness in an unfiltered, unprocessed way. So, knowing the sensitivity of the insecure partner, will the unaffected partner be able to generate memories that avoid the landmines of the insecure partner? If the insecure partner is terribly insecure about the way they are perceived in the neighborhood, will the unaffected partner know to stay away from memories that contain content related to that? And beyond sensitivity related to specific topics, the therapist will want to consider the unaffected partner's overall level of sensitivity in discussing certain issues. Is this a partner who will need more coaching in how to describe things in a sensitive, loving, and accepting way, or is this a partner who will come out of the gate (i.e., without much coaching) with words of affirmation and support? Knowing your clients' interaction styles will help you make a judgment call about whether the raw data (so to speak) is something you actually do want your insecure client to be exposed to.

Next I will offer a detailed example to illustrate this reasoning.

GARY AND ROBERT: WHEN ONE PARTNER IS INSECURE

I had been working with Robert and Gary, a middle-aged gay couple, for several sessions. Their pattern had emerged such that Gary was quite insecure about the value he brought to the relationship. Robert was more outgoing and quite successful in his profession (an up-and-coming lawyer), while Gary was struggling to start his own accounting practice, which was not doing well at the moment, and also felt more uncertain about his interpersonal skills. In addition to not feeling particularly close to Robert, Gary also struggled because he did not feel that he contributed much to the relationship. He did not earn as much money as Robert, and he felt that he couldn't contribute as much to organizing their social life because he hadn't made as many connections in their community as Robert. In addition, he felt self-conscious about his physical appearance because he had put on 15 pounds since they had started dating. Although Robert insisted this did not affect his level of attraction to Gary, mentioning many features about Gary that he loved and adored, Gary was not convinced.

Gary's insecurity spilled over into the couple's sex life: Gary was far less likely to initiate sex, and when he did, he often regretted doing so because he was preoccupied with feelings of insecurity throughout. When Robert wanted to be intimate, Gary worried he wasn't living up to Robert's desires. And because they were not engaging in intimacy as often, Gary worried about neglecting Robert's physical needs, making him concerned that Robert might look elsewhere.

In reality, Robert felt annoyed that Gary was so focused on his insecurities and wished he would focus on the moment. He felt Gary had lost this carefree sense of just being together that they used to have, and he missed that. To compensate for this, Gary started smoking pot or drinking before they would have sex, but this created a different concern for Robert, which was that Gary would be reliant on substances to be able to be intimate with him.

My goal in working with this couple was to use relational savoring to help increase Gary's sense of security in the relationship; I wanted to help Gary feel important, valued, cherished, and accepted by Robert. It seemed this was an important ingredient that was missing in their relationship. Gary's insecurity was fueling a whole set of problems within the relationship, and this insecurity was like a thirst that was not being quenched by anything that Robert was providing. And I saw that Robert was trying to provide Gary with reassurance of his love, though the ways in which he was trying were backfiring.

I initially chose to tackle this goal by conducting relational savoring with Gary using *caregiving* relational savoring because Gary's central concern was that he did not have a useful role in the relationship. The first session I conducted without Robert present, largely because Gary was very tentative and insecure, so insecure that it was difficult for him to even speak about a time when he had felt accepted by Robert because it brought up so much vulnerability. My hunch (and I checked this hunch by asking Gary directly about this) was that this insecurity would be greater with Robert in the room.

At the outset of my treatment planning, I intended to bring Robert into the second session, but the first session was so challenging for Gary that I made a change and did the second session with Gary alone. Already by the second session, Gary had gained confidence and qualified his statements a lot less—for instance, instead of saying things like "I think I felt loved," he would say, "I felt really heard and understood." He was less tentative in the way he recalled these memories. After this session, I asked for Gary's permission to bring Robert back into the sessions with us, and Gary granted it.

When Robert returned to the session, Gary and I told Robert what we had been working on together and what Gary had learned about himself as a result of doing these exercises. We then did a relational savoring exercise together in front of Robert so that Robert could see what it felt like for Gary when we did it. I noticed that when Gary was sharing his memories, Robert kept trying to jump in to share his impressions of how Gary should have felt and to remind him of details he had forgotten about the memory. I intervened and reminded Robert that this was Gary's chance to share his perspective about the experience, saying that in this circumstance, Gary is the expert. This comment made an impression on Robert, and he realized that he needed to let Gary be the expert of his own experience, including his experience in the relationship.

In the end, Gary shared with Robert that this process made him aware of the fact that he feels really secure when Robert treats him in a certain way. Gary shared that he feels safe when he has an important role in Robert's life, one that nobody else can fill because it's unique to him. And that these feelings extend to other domains of his life, such as how he feels about his work and his body. Robert expressed the strong desire to make Gary feel loved, valued, and secure, saying how important this was to him. And he heard from Gary how important it was to make him aware of how he is unique and special.

At that point we decided that Gary was going to continue working on the relational savoring on his own at home because he felt he had mastered the technique to the point where he could do it on his own. And we also decided that I would begin some work with Robert to help him share some of his memories of times when Gary was really there for him (*care-receiving* relational savoring). My thought was that this would complement the work I had already done with Gary because it would provide collateral data from Robert's perspective about the role Gary was filling in his life. Gary might be able to guess about the positive impact he had on Robert, but hearing Robert actually talk about it was a whole different ballgame.

I was a bit torn about whether to have Robert engage in the relational savoring "live" with Gary. I thought that their relationship was in a pretty good place; they did not have a lot of conflict (i.e., no yelling or domestic violence), there had not been any infidelity in the relationship, and they had relatively few stressors in their lives (e.g., they were financially stable and both had jobs). But I was concerned about Gary's relatively high level of insecurity; it seemed there were quite a few landmines that could be triggered. Further, I was concerned about some of the nonchalance that Robert had exhibited in his discussion about certain topics, particularly in the domain of body-related issues and sexuality. Robert had previously been a fitness guru and was very muscular and trim, which I had guessed was quite challenging for Gary. I wondered whether this contributed to part of his difficulty in imagining the feelings that Gary had in navigating the world as a person who did not have that body type. At any rate, Robert's lack of sensitivity to Gary's feelings about his body made me a bit nervous about having him do the relational savoring live, so I elected to do some individual sessions with him first.

As it turned out, Robert turned out to be an excellent first-time savorer. It is also possible that this session went so well because both Robert and I were ultra-relaxed as it was just the two of us. At the outset of the session, Robert made a comment about feeling nervous all the time when he is around Gary because he doesn't want to inadvertently hurt Gary's feelings or make him feel "less than." This comment made me think that the decision to work individually with Robert at first was a sound one.

In the savoring session, Robert focused on one time earlier in their relationship when he was struggling with a work challenge (feeling unprepared for a presentation) and Gary really went the extra mile and helped him prepare and feel more confident; Gary helped him get materials together, helped him rehearse, talked him down from feeling so anxious, and then got up early the next morning and brought home bagels and coffee to give him a fresh start. Robert was so grateful for Gary's support and really felt Gary was behind him; having his support meant the world to him, especially at this time in his career, when he was just starting out and trying to make a name for himself. He shared that he really felt he owed a lot of his successes to Gary.

After the success of this initial session, which went so smoothly and contained no hints of anything I was concerned would be activating to Gary, I suggested we consider reuniting with Gary in the next session and sharing some of this work with Gary. Robert was amenable to the idea based on my recommendation, so we followed this plan. When Robert shared this memory with Gary, Gary wept for the first time in our work together. He said that he had forgotten about that time but that he remembered it fondly and loved feeling a part of Robert's team in that way. And then Robert was able to say things like "You are a part of my team. You've always been a part of my team." I ended up asking Robert to continue to share memories of this kind to Gary on a regular basis to help remind Gary of the important role that he has in Robert's life, and especially to share his perspective on this role. We continued our work together for a while with this emphasis of really trying to underscore the importance of Gary in Robert's life as a way of increasing Gary's emotional security in the relationship.

In this case example, I made two decisions that are worth commenting on. I chose to do individual sessions initially with Gary (Decision 1) and with Robert (Decision 2). I chose to do this with both Gary and Robert for more or less the same reason: Gary's insecurity (real and perceived). We then had joint sessions in which each partner shared what they had savored.

Another strategy I sometimes use in joint sessions is bringing in audio or videorecording (with client permission, of course) for the individual sessions and then using them if they end up including data that are usable. The data must be unlikely to set off client landmines or negatively affect the goal of the intervention in any other way. Of course, as a therapist, you do not know this ahead of time, so I never make promises or comments about the recordings until after the session. We can always use a recap by the client or a therapist-assisted recap instead of a recording if that is a therapeutically indicated choice.

In comparison to the case of Robert and Gary, sometimes both members are contending with their own issues of insecurity. This almost always points in the direction of conducting individual sessions with each member of the couple before bringing them together to share the insights that were revealed during the savoring sessions. The reason for this is precisely what I described above: It is unlikely that the conditions have been met under which it is advisable to bring the savoring of one member into the room without having had a preview of what this might look like beforehand. Once the therapist has had a preview of what this looks like with a particular client, and if they have deemed this to be a safe therapeutic exercise (by which I mean it is not likely to raise the insecurities of the other client) as well as likely to be productive therapeutically (as in likely to achieve the goals of the therapy, which is increasing the security and closeness of one or both members of the couple), then the therapist can make the decision to conduct these sessions in vivo.

MAX AND REBECCA: WHEN BOTH PARTNERS ARE INSECURE

Next I am going to present a case of a couple in which both members of the dyad struggle with insecurity. This is a heterosexual middle-aged couple, Max and Rebecca. They have three children and have been together for many years. Max works as a successful business executive, and Rebecca does not work. Two central tensions in the relationship are that Rebecca feels that Max is not attracted to her, and Max feels that Rebecca does not give him credit for the stability and effort he brings to their lives.

Both contend with high levels of attachment insecurity. Rebecca has threatened to leave Max on multiple occasions and has developed feelings for other men at various times, which she has pursued. Her infidelity contributes to the insecurity that Max feels. Rebecca does not feel adequately noticed and appreciated by Max in other ways, which contributes to her seeking the attention of other men. The couple also struggle in their parenting and coparenting relationship, but for the moment we are going to focus on their relationship as a couple. Because neither of them feels appreciated or seen in their relationship, their therapist uses *care-receiving* relational savoring for both of them.

We will visit them in their therapy session with their therapist, Gloria, who elected to meet with each client individually first, as part of her ongoing work with them as a couple. Gloria conducted the sessions individually for the reasons described above, with the intention of bringing them back together to then share the results of the savoring with the other member of the couple. She began her work with Max.

Max's Individual Relational Savoring Session

THERAPIST: So for the next few minutes, I'm going to help you come up with a memory of a time when you felt extremely close, connected, or in sync with Rebecca. I am especially interested in hearing about a time when you needed Rebecca and Rebecca was really there for you. It may also be a time when Rebecca's support allowed you to do something you might not have been able to do otherwise. This can be a time when you felt especially cherished, protected, accepted, or loved by Rebecca in a way that you would like to hold on to. Feel free to choose something you felt as a milestone or something simple that happens on a daily basis. So what I'd like for you to do is try to come up with some memories and then I'll help you decide which one to focus on for the next part of the activity. Some people can think of just one, and some people can think of several, and it really doesn't matter how many he can think of. We're just gonna be brainstorming together. So can you tell me this time when you felt this?

MAX: I mean a—I mean, last night, I—so—we were watching, we were watching a show last night and I—we were lying in bed, and we were—I guess we were watching the first episode of a reboot show that came out of [TV network].

THERAPIST: Mmhm.

MAX: Um, in the first episode, um, I mean, I don't know if you seen it, and I don't mean to spoil it for you but I don't know how to tell the story without doing it.

THERAPIST: That's OK.

MAX: Um, you know, the main character's husband dies of a heart attack, um, on the first episode, and I don't know it really—it just really, like drove home, you know, my mother's death.

THERAPIST: Hmm.

MAX: And it was like, in that moment, it was like pretty upsetting to me, um, and, you know and—and, you know, Rebecca was like—I told her that I was upset and she was like very, um, she embraced me, and she hugged me, um. And we had like—I think I fell asleep with her holding me last night. And it was very—um, she was very comforting and I don't know, it felt like we had a really warm embrace. And I kind of like, fell asleep with her, you know—wrapped around me. Um, that was very recent. Yeah, that was last night.

THERAPIST: Wow.

MAX: I felt very supported by her in that moment.

THERAPIST: Absolutely, it sounds like a really beautiful moment. Yeah, if you want to brainstorm a few more, we could. I also think that one is really beautiful so we could definitely just move forward with that one. OK. OK, um, so, what I'd like for you to do now is um, we're gonna kind of spend some time thinking about the memory, um, and what I want you to really do is focus on the positive aspects of the event so I really want you to focus on, you know, this specific kind of moment of when Rebecca was there for you, right? And she was holding you and you were about to fall asleep in her arms you felt super comforted and supported. And if your mind kind of seems that it wants to go in the direction of the negative just gently bring it back to the positive aspects. So I want you to bring this memory to mind and it's great that it was last night, uh, and I want you to recall all of the details of the experience. So, where were you? What were you wearing? What was Rebecca wearing? What was the air like? What smells did you notice? What was the temperature like? What happened in that moment that made it special? What did you or, um, what did Rebecca say or do? And what did you say or do? And what about the connection between you and your partner allowed that special moment to happen?

MAX: Uh, wh—, I don't I don't remember any negative feelings. Um, at the moment.

THERAPIST: Do you remember what the air was like? What you were wearing? What she was wearing?

MAX:	We were in bed, so we were dressed for bed.
THERAPIST:	Um hum. OK.
MAX:	We were under the sheets, and I—I don't remember it smells or I don't—I don't remember any sense of temperature although I—uh, I was physically comfortable, as far as I can remember.
THERAPIST:	Wonderful. OK and uh, so you guys are both wearing pajamas?
MAX:	No, I was just wearing, I usually just wear a T-shirt, a white T-shirt, and boxer briefs to bed. That's normally how I dress for bed.
THERAPIST:	OK.
MAX:	No pajamas.
THERAPIST:	OK, and, but you were both wearing clothes for bed? OK.
MAX:	Yes.
THERAPIST:	Perfect. OK. Wh—What happened in the moment that made it so special? What did Rebecca say or do?
MAX:	She, well, she didn't understand why I was so upset at first, and then I just told her that I—it just—I mean, that I guess, I guess this is a negative aspect of it right, like, when I saw that scene, I, um, you know, it just occurred to me, like, just thinking about you know my you know how my mother died. How my mother died.
THERAPIST:	OK, perfect, OK what happened in the moment that made it so special, like what did Rebecca say or do?
MAX:	She . . . well . . . she didn't understand why I seemed so upset at first and I just told her, that it kind of, this, I mean, I guess, I—I guess, it's I mean I guess this is a negative aspect of it right like when I saw that scene you know, I, it just occurred to me like just thinking about you know my you know how my mother died
THERAPIST:	Um hum [*softly*].
MAX:	It's just, it's just, I mean I don't have a specific memory about how my mother died there because I wasn't there, but you know I've obviously heard from my father what happened. Um, and you know, she—she had a heart attack on the couch right beside him.
THERAPIST:	Aw [*softly*].
MAX:	Um, and that was the last time my father saw her alive.

THERAPIST: Wow [*softly*].

MAX: And you know, was, it was it was very upsetting memory that kind of just like, thought.

THERAPIST: Um hum.

MAX: And Rebecca saw that I was upset and I told her like why. And I don't know why, I don't usually have like, I mean, I mean, what was weird about that is that I feel it's actually one of the strongest reactions I've had. I don't know, like, and, it was very upsetting and Rebecca knew I was sad and she asked what was wrong and I told her. And she just, like she just rolled over and embraced me and I turned on my side and she was just spooning me.

THERAPIST: Aw. Yeah. Wow. So she was really, you know, there for you in that moment and she was able to see that you were you were upset and able to hear why and then to just show up for you and be there with you.

MAX: Yeah. Yeah that's really beautiful.

THERAPIST: Um, I guess one thing I wanna do next is like turn your attention to how you felt at that time. So what kinds of things were you feeling in your body when Rebecca was holding you and spooning you, were you feeling—

MAX: I was there, I was very like I don't know like I actually had some good, I was I got I—I felt like I don't know I actually felt, like for a few minutes there, I almost felt short of breath.

THERAPIST: Hmm.

MAX: And like, just, very, very physically uncomfortable.

THERAPIST: Um hmm.

MAX: And, and I think what I was feeling in that moment was like maybe this sort of like, empathy for what my dad must have been going through.

THERAPIST: Hmm.

MAX: In those minutes as he just kind of like feeling that very viscerally.

THERAPIST: Wow.

MAX: And it was a very, very upsetting feeling this and there was, I guess, something about watching that scene of the show, that kind of just like really made me sort of like, think about, like how, upsetting.

THERAPIST: Uh hmm.

MAX: You know or how traumatic that must have been for my father.

THERAPIST: Um hmm. Absolutely.

MAX: Right, I guess, I guess I was just like really feeling that viscerally and I felt very physically bad, like a tightness in my chest, having a hard time breathing.

THERAPIST: Totally.

MAX: So I had a very intense response to it.

THERAPIST: What were you feeling though when Rebecca was holding you because I'm curious like, I'm wondering how it was to feel like she was showing up for you? And that she cared for you and supported you? And I, I want you to kind of think about where in your body you felt those specific emotions and I want you to try to feel them again.

MAX: Well, I felt the warmth of her body.

THERAPIST: Hm hum.

MAX: I felt . . . well . . . I actually, I guess, like I mean there was a there was like a moment where I felt you know I was also thinking about, you know, I, I, was actually thinking too I was like what if something like that happened with us. Um, between Rebecca and I. And I, I guess there was that as well. I guess in that moment I was just trying to like, you know . . . I was almost sort of like simultaneously happy that we were just like there together.

THERAPIST: Aw, where did you feel that happiness?

MAX: Uh.

THERAPIST: In your body?

MAX: I don't know. Maybe like all over.

THERAPIST: Yeah.

MAX: Um.

THERAPIST: That's really nice. After just feeling these really intense emotions—the shortness of breath and, and dealing with this, these are really negative and difficult thoughts of the loss of your mother and then to have Rebecca right there . . . comforting you and holding you and being able to kind of you know show up and soothe those negative emotions that you were feeling. Uh, that's really beautiful. Oh. Yeah. Try to recall, you know we kind of already touched on this but I want you to try to recall the thoughts you were having at the time when Rebecca was holding you, specifically in that moment when she was spooning you and maybe right before you fell asleep. For example, were you thinking, "I really need Rebecca right now"? "Rebecca is really here for me"? Or were you thinking, "I feel so close to Rebecca at this moment"? "I feel comfortable relying on Rebecca"? And I want you to take a moment to reflect upon what your thoughts are about the memory now.

MAX: I felt very grateful that she was there with me.

THERAPIST: Aw, I bet.

MAX: It felt good. I mean . . . I . . . I mean . . . I was . . . I was definitely like savoring the moment, was like, like feeling her body against mine.

THERAPIST: Um hm.

MAX: And, and knowing that she was there and that she that she cared and . . .

THERAPIST: Yeah, absolutely . . . that sounds really nice that you were able to experience that. Finally I want you to turn your focus to the future I want you to focus on how close you felt to Rebecca at that time when this memory occurred and I want you to kind of consider how, how will the bond that you have together affect your relationship in the future. So like what positive things could you imagine happening as a result of your bond to one another. In order . . . yeah . . .

MAX: Honestly, my—my mind was drifting into the memory, sorry.

THERAPIST: No, no, no, it's OK. Yeah, yeah, yeah. So I want you to turn your focus to the future so focus on how close you felt to Rebecca at the time this memory occurred and how will the bond that you have together affect your relationship in the future? What positive things can you imagine happening as a result of your bond to one another?

MAX: I hope that my biggest hope is that you know the strengthening of our bond will . . . you know leave a more positive legacy for our children . . . um.

THERAPIST: Wow, that's beautiful.

MAX: You know, I—I think that, you know, I hope that . . . we continue to build on the progress that we've already had. And, and I hope to make many more positive memories.

THERAPIST: Absolutely, I mean that's wonderful, it's wonderful that you guys could share like this and I love what you're saying about it having a positive effect on your family as a whole. Yeah, wonderful. Thank you. Yeah. I'm just curious, how was that for you?

MAX: Well, I guess it's good, I mean, it re—it definitely reminds me of the bond that we have. That has survived throughout this tumult-, tumalt-, tulmatu-. Sorry.

THERAPIST: [*Giggles.*]

MAX: Um, my fatigue is showing.

THERAPIST: Aw, OK. Yeah, I appreciate.

MAX: Um.

THERAPIST: You doing this.

MAX: But . . . and uh . . . yeah . . . I mean . . . I mean moments like that, do, you know, remind me of why I'm fighting so hard for us.

THERAPIST: Absolutely, you guys are working so hard and it's it's really beautiful, you guys are progressing like this and like you guys are getting to like this is part of like this is why people get married right like you want to have somebody on your team like through the hard times and this was a really tough time when you lost your you know and to be reminded of that and, and then to have to feel all of that and then to think of like to put yourself in your father's shoes, right? I mean that's a really . . . emotionally taxing experience and it's beautiful that Rebecca was able to show up for you . . .

MAX: She was.

THERAPIST: And exactly—and it seems like, in the way that you needed.

MAX: Hm hum.

236 • *Relational Savoring*

THERAPIST: And the fact that you were able to fall asleep with her is just really beautiful.

MAX: Yeah.

THERAPIST: Awesome.

MAX: I agree.

As it turns out, although this session was primarily about Rebecca being emotionally supportive of Max, it also contained elements of physical and sexual intimacy, which would undoubtedly help to increase Rebecca's feelings of security given her aforementioned insecurity regarding Max's feelings for her sexually. Further, the memory overall was about the important role that Rebecca played in Max's life, which allowed Max to feel supported in this moment as he experienced a moment of grief, and how cognizant Max was about the connection they had despite the difficulties they experienced together. Working with two members of a couple using this technique can help address both members' concerns in tandem.

Now let's take a look at Rebecca's session with Gloria.

Rebecca's Individual Relational Savoring Session

THERAPIST: OK, so I'm going to help you come up with a memory of a time when you felt extremely connected, close, or in sync with Max. I'm especially interested in hearing about a time when you needed Max, and Max was really there for you. It may also be a time when Max's support allowed you to do something that you might not have been able to do otherwise. This can be a time when you felt especially cherished, protected, accepted, or loved by Max in a way that you would really like to hold on to. Feel free to choose something that you felt was a milestone or something simple that happens on a daily basis. What I'd like for you to do is to try come up with some memories and then I'll help you decide which one to focus on moving forward. So some people can think of just one and some people can think of several and it really doesn't matter how many you think of, we're just going to be brainstorming together. Uh, so can you tell me of a time when you felt this way with Max?

REBECCA: Ummmm, yes, is it better how brazen it is? 'Cause for some reason I, my mind had went to, probably 'cause I was already thinking about ummm, you know, feeling kinda anxious lately ummm it reminded me of a long time ago when Max and I you know first started dating umm.

THERAPIST: Mmmhmm.

REBECCA: Or, it was within that first year, it was still like when we first started dating 'cause I think we were you know already emotionally closer umm so maybe it was later than a year but anyway ummm. When I—I still had really bad umm social phobia and so I was having a lot of anxiety about going to my class because for some reason that's the way it it expressed it was very specific to like my college class, uhh.

THERAPIST: OK.

REBECCA: Umm, like a like lecture umm and so he so Max basically drove me there and just like sat with me in the car and talked with me and kind of like calmed me down so that I can go into my class.

THERAPIST: Awwww.

REBECCA: Umm yea [*inaudible*].

THERAPIST: That's really nice.

REBECCA: [*Laughs.*]

THERAPIST: That's so sweet. Yeah.

REBECCA: Yeah.

THERAPIST: Umm yeah, that's a great that's a really great memory, umm I think that like ideally umm if we can brainstorm a little bit more and try to think about something that was in the past two weeks that would be great umm but that was like, that kind of content that was beautiful. Umm.

REBECCA: OK, yeah, Uhhh hmm. The last two weeks uhhh [*24-second pause*]. I mean yeah I don't know, well. I don't know like how what am I trying to say [*laughs*]. I means it's like little things, I guess, but I don't know how big they need to be I mean I guess like you know, you have this you have this morning umm like I—actually I wasn't I didn't I didn't get stu—[*laughs*] good thing this is anonymous I didn't get stuck on the toilet picking [idiosyncratic term client uses to refer to picking skin while on the toilet]. This time it was picking that was good at least umm but I did basically like I was like super anxious this morning and I was just like sitting on the toilet but then like I was just you know mindlessly doing whatever on my phone and then I realized I was just still sitting on the toilet for like an hour later umm and then Max texted me and was like, oh umm, "where are you?" or whatever and then when I told him like I texted him I totally told him through text back I actually was worried he was actually going to be kind of judgmental and he wasn't at all.

THERAPIST: Umhmm.

REBECCA: And like I told him the truth that I was feeling really anxious for some reason umm and I was kinda like stuck in the bathroom but actually like just the fact that he texted me asking where I was and then also said something something empathetic where I like I'm started feeling really anxious or something like that like just that was enough to kind of like break me out of the stuck there and like I was able to get up and move on so.

THERAPIST [*quietly*]: Wow.

REBECCA: So that just happened this morning [*laughs*].

THERAPIST: Rebecca, that's wonderful, I mean that's like a beautiful like I mean like how wonderful right that he was able you know that fear of that he could've been judgmental right umm and instead he came to you right like in this very appropriate way like a way that you really needed and and he was really able kind of like meet your needs in that moment.

REBECCA: Yeah.

THERAPIST: Yeah, ummm that's a great, and that's like spot on like what we're looking for so umm yeah do you want to think of maybe one more.

REBECCA: Yeah, umm I have a horrible short-term memory [*laughs*] so in the last two weeks is hard.

THERAPIST: I—I know this is like the hardest part, just so you know [*laughs*] umm yeah.

REBECCA: So wait, tell me again what exactly I am supposed to be thinking of so a time when we—when I felt close to him or supported or . . .

THERAPIST:	Yeah, maybe he helped you see things in a new way umm maybe you did something that you wouldn't have been able to do without the confidence of knowing that he were there. Umm, times in which you felt like accepted or loved, cherished, protected umm even like in sync close connected, and it doesn't have to be big. It doesn't have to be a milestone, it can be something simple that happens such as you feel good when it happens but it can be it can be whatever.
REBECCA:	For some reason now, my mind is going a little bit negative; now I'm like remembering other things as I'm trying to think about this umm.
THERAPIST:	Oh OK, totally natural. Yeah, that's really hard I think like umm it's kind of like that activity we did where we think about the good parts but then it also can be kind of challenging to stay focused on the positive parts. Mmhmm.
REBECCA:	'Cause sad parts come up too.
THERAPIST:	Umm [*29-second pause*].
REBECCA:	I don't know, I just can't I don't know what counts and what doesn't. I mean I don't know I guess this is kinda well . . .
THERAPIST:	You're feeling unsure about a memory.
REBECCA:	Yeah I guess like yesterday night umm . . . I was also just feeling really overtired and anxious.
THERAPIST:	Ummhmm.
REBECCA:	And then yeah I don't know if this is kinda you know counts for what we're doing but I guess like he made me feel better because again like I thought maybe he was gonna be upset that like you know we were gonna watch a show, but then I was like well I'm too tired umm and then he he kind of didn't like pressure it. He—he just didn't push it he kind of just umm was like oh I acknowledge that you're upset or that you're anxious and that you're not feeling that well. So I—I really like to have my back rubbed 'cause like I used to when I when we were kids like our mom would sometimes do it or sometime we would like rub each other's back. My sister and I so sometimes Max will do that so like he just did that instead so I—so I felt really I was like safe and just like you know again was like not like judgmental and was accepting that I wasn't doing that well.

THERAPIST: Wow, that's a really great memory too. Those are both I mean all three of these are great, ummm yeah umm. Yeah, I think really any of them would be great. The last two I think are are really nice because they're so recent. Umm, I guess is there is there one of those last two that you feel you would rather focus on—what we're going to be doing is reexperiencing the positive aspects of like that moment when Max like showed up for you so it would either be when he texted you and in a nonjudgmental way or when he showed up and was like accepting of you and then kind of uhh was able to rub your back and-and spend time with you in that way?

REBECCA: Yeah. We'll use the second one then.

THERAPIST: Yeah OK. Umm yeah I think that one's really sweet. I like that one a lot. OK, umm wonderful OK so we'll do that one and then umm so umm I really want you to focus umm on this memory and we're gonna do this together so I want you to bring the memory to mind umm when you are feeling calm and you are able to deeply relax um I want us to both deeply reflect on this together. Umm and so first I want us to recall all the details of the event. So where were you, what were you wearing, what was Max wearing, what was the air like, what smells did you notice, what was the temperature like? What happened in that moment that made it so special, what did Max say or do, what did you say or do, and what about the connection between you and Max allowed that special moment to happen? And I'll remind you of these so don't feel like you have to like you have to answer all of them but umm yeah just to give you an overview.

REBECCA: Yes [laughs]. Yes [laughs], I have horrible memory. Umm OK umm so hmmm I'm like what was I wea—What we were each wearing he was probably wearing underwear and a T-shirt and I was probably wearing I was also wearing underwear and one of his T-shirts 'cause I sleep in his T-shirts [laughs; inaudible].

THERAPIST: Aww cute.

REBECCA: Kind of like built-in nighties umm.

THERAPIST: [Laughs.]

REBECCA: Yeah so yeah that's what we were wearing and I don't know what it smelled like probably smelled fine because the sheets were pretty clean and the dogs weren't there [laughs] so it smelled fine.

THERAPIST: [*Laughs.*] Nice.

REBECCA: Umm actually the kitty may have come to visit us, she likes to visit us at night.

THERAPIST: Aww.

REBECCA: Yeah she may have been there actually I think that was 'cause sometimes that's the funny thing that if if Max is rubbing my back. The cat comes and tries to as I say steal my pets so [*laughs*] I have to jokingly jokingly say don't pet the—don't pet the kitty, pet me [*laughs*] so yeah [*laughs*] umm.

THERAPIST: [*Laughs.*] That's so cute.

REBECCA: So he was like that happened umm and so yeah I guess before that moment well I guess there was a little bit more to the moment. I mean I guess umm you know I think Max actually was feeling in the mood for sex and so he was kind of like you know anticipating that that might happen or kind of trying to hold on to me a little bit and then when I was I mean not that he's not normally like you know fairly accepting of like if I'm you know don't want to do it he's not really pressuring me or anything.

THERAPIST: Sure, OK.

REBECCA: Umm, as soon as I said that I wasn't that I was really tired and that like it was just you know it was really the last few days of the week have been really hard and umm you know and that I was also feeling kind of anxious, he pretty much immediately just like shifted umm gears yeah and was like OK well like it's fine like you know we can try tomorrow or whatever we can try that tomorrow but like I can just you know rub your back now just to help you fall asleep umm.

THERAPIST: Aww.

REBECCA: So yes so that was really sweet.

THERAPIST: Wow.

REBECCA: Umm.

THERAPIST: So you guys were in your bedroom?

REBECCA: Yeah no yeah we were—so we were already in . . . in the bed. Yeah.

THERAPIST: OK, OK.

REBECCA: Yup.

THERAPIST: Umm, what was the temperature like that day, or yesterday?

REBECCA: [*Laughs.*] Well, Max likes to Max is a little a little um, uhh possessive over the temperature but I've gotten used to it. He's he's—he's read the research of course he has he's read the research on umm what temperature it should be [*laughs*].

THERAPIST: [*Laughs.*] Absolutely.

REBECCA: Umm at night and umm it's supposed to be cold so umm so our house is usually pretty cold at night.

REBECCA: OK [*soft*]. Um and we also have this weird high-tech mattress topper thing that runs water through it and you can put it on heating or cooling.

THERAPIST: Ooooo.

REBECCA: And so it's cold umm but at least uhh each side can be different so usually my side is not so cold and his side is cold, right? [*Laughs.*]

THERAPIST: [*Laughs.*] That is.

REBECCA: Right in the middle so but still pretty but still cold. Let's just call it cold [*laughs*].

THERAPIST: [*Laughs.*] Yeah alright. Umm OK well I think you did a really great job like laying everything out, so it sounds like like you know he kind of came to you umm wanting some kind of connection. I mean initially it was sex and when you were kind of like oh I'm you know not feeling it he was really receptive and he wanted to just spend time with you umm and rub your back until you fell asleep.

REBECCA: Yeah.

THERAPIST: Yeah that's really sweet. Umm I guess for next right like I—I kind of want us to turn your attention to how you felt at that time and so what kind of things were you feeling in your body were you feeling happy and excited when he was rubbing your back and when he kind of accepted you an—and didn't push you know for sex or anything like that or were you feeling really deeply calm and relaxed umm I want you to think about where in your body you felt these emotions and I want you to try to feel them again.

REBECCA: Yeah I think at first I was still feeling, I was feeling like a— a weird combination right because . . .

THERAPIST: Mmhmm.

REBECCA: Like fatigue you know actually I have been feeling like that fatigue and I may have to get my blood work done again but we also know that I've been having trouble sleeping.

THERAPIST: Aww.

REBECCA: Umm and so I was feeling that but then simultaneously I was kind of feeling anxious too so I'm not really sure where I was feeling the anxiety in my body see yeah so I was feeling kinda like a crushing feeling in the back like the heaviness and then also I guess I usually feel my anxiety like in my stomach I guess umm maybe also like the shoulders so it's like crushing and tense at the same time.

THERAPIST: Aww.

REBECCA: I don't know how that's possible but uhh . . .

THERAPIST: Yeah that's miserable. Did it change at all when Max started kind of?

REBECCA: Yeah yeah.

REBECCA: Oh.

REBECCA: Definitely so like at first I definitely felt well—in—in the bed's defense—as soon as I hit the bed usually the fatigue kind of goes away on its own you know so that kind of you know umm.

THERAPIST: Nice.

REBECCA: But yeah but that anxiety feeling definitely as soon as he started like rubbing my back and like I could kind of focus on that sensation instead umm then like I started feeling less anxious.

THERAPIST: Yeah, how was it when he was rubbing your back—was it like umm was that like soothing—was it "enjoyable"?

REBECCA: Umm, calming and soothing.

THERAPIST: Yeah, OK.

REBECCA: Yeah.

THERAPIST: Got it and so you just the fatigue was gone you were just relaxed and you were kind of in the soothing umm calming space.

REBECCA: Yeah yeah, exactly.

THERAPIST: Awesome OK.

REBECCA: Umm yeah and then like it you know became pretty-pretty easy to fall asleep after that like so probably within 10 minutes I was asleep.

THERAPIST: Aww so you were really relaxed.

REBECCA: Yeah.

THERAPIST: Nice.

REBECCA: Hopefully, yeah.

THERAPIST: Yeah I'm wondering—I know some people when they feel calm or relaxed it can be like a whole body experience they can feel like you know kind of like the stress off their off their shoulders they kind of feel like heavy what was what was happening in your body when you were feeling relaxed and calm.

REBECCA: Umm yeah I mean it's kind of a combination because like it's like it's like relaxing but it's also like very pleasurable as well because there were so many nerve endings in your back right.

THERAPIST: Absolutely.

REBECCA: So it's kind of like it was like a com—a combined kind of feeling umm so and I think then I think that it starts at first it seemed more pleasurable and then you know as you kind of like I guess then the endorphins are released in your body it's ohh OK go to sleep like you want to enjoy it a little bit first.

THERAPIST: Yeah.

REBECCA: And like then the relaxation comes so that's kind of what happened.

THERAPIST: Nice, OK umm yeah take a minute just to feel that again. . . . OK umm so next I want you to try to recall what thoughts you were having at the time. Umm, for example, were you thinking, "I really need Max right now"? "Max is really there for me"? or were you thinking, "I feel so close to Max at this moment"? or "I feel comfortable relying on Max"? I want you to take a moment to reflect upon what your thoughts are about the memory now.

REBECCA: Yeah I don't know, this is a hard one because I don't know that my thoughts were necessarily very like . . . it's more like, what am I trying to say? Like I think I was still thinking about other things that were making me anxious. It's just it's almost like more like i—it was it is more like on an emotional or like almost like a like you know like a—like a on a body kind of sensation level because it's . . .

THERAPIST: Mmhmm.

REBECCA: Yeah it's like the—it's like the anxiety is still there or still my mind is kind of still racing or it's thinking about you know other things like [child's name] is starting today and . . .

THERAPIST: Mmhmm.

REBECCA: Umm. But then . . . I guess it well it probably has like to do with the fact that yeah like it was you know that's like was what was done to calm me down as a child umm so it almost like isn't like rational at all like it's thought based like it just works [*laughs*] right like it yeah.

THERAPIST: Yeah.

REBECCA: Umm, so I guess probably I was just feeling like you know this is like this is kind of like my person this is like my close family like you know I'm not going to ask a st-stranger to rub my back [*laughs*] while I fall asleep so umm so yeah so it's more just like I'm more like intuitive I guess yeah.

THERAPIST: Yeah OK umm so it sounds like you were kind of really just feeling the like you were in the moment really right like you were and your mind was still maybe . . . going to these other topics but you were really still getting like the benefits of being close to Max in that moment and like having him kind of show up for you.

REBECCA: Yeah.

THERAPIST: Yeah, yeah.

REBECCA: Yeah and also I guess like I guess I felt like a bit grateful because you know it's not that easy rubbing someone's back and your arm starts hurting so [*giggles*] I have one moment where he kind of stopped and I was like [*makes crying noise*] uhh more you know kind of like what a cat does [*laughs*].

THERAPIST: Aww.

REBECCA: And like he did it more and I was like, uhh OK, like I was kinda being ungrateful like oh his arm is probably hurting uhh poor guy but yeah so . . .

THERAPIST: Aww but he really cared about you and he wanted you to feel better.

REBECCA: Yeah.

THERAPIST: Yeah awesome.

REBECCA: Nice.

THERAPIST: Umm OK, so finally I want you to turn your focus to the future. I want you to focus on how close you felt to Max at the time. How will the bond that you have together affect your relationship in the future? What positive things can you imagine happening as a result of your bond to one another?

REBECCA: OK, umm well I mean every time that we have you know a moment like that, I think that yeah like for me that moment almost is like a little bit like how sex kind of works [*laughs*]. You know it's the same thing, it's like very physical it's not necessarily like the person is you know showing you empathy or they're not—it's not like very words-based, but umm but yeah I think it's just like releasing a lot of oxytocin so it's just like making you feel like safe with them that person and close. Umm umm so I think that probably the long-term benefits of that it would make sense that you know like like probably like be in a better mood like less fighting with that person and umm probably like if I feel in the future like I feel anxious or I feel you know like I need someone to help calm me down like, you know, Max has shown that like he's the kind of per—like he's the person I can call kind of right to like help me do that umm so I think that's like what yeah like the future effect could be umm yeah.

THERAPIST: Absolutely, umm what other positive things can you imagine happening as a result of your bond with Max?

REBECCA: Do you mean like just in general or?

THERAPIST: Yeah.

REBECCA: Hmmm.

THERAPIST: As a result of this like strong connection that the two of you have.

REBECCA: I don't know, I mean I hope you know that that our strong bond means that you know we'll want to spend the rest of our lives with each other umm and I don't know who knows even that I don't why this is coming to my head but like you know we could—if—if were not too old yet we can eventually have another kid or something or who knows umm. So if you ask him though he might say no ha-ha [laughs].

THERAPIST: [Laughs.]

REBECCA: But umm yeah or you know really really anything I guess like if either of us wants to do do anything and we'll kind of just know like the other person is there umm . . . you know both like emotionally and and like in proximity like you know like I—I guess I'm thinking like you know I—I moved to the U.S. with Max for you know for his job like stuff like that like I feel like the closer we—the closer you are with someone the more willing we are to do things like that as well umm so if that ever has to happen in the future too like now we'll be more likely as well.

THERAPIST: Yeah yeah, that one sounds kind of like the sky is kind of the limit like when you guys are connected and close, like you guys can kind of tackle anything that comes up yeah.

REBECCA: Yeah.

This session with Rebecca is a bit more challenging in the sense that it is more difficult for Gloria to keep her focused on the positive memory. Rebecca tends to be drawn toward tangential topics and also toward negative topics, which she herself acknowledges. For instance, when asked how she felt (during the positive memory that she chose), she begins talking about her back pain and then she talks about her anxiety—saying that

> [she] was kind of feeling anxious too so [she's] not really sure where [she] was feeling the anxiety in [her] body see yeah so [she] was feeling kinda like a crushing feeling in the back like the heaviness and then also [she] guess[es] [she] usually feel[s] [her] anxiety like in [her] stomach.

However, Gloria is persistent and continues to remind Rebecca of the positive aspects of the event, asking her how she felt when Max began to touch her, and then Rebecca turns toward her positive feelings, which she vividly describes. But even in the next section on thoughts associated with the memory, Rebecca returns to a focus on her anxiety, saying that the "anxiety is still there or still [her] mind is kind of still racing or it's thinking about you know other things like [child's name] is starting today."

Deeper into the reflection, Rebecca comes to a place where she is more focused on the feelings and thoughts associated with positive connectedness with Max; these feelings are relatively untouched by anxiety and negativity in this latter section of the savoring. She makes comments such as the "strong bond [they have] can actually mean that you know . . . we'll want to spend the rest of our lives with each other." It is unclear whether she gets to this point because she has recently described their having sex and has experienced the emotional security she feels as a result of reliving that experience or whether she has simply been guided through the savoring process to the point where she has weeded through the anxiety and has whittled down to the more primary, vulnerable, and authentic feelings. But regardless of the explanation, Rebecca enters a much more vulnerable and open place, ready to express these feelings, at least to Gloria.

Let's now look at the session in which Gloria brought the couple together and played the audio of Max savoring a memory with Rebecca to both of them. They then discussed Rebecca's reaction to hearing the memory together. She also played the audio of Rebecca savoring her memory, but we had some technical difficulties with that audio, so I am lacking a transcript for that portion of the therapy session.

Max and Rebecca's Couples Session: Listening to Max's Savoring of Care-Receiving From Rebecca

THERAPIST: Rebecca how was it for you to hear . . . that Max chose that memory to savor? [3-second pause]

REBECCA: Yeah that was, that was really sweet. Actually, I was thinking in the beginning, I can't remember, but I feel like he left out the part where I think it's, I don't really know, because in my story [*laughs*], he was trying to have sex with me, and then I actually just needed like emotional comfort, pretty sure I was trying to have sex with him, then he was like, "actually I don't feel good, I just need emotional comfort," so it's kind of funny that both our stories are—were like that. Um . . . but yeah, so that's what I was—yeah, first, um . . . and then, I was also um . . . laughing at the fact that he worried he was going to ruin the episode for you [*laughs*] um—

THERAPIST: Oh, that's very interesting.

REBECCA: Which I mean, I'm laughing but really that's actually just like, coming from a very, cute place, I—where I'm like, "Ugh, why is he so cute" [*laughs*] so even that was just very like OK. Um, and then like it was just very nice, to hear what he said, um . . . and I was just really happy to be there for him, of course like, that's my job, right? What kind of wife would I be if I wasn't there for him when he was sad that his mom dying? I mean, so, um. Yeah, oh actually, it was also kind of interesting, um, I uh—I just assumed that he was sad, because his mom died and that's how his, you know, mom died, and so reminded him, but, when I heard it was that—kind of talk about how he actually was feeling, you know like, a lot of empathy, for his father, because in the scene, you know, kind of like, obviously he dies, but it's also a very—about like [actress's] character, kind of like finding him like that, um, and then like being destroyed, so um, I didn't think about that, you know I didn't—so it's interesting that he kind of clarified like, what was going on for him, um, in that moment [*2-second pause*]. Yeah.

THERAPIST: That's wonderful. So you feel like you kind of got to learn a little bit more . . . about his experience—

REBECCA: Yeah.

THERAPIST: [*Inaudible*]—

REBECCA: Yeah. I also didn't know that like, his heart was racing, and that he felt, it s-seems like . . . like anxiety symptoms too . . . um, because he kind of just, presented very much like . . . he kind of just like, he—he, you know, he didn't he doesn't really come out and say like, "I feel anxious right now" or like, this, you know, this sort of like stuff in the moment, so, it's, interesting to like hear, now, what what, he was actually feeling. Um, 'cause in the moment, he's just sort of like . . . like, "no, like please," you know, "stop what you're doing like, I actually, you know, don't feel good, because I'm, feel sad like right now that my mom died" or whatever. So, um. So yeah it's interesting to hear like, the extended version . . . um, of that [*2-second pause*].

THERAPIST: Yeah that's, such a beautiful point. We don't actually know what's happening inside somebody's body. Right. The same way we don't know what's happening inside their mind, and we only really go off of like, a few cues that we have. Unless, somebody really gives us all of that information. Right. And I'm sure in that moment—

REBECCA: Right.

THERAPIST: He's trying to manage all of that. Right. And he's trying to interact with you, but, you know it sounds like there . . . oftentimes, right, there's a lot more going on than, than we share. Um. And I—you know I guess, one thing that I'm curious about is like, did you, realize, like how, grateful Max was and how significant that was for you to be there for him?

REBECCA: Um, I don't know actually. I guess maybe not, 'cause that's another thing that, you know, people kind of don't . . . don't do, I mean yeah, we just kind of assume that the other person knows, that we're, well . . . that we're like, you know, grateful, uh, we feel really safe and good, but we don't necessarily say it. So, I mean I think I . . . kind of knew, but, um, you know . . . it's nice to hear still though.

THERAPIST: Yeah. [*3-second pause*] Max, how is it for you, to, have Rebecca here listening, and to hear that again? [*3-second pause*]

MAX: Um. [*5-second pause*] I'm glad she heard it . . . um um . . . glad that she knows, the full context of my feelings. [*14-second pause*]

THERAPIST: Yeah, sounds like there was like, a lot happening for you. Right, and it might have been something where . . . maybe it would, too much to say all about it in that moment. Or, right, like, you know . . . you, were dealing with a lot of anxiety, and negative thoughts and, you know, feelings about your mom and her experience, and, um . . . and oftentimes that can be, a little overwhelming to share that in the moment. Right, when you're just kind of

	trying to like, maintain. Um, and feel a little bit better and it sounds like . . . it sounds like it's really important for you—for you, to know that Rebecca knows all of that.
MAX:	Mhm. [*3-second pause; inaudible*]—
THERAPIST:	And plus, you guys got to share that too. I thought that was such a like . . . such an important um . . . moment, and Max, one thing that I didn't have a chance to say to you, um, when I was talking to Rebecca about this before, um . . . you came back into the room, but uh, we, you know, I was just telling Rebecca about how we've been, trying to set up this connection time for you guys. Right, um . . . and . . . you know, Rebecca—oh, we don't have time to listen to all of Rebecca's today, so we can like, listen to hers on Wednesday, but, um you know . . . Rebecca had like, multiple memories 'cause we had a little bit more time to brainstorm, Max, so I didn't just go with, the first memory she chose, um, but . . . out of the three memories, um, one of them was from a long time ago, one of them was from, I think this morning, and then the other one was from last night. Um, but we were just talking about how like . . . the importance of you guys like, making that time, like you guys make this time for one another, and when you do that, you really open up the possibility to show up for each other, in these ways that are just so critical. Right like . . . you guys both . . . if I'm understanding the stories correct, both of you were kind of seeking connection, right. Sexual connection and intimacy from your partner, and in the moment, that person, your partner, needed somebody else—something else, and you both just, were right there, and showed up, with like exactly what the other person needed. And Max, you don't actually know exactly what Rebecca, it might, it—that's not really helpful 'cause you don't know exactly the memory, but i—it, it was last night right, the memory she chose—
MAX:	[*Laughs.*]
THERAPIST:	[*Inaudible*] Y—you guys basically both had really similar experiences and, and you guys both really showed up for the other person. You know, and you guys, you know I—I just want to kind of remind you like, all of this work is coming from you guys. Right, y-you, both of you are the people who are showing up every night, at 10:15. Right and, both of you are doing all of the hard

work, that's really allowing your relationship to really, start to flourish. [5-second pause] It's not easy [laughs]. Right. Rebecca and I were talking about that, it's, definitely not easy, it's super hard, um . . . but you guys have these two really, really important moments in which you guys were . . . I would almost argue like a safe haven, for the other person, right, like, both of you were in, emotional distress . . . and despite your par—your partner bidding for something else, right. Your partner then was able to do a one eighty and say like, "Oh wait let me come here and be here for your needs" . . . and you guys both did that seamlessly. Like, "No, but I didn't have to be there, we didn't have to have"—like right, you guys just knew exactly what to do. That's really impressive, guys. [8-second pause] Makes me think of um . . . the importance of, like your relationship how—I was thinking about when you guys were telling me, how . . . your relationship was, you guys had a very strong connection at the beginning . . . and, often times . . . that's so important, you know, like when you don't have that . . . it's a lot harder when you're, having marital challenges, to get through it. Knowing that you guys had this passion, and this like connection, and this, um, intensity, right. That was really, strong for both of you. I just, I don't know if I had told you guys this before, but it's actually a really important indicator in terms of you guys healing and getting to a better place. Right 'cause if you guys—

REBECCA: Oh that's so interesting.

THERAPIST: Mhm.

REBECCA: Yeah no just, uh uh, a comment on that, 'cause sometimes . . . sometimes I would—I mean I definitely think it's a good thing . . . but sometimes you know, like, we all kind of like, you know, I guess I kind of like second guess that or I'm like, "well, you know," especially since I think I mentioned to you that my sister kind of mentioned that like her and her husband, didn't really have that, um, they had kind of more like a slow, kind of like building, and they were like, "OK like, I love you" not like, "I am in love with you" even, or it wasn't, 'cause it wasn't that sort of, kind of like—so sometimes—and then I think also, you know, in our society, we sometimes make fun of that whole like, oh that, initial chemical reaction or whatever, we kind of dismiss it a little bit?

THERAPIST: Mhm.

REBECCA: Um—

THERAPIST: Mhm.

REBECCA: And so maybe, you know, yeah so sometimes I feel like my mind goes there, or I'm like, "Oh well, you know, maybe we were being irrational" or like, "We moved in with each other too, too early" or like, you know it can go very negative it can—like my mind can go to a very negative place sometimes when it comes to like, you know, how we like fell in love, and like how strong it was, um, but I think that it's really . . . it's—that it's really, you know, interesting, and important point to bring up that like, um, but yeah like, when you, when you've been, when you know, when you've . . . been with someone for a really long time, like, what are—what's gonna be, what's kind of gonna be, um, better I guess, like in times of, of conflict, like to think back and go like, "Well we had a slow buildup" like you know [*laughs*] or is it gonna be you know like, "Oh actually we had like this passionate like, falling in love period, and like we have those memories, and like remember and" um, so yeah, so I think like, it is definitely, helpful to have that, especially like when you're, when you are struggling in a relationship. Um. It's definitely been helpful before for us to, I mean that's what we kind of did, even though we were separated . . . we did, we we we did a lot of that, kind of like reminiscing about that, about our early relationship, when we were working with—I cannot remember her name right now, that couples therapist, um. So yeah, so like even, even though we were literally separated like that it was s-super helpful. You know even in that moment, um, so, yeah.

THERAPIST: Yeah, and I think, you know that's like . . . and you kind of nailed it right, that's like relational savoring. Right, and we're doing a form of that now, right, where we're [*inaudible*] like, "let's look back" um, part of the reason that I ask you guys to think of a more recent event is 'cause you do have to relive it. "What was I wearing," right, all of those d-details 'cause we're really . . . idea of something is you're like, reexperiencing it, right, you're re-um, you're trying to feel those emotions again, think those thoughts. Use all of that to kind of . . . you know, optimistically look into the future, and see like, what could happen, right? Um . . . and,

I think that's actually a really important... you know, kind of tool you guys have in your tool chest, right like, you guys can reminisce, about, a lot of wonderful things, right, you have two beautiful children, you have like, this "falling in love" period, right, and you guys are—even now, right, when things are kind of... you guys have... a large amount of demands on you, at all times, um, and you're still able to... create moments like this... that are really important. Um, you know and I think moving forward if you guys can, you know, create a space right, where, you know, Max you can kind of [*3-second pause*] m-maybe not do the whole savoring experience, but you can tell Rebecca how important it was for her to be there for you. Right, because I think sometimes, we do assume, that the person knows we're grateful, or we assume they know 'cause it's like, "Well of course you know how much I love you, and how much that meant to me," but in reality like, no one knows unless we tell them, right? Like nobody can look into our mind and know what we're thinking. We have to be so explicit. Right, with everything, um, you know, even Max, like how Rebecca didn't realize you were as anxious as you were. You know I'm wondering, was that surprising for you to hear or are you aware of that? [*3-second pause*]

MAX: I'm not... surprised... mean obviously I didn't share all my thoughts. I didn't, feel like I could in that moment.

THERAPIST: Yeah... yeah.

REBECCA: Yeah, I think that sometimes, like what people do, especially like... you know, people who are—I think people who have social phobia, like me or like... we, we are almost like so, like attuned to what, we think or like, we're getting so much mind reading that we think like other people can mind read us, or like, "Oh, of course you knew I was anxious" like, "You could tell my body was tense" or like some weird thing to like know right like—

THERAPIST: Right.

REBECCA: Yeah, like I think that that's really common so, um, yeah... it was just a really good—

THERAPIST: Totally.

REBECCA: —point.

THERAPIST: Totally. Well—

REBECCA: Yeah, so sometimes I think Max like, might know that I'm like anxious, or like yeah he probably has no idea . . . so, but yeah—

THERAPIST: Totally.

REBECCA: [*Inaudible 2 seconds*] It is better to just be you know, as explicit as possible. Of course like, within reason like, sometimes in the moment right, you can't, you can't be that explicit in the moment, 'cause you're like, it's just too hard to verbalize it. Um, but.

THERAPIST: Yeah and all we can do is, right, try our best. You know, and like, you know, whatever we can do in that moment, is, is great. Um . . . but yeah I think it is really tough, I mean, especially when you have such a history with somebody and you know them so well. Right, it's like, you just kind of have this assumption like, "Oh they get it" or like, "They know I'm—they know I'm appreciative," right? But it's like . . . sometimes, you are way more appreciative than that person even understands. Right like, um—

REBECCA: Mhm.

THERAPIST: The times in which people show up for us can be so much more important than, um . . . than we really, even kind of share. Right like, um . . . not always right, but I think that's like, you know, ideally [*inaudible*] we would work . . . toward, right? It's like how can we make sure that we're being, as explicit with each other as possible.

REBECCA: Mhm.

THERAPIST: Which it sounds like guys, by the way, you guys totally did that. Right. Because you guys were able to communicate really clearly in that moment what you needed from the other person and then they were able to show up for you.

REBECCA: Yeah.

In this final couples session, it is apparent how Gloria, the couples therapist, takes the time to really drive home the central points of the savoring. The first point Gloria hits is that Max and Rebecca were really there for one another during times of need and the fact that they were there for one another means something significant for their relationship. The second point she hits is that the act of savoring is really important for the relationship—that taking the time to notice what is good in the relationship will strengthen the relationship. In so doing, she helps to underscore the importance and utility of relational savoring as an effective emotion regulation tool that has relational benefits. The third point she makes is that it is impossible to know what the other person in the relationship is thinking and that if we make assumptions about this, we are often wrong.

This type of work is consistent with mentalization-based therapeutic approaches—relational savoring is grounded in an attachment- and mentalization-based approach—and this emphasis in this final session on expanding the clients' ability to adopt a more flexible approach to viewing others' states is what mentalizing theorists refer to as *opacity*. Opacity is the principle that one must be tentative in inferring the mental states of others because, after all, we can never be sure what another person is thinking or feeling; people have different ways of expressing their feelings/thoughts, and people can also hide or mask their feelings/thoughts (Fonagy, 1989, 1991). In emphasizing this point, she is helping them see that making an assumption about the mental states of the other person, particularly a hostile assumption, would be an error because we cannot know for sure what others are thinking or feeling. So it's better to err on the side of assuming we do not know and trying to gather more information about the situation, as well as assuming good intentions on behalf of the other person.

I refer to the work that Gloria demonstrated in this final session as closing the loop following dyadic savoring. This therapeutic work is the therapist's opportunity to underscore the clinical lessons that have been achieved. In other words, in the savoring sessions, the therapeutic work is accomplished, but in the final conversations, the therapist has the opportunity to share these lessons with the clients. *Savoring the savoring*, we might call it, which allows a multidimensional and multilayered experience for the client.

WRAP-UP

With its emphasis on moments of positive connectedness, relational savoring is a natural fit for work with couples and families. There are myriad ways in which you might want to integrate this brief intervention into your work with couples and families. In this chapter, I sought to provide some initial ideas and a framework for how to begin thinking about this process of integrating relational savoring into your work with couples and families. As you contemplate how to fit this intervention within a specific relational context, focusing on your therapeutic goals is of the utmost importance. In the next chapter, I examine how relational savoring can be adapted to fit within specific clinical contexts.

10

THE CULTURAL CONGRUENCE OF RELATIONAL SAVORING AND PARTNERING WITH COMMUNITY AGENCIES TO HEIGHTEN IT

Although initial research on attachment involved fieldwork by Mary Ainsworth in Uganda, which was important because it meant that the early theorizing included a more global perspective, the majority of the research since that point has relied on Western, middle-class, and predominantly White samples (Agishtein & Brumbaugh, 2013). In recent years there has been a move to broaden the research base by conducting studies in other cultural contexts (in understudied countries and in understudied groups within highly studied countries). The findings that have emerged have revealed that intimate relationships are important across cultures, and attachment relationships are a crucial component of the intimate relationship landscape.

Attachment theorists argue that the propensity to become attached to one or more caregivers is a universal drive. This means that across diverse cultural contexts, if given the opportunity to do so, children will become attached to caregivers. However, there is cultural variability in the way attachment relationship forms—for example, there are differences in the number of attachments formed and with whom they are formed as a function of cultural context (Mesman et al., 2016). Further, adult attachment patterns vary cross-culturally as a function of cultural values and religion

https://doi.org/10.1037/0000372-010
Relational Savoring: Using Guided Reflection to Strengthen Relationships and Improve Outcomes in Therapy, by J. L. Borelli
Copyright © 2024 by the American Psychological Association. All rights reserved.

(Agishtein & Brumbaugh, 2013), as well as within cultures as a function of race and ethnicity (Arbona & Power, 2003; Fiori et al., 2009; Lopez et al., 2000; Wei et al., 2004).

An important part of providing high-quality treatment is being sensitive to cultural differences in our clients, which includes differences in the ways interpersonal needs are perceived, experienced, and expressed. Awareness of cultural differences can come from lived experiences or training, but therapists should be aware that the interpersonal landscape of clients from different cultural groups may vary and be ready to discuss the intersection of culture, interpersonal relationships, and mental health in the therapy. Relatedly, identifying interventions that are culturally congruent with the values of the cultural groups of the clients a therapist is serving is an important component of this process.

RELATIONAL SAVORING WITH MINORITIZED COMMUNITIES

In this chapter, I discuss the research I have done in my laboratory on relational savoring and in minoritized communities. Relational savoring is a technique that has been shown to have widespread efficacy in samples with considerable diversity in terms of racial, ethnic, and socioeconomic dimensions, as well as ages and life stages (Borelli et al., 2015; Borelli, Smiley, et al., 2020; Burkhart et al., 2015), suggesting that this intervention technique affects its treatment targets when tested within diverse samples. In addition, my colleagues and I have taken steps within our work to examine the unique impacts of relational savoring when tested within specific cultural and/or racial/ethnic groups. Our culture-specific work thus far has mostly focused on Latino/a/x individuals. The reason for this is twofold: First, I had a long-standing interest in working with Latino/a/x families, as this group is the largest and most rapidly growing minority community in the United States (Takeuchi et al., 2007), particularly in southern California, where my laboratory is based. Second, early on, I found evidence supportive of the efficacy of the intervention modality within this population.

As discussed in Chapter 3, although I did not develop the relational savoring intervention with the Latino/a/x population in mind, in hindsight, it is not surprising that this intervention is particularly appealing to this cultural group. An intervention that involves relishing the positive moments of interpersonal connectedness and savoring moments of felt closeness within relationships seems ideal for a cultural group that celebrates relational closeness as much as Latinos/as do. This celebration of relationship and familial roles in particular is reflected in Hispanic and Latino/a/x media, music, food, and cultural and religious celebrations. As just one bit of evidence of this, if you look around Tik Tok or Instagram, the majority of the funny videos from Latino/a/x young adults pertain to the size and closeness of their families and the fact that everyone shows up for every family event—for instance, I found one that says, "Graduation tickets? Yes, I need 43 for my family."

Relational savoring is consistent with Latino/a/x cultural values related to positive emotion, familial relationships, and the intersection between the two. One dimension of culture that has been discussed extensively in the literature is collectivism versus individualism, with *collectivism* referring to the tendency to view the self as part of a larger group and *individualism* referring to the tendency to view the self as an individual unit (Triandis, 2001). In collectivist societies, social roles are an important part of one's identity, whereas in individualistic societies, individual characteristics play a prominent role in one's identity (Triandis, 2001).

This distinction between collectivism and individualism has broad utility in differentiating values across cultures. These cultural values also have implications for the values people place on emotional experience, which vary cross-culturally. Latino/a/x cultural values place priority on positive emotional experience, particularly that which is experienced in the context of familial relationships (Campos & Kim, 2017).

Social relationships are developed and maintained through the open expression of positive emotions, respect for the dignity of others, and frequent social interactions (Campos & Kim, 2017; Senft et al., 2021). *Simpatía* is a cultural value that pertains to the expression of emotion and that is commonly held by Latinos/as; it refers to the desire to prefer social interactions that are full of warmth, love, and positive emotion, on the one hand, and to avoid social interactions that are characterized by conflict, hostility, and negativity, on the other (Acevedo et al., 2020). This cultural value is apparent when a client wishes to talk at length about the time they reunited with their family member, soaking up all of the things they had missed about them, taking them around and reintroducing them to the other members of their family, and reliving the joy they experience in being together.

This willingness to share with reckless abandon about these positive moments of interpersonal connection may be accompanied by a reluctance to speak about the difficulties they are having in the relationship with this relative, or the difficulties that another relative in their family is having with the reintroduction of this relative in their life (Acevedo et al., 2020). Instead, they may wish to push these topics under the rug, so to speak, not wanting to look at them because they bring up unpleasant feelings and thoughts that are better forgotten about.

I hope from illustrating these cultural values of simpatía and familism that it is easy to see why relational savoring is such a natural fit for the Latino/a/x population. It provides people with the opportunity to reflect on moments of closeness and positivity with another person with whom they have a cherished relationship and to really focus on their role in this relationship. In contrast, intervention/prevention programs that lead clients to focus on negatively valenced interactions, or on moments of disconnect in relationships, might be exceedingly difficult and culturally incongruent for people from this background. If the basic premise of an intervention program is that it will entail a person talking about their problems in a relationship, particularly with a stranger (the therapist), this will be at odds with core cultural values of Latino/a/x families.

Indeed, as I described in Chapter 3, we have now found in two studies that Latino/a/x parents show unique benefits from relational savoring in terms of their reflective functioning (Borelli, Kerr, et al., 2023; Goldstein et al., 2019) and the likelihood they are to continue using savoring following the intervention (Borelli, Kerr, et al., 2023), while demonstrating equally strong responses as non-Latino/a/x parents have to the intervention on other outcomes that were measured. This is especially important given that in response to many prevention/intervention programs, ethnic minority parents, including Latino/a/x parents, are disadvantaged, showing worse outcomes. This may be because the programs are inconsistent with their cultural values or stigmatize them as being inadequate or overly strict parents (Calzada, 2010; Cardona et al., 2009; Updegraff et al., 2016). We considered these findings to be very encouraging in terms of the promise of relational savoring for this population.

This recognition that the intervention was a particularly good fit for this cultural group led me to want to work more closely with this population, and as I had stated above, I already had a strong interest in working with Latino/a/x families. A little bit about me: Ever since I started learning Spanish in junior high school and high school, I basically fell in love with Hispanic/Latino/a/x culture and language. At that time, I decided I wanted to become a Spanish teacher (as a career). I went all the way to AP Spanish 5 in high school, and as a senior, I received an award for the student in the school who excelled the most in Spanish.

By the time I got to college, I had transitioned my career dreams to those of becoming a psychologist, but I was still holding onto my passion for Spanish, and I wanted to double major in Spanish. However, once I learned that majoring in Spanish was more like majoring in history or English literature (except that you were doing it in Spanish), I decided not to do it anymore. It took only a few classes of me reading "old Spanish" (in other words, Spanish from the 1400s) and analyzing these texts from various literary and historical perspectives for me to realize that perhaps what I really loved was speaking Spanish, learning the language, and being exposed to the culture. So this ended my dream of majoring in Spanish, but still I managed to speak it whenever I could up until the present day, with basically anyone who would allow me to speak Spanish to them. Imagine my delight when I realize that the relational savoring intervention worked best with Latino/a/x participants. Perhaps this was a chance for me to marry my passions?

PARTNERING WITH LATINO HEALTH ACCESS TO ADAPT RELATIONAL SAVORING

In this next section, I'm going to tell you a bit about my experience of working to adapt the relational savoring intervention to fit within the goals of a community agency. In total, I have administered relational savoring within three community agencies: River Stones Residential Treatment Facility in Redlands, California, a residential treatment facility that used to serve foster youth and postadoption youth (all male) but has now transitioned to serving adolescents with psychiatric impairments who have health insurance as well; the Center for Discovery, a national network of residential treatment facilities that provides treatment to adults and adolescents with eating disorders; and Latino Health Access (LHA) in Santa Ana, California, a community health agency that works with low-income Latino/a/x families in Orange County.

The experiences delivering the intervention at these different sites were dramatically different. I'm going to tell you about my experiences of adapting and delivering the intervention at LHA because I think it is the most instructive of the three, at least for those of you who wish to work with people from minoritized cultural groups. This was by far the most challenging of the three experiences and also the one from which I learned the most.

Let me provide a tiny more context on the community agency before I tell you about my experiences working with them. LHA is embedded in one of the lowest income, highest risk (in terms of levels of poverty and community violence) neighborhoods in the United States. The families who live in the area are majority Latino/a/x, and based on our studies, most of the adults are first-generation immigrants from Mexico or Central America and low income (Borelli, Russo, et al., 2021; Borelli, Yates, et al., 2021).

LHA delivers services using a promotor/a de salud model; *promotores* are trained community workers (Bracho et al., 2016). By definition, they are people who reside in the community they serve. Promotores are not professionals (e.g., doctors and nurses); they share similar income levels, ethnic identities, and education levels of the families who receive services at LHA. This is by design, as the guiding principle of the service delivery model is that treatments and programs are delivered by people who reside in the community they serve (promotores).

This model of treatment delivery has several advantages for this community: It is cost-effective, so the services are more sustainable. Further, the services are often better received by the community, as the providers are trusted members of the community rather than people who come from outside the community and cannot relate to community experiences (Barnett et al., 2019; Messias et al., 2013; Sternberg et al., 2019). The promotores receive training in delivering the programs they deliver (e.g., diabetes care, healthy weight, emotional wellness), and they deliver programs and engage with the community. They are masterful at developing relationships with community members and refer them to licensed professionals for higher levels of care when needed. LHA is directed by Dr. America Bracho (Bracho et al., 2016), who is a visionary in terms of community organizing, social justice, and health promotion.

When I came to LHA, it was at the introduction of my colleague and friend, Dr. Nancy Guerra, who had worked with America and LHA for many years. She had developed and evaluated a mothers' group with them many years before and had years of collaboration with them to build upon. Together, she and I applied for and got a grant from the Centers for Disease Control and Prevention with LHA to develop and implement a family resilience program that would incorporate relational savoring and be delivered by promotores.

During this time, Nancy was the dean of the School of Social Ecology at the University of California, Irvine, and not able to devote much time to the collaboration at LHA, leaving me to spearhead the project, intervention development, and the university–community partner relationship. However, I did not have the years and years of history that Nancy had with this organization or the mountains of trust she had built with them. It was just me, and I had very little experience building solid partnerships with community agencies, particularly those serving low-income Latino/a/x families.

I had recently transitioned academic institutions from Pomona College to UC Irvine and had previously spent years trying to build a partnership with a community agency without success. However, suddenly finding myself in the position of having a partnership was a tremendous responsibility. This was thrilling, for sure—I felt I had landed a huge jackpot—but also terrifying because I was far from steady in my skills for developing and maintaining this partnership.

But I jumped in headfirst and gave it my all, making plenty of mistakes along the way. I won't bore you with all of the details of all of the mistakes I made, but if you are interested in hearing more about those details, I refer you to other papers regarding our experience of partnering together to build this intervention—the lessons learned, the benefits, and the difficulties (Borelli, Cervantes, et al., 2022; Borelli, Russo, et al., 2022).

I focus here on the adaptation we made to the relational savoring intervention to adjust it for this treatment model. The intervention was codeveloped by myself, the members of my research team (my study coordinators), and the administrators and promotores at LHA. What that meant is that this was not a process of me, the lead researcher, coming to LHA with my manualized intervention and saying, "Here, this is what we should do with your community!" Far from it. This was a dialogue that extended over 1.5 years and involved all of us coming to the table with our ideas and discussing, refining, sharing, and going back to the drawing board again.

I brought in a tentative set of ideas (a manual or curriculum, as they preferred to call it) and then they would mark it up and recommend what they would like to keep and discard, what felt wrong and at odds with their values, and what they would like to revise. And then my team and I would go back to the drawing board and come back with fresh ideas, based on what they had shared, and try again. And they would try again, offering their wisdom and ideas, and tell me how what I had shared struck them. And we went back and forth like this over the 1.5-year period until we felt ready to proceed, at which point I began training more promotores in the agreed-upon curriculum, which was a true amalgam of our shared vision.

I will note that I grew as much or more than the promotores and administrators did as a result of learning from them; I learned about their community, the local wisdom, and their model of listening to the community members and what they need before offering help.

We made several major modifications to the intervention. First, we adapted it to be delivered in groups. The therapy intervention, *Confía en mí, Confío en ti* (Borelli, Yates, et al., 2021), which translates to "Trust Me, for I Trust You," is a group-based therapy designed to be delivered to parents and youth (ages 8–18). Originally we began with youth ages 10 to 18, but we lowered the age range when we were having recruitment difficulties.

There was a mothers' group and a youth group that were conducted in tandem. Both groups were led by promotores, who often led the groups in pairs. Sometimes the promotores were accompanied by a student (research assistant) from our team who was bilingual/bicultural (we referred to them as promotores as well). The youth groups were typically led by promotores who were younger than the mother groups because the younger promotores appeal more to the youth.

The groups would run for eight weekly sessions in total. However, of this 8-week program, only two sessions of the mother groups and two sessions of the youth groups focused exclusively on relational savoring. The other sessions focused on psychoeducational content (teaching attachment concepts like secure base and safe haven and teaching about social determinants of health), and the last session focused a bit on savoring the group context.

To make the savoring amenable to the group context, in the mother groups, we first had the promotor leading the group describe the concept and provide the rationale for the technique. Next, the promotor demonstrated relational savoring in front of the group for the group participants. Then the group participants broke into pairs and did the savoring with one another. We created handouts for them that broke the concepts into simple steps (in Spanish) and had visual icons attached to the steps, distilling what we thought were the most central points from the intervention into the smallest number of words, and we had the mothers use these handouts as their "scripts" for the relational savoring exercise.

This strategy seemed successful, as the mothers were actively engaged in conversation throughout the exercises and came up with useful memories to discuss. We did not have them generate multiple memories to savor; we just had them come up with one memory and proceed through and follow the reflection steps for that memory (see Figure 10.1). In the two sessions focused on savoring, the mothers were instructed to focus on savoring caregiving for their children (based on the fact that the intervention program was designed to improve parent–child relationships).

Youth also engaged in two sessions of relational savoring. Their savoring occurred earlier in their 8-week curriculum (Sessions 3 and 4, as compared with Sessions 6 and 7 for the mothers) and was divided into two parts. In Session 3, the youth learned about the secure base concept (using films and metaphors) and then were taught to and asked to savor an experience of a time when their mother acted as a secure base for them. In Session 4, youth were taught about the safe haven concept (again using film and metaphor) and were then taught about and asked to savor a time when their mother acted as a safe haven for them.

Youth completed the memory selection phase of the savoring in the big group, led by the promotores, and then transitioned to working in pairs and using worksheets (see Figures 10.2 and 10.3) to guide their memory reflection. We reasoned that youth needed a bit more guidance/support to help guide their conversations and could benefit from having activities

FIGURE 10.1. Handout Provided to Mother Participants to Assist With Savoring

Disfrutar la relación

1. ¿Usted recuerda alguna vez que fue base segura o refugio seguro para su hijo/a? ¿Qué pasó?

   a. Si no puede pensar en un momento cuando fue base segura o refugio seguro, ¿recuerda alguna vez cuando se sintió conectada con su hijo/a?

2. Note y recuerde los detalles del evento. ¿Cómo estaba el tiempo ese día? ¿A qué hora del día ocurrió? ¿Cómo lucía su niño/a o que ropa tenía puesta? ¿Se recuerda que tenía puesta usted? ¿Qué sonidos oyó? ¿Qué cosas pudo ver?

(continues)

266 • *Relational Savoring*

FIGURE 10.1. Handout Provided to Mother Participants to Assist With Savoring (*Continued*)

3. Note como se sintió emocionalmente en ese momento cuando usted fue base segura o refugio seguro para su hijo/a. Piense en cual parte de su cuerpo sintió estas emociones y trate de sentirlas ahora.

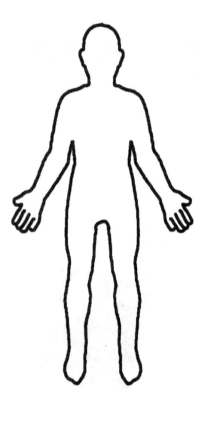

FIGURE 10.1. Handout Provided to Mother Participants to Assist With Savoring (Continued)

4. Recuerde lo que estaba pensando en el momento. ¿Piensa algo diferente ahora?

5. Puede identificar si este momento tuvo un efecto positivo en la relación con su hijo/a?

268 • *Relational Savoring*

FIGURE 10.2. Handout From Youth Reflection

Take a few moments to think about this memory that you shared with your mom. Using this memory, answer the following:

1. Draw this memory as if it were a movie scene. You may want to consider:
   - What the weather was like that day
   - The time of day that the event occurred
   - What your mom looked like or what she was wearing
   - What you were wearing
   - Sounds you could hear
   - Things you could see

2. How did you feel during this time? _____

   Circle where in your body you felt these emotions. You can feel free to draw them too!

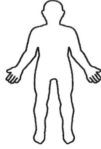

FIGURE 10.3. Handout From Youth Reflection

1. What were you thinking about when this moment happened? For example, were you thinking
   - "I really need my mom at this moment"
   - "I feel really close to my mom right now"
   - "I feel really comfortable and safe with my mom at this moment"

What does this mean about you as a person?
_____
_____
_____

2. Draw a scene of a future moment you can envision with your mom. Consider:
   - Can you imagine other ways you and your mom might be close in the future?
   - In what ways will that closeness be helpful to you?

to help support their conversation. Thus we provided them with some activities to help enhance their experience of doing the savoring memory reflection exercise. For instance, we had them draw the memory scene that they experienced with their mothers and had them circle where in their bodies they experienced the feelings they had. When it came to reflecting on the thoughts that they had during the time of the event, we asked them to fill their thoughts out within thought bubbles and then write out what these thoughts or experiences mean about them as a person. The goal of this subtask is for them to be able to generate meaning from the memory. Finally, for the future-oriented portion of reflection, we asked them to draw a scene of a moment they could envision occurring in the future with their mothers. We then asked them to share their responses on the worksheets with their partners.

We used handouts and worksheets for the mothers and youth because we knew we would not get the quality of savoring we were used to getting from the intervention as administered in a one-on-one format by a therapist or intervener when we were having an untrained peer administer it (a peer who was being introduced to the ideas in the same moment as the client and who was about to go through the experience themselves). We thought that the best compromise, the best way to try to preserve the integrity of the intervention within this context, would be to provide the cues of the most salient aspect of the intervention in a visual format so that both the person delivering the intervention and the recipient could see it. And we also thought it was best to simplify the intervention as much as possible so that the intervener and the client could focus on the most essential components. The reasoning was as follows: If you have to master a concept in 10 minutes, it is best to have that concept be as simple as possible. Plus, we did not want the participants to be focused on getting it right; we wanted them to be focused on savoring their memories. Thus, we stepped back and thought carefully about what the most essential components were to the intervention and dropped the rest.

I cannot lie and say this was an easy thing to do, certainly not for me, when I had poured so much heart into developing this therapy protocol just so. But I tried to console myself by telling myself that if I didn't drop these pieces of the intervention, all would be lost, and it was better for them to get something than to get nothing. I also must confess that we did not go about this the "right way," in that we did not do therapy-dismantling studies in which we identified which aspects of the intervention were essential and which could be left out without affecting the outcome. Rather, we were operating in a boots-on-the-ground mentality, having gotten a grant to build an intervention, knowing that the relational savoring intervention worked well for Latino/a/x families, and wanting to be responsive to this community agency. So we built the intervention with this in mind and held our breath, hoping this approach would work.

And did it? We conducted an evaluation trial of the intervention we had built. The study was originally intended to be a randomized, controlled trial involving an intervention group and a waitlist control group. This means the control group was going to eventually receive the intervention, but at a delayed interval; they would receive multiple baseline assessments and then receive the intervention. We designed the study this way because the team at LHA is opposed to the use of control groups in which participants do not get access to the intervention. From their perspective, this unfairly deprives half of the participating people from receiving the program, even after they are contributing to the research. The idea of a waitlist control was appealing to them because it meant that everyone would receive the intervention but we could still evaluate its effects in comparison with a group that received it in a delayed way.

However, the waitlist control group did not function as intended, mostly because we were unable to effectively engage the participants in this group. By design, the participants in the waitlist control group only completed assessments over a period of many months, and this was insufficient to keep them connected to the research study. So when it came time for them to be enrolled in the intervention, they were not available or interested— we could not enroll them. After we discovered this was a challenge, we tried everything we could think of to increase engagement of this group—pamphlets, flyers, monthly social events, and phone calls with the research team—but none of our efforts solved the problem. We were unable to make significant headway on this issue before the COVID-19 pandemic hit, which precluded us from trying anything else creative. At that point, we stopped devoting efforts to recruiting this waitlist control group and focused on the intervention group.

The resulting data are part of a pre–post design of 112 mothers and youth. Our findings revealed that some things worked well and some didn't work as well as we would have liked. Overall, the program was a success from the perspective of how the families served felt about it. The mothers in particular raved about it and continued to seek services at the agency. The promotores felt it was a success overall; they reported that the mothers in particular enjoyed the program, learned a lot, and became very close during the groups. In one of our analyses, we examined the promotores' assessments of the group members' dynamic at the end of each of the groups. The promotores reported that the mothers' groups had higher levels of connection, higher quality relationships, and lower levels of conflict and found the program content to be more relevant than did the youth participation in the program (Borelli, Russo, et al., 2022).

The youth were more difficult to engage overall in the curriculum. This is not surprising; youth, especially youth in this age range, can be notoriously difficult to engage in therapy. In most instances, they were also not the ones who made the choice to join the program, as mothers were typically the driving forces for enrollment in our program. In our therapy groups, the youth were less likely to engage in the discussion tasks; they enjoyed the tasks that involved multimedia more.

In hindsight, we think we should have designed the youth program to include a greater focus on multimedia (e.g., social media, videos songs, activities). The curriculum was primarily designed according to the cultural needs of low-income Latina mothers who were recent immigrants, but we realized we did not pay enough attention to the cultural factors (and particularly the acculturation gap) facing the youth of these mothers.

In future iterations of this intervention and other work we do with this population, we need to attend more carefully to these divergent cultural values. These issues partly arose because we involved promotores in the codesign of the intervention, but the promotores largely matched the cultural background of the mothers in the mother group, not the youth in the youth group. We recognized in hindsight that we had neglected to involve youth in our codesign process, an omission that cost us. This is particularly striking because our intervention and study codesign involved members of every contingent except youth, so their voice was noticeably absent.

In terms of the relational savoring in particular, overall the feedback was very positive. Mothers and youth reported that they enjoyed the activity and felt it taught them to notice and appreciate these positive moments with one another. There were some elements that we felt needed some tinkering, some of which we did during the intervention trial. For instance, although the relational savoring for the mothers was focused on caregiving, not care-receiving, during the first relational savoring session, the promotores often discussed experiences of receiving secure base and safe haven care.

This topic naturally came about for some mothers as well when they were discussing their own experiences of providing care for their children. The promotores and mothers would discuss experiences of secure base and safe haven care they had themselves received. However, for some of the mother participants in our study, this brought up difficult experiences, such as trauma or abuse. Of note, this sample experienced a high incidence of abuse overall

(Russo et al., 2022), which is not surprising given that it was a low-income, immigrant, ethnic minority sample.

During our weekly supervision meeting, the promotores brought to my attention that it was at times difficult for some of the mothers to engage in savoring when they felt they had never had these experiences with their own mothers—that it brought up experiences of pain, sadness, and loss for them. Further, the promotores could relate; they had memories of similar experiences, and it brought up difficult feelings for them of wishing they had had more positive experiences.

To address this issue, we had mothers who were unable to remember any experiences of secure base/safe haven care-receiving imagine the ways they would have liked to have been taken care of and to savor those imagined experiences. The promotores also validated the emotional pain and sadness associated with not having had these experiences, as well as the fact that the mother was deserving of these experiences and should have had them. We came up with the idea collaboratively during a supervision session, and the promotores thought it was a good solution to this difficulty; they implemented it during their groups, and it worked well (Borelli, Kazmierski, et al., 2023; Borelli, Russo, et al., 2022). At this juncture we also discussed the utility of providing promotores with more training in how to assess and respond to trauma-exposed populations, as it was clear that this type of intervention activated both positive and painful memories for some of the mothers, and at times the promotores felt that additional training in trauma-informed care would have benefited them.

The outcomes we reported in our intervention trial are reported in one of our outcome papers (Borelli, Yates, et al., 2021). When comparing how participants in the program did in terms of their pre-to-post outcomes, we saw reductions in psychopathology in mothers and youth, increases in attachment security, and increases in reflective functioning. However, we cannot speak to the portions of these outcomes that are attributable to relational savoring specifically, since this was just a component of the larger intervention.

In terms of the community partnership aspect of the collaboration, although there were bumps in the road, the promotores reported that they felt included in the intervention codevelopment process. They expressed the belief that the resultant curriculum reflected their wisdom, input, and beliefs, which was very important from the university research team side of things (Borelli, Russo, et al., 2022).

Also of note, the promotores acknowledged that they themselves benefited from learning about the curriculum. They incorporated the principles they learned through the psychoeducational component of the curriculum (e.g., learning about the basics of attachment theory, the importance of parent–child relationships, the secure base and safe haven concepts, and learning about the social determinants of health) as well as the experiential components of the intervention into their own lives (e.g., relational savoring). Promotores described that the lessons they learned from codeveloping and delivering the intervention affected their own families and parenting, saying they "feel that [they] have a lot of tools" and "put what they learned into practice" (Borelli, Russo, et al., 2022, p. 51). We considered this to be additional evidence of the cultural congruence of the relational savoring intervention; not only was it a positive fit with the community members that it was provided to, but also the promotores who were delivering it felt that the principles of the intervention resonated with them.

FUTURE COLLABORATIONS: EL CORAZÓN DE LA COMUNIDAD STUDY

The promotores' comments about the intervention were germinating inside me, planting seeds of ideas regarding future program development. In addition, watching the promotores in their role during the COVID-19 pandemic was nothing short of heroic. They were absolutely essential in serving as a lifeline to the community. Especially during a time of global distrust, the promotor network revealed how crucial it was to have local health care providers whom the community trusted. This community was not listening first and foremost to CNN or Fauci; they were listening to the people whom they had already trusted to provide them with health care advice: their local promotores, the people who lived in their communities, walked their neighborhoods, and spoke their language.

This was a tremendous honor for promotores yet also placed a great deal of responsibility on the promotores of LHA, leading to higher rates of overwork and burnout in the same way that we observed with other frontline responders (Marquez et al., 2023). The promotores were the voice of their community, advocating for their needs, absorbing their pain as the pandemic accelerated, and working as diligently as possible to get them the information and resources they needed to protect them. The promotores at LHA felt unsupported by their government and felt that the agency support did not keep pace with the demand for services from the community, which is unsurprising given the intensity of the demand (Marquez et al., 2023).

We have seen this pattern in frontline responders in general (doctors, nurses, etc.); the difference between these frontline responders and promotores is that the promotores are members of the community they serve, so in some senses, they are doubly disadvantaged. They experience the same levels of poverty, discrimination, and crime as the other members of their community, and then they have the added difficulty of absorbing the community's pain. The combination of all of these factors created the perfect storm for this workforce—burnout and compassion fatigue—which is what these agencies were telling us.

As a result, I decided that I wanted to adapt relational savoring for use with the promotores at LHA and other similar agencies that serve low-income Latino/a/x families. So with the support of a grant from UC End Disparities and with the help of my colleagues Kelly Kazmierski, Lyric Russo, Nancy Guerra, DeWayne Williams, Briana Woods-Jaeger, Maryam Kia-Keating, and Alyson Zalta, I have been working toward this goal, adapting the intervention so it is focused on helping promotores and community service providers (essentially anyone who works within one of these agencies) savor moments in which they have provided support for the community.

We help them focus on secure base support (times when they supported someone in achieving a goal or accomplishing a milestone, such as helping someone get access to resources or clear an obstacle that was in their path), safe haven support (times when they provided emotional support for someone who needed respite from a difficult situation or force in their lives, such as when they needed a shoulder to cry on or someone to talk to about their fears of deportation), or moments of connection (such as when they felt close to someone in sharing a positive moment together or joining together as community). We are presently testing the efficacy of this intervention as a means of increasing job satisfaction, reducing burnout, and improving cardiometabolic health in these promotores.

The data for this study are just now rolling into my laboratory, but our initial sneak peek suggests promise from this approach. The participants have been engaged and have enjoyed the intervention, often making comments during the sessions about how they value the chance to share their experiences in this way. Here's a small excerpt from a relational savoring session with Mira, first in the original Spanish and then translated into English. You will hear that Mira expresses that she values the opportunity to engage in this sort of sharing about her work experiences:

Original Spanish

MIRA: Bueno, ahorita ya me siento más contenta.

RESEARCHER: [*Pequeña risa.*]

MIRA: Me ayuda mucho que qué lástima que es un estudio, pero creo que en este momento yo puedo hablar, y sacar; por ejemplo,

	los sentimientos que por lo que pasó con la señora [miembro de la comunidad] que me puse a llorar, yo llego con mi esposo y le platico, pero no le platico como me afectó.
MIRA:	Pero contigo sí.
RESEARCHER:	Mmm-hmm—
MIRA:	Contigo sí, sí, me siento, así como libre de platicar. Y gracias por este momento. Sí la voy a extrañar cuando ya no esté en este estudio—
RESEARCHER:	[*Pequeña risa.*]
MIRA:	Sabes por qué, porque me haces ver de otra manera lo que uno no ve. A lo mejor el cansancio o el estrés, la frustración, pero tus haces, me haces ver el otro lado, el lado más positivo. Entonces, mira, al principio estaba yo *uyyy*—ahorita ya como que me sale la sonrisa mejor.
RESEARCHER:	Qué bueno, qué bueno, y en realidad ese es el propósito de este estudio . . .

Translated English

MIRA:	Well, right now I feel happier.
RESEARCHER:	[*Little laugh.*]
MIRA:	It helps me a lot that what a pity that this is just a study, but I think that at this moment I can speak, and take out; for example, the feelings that for what happened with the lady [member of the community] that I started crying, I arrive with my husband and tell him, but I do not tell him how it affected me.
MIRA:	But with you yes.
RESEARCHER:	Mmm-hmm—
MIRA:	With you yes, yes, I feel, as well as free to talk. And thank you for this moment. Yes, I'm going to miss you when I'm no longer in this study—
RESEARCHER:	[*Little laugh.*]
MIRA:	You know why, because it makes me see differently, what you don't see, maybe fatigue or stress, frustration, but you do, you

	make me see the other side, the more positive side. So, look, at the beginning I was like *uyyy*—now I like I smile better.
RESEARCHER:	That's good, that's good, and in reality that is the purpose of this study . . .

My work with LHA has taught me a lesson, which is the importance of listening to the community to truly hear what they need and working first and foremost to be responsive to their needs. This may mean shifting course in my research, and it may mean forfeiting a prettily packaged research portfolio, but the trade-off is truly showing up for the community. In my view, that's worth it.

ADAPTING RELATIONAL SAVORING TO BE CULTURALLY CONGRUENT WITH OTHER GROUPS

I have focused in this chapter on my work adapting relational savoring for use with an agency serving low-income Latino/a/x families. The intervention is an intuitive cultural fit with the values of this community. I also have the aspiration of being able to adapt this intervention to other minoritized communities if the cultural fit makes sense.

For instance, I have the personal goal of adapting this intervention for use with Black/African American families; I think that the cultural values of these families will also align well with relational savoring. These families tend to emphasize strong family ties and closeness (Chao, 1994; Chen et al., 2012; Gorman, 1998), and I think we could appeal to these values within the intervention and that this would work well. I have not tested relational savoring with this community, but my hunch after meeting with some community groups and colleagues who work in this area is that with some minor modifications, this intervention could also be culturally congruent with the values of Black/African American families.

In contrast to the relatively simple adaptation made for Latino/a/x families, I think the steps needed to adapt this intervention to be culturally congruent with Asian cultural values may be less clear. Whereas Western cultures express positive emotions and emphasize pleasure and happiness, Eastern cultures tend to focus on the importance of experiencing harmony, focus on fears of happiness, and dampen positive feelings (Smith et al., 2019). This emphasis may serve to promote social cohesion and a sense of community and to prevent things that threaten a sense of community, such as jealousy (Miyamoto & Ma, 2011; Safdar et al., 2009).

Given the connection that people from Asian cultures feel with their community and relationships, savoring experts like Fred Bryant have argued that relational savoring may work well with Asian populations (Smith et al., 2019). In fact, they argue that relational savoring may be the best place to start in terms of adapting savoring interventions for Asian populations. However, my experience leads me to think that relational savoring may need to be more extensively adapted in order to be culturally congruent. I say this because my preliminary work in testing relational savoring with Asian and Asian American samples has led me to believe that the focus on positive emotion and constructs such as "closeness" and "pleasure" may not be culturally resonant with Asian and Asian American clients.

My colleagues and I have conducted a preliminary investigation on relational savoring among Asian samples, finding less efficacy from the approach than we would like (Pereira et al., 2021). In one study we found that both relational savoring and personal savoring increased significantly in positive emotion, but we did not find any differences between the two approaches (Pereira et al., 2021). This study was an online study, in which the participants were parents with children with autism spectrum disorder; they were administered a single session of relational or personal savoring online. Given this, it is difficult to know whether the outcomes would have been the same had the intervention been done in person.

In another unpublished study (Lee et al., 2019), the research team (of which I was a part but not the lead) worked with Asian American (Vietnamese American and Korean American) caregivers (of people with dementia), using relational savoring and a mindfulness intervention, and we found that the caregivers preferred the mindfulness intervention. In fact, initially the caregivers were asked to speak about a connected memory they had with the person with dementia, but they refused to discuss this happy memory. The principal investigator (Dr. Jung-Ah Lee) made the decision to convert the relational savoring condition into an active compassionate listening condition. This pilot study was extremely small, intended only to provide data to be used to inform intervention development, and it ended up directing the lead researcher away from using relational savoring as her main intervention approach.

What is a takeaway from this study? At the very least, these findings suggest that in order to be culturally congruent with this population, relational savoring might need to be modified more extensively to fit with the cultural values of East Asian cultures, such as through collaboration with community partners and by finding out how East Asian people best express pleasant feelings of connection to one another. One untested hunch I have is that there may need to be more of a focus on ideals of respect and honor within relationships rather than closeness and joy. If the intervention were modified to emphasize respect and honor, then it might fit more with Asian/Asian American cultural values. Another idea I have is to focus on feelings of calm and tranquility/peace within relationships rather than on excitement and pleasure (in other words, focusing on lower-arousal positive emotions); turning the nozzle down on the emotional intensity may make the intervention more in line with cultural values. This would be an interesting recommendation in light of other findings suggesting that higher arousal yields greater effects for participants high in depressive symptoms (Straszewski & Siegel, 2020). However, this study did not examine these effects as a function of participant race or ethnicity, making it impossible to know whether the effects are conserved across groups. We are in the process of developing a plan to pursue these questions.

The majority of the studies we have conducted on this intervention have involved female-identifying participants. This has occurred mostly because many of our studies have focused on mothers, but it has resulted in an uneven sampling of participants. This uneven sampling may mean that this intervention is more suitable for clients who are more verbal, more comfortable discussing relationships and moments of positive connection, and more comfortable sharing emotion. We have not examined participant gender as a moderator in our studies to evaluate whether this intervention works better for clients who are female, but just the fact that many of our studies have predominantly included female-identifying participants has led the effects to be biased in this direction.

Thus, it is possible that the intervention as it is currently written is more culturally congruent with traits that females, on average, tend to have. I acknowledge that gender is a continuum, differs from biological sex, and can be fluid. But for the sake of discussing tailoring this intervention, we may want to consider gender to be part of a client's cultural makeup. If this is the case, I may want to seek to make modifications to the intervention to allow it to be more culturally congruent with traditionally male cultural values. Said differently, I would want to modify it so that the intervention matched what male clients want from a relationship-based intervention.

To go about this process of modifying the intervention, I would probably introduce the idea of the intervention to a group of male-identifying clients (either in one-on-one meetings or in a focus group) and then gather their feedback on the intervention overall and on ways to tailor it to their values, needs, and interests. To make this more applicable to the clients, it might make sense to restrict the identities of the male clients to the population of interest, by role (e.g., male fathers, male members of romantic partnerships), racial/ethnic dimensions (e.g., Latino males), or other cultural groups (e.g., gay males). After this feedback solicitation, I would modify the intervention and then pilot it with males who matched the description of the males who had provided the feedback and solicit more feedback from these participants. I believe that this iterative process would lead to a more culturally congruent intervention for this population.

TAKE-HOME MESSAGES

I was not someone who had all of the right tools to do community-engaged work, nor was I someone who was equipped with loads of knowledge about community-based participatory research or community–academic partnerships. It would certainly be possible for many people to do a far better job of taking an intervention and adapting it within the community than I did.

I stumbled my way through this process as someone who had a lot of commitment to work with this community and who wanted to put my whole heart into it. I made a lot of mistakes along the way (reviewed comprehensively elsewhere; Borelli, Cervantes, et al., 2022), and I also learned a lot about myself through the process. I was scared throughout pretty much the whole experience. I was scared I would let everyone down, that the project would be a failure, that the intervention would flop, that I would waste the CDC's money, and that the program wouldn't work and would be a waste of time for community members. And as you can see from my comments here, I still have a long way to go in terms of the future modifications I would like to make to this intervention.

I would be lying if I didn't acknowledge that I'm still scared. But I am still committed to wanting to work with this community. When I watch videos of therapists doing this intervention with this community in Spanish, it gives me goosebumps. I feel I am doing the exact kind of work I was meant to be doing. I understand enough Spanish to be able to give the therapists feedback on their therapy techniques but do not speak it well enough to be able to do the intervention sessions myself (I wish! Maybe in another 5 years!). I know it's not going to be perfect, and I know there is a very good chance I am going to say or do something that could offend the agency I am working with, but I also know that the work matters enough for me to continue trying.

My advice for doing this work of taking an intervention, such as relational savoring, and adapting it for use with a community agency, is the following. Identify an agency with whom you would like to work. Ideally, that agency should serve a population whose cultural values align with the values of the intervention you would like to use. If it is relational savoring that you want to implement within the agency, these values tend to be values of collectivism/familism, as well as valuing positive emotion, particularly in the context of close relationships.

Once you have identified an agency, meet with that agency to find out what their goals are for serving their community. Figure out how they envision your work with them and the holes they are trying to fill in their programming. For instance, if you meet with your agency and you learn that what they really want to do is work on homelessness prevention and they were hoping you could help them with that, then you coming in and asking to start your own program that goes in a completely different direction might not be a good fit, at least not at this time. However, if they have a goal for identifying an emotional wellness program or a parenting or couples program in their agency, then this could be a very good fit.

Next, have conversations about resources; by resources, I mean funds, person hours, supervision hours, collaboration hours, supplies, transportation costs, administration overhead, and food. Namely, [get] get a sense of how many resources they would like to contribute to the development and implementation of the program and how many resources they want you to contribute to the same. There can be misunderstandings about this along the way, and these misunderstandings can lead to resentment and anger if not addressed, so it is best to be clear about this from the outset. They will have ideas about how many resources it takes to run a program, and you may also have ideas about how many resources it takes to run a program. If you have goals for collecting data alongside your program, it is also a great idea to make that clear at this juncture.

Community agencies, particularly those agencies that work with disenfranchised communities, can harbor negative feelings (e.g., resentment, fear, hurt) toward researchers. They have been harmed by researchers in the past and may justifiably feel that researchers are there to objectify them, to use them, or to victimize them in some way. It is crucial to explain the purpose of the research in a way that everyone can understand. At this point, you may want to do that in a big-picture way, but you might also want to specify what you would need from them and from program participants. In my experience, this led to the greatest amount of friction between my community partner and me—differences between what each of us thought was reasonable and expected on the research front. Here I found that it can help to talk about what the funder requires from a reporting perspective, but I also think it helps (probably more) to talk about what the benefits will be to the community once we have information about how something works or does not work. You can also do them one better and tell them what you will do with that information when you have it, such as how you will tell the community members about your findings.

One important point I want to make here is the attitude and approach one must have in forming these relationships. The agreements that are formed must be mutually beneficial to both parties, so if the community agency is uncomfortable with some of the terms the mental health practitioner/researcher has offered, then the mental health practitioner/researcher should reconsider those terms. And likewise, if what the agency is asking for seems like too far of a stretch for the mental health practitioner/researcher, the mental health practitioner/researcher should take that into consideration and tell the community agency that this might not be a good fit for them because it might not fit the requirements of their project.

In the end, neither the community agency nor the mental health practitioner/researcher should be in a position of entering into an agreement with which they are uncomfortable. It is not uncommon for groups to create memoranda of understandings or other collaborative agreements, so complex are these relationships. I have never done this before myself, but I understand why they come to be. Often these arrangements also involve complex financial agreements, which include agreements about who is going to do what (or pay for what) in the relationship, and people are not infallible, so it can be beneficial to have a formal agreement in place. At the very least, meeting minutes or notes from meetings will help increase accountability.

At this juncture, I think it can also be helpful to discuss each entity's desired degree of involvement in program development. I referred to this above as intervention codevelopment. In my involvement with LHA, the promotores were very involved in intervention co-development, which was very consistent with the mores of that community agency. Not all agencies will value participation in program development to the same degree. In fact, in some agencies, asking for staff involvement in program development could feel like an added burden, more time that you are adding to their to-dos. So asking whether they would like to be involved is wise. Similarly, you as a mental health practitioner/researcher may not wish to have staff or community member input into the development of your intervention. This will undoubtedly change the intervention, and if you have something set as is and do not wish to alter it, even with the desire to make it more culturally congruent, you may not wish to offer this.

Once you have a plan in place for how much involvement each key stakeholder will have and what the big-picture plan will be, scheduling regular check-ins is another must. The check-ins should be efficient because people working at these agencies are busy. Coming to the meetings with an agenda is important and will help increase your efficiency. It is important at these meetings to also assess the agency member's satisfaction with the collaborative process; that way you can address problems that emerge before they become too large.

Follow through with what you promised the agency: If you said you would complete an evaluation, ensure that you do that. If you said you would stick with them through a certain period of time, make sure you do that. Also, make sure you show up in other ways for the agency so that you show them you do not only care about your program. Attend community events, and donate money (if you can, even in small amounts) to the agency. Send birthday cards to agency members. Show up as a person first and foremost at the agency so that you are present. Remember that agency members are sensitive to this idea of outsiders coming in to use them and their access to community members for their purposes and then leaving. Make sure that you break that stereotype by going above and beyond in the opposite direction. Essentially, make sure you show up in an authentic, enduring, and present way for your agency and not just for your program or project.

WRAP-UP

This is a rich and promising area, and doing this work within the context of community agencies presents so many opportunities for enrichment. My own work has only been enhanced by these experiences, and I hope that others of you will take a similar step in your work. Partnering with different communities to meet their needs will not only enhance the development of our existing interventions, making them more culturally responsive but also improve our ability to provide clinical services to these communities as well as heighten our knowledge about best practices in working with different communities.

AFTERWORD
Relational Savoring for Therapists

In the brief informal survey I mentioned doing in Chapter 10 with colleagues who had learned about relational savoring, the last question I asked them was whether learning about relational savoring has affected their approach to their clinical work; 89% said it made them make a conscious effort to focus on moments of positive connectedness with their clients more, while 11% said it had not affected how they process their clinical experiences. I am hoping that learning about relational savoring will do the same for you—that it will affect how you not only approach your own clients but also think and feel about your work.

This benefit can be twofold. First, much as I discussed in Chapter 10 with our study of using relational savoring to help promotores stay engaged with their work in the community, I believe that using this technique can help therapists stay engaged in our work as helpers. Because let's be honest: Being a therapist is not an easy gig. It is not uncommon to feel challenged by clients, ineffective, or discouraged, or to wonder if anything you are doing is making a difference.

---

https://doi.org/10.1037/0000372-011
Relational Savoring: Using Guided Reflection to Strengthen Relationships and Improve Outcomes in Therapy, by J. L. Borelli
Copyright © 2024 by the American Psychological Association. All rights reserved.

A common problem among therapists is compassion fatigue, a form of burnout that can occur among people who are involved in providing care for people who are experiencing trauma, crisis, or high levels of emotional distress (Bride et al., 2007; Figley, 1998, 2002; McCann & Pearlman, 1990; Negash & Sahin, 2011). This can result in a range of psychological and physiological symptoms, including exhaustion, negative sentiment toward work, and physical symptoms (e.g., headaches, chronic pain). According to a nationally representative study of therapists conducted in 2009, 5% of therapists met the criteria for compassion fatigue (Craig & Sprang, 2010).

Unsurprisingly, rates of compassion fatigue among mental health professionals have been on the climb during the COVID-19 pandemic. The demand for mental health services has been extremely high (Holmes et al., 2021), and with fewer outlets for self-care and joy, as well as more demands on therapists in all aspects of our lives, therapists are overburdened.

In support of this theorizing that the pandemic worsened compassion fatigue among mental health providers, a study of social workers conducted during the COVID-19 pandemic found that 63% reported experiencing burnout (Holmes et al., 2021). Likewise, a study of psychotherapists working in the VA hospital context found that burnout increased from 40% to 56% during the COVID-19 pandemic among posttraumatic stress disorder therapists (Rosen et al., 2023; note that this study used a different measure of burnout than the previous study). These figures from pre- to postpandemic are not directly comparable because they are not from the same samples; however, they were all from large samples of mental health professionals, and the differences in the percentage of mental health professionals reporting burnout are so great from pre- to postpandemic that we likely can draw the conclusion that the pandemic increased therapists' risk for burnout.

There are many powerful antidotes against compassion fatigue and burnout. For example, taking breaks, exercising regularly, and taking restorative vacations can be a wonderful way to buffer yourself against the ills of stress buildup. But more on theme, reflecting on what matters to us can also be a way to ground ourselves in why we do what we do. One of the ways to do this is to pose the following question to yourself in one way or another: *What am I proud of having done in my life? How have I made a positive impact on the world?* I ask myself this because having a positive impact on others keeps me going. So for me, part of making my work feel meaningful lies in reminding myself that my work in fact has meaning for myself and others.

This has certain parallels to the values reflection that is often undertaken in acceptance and commitment therapy (Hayes & Strosahl, 2005; Hayes et al., 1999). And for me, the answer to this question often comes down to the people whose lives I have made an impact on. I think about my children and how I have positively shaped their lives and I also think about my clients. I think about the instances in which I might have actually saved people's lives, and I also think about times I might have helped change the course of clients' lives. I hold these memories close to my heart, letting them sink in, feeling deep waves of gratitude pass over me that I got to be the person in these people's lives.

Standing beside people during the toughest time in their lives is such a privilege, despite all of its challenges. Sometimes I look through cards I have saved from former clients in which they have written me particularly meaningful messages; I reread these messages, savoring the words from the client about the impact I have had on their lives. One of my clients wrote all of her college essays about the way that therapy changed her life. A former client left a Yelp review on my practice. This one I go back to and reread regularly because it warms my heart:

> She helped me to grow by showing how much she cared that I lived. She was always available to support me, even if we did not have a scheduled session. She encouraged me to live when I didn't want to. She taught me skills to love myself for the first time in my life. She taught me how to heal from a horrific life. She taught me how to have confidence. She taught me how to have successful personal relationships. Sometimes there were setbacks because I had a hard time stopping my toxic behaviors that hurt me. She taught me to forgive myself. She taught me how to be happy. She taught me how to trust in myself. I was a hard case and a difficult patient so it took ten years. I now have a beautiful marriage, a very successful career, many wonderful friends (I had to trust her and remove the negative people from my life), and personal joy. I now love life. I love me. I love my life and I never thought that was even a remote possibility.

This *is* relational savoring—bringing to mind these cherished memories of connection, and specifically, of how my connection to others has positively affected their lives. It does not have to be a five-step process to be relational savoring; just ensuring that I am allowing my mind to pause on these positive moments means I am engaging in the process. And I believe that engaging in this reflective process from time to time can bring more positive emotions and meaning to your life and your work. It might rejuvenate you, increasing your job satisfaction and satisfaction. It might remind you of why you do the work that you do. Rather than review your greatest failures as a therapist, you could regularly review your greatest hits. Instead of allowing them to just quickly pass by, you could really make a point to savor them, to marinate in their juices. Stay a while, allow yourself to linger and really enjoy. If you are so inclined, you could even go through all of the steps of the relational savoring to reflect deeply on the feeling and meaning associated with the experience.

There is one other way in which you as a therapist might wish to use relational savoring: You could accentuate a relational or intersubjective dynamic between you and your clients. You might wish to heighten the moment of connectedness between you and your client. For instance, you could highlight for them how they feel in the moment of being so close to them. Or you could ask them how it felt for you to be aware of their need to be noticed or taken care of in that way: How did it feel? Where did they feel it in their body? And what did it make them think? What does it mean about their relationship with you? What does it mean for their future and for their relationship with you?

Depending on the client's relational history, the therapist may also wish to underline how this interaction differs from other types of interactions the client has had in the past. Finally, the therapist might want to share how they feel in the situation; this sharing could further enhance the bonding that occurs in the encounter.

Hopefully, this example has illustrated how one can flexibly weave some of the content of relational savoring to underscore the connection between the therapist and the client in a way that feels natural and unscripted. This approach allows the therapist to emphasize the relationship the therapist and client are building in a very present-oriented, in-the-moment way.

CLOSING

I want to close by returning to an argument we discussed at the beginning of the book. Figure 1 presents the bidirectional connection between caregiving and care-receiving. One important tenet represented by this figure is that experiences in care-receiving relationships have important downstream effects on our ability to engage in caregiving. This argument has been supported by half a century of theorizing by Bowlby (1973) and Ainsworth et al. (1978a), and more recently through animal epigenetic models that demonstrate that experiences of being parented have impacts on DNA, which in turn affects their caregiving behavior later in life (Caldji et al., 1998). But it is actually more complex than this; there is not just a relationship between how we are cared for and learn to care for others. There is also a connection between how we provide care and how we believe we deserve to be cared for. These relationships are truly transactional.

FIGURE 1. Bidirectional Connection Between Caregiving and Care-Receiving

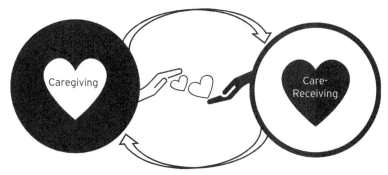

This principle also has important implications for us as therapists. Our work has the potential to be transformative for us; it can fulfill us and even heal us by helping to change our own internal working model of how we deserve to be cared for. Engaging in reflective practices, like relational savoring, that seek to maximize the meaning we derive from the work is a piece of this puzzle, as it can help us arrive at this place.

However, the cycle can also operate in the reverse direction. Following this logic that there is a bidirectional path of influence between care-receiving and caregiving, in order to be effective providers of care (e.g., in our roles as therapists), we must also receive sufficient care in other ways, whether from other people in our lives or from other outlets (e.g., self-care). Receiving the kind of care that we deserve to receive (loving, sensitive care) will enable us to be sensitive caregivers to others, helping to prevent compassion fatigue. We as therapists are also people who have needs and deserve to be nurtured. We may find that a combination of seeking concrete ways to meet those needs and engaging in reflective practices to heighten our awareness of those needs being met (e.g., relational savoring) will help to increase our felt sense of having been cared for, which ultimately enhances the ability to help.

References

Aber, J. L., Slade, A., Berger, B., Bresgi, I., & Kaplan, M. (1985). *The parent development interview* [Unpublished manuscript]. Barnard College, Columbia University.

Abramovitch, A., Pizzagalli, D. A., Reuman, L., & Wilhelm, S. (2014). Anhedonia in obsessive–compulsive disorder: Beyond comorbid depression. *Psychiatry Research, 216*(2), 223–229. https://doi.org/10.1016/j.psychres.2014.02.002

Abrams, K. Y., Rifkin, A., & Hesse, E. (2006). Examining the role of parental frightened/frightening subtypes in predicting disorganized attachment within a brief observational procedure. *Development and Psychopathology, 18*(2), 345–361. https://doi.org/10.1017/s0954579406060184

Acevedo, A. M., Herrera, C., Shenhav, S., Yim, I. S., & Campos, B. (2020). Measurement of a Latino cultural value: The Simpatía scale. *Cultural Diversity & Ethnic Minority Psychology, 26*(4), 419–425. https://doi.org/10.1037/cdp0000324

Agishtein, P., & Brumbaugh, C. (2013). Cultural variation in adult attachment: The impact of ethnicity, collectivism, and country of origin. *Journal of Social, Evolutionary, and Cultural Psychology, 7*(4), 384–405. https://doi.org/10.1037/h0099181

Ahmed, A. O., Murphy, C. F., Latoussakis, V., McGovern, K. E., English, J., Bloch, A., Anthony, D. T., & Savitz, A. J. (2016). An examination of neurocognition and symptoms as predictors of post-hospital community tenure in treatment resistant schizophrenia. *Psychiatry Research, 236*, 47–52. https://doi.org/10.1016/j.psychres.2016.01.001

Ahmedani, B. K. (2011). Mental health stigma: Society, individuals, and the profession. *Journal of Social Work Values and Ethics, 8*(2), 4-1–4-16.

Ainsworth, M. D. S. (1974). *Infancy in Uganda: Infant care and the growth of love*. Johns Hopkins University Press.

Ainsworth, M. D. S., & Bell, S. M. (1970). Attachment, exploration, and separation: Illustrated by the behavior of one-year-olds in a strange situation. *Child Development, 41*(1), 49–67. https://doi.org/10.2307/1127388

Ainsworth, M. D. S., Bell, S. M., & Stayton, D. J. (1974). Infant–mother attachment and social development: Socialisation as a product of reciprocal responsiveness to social signals. In M. P. M. Richards (Ed.), *The introduction of the child into a social world* (pp. 99–135). Cambridge University Press.

Ainsworth, M. D. S., Blehar, M. C., Waters, E., & Wall, S. (1978a). *Patterns of attachment: A psychological study of the Strange Situation*. Erlbaum.

Ainsworth, M. D. S., Blehar, M. C., Waters, E., & Wall, S. (1978b). Strange Situation Procedure. *Clinical Child Psychology and Psychiatry*. Advance online publication. https://doi.org/10.1037/t28248-000

Allen, J. P., & Miga, E. M. (2010). Attachment in adolescence: A move to the level of emotion regulation. *Journal of Social and Personal Relationships, 27*(2), 181–190. https://doi.org/10.1177/0265407509360898

American Psychological Association. (2017). *Ethical principles of psychologists and code of conduct* (2002, amended effective June 1, 2010, and January 1, 2017). https://www.apa.org/ethics/code/index.aspx

Amstadter, A. (2008). Emotion regulation and anxiety disorders. *Journal of Anxiety Disorders, 22*(2), 211–221. https://doi.org/10.1016/j.janxdis.2007.02.004

Arbona, C., & Power, T. G. (2003). Parental attachment, self-esteem, and antisocial behaviors among African American, European American, and Mexican American adolescents. *Journal of Counseling Psychology, 50*(1), 40–51. https://doi.org/10.1037/0022-0167.50.1.40

Areni, C. S., & Black, I. (2015). Consumers' responses to small portions: Signaling increases savoring and satiation. *Psychology and Marketing, 32*(5), 532–543. https://doi.org/10.1002/mar.20798

Ashby, F. G., Isen, A. M., & Turken, A. U. (1999). A neuropsychological theory of positive affect and its influence on cognition. *Psychological Review, 106*(3), 529–550. https://doi.org/10.1037/0033-295x.106.3.529

Assaad, L. (2016). *The association of social anhedonia with romantic relationship processes* [Doctoral dissertation, University of Maryland, College Park]. Digital Repository at the University of Maryland. https://doi.org/10.13016/M29J5V

Assaad, L., & Lemay, E. P., Jr. (2018). Social anhedonia and romantic relationship processes. *Journal of Personality, 86*(2), 147–157. https://doi.org/10.1111/jopy.12300

Atherton, B. D., Nevels, R. M., & Moore, M. T. (2015). Predicting symptoms of depression from social anhedonia and emotion regulation. *Journal of Nervous and Mental Disease, 203*(3), 170–174. https://doi.org/10.1097/nmd.0000000000000262

Ayduk, Ö., & Kross, E. (2010). Analyzing negative experiences without ruminating: The role of self-distancing in enabling adaptive self-reflection. *Social and Personality Psychology Compass, 4*(10), 841–854. https://doi.org/10.1111/j.1751-9004.2010.00301.x

Baer, R. A., Smith, G. T., Hopkins, J., Krietemeyer, J., & Toney, L. (2006). Using self-report assessment methods to explore facets of mindfulness. *Assessment, 13*(1), 27–45. https://doi.org/10.1177/1073191105283504

Barkus, E., & Badcock, J. C. (2019). A transdiagnostic perspective on social anhedonia. *Frontiers in Psychiatry, 10*, Article 216. https://doi.org/10.3389/fpsyt.2019.00216

Barnett, M., Miranda, J., Kia-Keating, M., Saldana, L., Landsverk, J., & Lau, A. S. (2019). Developing and evaluating a lay health worker delivered implementation intervention to decrease engagement disparities in behavioural parent training: A mixed methods study protocol. *BMJ Open, 9*(7), Article e028988. https://doi.org/10.1136/bmjopen-2019-028988

Barnett, M. L., Gonzalez, A., Miranda, J., Chavira, D. A., & Lau, A. S. (2018). Mobilizing community health workers to address mental health disparities for underserved populations: A systematic review. *Administration and Policy in Mental Health, 45*(2), 195–211. https://doi.org/10.1007/s10488-017-0815-0

Beidas, R. S., Podell, J., & Kendall, P. C. (2008). Cognitive-behavioral treatment for child and adolescent anxiety: The Coping Cat Program. In C. W. LeCroy (Ed.), *Handbook of evidence-based treatment manuals for children and adolescents* (2nd ed., 405–411). Oxford University Press.

Beijersbergen, M. D., Juffer, F., Bakermans-Kranenburg, M. J., & van IJzendoorn, M. H. (2012). Remaining or becoming secure: Parental sensitive support predicts attachment continuity from infancy to adolescence in a longitudinal adoption study. *Developmental Psychology, 48*(5), 1277–1282. https://doi.org/10.1037/a0027442

Ben-Tovim, D. I., Walker, M. K., Fok, D., & Yap, E. (1989). An adaptation of the Stroop test for measuring shape and food concerns in eating disorders: A quantitative measure of psychopathology? *International Journal of Eating Disorders, 8*(6), 681–687. https://doi.org/10.1002/1098-108X(198911)8:6%3C681::AID-EAT2260080609%3E3.0.CO;2-%23

Berry, O. O., Londoño Tobón, A., & Njoroge, W. F. (2021). Social determinants of health: The impact of racism on early childhood mental health. *Current Psychiatry Reports, 23*(5), 1–10. https://doi.org/10.1007/s11920-021-01240-0

Bharadwaj, P., Pai, M. M., & Suziedelyte, A. (2017). Mental health stigma. *Economics Letters, 159*, 57–60. https://doi.org/10.1016/j.econlet.2017.06.028

Blais, R. K. (2020). Higher anhedonia and dysphoric arousal relate to lower relationship satisfaction among trauma-exposed female service members/veterans. *Journal of Clinical Psychology, 76*(7), 1327–1338. https://doi.org/10.1002/jclp.22937

Blanchard, J. J., Mueser, K. T., & Bellack, A. S. (1998). Anhedonia, positive and negative affect, and social functioning in schizophrenia. *Schizophrenia Bulletin, 24*(3), 413–424. https://doi.org/10.1093/oxfordjournals.schbul.a033336

Bland, A. R., Williams, C. A., Scharer, K., & Manning, S. (2004). Emotion processing in borderline personality disorders. *Issues in Mental Health Nursing, 25*(7), 655–672. https://doi.org/10.1080/01612840490486692

Bond, D. K., & Borelli, J. L. (2017). Maternal attachment insecurity and poorer proficiency savoring memories with their children: The mediating role of rumination. *Journal of Social and Personal Relationships, 34*(7), 1007–1030. https://doi.org/10.1177/0265407516664995

Borelli, J. L., Bond, D. K., Fox, S., & Horn-Mallers, M. (2020). Relational savoring reduces physiological reactivity and enhances psychological agency in older adults. *Journal of Applied Gerontology, 39*(3), 332–342. https://doi.org/10.1177/0733464819866972

Borelli, J. L., Burkhart, M. L., Rasmussen, H. F., Brody, R., & Sbarra, D. A. (2017). Secure base script content explains the association between attachment avoidance and emotion-related constructs in parents of young children. *Infant Mental Health Journal, 38*(2), 210–225. https://doi.org/10.1002/imhj.21632

Borelli, J. L., Cervantes, B. R., Hecht, H. K., Marquez, C. M., DePrado, R., Torres, G., Robles, A., Chirinos, N., Leal, F., Montiel, G. I., Pedroza, M., & Guerra, N. (2022). Barreras y Soluciones: Lessons learned from integrating research-based clinical techniques into a community agency serving low-income Latinx immigrant families. *Family Process, 61*(1), 108–129. https://doi.org/10.1111/famp.12712

Borelli, J. L., Hong, K., Kazmierski, K. F. M., Smiley, P. A., Sohn, L., & Guo, Y. (2022). Parents' depressive symptoms and reflective functioning predict parents' proficiency in relational savoring and children's physiological regulation. *Development and Psychopathology*, 1–14. https://doi.org/10.1017/s095457942200102x

Borelli, J. L., Kazmierski, K. F. M., Gaskin, G. E., Kerr, M. L., Smiley, P. A., & Rasmussen, H. F. (2023). Savoring interventions for mothers of young children: Mechanisms linking relational savoring and personal savoring to reflective functioning. *Infant Mental Health Journal, 44*(2), 200–217. https://doi.org/10.1002/imhj.22038

Borelli, J. L., Kerr, M. L., Smiley, P. A., Rasmussen, H. F., Hecht, H. K., & Campos, B. (2023). Relational savoring intervention: Positive impacts for mothers and evidence of cultural compatibility for Latinas. *Emotion, 23*(2), 303–320. https://doi.org/10.1037/emo0001102

Borelli, J. L., Pedroza, M., Gaskin, G. E., Smiley, P. A., Kernick, C., Brachman, A., & Mehl, M. (2018). School-aged children's cognitive interdependence as a prospective link between their depressive symptoms and physiological stress reactivity. *Journal of Social and Clinical Psychology, 37*(5), 325–355. https://doi.org/10.1521/jscp.2018.37.5.325

Borelli, J. L., Rasmussen, H. F., Burkhart, M. L., & Sbarra, D. A. (2015). Relational savoring in long-distance romantic relationships. *Journal of Social and Personal Relationships, 32*, 1083–1108. https://doi.org/10.1177/0265407514558960

Borelli, J. L., Russo, L. N., Arreola, J., Cervantes, B. R., Hecht, H. K., Leal, F., Montiel, G., Paredes, P., & Guerra, N. (2021). Más Fuertes Juntos: Attachment relationship quality, but not demographic risk, predicts psychopathology in Latinx mother-youth dyads. *Journal of Community Psychology, 49*(6), 2086–2105. https://doi.org/10.1002/jcop.22535

Borelli, J. L., Russo, L. N., Arreola, J., Cervantes, B. R., Marquez, C. M., Montiel, G., Avalos, V., Carballo, J., Garcia, J., Bhatt, I., Torres, G., Leal, F., & Guerra, N. (2022). Saving a seat at the table for community members: Co-creating an attachment-based intervention for low-income Latinx parent-youth dyads using a promotor/a model. *Research in Psychotherapy, 25*(1), 39–56. https://doi.org/10.4081/ripppo.2022.598

Borelli, J. L., Sbarra, D. A., Snavely, J. E., McMakin, D. L., Coffey, J. K., Ruiz, S. K., Wang, B. A., & Chung, S. Y. (2014). With or without you: Preliminary evidence that attachment avoidance predicts nondeployed spouses' reactions to relationship challenges during deployment. *Professional Psychology, Research and Practice, 45*(6), 478–487. https://doi.org/10.1037/a0037780

Borelli, J. L., Smiley, P. A., Kerr, M. L., Hong, K., Hecht, H. K., Blackard, M. B., Falasiri, E., Cervantes, B. R., & Bond, D. K. (2020). Relational savoring: An attachment-based approach to promoting interpersonal flourishing. *Psychotherapy, 57*(3), 340–351. https://doi.org/10.1037/pst0000284

Borelli, J. L., Yates, T. M., Hecht, H. K., Cervantes, B. R., Russo, L. N., Arreola, J., Leal, F., Torres, G., & Guerra, N. (2021). Confía en mí, Confío en ti: Applying developmental theory to mitigate sociocultural risk in Latinx families. *Development and Psychopathology, 33*(2), 581–597. https://doi.org/10.1017/s0954579420001364

Bowlby, J. (1969). *Attachment and loss: Vol. 1. Attachment*. Basic Books.

Bowlby, J. (1973). *Attachment and loss: Vol. 2. Separation*. Basic Books.

Bowlby, J. (1980). *Attachment and loss: Vol. 3. Loss*. Basic Books.

Bowlby, J. (1988). *A secure base: Parent-child attachment and healthy human development*. Basic Books.

Bracho, A., Lee, G., Giraldo, G. P., & De Prado, R. M. (2016). *Recruiting the heart, training the brain*. Hesperian Health Guides.

Bradley, M. M., & Lang, P. J. (1994). Measuring emotion: The self-assessment manikin and the semantic differential. *Journal of Behavior Therapy and Experimental Psychiatry, 25*(1), 49–59. https://doi.org/10.1016/0005-7916(94)90063-9

Braithwaite, S., & Holt-Lunstad, J. (2017). Romantic relationships and mental health. *Current Opinion in Psychology, 13*, 120–125. https://doi.org/10.1016/j.copsyc.2016.04.001

Breslau, J., Miller, E., Jin, R., Sampson, N. A., Alonso, J., Andrade, L. H., Bromet, E. J., de Girolamo, G., Demyttenaere, K., Fayyad, J., Fukao, A., Gălăon, M., Gureje, O., He, Y., Hinkov, H. R., Hu, C., Kovess-Masfety, V., Matschinger, H., Medina-Mora, M. E., . . . Kessler, R. C. (2011). A multinational study of mental disorders, marriage, and divorce. *Acta Psychiatrica Scandinavica, 124*(6), 474–486. https://doi.org/10.1111/j.1600-0447.2011.01712.x

Bretherton, I. (1992). The origins of attachment theory: John Bowlby and Mary Ainsworth. *Developmental Psychology, 28*(5), 759–775. https://doi.org/10.1037/0012-1649.28.5.759

Bride, B. E., Radey, M., & Figley, C. R. (2007). Measuring compassion fatigue. *Clinical Social Work Journal, 35*(3), 155–163. https://doi.org/10.1007/s10615-007-0091-7

Broome, M. R., Woolley, J. B., Tabraham, P., Johns, L. C., Bramon, E., Murray, G. K., Pariante, C., McGuire, P. K., & Murray, R. M. (2005). What causes the onset of psychosis? *Schizophrenia Research, 79*(1), 23–34. https://doi.org/10.1016/j.schres.2005.02.007

Brosschot, J. F., Verkuil, B., & Thayer, J. F. (2016). The default response to uncertainty and the importance of perceived safety in anxiety and stress: An evolution-theoretical perspective. *Journal of Anxiety Disorders, 41*, 22–34. https://doi.org/10.1016/j.janxdis.2016.04.012

Brown, B. (2010a). *The gifts of imperfection: Let go of who you think you're supposed to be and embrace who you are*. Simon & Schuster.

Brown, B. (2010b). *The power of vulnerability* [Video]. TED Conferences. https://www.ted.com/talks/brene_brown_the_power_of_vulnerability/c

Brown, B. (2012). *Daring greatly: How the courage to be vulnerable transforms the way we live, love, parent, and lead*. Gotham.

Brown, K. W., & Ryan, R. M. (2003). The benefits of being present: Mindfulness and its role in psychological well-being. *Journal of Personality and Social Psychology, 84*(4), 822–848. https://doi.org/10.1037/0022-3514.84.4.822

Brown, L. H., Silvia, P. J., Myin-Germeys, I., & Kwapil, T. R. (2007). When the need to belong goes wrong: The expression of social anhedonia and social anxiety in daily life. *Psychological Science, 18*(9), 778–782. https://doi.org/10.1111/j.1467-9280.2007.01978.x

Bryant, F. B. (2003). Savoring Beliefs Inventory (SBI): A scale for measuring beliefs about savouring. *Journal of Mental Health, 12*(2), 175–196. https://doi.org/10.1080/0963823031000103489

Bryant, F. B. (2021). Current progress and future directions for theory and research on savoring. *Frontiers in Psychology, 12*, Article 771698. https://doi.org/10.3389/fpsyg.2021.771698

Bryant, F. B., Chadwick, E. D., & Kluwe, K. (2011). Understanding the processes that regulate positive emotional experience: Unsolved problems and future directions for theory and research on savoring. *International Journal of Wellbeing, 1*(1), 107–126. https://doi.org/10.5502/ijw.v1i1.18

Bryant, F. B., Ericksen, C. L., & DeHoek, A. H. (2008). Savoring. In S. J. Lopez (Ed.), *Encyclopedia of positive psychology* (Vol. 2, pp. 857–859). Wiley/Blackwell.

Bryant, F. B., Smart, C. M., & King, S. P. (2005). Using the past to enhance the present: Boosting happiness through positive reminiscence. *Journal of Happiness Studies, 6*, 227–260. https://doi.org/10.1007/s10902-005-3889-4

Bryant, F. B., & Veroff, J. (2007). *Savoring: A new model of positive experience*. Lawrence Erlbaum.

Burbridge, J. A., & Barch, D. M. (2007). Anhedonia and the experience of emotion in individuals with schizophrenia. *Journal of Abnormal Psychology, 116*(1), 30–42. https://doi.org/10.1037/0021-843x.116.1.30

Burkhart, M. L., Borelli, J. L., Rasmussen, H. F., Brody, R., & Sbarra, D. A. (2017). Parental mentalizing as an indirect link between attachment anxiety and parenting satisfaction. *Journal of Family Psychology, 31*(2), 203–213. https://doi.org/10.1037/fam0000270

Burkhart, M. L., Borelli, J. L., Rasmussen, H. F., & Sbarra, D. B. (2015). Cherish the good times: Relational savoring in parents of infants and toddlers. *Personal Relationships, 22*(4), 692–711. https://doi.org/10.1111/pere.12104

Caldji, C., Tannenbaum, B., Sharma, S., Francis, D., Plotsky, P. M., & Meaney, M. J. (1998). Maternal care during infancy regulates the development of neural systems mediating the expression of fearfulness in the rat. *Proceedings of the National Academy of Sciences of the United States of America, 95*(9), 5335–5340. https://doi.org/10.1073/pnas.95.9.5335

Calhoun, L. G., & Tedeschi, R. G. (1999). *Facilitating posttraumatic growth: A clinician's guide*. Routledge. https://doi.org/10.4324/9781410602268

Calhoun, L. G., & Tedeschi, R. G. (2001). Posttraumatic growth: The positive lessons of loss. In R. A. Neimeyer (Ed.), *Meaning reconstruction and the experience of loss* (pp. 157–172). American Psychological Association. https://doi.org/10.1037/10397-008

Calzada, E. J. (2010). Bringing culture into parent training with Latinos. *Cognitive and Behavioral Practice, 17*(2), 167–175. https://doi.org/10.1016/j.cbpra.2010.01.003

Campos, B., & Kim, H. S. (2017). Incorporating the cultural diversity of family and close relationships into the study of health. *American Psychologist, 72*(6), 543–554. https://doi.org/10.1037/amp0000122

Cannon, M. F., & Weems, C. F. (2006). Do anxiety and depression cluster into distinct groups? A test of tripartite model predictions in a community sample of youth. *Depression and Anxiety, 23*(8), 453–460. https://doi.org/10.1002/da.20215

Capps, L., Sigman, M., & Mundy, P. (1994). Attachment security in children with autism. *Development and Psychopathology, 6*(2), 249–261. https://doi.org/10.1017/s0954579400004569

Cardona, J. P., Holtrop, K., Córdova, D., Jr., Escobar-Chew, A. R., Horsford, S., Tams, L., Villarruel, F. A., Villalobos, G., Dates, B., Anthony, J. C., & Fitzgerald, H. E. (2009). "Queremos aprender": Latino immigrants' call to integrate cultural adaptation with best practice knowledge in a parenting intervention. *Family Process, 48*(2), 211–231. https://doi.org/10.1111/j.1545-5300.2009.01278.x

Carl, J. R., Soskin, D. P., Kerns, C., & Barlow, D. H. (2013). Positive emotion regulation in emotional disorders: A theoretical review. *Clinical Psychology Review, 33*(3), 343–360. https://doi.org/10.1016/j.cpr.2013.01.003

Carnelley, K. B., & Rowe, A. C. (2007). Repeated priming of attachment security influences later views of self and relationships. *Personal Relationships, 14*(2), 307–320. https://doi.org/10.1111/j.1475-6811.2007.00156.x

Carver, C. S., & Johnson, S. L. (2009). Tendencies toward mania and tendencies toward depression have distinct motivational, affective, and cognitive correlates.

Cognitive Therapy and Research, 33(6), 552–569. https://doi.org/10.1007/s10608-008-9213-y

Cassidy, J. (1994). Emotion regulation: Influences of attachment relationships. *Monographs of the Society for Research in Child Development, 59*(2–3), 228–249. https://doi.org/10.1111/j.1540-5834.1994.tb01287.x

Cassidy, J., & Berlin, L. J. (1994). The insecure/ambivalent pattern of attachment: Theory and research. *Child Development, 65*(4), 971–991. https://doi.org/10.1111/j.1467-8624.1994.tb00796.x

Cassidy, J., & Kobak, R. R. (1988). Avoidance and its relation to other defensive processes. In J. Belsky & T. Nezworski (Eds.), *Clinical implications of attachment* (pp. 300–323). Lawrence Erlbaum.

Chao, R. K. (1994). Beyond parental control and authoritarian parenting style: Understanding Chinese parenting through the cultural notion of training. *Child Development, 65*(4), 1111–1119. https://doi.org/10.1111/j.1467-8624.1994.tb00806.x

Chapman, G. D. (1992). *The five love languages: How to express heartfelt commitment to your mate.* Northfield Publishing.

Cheetham, A., Allen, N. B., Yücel, M., & Lubman, D. I. (2010). The role of affective dysregulation in drug addiction. *Clinical Psychology Review, 30*(6), 621–634. https://doi.org/10.1016/j.cpr.2010.04.005

Chen, J. J. L., Chen, T., & Zheng, X. X. (2012). Parenting styles and practices among Chinese immigrant mothers with young children. *Early Child Development and Care, 182*(1), 1–21. https://doi.org/10.1080/03004430.2010.533371

Cho, H., Gonzalez, R., Lavaysse, L. M., Pence, S., Fulford, D., & Gard, D. E. (2017). Do people with schizophrenia experience more negative emotion and less positive emotion in their daily lives? A meta-analysis of experience sampling studies. *Schizophrenia Research, 183,* 49–55. https://doi.org/10.1016/j.schres.2016.11.016

Choi, H. J., & Smith, R. A. (2013). Members, isolates, and liaisons: Meta-analysis of adolescents' network positions and their smoking behavior. *Substance Use & Misuse, 48*(8), 612–622. https://doi.org/10.3109/10826084.2013.800111

Chu, J. A. (1994). The rational treatment of multiple personality disorder. *Psychotherapy: Theory, Research, & Practice, 31*(1), 94–100. https://doi.org/10.1037/0033-3204.31.1.94

Clark, D. A., Beck, A. T., & Alford, B. A. (1999). *Scientific foundations of cognitive theory and therapy of depression.* John Wiley & Sons Inc.

Clark, D. C., & Fawcett, J. (Eds.). (1987). *Anhedonia and affect deficit states.* PMA Publishing Corporation.

Clark, L. A., & Watson, D. (1991). Tripartite model of anxiety and depression: Psychometric evidence and taxonomic implications. *Journal of Abnormal Psychology, 100*(3), 316–336. https://doi.org/10.1037/0021-843x.100.3.316

Coles, N. A., Larsen, J. T., & Lench, H. C. (2019). A meta-analysis of the facial feedback literature: Effects of facial feedback on emotional experience are small and variable. *Psychological Bulletin, 145*(6), 610–651. https://doi.org/10.1037/bul0000194

Collins, N. L., & Read, S. J. (1990). Adult attachment, working models, and relationship quality in dating couples. *Journal of Personality and Social Psychology, 58*(4), 644–663. https://doi.org/10.1037/0022-3514.58.4.644

Connolly, J., McIsaac, C., Shulman, S., Wincentak, K., Joly, L., Heifetz, M., & Bravo, V. (2014). Development of romantic relationships in adolescence and emerging adulthood: Implications for community mental health. *Canadian Journal of Community Mental Health, 33*(1), 7–19. https://doi.org/10.7870/cjcmh-2014-002

Conway, M., Csank, P. A., Holm, S. L., & Blake, C. K. (2000). On assessing individual differences in rumination on sadness. *Journal of Personality Assessment, 75*(3), 404–425. https://doi.org/10.1207/s15327752jpa7503_04

Copeland, M., Fisher, J. C., Moody, J., & Feinberg, M. E. (2018). Different kinds of lonely: Dimensions of isolation and substance use in adolescence. *Journal of Youth and Adolescence, 47*(8), 1755–1770. https://doi.org/10.1007/s10964-018-0860-3

Corrigan, P. W., Mittal, D., Reaves, C. M., Haynes, T. F., Han, X., Morris, S., & Sullivan, G. (2014). Mental health stigma and primary health care decisions. *Psychiatry Research, 218*(1–2), 35–38. https://doi.org/10.1016/j.psychres.2014.04.028

Costa-Ramalho, S., Marques-Pinto, A., Ribeiro, M. T., & Pereira, C. R. (2015). Savoring positive events in couple life: Impacts on relationship quality and dyadic adjustment. *Family Science, 6*(1), 170–180. https://doi.org/10.1080/19424620.2015.1082047

Craig, C. D., & Sprang, G. (2010). Compassion satisfaction, compassion fatigue, and burnout in a national sample of trauma treatment therapists. *Anxiety, Stress, and Coping, 23*(3), 319–339. https://doi.org/10.1080/10615800903085818

Craske, M. G., Meuret, A. E., Ritz, T., Treanor, M., Dour, H., & Rosenfield, D. (2019). Positive affect treatment for depression and anxiety: A randomized clinical trial for a core feature of anhedonia. *Journal of Consulting and Clinical Psychology, 87*(5), 457–471. https://doi.org/10.1037/ccp0000396

Craske, M. G., Meuret, A. E., Ritz, T., Treanor, M., & Dour, H. J. (2016). Treatment for anhedonia: A neuroscience driven approach. *Depression and Anxiety, 33*(10), 927–938. https://doi.org/10.1002/da.22490

Cullinan, C. C. (2018). *Taking your child to a therapist*. KidsHealth. https://kidshealth.org/en/parents/finding-therapist.html

Cunningham, M. R. (1988). What do you do when you're happy or blue? Mood, expectancies, and behavioral interest. *Motivation and Emotion, 12*, 309–331. https://doi.org/10.1007/bf00992357

Dallos, R., Grey, B., & Stancer, R. (2022). Anger without a voice, anger without a solution: Parent–child triadic processes and the experience of caring for a child with a diagnosis of autism. *Human Systems, 3*(1), 51–71. https://doi.org/10.1177/26344041221115255

Darwin, C. R. (1872). *The expression of the emotions in man and animals.* John Murray. https://doi.org/10.1037/10001-000

Davidson, E. J., & Wright, P. (2002). Selective processing of weight-and shape-related words in bulimia nervosa: Use of a computerised Stroop test. *Eating Behaviors, 3*(3), 261–273. https://doi.org/10.1016/s1471-0153(02)00064-8

Davis, N. O., & Carter, A. S. (2008). Parenting stress in mothers and fathers of toddlers with autism spectrum disorders: Associations with child characteristics. *Journal of Autism and Developmental Disorders, 38*(7), 1278–1291. https://doi.org/10.1007/s10803-007-0512-z

Denham, S. A., & Couchoud, E. A. (1990). Young preschoolers' understanding of emotions. *Child Study Journal, 20*(3), 171–192.

Denham, S. A., McKinley, M., Couchoud, E. A., & Holt, R. (1990). Emotional and behavioral predictors of preschool peer ratings. *Child Development, 61*(4), 1145–1152. https://doi.org/10.2307/1130882

Denham, S. A., Renwick-DeBardi, S., & Hewes, S. (1994). Emotional communication relation between mothers and Preschoolers: Relations with emotional competence. *Merrill-Palmer Quarterly, 40*(4), 488–508.

Denham, S. A., & Zoller, D. (1991). "When my hamster died, I cried": Preschoolers' attributions of the causes of emotions. *The Journal of Genetic Psychology, 152*(3), 371–373. https://doi.org/10.1080/00221325.1991.9914693

Denham, S. A., Zoller, D., & Couchoud, E. A. (1994). Socialization of preschoolers' emotion understanding. *Developmental Psychology, 30*(6), 928–936. https://doi.org/10.1037/0012-1649.30.6.928

De Stefano, R., Muscatello, M. R. A., Bruno, A., Cedro, C., Mento, C., Zoccali, R. A., & Pandolfo, G. (2021). Complicated grief: A systematic review of the last 20 years. *The International Journal of Social Psychiatry, 67*(5), 492–499. https://doi.org/10.1177/0020764020960202

Di Pierro, R., Benzi, I. M. A., & Madeddu, F. (2015). Difficulties in emotion regulation among inpatients with substance use disorders: The mediating effect of mature defenses mechanisms. *Clinical Neuropsychiatry: Journal of Treatment Evaluation, 12*(4), 83–89.

Doss, B. D., Simpson, L. E., & Christensen, A. (2004). Why do couples seek marital therapy? *Professional Psychology, Research and Practice, 35*(6), 608–614. https://doi.org/10.1037/0735-7028.35.6.608

Dozier, M., & Kobak, R. R. (1992). Psychophysiology in attachment interviews: Converging evidence for deactivating strategies. *Child Development, 63*(6), 1473–1480. https://doi.org/10.1111/j.1467-8624.1992.tb01708.x

Eddy, K. T., Tabri, N., Thomas, J. J., Murray, H. B., Keshaviah, A., Hastings, E., Edkins, K., Krishna, M., Herzog, D. B., Keel, P. K., & Franko, D. L. (2017). Recovery from anorexia nervosa and bulimia nervosa at 22-year follow-up. *Journal of Clinical Psychiatry, 78*(2), 184–189. https://doi.org/10.4088/JCP.15m10393

Eisenhower, A. S., Baker, B. L., & Blacher, J. (2005). Preschool children with intellectual disability: Syndrome specificity, behaviour problems, and maternal well-being. *Journal of Intellectual Disability Research, 49*(9), 657–671. https://doi.org/10.1111/j.1365-2788.2005.00699.x

Ekman, P., Davidson, R. J., & Friesen, W. V. (1990). The Duchenne smile: Emotional expression and brain physiology: II. *Journal of Personality and Social Psychology, 58*(2), 342–353. https://doi.org/10.1037/0022-3514.58.2.342

Elder, J. P., Ayala, G. X., Parra-Medina, D., & Talavera, G. A. (2009). Health communication in the Latino community: Issues and approaches. *Annual Review of Public Health, 30*, 227–251. https://doi.org/10.1146/annurev.publhealth.031308.100300

Figley, C. R. (1998). Burnout as systemic traumatic stress: A model for helping traumatized family members. In C. R. Figley (Ed.), *Burnout in families: The systemic costs of caring* (pp. 15–28). CRC Press.

Figley, C. R. (2002). *Treating compassion fatigue.* Brunner/Rutledge. https://doi.org/10.4324/9780203890318

Fincham, F. D., & Beach, S. R. H. (2010). Of memes and marriage: Toward a positive relationship science. *Journal of Family Theory & Review, 2*(1), 4–24. https://doi.org/10.1111/j.1756-2589.2010.00033.x

Fiori, K. L., Consedine, N. S., & Magai, C. (2009). Late life attachment in context: Patterns of relating among men and women from seven ethnic groups. *Journal of Cross-Cultural Gerontology, 24*(2), 121–141. https://doi.org/10.1007/s10823-008-9078-2

Fonagy, P. (1989). On tolerating mental states: Theory of mind in borderline personality. *Bulletin of the Anna Freud Centre, 12*(2), 91–115.

Fonagy, P. (1991). Thinking about thinking: Some clinical and theoretical considerations in the treatment of a borderline patient. *The International Journal of Psycho-Analysis, 72*(4), 639–656.

Forgas, J. P., Bower, G. H., & Krantz, S. E. (1984). The influence of mood on perceptions of social interactions. *Journal of Experimental Social Psychology, 20*(6), 497–513. https://doi.org/10.1016/0022-1031(84)90040-4

Fox, N. A., Kimmerly, N. L., & Schafer, W. D. (1991). Attachment to mother/attachment to father: A meta-analysis. *Child Development, 62*(1), 210–225. https://doi.org/10.1111/j.1467-8624.1991.tb01526.x

Fraley, R. C. (2002). Attachment stability from infancy to adulthood: Meta-analysis and dynamic modeling of developmental mechanisms. *Personality and Social Psychology Review, 6*(2), 123–151. https://doi.org/10.1207/s15327957pspr0602_03

Fraley, R. C., Heffernan, M. E., Vicary, A. M., & Brumbaugh, C. C. (2011). The experiences in close relationships—Relationship Structures Questionnaire: A method for assessing attachment orientations across relationships. *Psychological Assessment, 23*(3), 615–625. https://doi.org/10.1037/a0022898

Fraley, R. C., Waller, N. G., & Brennan, K. A. (2000). An item response theory analysis of self-report measures of adult attachment. *Journal of Personality and Social Psychology, 78*(2), 350–365. https://doi.org/10.1037/0022-3514.78.2.350

Frank, R. G., & Gertler, P. (1991). Mental health and marital stability. *International Journal of Law and Psychiatry, 14*(4), 377–386. https://doi.org/10.1016/0160-2527(91)90016-g

Fredrickson, B. L. (1998). What good are positive emotions? *Review of General Psychology, 2*(3), 300–319. https://doi.org/10.1037/1089-2680.2.3.300

Fredrickson, B. L. (2001). The role of positive emotions in positive psychology. The broaden-and-build theory of positive emotions. *American Psychologist, 56*(3), 218–226. https://doi.org/10.1037/0003-066x.56.3.218

Fredrickson, B. L. (2005). The broaden-and-build theory of positive emotions. In F. A. Huppert, N. Baylis, & B. Keverne (Eds.), *The science of well-being* (pp. 217–238). Oxford University Press.

Fredrickson, B. L., & Levenson, R. W. (1998). Positive emotions speed recovery from the cardiovascular sequelae of negative emotions. *Cognition and Emotion, 12*(2), 191–220. https://doi.org/10.1080/026999398379718

Fredrickson, B. L., Mancuso, R. A., Branigan, C., & Tugade, M. M. (2000). The undoing effect of positive emotions. *Motivation and Emotion, 24*(4), 237–258. https://doi.org/10.1023/a:1010796329158

Freedman, A. (1987). Development in story writing. *Applied Psycholinguistics, 8*(2), 153–170. https://doi.org/10.1017/s0142716400000187

Frewen, P. A., Dozois, D. J., & Lanius, R. A. (2012). Assessment of anhedonia in psychological trauma: Psychometric and neuroimaging perspectives. *European Journal of Psychotraumatology, 3*(1), Article 8587. https://doi.org/10.3402/ejpt.v3i0.8587

Froidevaux, N. M., Sanchez Hernandez, H., Pourmand, V., Yunusova, A., Sbarra, D. A., & Borelli, J. L. (2023). Psychological distress with relationship satisfaction is moderated by anticipatory relational savoring among non-deployed military partners. *Personal Relationships, 30*(2), 636–659. https://doi.org/10.1111/pere.12469

Frostad, S., Rozakou-Soumalia, N., Dârvariu, Ş., Foruzesh, B., Azkia, H., Larsen, M. P., Rowshandel, E., & Sjögren, J. M. (2022). BMI at discharge from treatment predicts relapse in anorexia nervosa: A systematic scoping review. *Journal of Personalized Medicine, 12*(5), 836–852. https://doi.org/10.3390/jpm12050836

Furman, W., & Simon, V. A. (2004). Concordance in attachment states of mind and styles with respect to fathers and mothers. *Developmental Psychology, 40*(6), 1239–1247. https://doi.org/10.1037/0012-1649.40.6.1239

Furman, W., Simon, V. A., Shaffer, L., & Bouchey, H. A. (2002). Adolescents' working models and styles for relationships with parents, friends, and romantic partners. *Child Development, 73*(1), 241–255. https://doi.org/10.1111/1467-8624.00403

Gaskin, G. E. (2021). *Relational savoring in mothers of children with autism spectrum disorders: An attachment-based intervention* [Unpublished doctoral dissertation]. Claremont Graduate University. ProQuest Dissertations and

Theses Global. https://www.proquest.com/dissertations-theses/relational-savoring-mothers-children-with-autism/docview/2617227920/se-2

Geiger, P. J., Morey, J. N., & Segerstrom, S. C. (2017). Beliefs about savoring in older adulthood: Aging and perceived health affect temporal components of perceived savoring ability. *Personality and Individual Differences, 105*, 164–169. https://doi.org/10.1016/j.paid.2016.09.049

Gentzler, A., & Kerns, K. (2006). Adult attachment and memory of emotional reactions to negative and positive events. *Cognition and Emotion, 20*(1), 20–42. https://doi.org/10.1080/02699930500200407

Gentzler, A. L., Kerns, K. A., & Keener, E. (2010). Emotional reactions and regulatory responses to negative and positive events: Associations with attachment and gender. *Motivation and Emotion, 34*(1), 78–92. https://doi.org/10.1007/s11031-009-9149-x

George, C., Kaplan, N., & Main, M. (1996). *The adult attachment interview* [Unpublished manuscript]. Department of Psychology, University of California at Berkeley. https://doi.org/10.1037/t02879-000

Gillath, O., & Karantzas, G. (2019). Attachment security priming: A systematic review. *Current Opinion in Psychology, 25*, 86–95. https://doi.org/10.1016/j.copsyc.2018.03.001

Gillath, O., Selcuk, E., & Shaver, P. R. (2008). Moving toward a secure attachment style: Can repeated security priming help? *Social and Personality Psychology Compass, 2*(4), 1651–1666. https://doi.org/10.1111/j.1751-9004.2008.00120.x

Glenberg, A. M., Schroeder, J. L., & Robertson, D. A. (1998). Averting the gaze disengages the environment and facilitates remembering. *Memory & Cognition, 26*(4), 651–658. https://doi.org/10.3758/bf03211385

Gold, A. K., Stathopoulou, G., & Otto, M. W. (2020). Emotion regulation and motives for illicit drug use in opioid-dependent patients. *Cognitive Behaviour Therapy, 49*(1), 74–80. https://doi.org/10.1080/16506073.2019.1579256

Goldstein, A., Kerr, M. L., Li, F., Campos, B., Sbarra, D., Smiley, P., & Borelli, J. L. (2019). Intervening to improve reflective functioning and emotional experience among Latino/a parents. In A. G. Goldstein (Chair), *A basic and applied understanding of the bidirectional links between parents' emotions and child well-being* [Symposium]. Biennial Meeting of the Society for Research in Child Development, Baltimore, MD, United States.

Gooding, D. C., Tallent, K. A., & Matts, C. W. (2005). Clinical status of at-risk individuals 5 years later: Further validation of the psychometric high-risk strategy. *Journal of Abnormal Psychology, 114*(1), 170–175. https://doi.org/10.1037/0021-843x.114.1.170

Gorman, J. C. (1998). Parenting attitudes and practices of immigrant Chinese mothers of adolescents. *Family Relations, 47*(1), 73–80. https://doi.org/10.2307/584853

Gorwood, P. (2022). Neurobiological mechanisms of anhedonia. *Dialogues in Clinical Neuroscience, 10*(3), 291–299. https://doi.org/10.31887/dcns.2008.10.3/pgorwood

Greenberg, L. S. (2015). *Emotion-focused therapy: Coaching clients to work through their feelings* (2nd ed.). American Psychological Association. https://doi.org/10.1037/14692-000

Grey, B., Dallos, R., & Stancer, R. (2021). Feeling "like you're on . . . a prison ship": Understanding the caregiving and attachment narratives of parents of autistic children. *Human Systems, 1*(1), 96–114. https://doi.org/10.1177/26344041211000202

Grisset, N. I., & Norvell, N. K. (1992). Perceived social support, social skills, and quality of relationships in bulimic women. *Journal of Consulting and Clinical Psychology, 60*(2), 293–299. https://doi.org/10.1037/0022-006x.60.2.293

Grossmann, K., Grossmann, K. E., & Kindler, H. (2005). Early care and the roots of attachment and partnership representations: The Bielefeld and Regensburg longitudinal studies. In K. E. Grossmann, K. Grossmann, & E. Waters (Eds.), *Attachment from infancy to adulthood: The major longitudinal studies* (pp. 98–136). Guilford Press.

Harris, R. B. (1990). Role of set-point theory in regulation of body weight. *The FASEB Journal, 4*(15), 3310–3318. https://doi.org/10.1096/fasebj.4.15.2253845

Hartmann, A., Zeeck, A., & Barrett, M. S. (2010). Interpersonal problems in eating disorders. *International Journal of Eating Disorders, 43*(7), 619–627. https://doi.org/10.1002/eat.20747

Harvey, A. G. (2002). Trouble in bed: The role of pre-sleep worry and intrusions in the maintenance of insomnia. *Journal of Cognitive Psychotherapy, 16*(2), 161–178. https://doi.org/10.1891/jcop.16.2.161.63992

Hayes, S. C., & Strosahl, K. D. (2005). *A practical guide to acceptance and commitment therapy*. Springer. https://doi.org/10.1007/978-0-387-23369-7

Hayes, S. C., Strosahl, K. D., & Wilson, K. G. (1999). *Acceptance and commitment therapy: An experiential approach to behavior change*. Guilford Press.

Heflin, C. M., & Ziliak, J. P. (2008). Food insufficiency, food stamp participation, and mental health. *Social Science Quarterly, 89*(3), 706–727. https://doi.org/10.1111/j.1540-6237.2008.00556.x

Herr, N. R., Rosenthal, M. Z., Geiger, P. J., & Erikson, K. (2013). Difficulties with emotion regulation mediate the relationship between borderline personality disorder symptom severity and interpersonal problems. *Personality and Mental Health, 7*(3), 191–202. https://doi.org/10.1002/pmh.1204

Ho, H. Y., Yeung, D. Y., & Kwok, S. L. (2014). Development and evaluation of the positive psychology intervention for older adults. *The Journal of Positive Psychology, 9*(3), 187–197. https://doi.org/10.1080/17439760.2014.888577

Hoffman, C. D., Sweeney, D. P., Hodge, D., Lopez-Wagner, M. C., & Looney, L. (2009). Parenting stress and closeness: Mothers of typically developing children and mothers of children with autism. *Focus on Autism and Other Developmental Disabilities, 24*(3), 178–187. https://doi.org/10.1177/1088357609338715

Hofmann, S. G., Sawyer, A. T., Fang, A., & Asnaani, A. (2012). Emotion dysregulation model of mood and anxiety disorders. *Depression and Anxiety, 29*(5), 409–416. https://doi.org/10.1002/da.21888

Holloway, R. A., Waldrip, A. M., & Ickes, W. (2009). Evidence that a simpático self-schema accounts for differences in the self-concepts and social behavior of Latinos versus Whites (and Blacks). *Journal of Personality and Social Psychology, 96*(5), 1012–1028. https://doi.org/10.1037/a0013883

Holm, A. L., & Severinsson, E. (2011). Struggling to recover by changing suicidal behaviour: Narratives from women with borderline personality disorder. *International Journal of Mental Health Nursing, 20*(3), 165–173. https://doi.org/10.1111/j.1447-0349.2010.00713.x

Holmes, M. R., Rentrope, C. R., Korsch-Williams, A., & King, J. A. (2021). Impact of COVID-19 pandemic on posttraumatic stress, grief, burnout, and secondary trauma of social workers in the United States. *Clinical Social Work Journal, 49*(4), 495–504. https://doi.org/10.1007/s10615-021-00795-y

Hopper, J. W., Pitman, R. K., Su, Z., Heyman, G. M., Lasko, N. B., Macklin, M. L., Orr, S. P., Lukas, S. E., & Elman, I. (2008). Probing reward function in posttraumatic stress disorder: Expectancy and satisfaction with monetary gains and losses. *Journal of Psychiatric Research, 42*(10), 802–807. https://doi.org/10.1016/j.jpsychires.2007.10.008

Horan, W. P., Harvey, P. O., Kern, R. S., & Green, M. F. (2011). Neurocognition, social cognition and functional outcome in schizophrenia. *Schizophrenia Research, 9*(1–3), 316–324. https://doi.org/10.1002/9780470978672.ch3

Horvath, A. O., & Luborsky, L. (1993). The role of the therapeutic alliance in psychotherapy. *Journal of Consulting and Clinical Psychology, 61*(4), 561–573. https://doi.org/10.1037/0022-006x.61.4.561

Howard, L. M., Trevillion, K., & Agnew-Davies, R. (2010). Domestic violence and mental health. *International Review of Psychiatry, 22*(5), 525–534. https://doi.org/10.3109/09540261.2010.512283

Hudson, N. W., & Fraley, R. C. (2018). Moving toward greater security: The effects of repeatedly priming attachment security and anxiety. *Journal of Research in Personality, 74*, 147–157. https://doi.org/10.1016/j.jrp.2018.04.002

Hughes, C., Devine, R. T., Mesman, J., & Blair, C. (2020). Understanding the terrible twos: A longitudinal investigation of the impact of early executive function and parent–child interactions. *Developmental Science, 23*(6), Article e12979. https://doi.org/10.1111/desc.12979

Hurley, D. B., & Kwon, P. (2013). Savoring helps most when you have little: Interaction between savoring the moment and uplifts on positive affect and satisfaction with life. *Journal of Happiness Studies, 14*, 1261–1271. https://doi.org/10.1007/s10902-012-9377-8

Isen, A. M. (1990). The influence of positive and negative affect on cognitive organization: Some implications for development. In N. Stein, B. Leventhal,

& T. Trabasso (Eds.), *Psychological and biological approaches to emotion* (pp. 75–94). Erlbaum.

Isen, A. M., & Daubman, K. A. (1984). The influence of affect on categorization. *Journal of Personality and Social Psychology, 47*(6), 1206–1217. https://doi.org/10.1037/0022-3514.47.6.1206

Isen, A. M., Daubman, K. A., & Nowicki, G. P. (1987). Positive affect facilitates creative problem solving. *Journal of Personality and Social Psychology, 52*(6), 1122–1131. https://doi.org/10.1037/0022-3514.52.6.1122

Isen, A. M., Johnson, M. M. S., Mertz, E., & Robinson, G. F. (1985). The influence of positive affect on the unusualness of word associations. *Journal of Personality and Social Psychology, 48*(6), 1413–1426. https://doi.org/10.1037/0022-3514.48.6.1413

Isen, A. M., & Means, B. (1983). The influence of positive affect on decision-making strategy. *Social Cognition, 2*(1), 18–31. https://doi.org/10.1521/soco.1983.2.1.18

Isen, A. M., Rosenzweig, A. S., & Young, M. J. (1991). The influence of positive affect on clinical problem solving. *Medical Decision Making, 11*(3), 221–227. https://doi.org/10.1177/0272989x9101100313

James, D. E., Schumm, W. R., Kennedy, C. E., Grigsby, C. C., Selectman, K., & Nichols, C. W. (1985). Characteristics of the Kansas parental satisfaction scale among two samples of married parents. *Psychological Reports, 57*(1), 163–169. https://doi.org/10.2466/pr0.1985.57.1.163

James, W. (1884). What is an emotion? *Mind, os-IX*(34), 188–205. https://doi.org/10.1093/mind/os-IX.34.188

Jiao, J., Kim, S., & Pitts, M. J. (2021). Promoting subjective well-being through communication savoring. *Communication Quarterly, 69*(2), 152–171. https://doi.org/10.1080/01463373.2021.1901758

Johnson, S. M. (2019). *Attachment theory in practice: Emotionally focused therapy (EFT) with individuals, couples, and families*. Guilford Press.

Jones, A. D. (2017). Food insecurity and mental health status: A global analysis of 149 countries. *American Journal of Preventive Medicine, 53*(2), 264–273. https://doi.org/10.1016/j.amepre.2017.04.008

Jones, J. D., Stern, J. A., Fitter, M. H., Mikulincer, M., Shaver, P. R., & Cassidy, J. (2022). Attachment and attitudes toward children: Effects of security priming in parents and non-parents. *Attachment & Human Development, 24*(2), 147–168. https://doi.org/10.1080/14616734.2021.1881983

Kabat-Zinn, J., & Hanh, T. N. (2009). *Full catastrophe living: Using the wisdom of your body and mind to face stress, pain, and illness*. Delta.

Kashdan, T. B., Elhai, J. D., & Frueh, B. C. (2006). Anhedonia and emotional numbing in combat veterans with PTSD. *Behaviour Research and Therapy, 44*(3), 457–467. https://doi.org/10.1016/j.brat.2005.03.001

Katsakou, C., & Pistrang, N. (2018). Clients' experiences of treatment and recovery in borderline personality disorder: A meta-synthesis of qualitative studies.

Psychotherapy Research, 28(6), 940–957. https://doi.org/10.1080/10503307.2016.1277040

Katzman, W., & Papouchis, N. (2022). Grief responses during the COVID-19 pandemic: Differences in attachment and emotion regulation. *Journal of Loss and Trauma, 27*(8), 761–772. https://doi.org/10.1080/15325024.2022.2040154

Kemper, S. (1984). The development of narrative skills: Explanations and entertainments. In S. A. Kuczaj II (Ed.), *Discourse development* (pp. 99–124). Springer. https://doi.org/10.1007/978-1-4613-9508-9_5

Kendall, P. C., & Hedtke, K. (2006a). *Cognitive-behavioral therapy for anxious children: Therapist manual* (3rd ed.). Workbook Publishing.

Kendall, P. C., & Hedtke, K. (2006b). *The coping cat workbook* (2nd ed.). Workbook Publishing.

Kerr, M. L., Charles, P., Massoglia, M., Jensen, S., Wirth, J., Fanning, K., & Poehlmann-Tynan, J. (2022). Development and implementation of an attachment-based intervention to enhance visits between children and their incarcerated parents. In J. Krysik & N. Rodriguez (Eds.), *Children of incarcerated parents* (pp. 135–151). Springer. https://doi.org/10.1007/978-3-030-84713-5_7

Kessler, R. C., Walters, E. E., & Forthofer, M. S. (1998). The social consequences of psychiatric disorders, III: Probability of marital stability. *The American Journal of Psychiatry, 155*(8), 1092–1096. https://doi.org/10.1176/ajp.155.8.1092

Keyes, C. L. M. (2016). Why flourishing? In D. W. Harward (Ed.), *Well-being and high education: A strategy for change and the realization of education's greater purposes* (pp. 99–107). Bringing Theory to Practice.

Kirkpatrick, L. A., & Davis, K. E. (1994). Attachment style, gender, and relationship stability: A longitudinal analysis. *Journal of Personality and Social Psychology, 66*(3), 502–512. https://doi.org/10.1037/0022-3514.66.3.502

Kok, B. E., & Fredrickson, B. L. (2010). Upward spirals of the heart: Autonomic flexibility, as indexed by vagal tone, reciprocally and prospectively predicts positive emotions and social connectedness. *Biological Psychology, 85*(3), 432–436. https://doi.org/10.1016/j.biopsycho.2010.09.005

Koren-Karie, N., Oppenheim, D., Dolev, S., & Yirmiya, N. (2009). Mothers of securely attached children with autism spectrum disorder are more sensitive than mothers of insecurely attached children. *Journal of Child Psychology and Psychiatry, and Allied Disciplines, 50*(5), 643–650. https://doi.org/10.1111/j.1469-7610.2008.02043.x

Kross, E., & Ayduk, O. (2011). Making meaning out of negative experiences by self-distancing. *Current Directions in Psychological Science, 20*(3), 187–191. https://doi.org/10.1177/0963721411408883

Kurtz, J. L. (2008). Looking to the future to appreciate the present: The benefits of perceived temporal scarcity. *Psychological Science, 19*(12), 1238–1241. https://doi.org/10.1111/j.1467-9280.2008.02231.x

Kwapil, T. R. (1998). Social anhedonia as a predictor of the development of schizophrenia-spectrum disorders. *Journal of Abnormal Psychology, 107*(4), 558–565. https://doi.org/10.1037/0021-843x.107.4.558

Kwapil, T. R., Barrantes-Vidal, N., & Silvia, P. J. (2008). The dimensional structure of the Wisconsin Schizotypy Scales: Factor identification and construct validity. *Schizophrenia Bulletin, 34*(3), 444–457. https://doi.org/10.1093/schbul/sbm098

Kwapil, T. R., Silvia, P. J., Myin-Germeys, I., Anderson, A. J., Coates, S. A., & Brown, L. H. (2009). The social world of the socially anhedonic: Exploring the daily ecology of asociality. *Journal of Research in Personality, 43*(1), 103–106. https://doi.org/10.1016/j.jrp.2008.10.008

Lang, P. J. (1980). Behavioral treatment and bio-behavioral assessment: Computer applications. In L. B. Sidowski, J. H. Johnson, & T. A. Williams (Eds.), *Technology in mental health care delivery* (pp. 119–137). Ablex.

Langston, C. A. (1994). Capitalizing on and coping with daily-life events: Expressive responses to positive events. *Journal of Personality and Social Psychology, 67*(6), 1112–1125. https://doi.org/10.1037/0022-3514.67.6.1112

Lavender, J. M., Wonderlich, S. A., Peterson, C. B., Crosby, R. D., Engel, S. G., Mitchell, J. E., Crow, S. J., Smith, T. L., Klein, M. H., Goldschmidt, A. B., & Berg, K. C. (2014). Dimensions of emotion dysregulation in bulimia nervosa. *European Eating Disorders Review, 22*(3), 212–216. https://doi.org/10.1002/erv.2288

Lee, J.-A., Hong, K., Borelli, J. L., & Rahmani, A. (2019, April). *A culturally sensitive dementia family caregiver pilot study* [Poster presentation]. Western Institute of Nursing's 52nd Annual Communicating Nursing Research Conference, San Diego, CA, United States.

Lejuez, C. W., Hopko, D. R., Acierno, R., Daughters, S. B., & Pagoto, S. L. (2011). Ten year revision of the brief behavioral activation treatment for depression: Revised treatment manual. *Behavior Modification, 35*(2), 111–161. https://doi.org/10.1177/0145445510390929

Liebke, L., Koppe, G., Bungert, M., Thome, J., Hauschild, S., Defiebre, N., Izurieta Hidalgo, N. A., Schmahl, C., Bohus, M., & Lis, S. (2018). Difficulties with being socially accepted: An experimental study in borderline personality disorder. *Journal of Abnormal Psychology, 127*(7), 670–682. https://doi.org/10.1037/abn0000373

Limbert, C. (2010). Perceptions of social support and eating disorder characteristics. *Health Care for Women International, 31*(2), 170–178. https://doi.org/10.1080/07399330902893846

Linville, D., Brown, T., Sturm, K., & McDougal, T. (2012). Eating disorders and social support: Perspectives of recovered individuals. *Eating Disorders, 20*(3), 216–231. https://doi.org/10.1080/10640266.2012.668480

Litz, B. T., Orsillo, S. M., Kaloupek, D., & Weathers, F. (2000). Emotional processing in posttraumatic stress disorder. *Journal of Abnormal Psychology, 109*(1), 26–39. https://doi.org/10.1037/0021-843x.109.1.26

Lopez, F. G., Melendez, M. C., & Rice, K. G. (2000). Parental divorce, parent–child bonds, and adult attachment orientations among college students: A comparison of three racial/ethnic groups. *Journal of Counseling Psychology, 47*(2), 177–186. https://doi.org/10.1037/0022-0167.47.2.177

Ludermir, A. B., Schraiber, L. B., D'Oliveira, A. F., França-Junior, I., & Jansen, H. A. (2008). Violence against women by their intimate partner and common mental disorders. *Social Science & Medicine, 66*(4), 1008–1018. https://doi.org/10.1016/j.socscimed.2007.10.021

Lyons-Ruth, K., Bronfman, E., & Parsons, E. (1999). Atypical attachment in infancy and early childhood among children at developmental risk: Part IV. Maternal frightened, frightening, or atypical behavior and disorganized infant attachment patterns. *Monographs of the Society for Research in Child Development, 64*(3), 67–96. https://doi.org/10.1111/1540-5834.00034

Lyubomirsky, S., & Lepper, H. S. (1999). A measure of subjective happiness: Preliminary reliability and construct validation. *Social Indicators Research, 46*(2), 137–155. https://doi.org/10.1023/a:1006824100041

Macy, A. S., Theo, J. N., Kaufmann, S. C., Ghazzaoui, R. B., Pawlowski, P. A., Fakhry, H. I., Cassmassi, B. J., & IsHak, W. W. (2013). Quality of life in obsessive compulsive disorder. *CNS Spectrums, 18*(1), 21–33. https://doi.org/10.1017/s1092852912000697

Main, M. (1981). Avoidance in the service of attachment: A working paper. In K. Ingelmann, G. Barlow, M. Main, & L. Petrinovich (Eds.), *Behavioral development: The Bielefeld interdisciplinary project* (pp. 651–693). Cambridge University Press.

Main, M. (1991). Metacognitive knowledge, metacognitive monitoring, and singular (coherent) vs. multiple (incoherent) models of attachment. In C. M. Parkes, J. Stevenson-Hinde, & P. Marris (Eds.), *Attachment across the life cycle* (pp. 127–159). Routledge.

Main, M. (2000). The organized categories of infant, child, and adult attachment: Flexible vs. inflexible attention under attachment-related stress. *Journal of the American Psychoanalytic Association, 48*(4), 1055–1096. https://doi.org/10.1177/00030651000480041801

Main, M., & Hesse, E. (1990). Parents' unresolved traumatic experiences are related to infant disorganized attachment status: Is frightened and/or frightening parental behavior the linking mechanism? In M. T. Greenberg, D. Cicchetti, & E. M. Cummings (Eds.), *Attachment in the preschool years: Theory, research, and intervention* (pp. 161–182). University of Chicago Press.

Main, M., Hesse, E., & Goldwyn, R. (2008). Studying differences in language usage in recounting attachment history: An introduction to the AAI. In H. Steele & M. Steele (Eds.), *Clinical applications of the Adult Attachment Interview* (pp. 31–68). Guilford Press.

Mangurian, C., Sreshta, N., & Seligman, H. (2013). Food insecurity among adults with severe mental illness. *Psychiatric Services, 64*(9), 931–932. https://doi.org/10.1176/appi.ps.201300022

Marissen, M. A., Arnold, N., & Franken, I. H. (2012). Anhedonia in borderline personality disorder and its relation to symptoms of impulsivity. *Psychopathology, 45*(3), 179–184. https://doi.org/10.1159/000330893

Marquez, C., Kazmierski, K., Carballo, J. A., Garcia, J., Avalos, V., Russo, L. N., Arreola, J., Rodriguez, A. H., Perez, A. A., Leal, F., Torres, G., Montiel, G., Guerra, G., & Borelli, J. L. (2023). COVID-19 and the Latinx community: "Promotoras represent a community in pain." *Journal of Latinx Psychology, 11*(2), 148–165. https://doi.org/10.1037/lat0000224

Matthews, T., Danese, A., Wertz, J., Odgers, C. L., Ambler, A., Moffitt, T. E., & Arseneault, L. (2016). Social isolation, loneliness and depression in young adulthood: A behavioural genetic analysis. *Social Psychiatry and Psychiatric Epidemiology, 51*(3), 339–348. https://doi.org/10.1007/s00127-016-1178-7

McAdams, D. P., Diamond, A., de St Aubin, E., & Mansfield, E. (1997). Stories of commitment: The psychosocial construction of generative lives. *Journal of Personality and Social Psychology, 72*(3), 678–694. https://doi.org/10.1037/0022-3514.72.3.678

McAdams, D. P., Reynolds, J., Lewis, M., Patten, A. H., & Bowman, P. J. (2001). When bad things turn good and good things turn bad: Sequences of redemption and contamination in life narrative and their relation to psychosocial adaptation in midlife adults and in students. *Personality and Social Psychology Bulletin, 27*(4), 474–485. https://doi.org/10.1177/0146167201274008

McCann, I. L., & Pearlman, L. A. (1990). Vicarious traumatization: A framework for understanding the psychological effects of working with victims. *Journal of Traumatic Stress, 3*(1), 131–149. https://doi.org/10.1007/bf00975140

McCarthy, J. M., Bradshaw, K. R., Catalano, L. T., Garcia, C. P., Malik, A., Bennett, M. E., & Blanchard, J. J. (2018). Negative symptoms and the formation of social affiliative bonds in schizophrenia. *Schizophrenia Research, 193*, 225–231. https://doi.org/10.1016/j.schres.2017.07.034

McDonagh, A., Friedman, M., McHugo, G., Ford, J., Sengupta, A., Mueser, K., Demment, C. C., Fournier, D., Schnurr, P. P., & Descamps, M. (2005). Randomized trial of cognitive-behavioral therapy for chronic posttraumatic stress disorder in adult female survivors of childhood sexual abuse. *Journal of Consulting and Clinical Psychology, 73*(3), 515–524. https://doi.org/10.1037/0022-006X.73.3.515

McGrath, J. J. (2006). Variations in the incidence of schizophrenia: Data versus dogma. *Schizophrenia Bulletin, 32*(1), 195–197. https://doi.org/10.1093/schbul/sbi052

McLean, C. P., & Foa, E. B. (2017). Emotions and emotion regulation in posttraumatic stress disorder. *Current Opinion in Psychology, 14*, 72–77. https://doi.org/10.1016/j.copsyc.2016.10.006

McMakin, D. L., Siegle, G. J., & Shirk, S. R. (2011). Positive affect stimulation and sustainment (PASS) module for depressed mood: A preliminary investigation of treatment-related effects. *Cognitive Therapy and Research, 35*(3), 217–226. https://doi.org/10.1007/s10608-010-9311-5

Meehl, P. E. (2017). Schizotaxia, schizotypy, schizophrenia. In A. H. Buss & E. H. Buss (Eds.), *Schizophrenia: Seven approaches* (pp. 21–46). Routledge.

Mehl, M. R., & Pennebaker, J. W. (2003). The social dynamics of a cultural upheaval: Social interactions surrounding September 11, 2001. *Psychological Science, 14*(6), 579–585. https://doi.org/10.1046/j.0956-7976.2003.psci_1468.x

Mesman, J., Van IJzendoorn, M. H., & Sagi-Schwartz, A. (2016). Cross-cultural patterns of attachment. In J. Cassidy & P. R. Shaver (Eds.), *Handbook of attachment: Theory, research, and clinical applications* (pp. 852–877). Guilford Press.

Messias, D. K., Parra-Medina, D., Sharpe, P. A., Treviño, L., Koskan, A. M., & Morales-Campos, D. (2013). Promotoras de salud: Roles, responsibilities, and contributions in a multisite community-based randomized controlled trial. *Hispanic Health Care International: The Official Journal of the National Association of Hispanic Nurses, 11*(2), 62–71. https://doi.org/10.1891/1540-4153.11.2.62

Mikulincer, M., Gillath, O., Halevy, V., Avihou, N., Avidan, S., & Eshkoli, N. (2001). Attachment theory and reactions to others' needs: Evidence that activation of the sense of attachment security promotes empathic responses. *Journal of Personality and Social Psychology, 81*(6), 1205–1224. https://doi.org/10.1037/0022-3514.81.6.1205

Mikulincer, M., Hirschberger, G., Nachmias, O., & Gillath, O. (2001). The affective component of the secure base schema: Affective priming with representations of attachment security. *Journal of Personality and Social Psychology, 81*(2), 305–321. https://doi.org/10.1037/0022-3514.81.2.305

Mikulincer, M., & Shaver, P. R. (2001). Attachment theory and intergroup bias: Evidence that priming the secure base schema attenuates negative reactions to out-groups. *Journal of Personality and Social Psychology, 81*(1), 97–115. https://doi.org/10.1037/0022-3514.81.1.97

Mikulincer, M., & Shaver, P. R. (2007). Boosting attachment security to promote mental health, prosocial values, and inter-group tolerance. *Psychological Inquiry, 18*(3), 139–156. https://doi.org/10.1080/10478400701512646

Mikulincer, M., & Shaver, P. R. (2010). *Attachment in adulthood: Structure, dynamics, and change*. Guilford Press.

Mikulincer, M., & Shaver, P. R. (2015). The psychological effects of the contextual activation of security-enhancing mental representations in adulthood. *Current Opinion in Psychology, 1*, 18–21. https://doi.org/10.1016/j.copsyc.2015.01.008

Mikulincer, M., Shaver, P. R., & Horesh, N. (2006). Attachment bases of emotion regulation and posttraumatic adjustment. In D. K. Snyder, J. A. Simpson, & J. N. Hughes (Eds.), *Emotion regulation in families: Pathways to dysfunction and health* (pp. 77–99). American Psychological Association. https://doi.org/10.1037/11468-004

Mikulincer, M., Shaver, P. R., & Pereg, D. (2003). Attachment theory and affect regulation: The dynamics, development, and cognitive consequences of attachment-related strategies. *Motivation and Emotion, 27*(2), 77–102. https://doi.org/10.1023/a:1024515519160

Mikulincer, M., & Sheffi, E. (2000). Adult attachment style and cognitive reactions to positive affect: A test of mental categorization and creative problem solving. *Motivation and Emotion, 24*(3), 149–174. https://doi.org/10.1023/a:1005606611412

Miljkovitch, R., Moss, E., Bernier, A., Pascuzzo, K., & Sander, E. (2015). Refining the assessment of internal working models: The Attachment Multiple Model Interview. *Attachment & Human Development, 17*(5), 492–521. https://doi.org/10.1080/14616734.2015.1075561

Miyamoto, Y., & Ma, X. (2011). Dampening or savoring positive emotions: A dialectical cultural script guides emotion regulation. *Emotion, 11*(6), 1346–1357. https://doi.org/10.1037/a0025135

Mohammadi, F., Rakhshan, M., Molazem, Z., & Gillespie, M. (2019). Parental competence in parents of children with autism spectrum disorder: A systematic review. *Investigacion y Educacion en Enfermeria, 37*(3), Article e03. https://pubmed.ncbi.nlm.nih.gov/31830401/

Mohammadi, F., Rakhshan, M., Molazem, Z., & Zareh, N. (2018). Parental competence among parents with autistic children: A qualitative study. *Nursing and Midwifery Studies, 7*(4), 168–173.

Monteiro, L., Veríssimo, M., Vaughn, B. E., Santos, A. J., & Bost, K. K. (2008). Secure base representations for both fathers and mothers predict children's secure base behavior in a sample of Portuguese families. *Attachment & Human Development, 10*(2), 189–206. https://doi.org/10.1080/14616730802113711

Monteleone, A. M., Pellegrino, F., Croatto, G., Carfagno, M., Hilbert, A., Treasure, J., Wade, T., Bulik, C. M., Zipfel, S., Hay, P., Schmidt, U., Castellini, G., Favaro, A., Fernandez-Aranda, F., Il Shin, J., Voderholzer, U., Ricca, V., Moretti, D., Busatta, D., & Solmi, M. (2022). Treatment of eating disorders: A systematic meta-review of meta-analyses and network meta-analyses. *Neuroscience & Biobehavioral Reviews, 142*, Article 104857. https://doi.org/10.1016/j.neubiorev.2022.104857

Mor, N., & Winquist, J. (2002). Self-focused attention and negative affect: A meta-analysis. *Psychological Bulletin, 128*(4), 638–662. https://doi.org/10.1037/0033-2909.128.4.638

Muñoz, R. F., Miranda, J., & Aguilar-Gaxiola, S. (2000). *Individual therapy manual for cognitive-behavioral treatment of depression*. Rand.

Nakajima, S., Masaya, I., Akemi, S., & Takako, K. (2012). Complicated grief in those bereaved by violent death: The effects of post-traumatic stress disorder on complicated grief. *Dialogues in Clinical Neuroscience, 14*(2), 210–214. https://doi.org/10.31887/DCNS.2012.14.2/snakajima

Negash, S., & Sahin, S. (2011). Compassion fatigue in marriage and family therapy: Implications for therapists and clients. *Journal of Marital and Family Therapy, 37*(1), 1–13. https://doi.org/10.1111/j.1752-0606.2009.00147.x

Nichols, C. W., Schumm, W. R., Schectman, K. L., & Grigsby, C. C. (1983). Characteristics of responses to the Kansas marital satisfaction scale by a sample of

84 married mothers. *Psychological Reports, 53*(2), 567–572. https://doi.org/10.2466/pr0.1983.53.2.567

Nolen-Hoeksema, S. (1991). Responses to depression and their effects on the duration of depressive episodes. *Journal of Abnormal Psychology, 100*(4), 569–582. https://doi.org/10.1037/0021-843x.100.4.569

Nolen-Hoeksema, S., Wisco, B. E., & Lyubomirsky, S. (2008). Rethinking rumination. *Perspectives on Psychological Science, 3*(5), 400–424. https://doi.org/10.1111/j.1745-6924.2008.00088.x

Okazaki, S. (2009). Impact of racism on ethnic minority mental health. *Perspectives on Psychological Science, 4*(1), 103–107. https://doi.org/10.1111/j.1745-6924.2009.01099.x

Ooi, J., Michael, J., Lemola, S., Butterfill, S., Siew, C. S. Q., & Walasek, L. (2020). Interpersonal functioning in borderline personality disorder traits: A social media perspective. *Scientific Reports, 10*(1), Article 1068. https://doi.org/10.1038/s41598-020-58001-x

Opie, J. E., McIntosh, J. E., Esler, T. B., Duschinsky, R., George, C., Schore, A., Kothe, E. J., Tan, E. S., Greenwood, C. J., & Olsson, C. A. (2021). Early childhood attachment stability and change: A meta-analysis. *Attachment & Human Development, 23*(6), 897–930. https://doi.org/10.1080/14616734.2020.1800769

Osher, F., & Thompson, M. (2020). Adults with serious mental illnesses who are arrested and incarcerated. In H. H. Goldman, R. G. Frank, & J. P. Morrissey (Eds.), *The Palgrave handbook of American mental health policy* (pp. 471–508). Palgrave Macmillan. https://doi.org/10.1007/978-3-030-11908-9_17

Padgett, D. K. (2007). There's no place like (a) home: Ontological security among persons with serious mental illness in the United States. *Social Science & Medicine, 64*(9), 1925–1936. https://doi.org/10.1016/j.socscimed.2007.02.011

Palmer, C. A., & Gentzler, A. L. (2018). Adults' self-reported attachment influences their savoring ability. *The Journal of Positive Psychology, 13*(3), 290–300. https://doi.org/10.1080/17439760.2017.1279206

Park, C., Rosenblat, J. D., Lee, Y., Pan, Z., Cao, B., Iacobucci, M., & McIntyre, R. S. (2019). The neural systems of emotion regulation and abnormalities in major depressive disorder. *Behavioural Brain Research, 367*, 181–188. https://doi.org/10.1016/j.bbr.2019.04.002

Parker-Pope, T., Caron, C., & Cordero Sancho, M. (2021, December 17). Why 1,320 therapists are worried about mental health in America right now. *The New York Times*. https://www.nytimes.com/interactive/2021/12/16/well/mental-health-crisis-america-covid.html

Pascual-Leone, A., & Greenberg, L. S. (2007). Emotional processing in experiential therapy: Why "the only way out is through." *Journal of Consulting and Clinical Psychology, 75*(6), 875–887. https://doi.org/10.1037/0022-006x.75.6.875

Pearson, J. L., Cohn, D. A., Cowan, P. A., & Cowan, C. P. (1994). Earned- and continuous-security in adult attachment: Relation to depressive symptomatology and parenting style. *Development and Psychopathology, 6*(2), 359–373. https://doi.org/10.1017/s0954579400004636

Pennebaker, J. W., Mehl, M. R., & Niederhoffer, K. G. (2003). Psychological aspects of natural language use: Our words, our selves. *Annual Review of Psychology, 54*(1), 547–577. https://doi.org/10.1146/annurev.psych.54.101601.145041

Pennebaker, J. W., & Stone, L. D. (2003). Words of wisdom: Language use over the life span. *Journal of Personality and Social Psychology, 85*(2), 291–301. https://doi.org/10.1037/0022-3514.85.2.291

Pereira, A. S., Azhari, A., Hong, C. A., Gaskin, G. E., Borelli, J. L., & Esposito, G. (2021). Savouring as an intervention to decrease negative affect in anxious mothers of children with autism and neurotypical children. *Brain Sciences, 11*(5), 652. https://doi.org/10.3390/brainsci11050652

Perfect, T. J., Andrade, J., & Eagan, I. (2011). Eye closure reduces the cross-modal memory impairment caused by auditory distraction. *Journal of Experimental Psychology: Learning, Memory, and Cognition, 37*(4), 1008–1013. https://doi.org/10.1037/a0022930

Peters, L., & Fallon, P. (1994). The journey of recovery: Dimensions of change. In P. Fallon, M. Katzman, & S. Wooley (Eds.), *Feminist perspectives on eating disorders* (pp. 339–354). Guilford Press.

Peterson, C., & McCabe, A. (2013). *Developmental psycholinguistics: Three ways of looking at a child's narrative*. Springer Science & Business Media. https://doi.org/10.1007/978-1-4757-0608-6

Phetrasuwan, S., & Shandor Miles, M. (2009). Parenting stress in mothers of children with autism spectrum disorders. *Journal for Specialists in Pediatric Nursing, 14*(3), 157–165. https://doi.org/10.1111/j.1744-6155.2009.00188.x

Piacentini, J., Langley, A., & Roblek, T. (2007). *Cognitive behavioral treatment of childhood OCD: It's only a false alarm therapist guide*. Oxford University Press.

Pinquart, M., Feussner, C., & Ahnert, L. (2012). Meta-analytic evidence for stability in attachments from infancy to early adulthood. *Attachment & Human Development, 15*(2), 189–218. https://doi.org/10.1080/14616734.2013.746257

Pourmotabbed, A., Moradi, S., Babaei, A., Ghavami, A., Mohammadi, H., Jalili, C., Symonds, M. E., & Miraghajani, M. (2020). Food insecurity and mental health: A systematic review and meta-analysis. *Public Health Nutrition, 23*(10), 1778–1790. https://doi.org/10.1017/s136898001900435x

Powell, B., Cooper, G., Hoffman, K., & Marvin, R. S. (2009). The circle of security. In C. H. Zeanah Jr. (Ed.), *Handbook of infant mental health* (pp. 450–467). Guilford Press.

Prenoveau, J. M., Zinbarg, R. E., Craske, M. G., Mineka, S., Griffith, J. W., & Epstein, A. M. (2010). Testing a hierarchical model of anxiety and depression in adolescents: A tri-level model. *Journal of Anxiety Disorders, 24*(3), 334–344. https://doi.org/10.1016/j.janxdis.2010.01.006

Pressman, S. D., Acevedo, A. M., Hammond, K. V., & Kraft-Feil, T. L. (2021). Smile (or grimace) through the pain? The effects of experimentally manipulated facial expressions on needle-injection responses. *Emotion, 21*(6), 1188–1203. https://doi.org/10.1037/emo0000913

Privizzini, A. (2017). The child attachment interview: A narrative review. *Frontiers in Psychology, 8*, Article 384. https://doi.org/10.3389/fpsyg.2017.00384

Puschner, B., Bauer, S., Horowitz, L. M., & Kordy, H. (2005). The relationship between interpersonal problems and the helping alliance. *Journal of Clinical Psychology, 61*(4), 415–429. https://doi.org/10.1002/jclp.20050

Quoidbach, J., Wood, A. M., & Hansenne, M. (2009). Back to the future: The effect of daily practice of mental time travel into the future on happiness and anxiety. *The Journal of Positive Psychology, 4*(5), 349–355. https://doi.org/10.1080/17439760902992365

Raes, F., Smets, J., Nelis, S., & Schoofs, H. (2012). Dampening of positive affect prospectively predicts depressive symptoms in non-clinical samples. *Cognition and Emotion, 26*(1), 75–82. https://doi.org/10.1080/02699931.2011.555474

Ralph-Nearman, C., Achee, M., Lapidus, R., Stewart, J. L., & Filik, R. (2019). A systematic and methodological review of attentional biases in eating disorders: Food, body, and perfectionism. *Brain and Behavior, 9*(12), Article e01458. https://doi.org/10.1002/brb3.1458

Raval, V. V., Luebbe, A. M., & Sathiyaseelan, A. (2019). Parental socialization of positive affect, adolescent positive affect regulation, and adolescent girls' depression in India. *Social Development, 28*(2), 274–289. https://doi.org/10.1111/sode.12325

Rawana, J. S., Flett, G. L., McPhie, M. L., Nguyen, H. T., & Norwood, S. J. (2014). Developmental trends in emotion regulation: A systematic review with implications for community mental health. *Canadian Journal of Community Mental Health, 33*(1), 31–44. https://doi.org/10.7870/cjcmh-2014-004

Rhodes, S. D., Foley, K. L., Zometa, C. S., & Bloom, F. R. (2007). Lay health advisor interventions among Hispanics/Latinos: A qualitative systematic review. *American Journal of Preventive Medicine, 33*(5), 418–427. https://doi.org/10.1016/j.amepre.2007.07.023

Rohrbaugh, M. J., Mehl, M. R., Shoham, V., Reilly, E. S., & Ewy, G. A. (2008). Prognostic significance of spouse *we* talk in couples coping with heart failure. *Journal of Consulting and Clinical Psychology, 76*(5), 781–789. https://doi.org/10.1037/a0013238

Roisman, G. I., Collins, W. A., Sroufe, L. A., & Egeland, B. (2005). Predictors of young adults' representations of and behavior in their current romantic relationship: Prospective tests of the prototype hypothesis. *Attachment & Human Development, 7*(2), 105–121. https://doi.org/10.1080/14616730500134928

Roisman, G. I., Padrón, E., Sroufe, L. A., & Egeland, B. (2002). Earned–secure attachment status in retrospect and prospect. *Child Development, 73*(4), 1204–1219. https://doi.org/10.1111/1467-8624.00467

Rosen, C. S., Kaplan, A. N., Nelson, D. B., La Bash, H., Chard, K. M., Eftekhari, A., Kehle-Forbes, S., Wiltsey Stirman, S., & Sayer, N. A. (2023). Implementation context and burnout among Department of Veterans Affairs psychotherapists prior to and during the COVID-19 pandemic. *Journal of Affective Disorders, 320*, 517–524. https://doi.org/10.1016/j.jad.2022.09.141

Rottenberg, J., Kasch, K. L., Gross, J. J., & Gotlib, I. H. (2002). Sadness and amusement reactivity differentially predict concurrent and prospective functioning in major depressive disorder. *Emotion, 2*(2), 135–146. https://doi.org/10.1037/1528-3542.2.2.135

Rowe, A. C., Gold, E. R., & Carnelley, K. B. (2020). The effectiveness of attachment security priming in improving positive affect and reducing negative affect: A systematic review. *International Journal of Environmental Research and Public Health, 17*(3), Article 968. https://doi.org/10.3390/ijerph17030968

Rude, S., Gortner, E., & Pennebaker, J. (2004). Language use of depressed and depression vulnerable college students. *Cognition and Emotion, 18*(8), 1121–1133. https://doi.org/10.1080/02699930441000030

Rüsch, N., Angermeyer, M. C., & Corrigan, P. W. (2005). Mental illness stigma: Concepts, consequences, and initiatives to reduce stigma. *European Psychiatry, 20*(8), 529–539. https://doi.org/10.1016/j.eurpsy.2005.04.004

Russo, L. N., Arreola, J., Montiel, G., Torres, G., Leal, F., Guerra, N., & Borelli, J. L. (2022). Examining interpersonal traumas across low income Latinx mother-youth dyads: Associations between maternal child abuse exposure and racial discrimination with mother and youth psychopathology. *Child Psychiatry and Human Development*, 1–14. https://doi.org/10.1007/s10578-022-01483-9

Rutgers, A. H., Bakermans-Kranenburg, M. J., van Ijzendoorn, M. H., & van Berckelaer-Onnes, I. A. (2004). Autism and attachment: A meta-analytic review. *Journal of Child Psychology and Psychiatry, and Allied Disciplines, 45*(6), 1123–1134. https://doi.org/10.1111/j.1469-7610.2004.t01-1-00305.x

Rutgers, A. H., van Ijzendoorn, M. H., Bakermans-Kranenburg, M. J., Swinkels, S. H., van Daalen, E., Dietz, C., Naber, F. B., Buitelaar, J. K., & van Engeland, H. (2007). Autism, attachment and parenting: A comparison of children with autism spectrum disorder, mental retardation, language disorder, and non-clinical children. *Journal of Abnormal Child Psychology, 35*(5), 859–870. https://doi.org/10.1007/s10802-007-9139-y

Ryff, C. D., & Keyes, C. L. M. (1995). The structure of psychological well-being revisited. *Journal of Personality and Social Psychology, 69*(4), 719–727. https://doi.org/10.1037/0022-3514.69.4.719

Safdar, S., Friedlmeier, W., Matsumoto, D., Yoo, S., Kwantes, C., Kakai, H., & Shigemasu, E. (2009). Variations of emotional display rules within and across cultures: A comparison between Canada, USA, and Japan. *Canadian Journal of Behavioural Science, 41*(1), 1–10. https://doi.org/10.1037/a0014387

Salsman, N. L., & Linehan, M. M. (2012). An investigation of the relationships among negative affect, difficulties in emotion regulation, and features of borderline personality disorder. *Journal of Psychopathology and Behavioral Assessment, 34*, 260–267. https://doi.org/10.1007/s10862-012-9275-8

Salzer, S., Pincus, A. L., Winkelbach, C., Leichsenring, F., & Leibing, E. (2011). Interpersonal subtypes and change of interpersonal problems in the treatment of patients with generalized anxiety disorder: A pilot study. *Psychotherapy: Theory, Research, & Practice, 48*(3), 304–310. https://doi.org/10.1037/a0022013

Samios, C., & Khatri, V. (2019). When times get tough: Savoring and relationship satisfaction in couples coping with a stressful life event. *Anxiety, Stress, and Coping, 32*(2), 125–140. https://doi.org/10.1080/10615806.2019.1570804

Sartorius, N., Jablensky, A., Korten, A., Ernberg, G., Anker, M., Cooper, J. E., & Day, R. (1986). Early manifestations and first-contact incidence of schizophrenia in different cultures. A preliminary report on the initial evaluation phase of the WHO Collaborative Study on determinants of outcome of severe mental disorders. *Psychological Medicine, 16*(4), 909–928. https://doi.org/10.1017/s0033291700011910

Schick, M. R., Weiss, N. H., Contractor, A. A., Suazo, N. C., & Spillane, N. S. (2020). Post-traumatic stress disorder's relation with positive and negative emotional avoidance: The moderating role of gender. *Stress and Health, 36*(2), 172–178. https://doi.org/10.1002/smi.2920

Schuster, T. L., Kessler, R. C., & Aseltine, R. H., Jr. (1990). Supportive interactions, negative interactions, and depressed mood. *American Journal of Community Psychology, 18*(3), 423–438. https://doi.org/10.1007/bf00938116

Segal, Z., Williams, M., & Teasdale, J. (2018). *Mindfulness-based cognitive therapy for depression.* Guilford Press.

Seligman, M. E. P. (2011). *Flourish: A visionary new understanding of happiness and well-being.* Free Press.

Senchak, M., & Leonard, K. E. (1992). Attachment styles and marital adjustment among newlywed couples. *Journal of Social and Personal Relationships, 9*(1), 51–64. https://doi.org/10.1177/0265407592091003

Senft, N., Campos, B., Shiota, M. N., & Chentsova-Dutton, Y. E. (2021). Who emphasizes positivity? An exploration of emotion values in people of Latino, Asian, and European heritage living in the United States. *Emotion, 21*(4), 707–719. https://doi.org/10.1037/emo0000737

Sharac, J., McCrone, P., Clement, S., & Thornicroft, G. (2010). The economic impact of mental health stigma and discrimination: A systematic review. *Epidemiology and Psychiatric Sciences, 19*(3), 223–232. https://doi.org/10.1017/s1121189x00001159

Shmueli-Goetz, Y., Target, M., Fonagy, P., & Datta, A. (2008). The Child Attachment Interview: A psychometric study of reliability and discriminant validity. *Developmental Psychology, 44*(4), 939–956. https://doi.org/10.1037/0012-1649.44.4.939

Sichko, S., Borelli, J. L., Rasmussen, H. F., & Smiley, P. A. (2016). Relational closeness moderates the association between maternal overcontrol and children's depressive symptoms. *Journal of Family Psychology, 30*(2), 266–275. https://doi.org/10.1037/fam0000155

Sickel, A. E., Seacat, J. D., & Nabors, N. A. (2014). Mental health stigma update: A review of consequences. *Advances in Mental Health, 12*(3), 202–215. https://doi.org/10.1080/18374905.2014.11081898

Siegel, J. T., & Thomson, A. L. (2016). Positive emotion infusions of elevation and gratitude: Increasing help-seeking intentions among people with heightened levels of depressive symptomatology. *The Journal of Positive Psychology, 12*(6), 509–524. https://doi.org/10.1080/17439760.2016.1221125

Silvia, P. J., & Kwapil, T. R. (2011). Aberrant asociality: How individual differences in social anhedonia illuminate the need to belong. *Journal of Personality, 79*(6), 1315–1332. https://doi.org/10.1111/j.1467-6494.2010.00702.x

Simpson, J. A. (1990). Influence of attachment styles on romantic relationships. *Journal of Personality and Social Psychology, 59*(5), 971–980. https://doi.org/10.1037/0022-3514.59.5.971

Şimşek, O. F. (2013). The relationship between language use and depression: Illuminating the importance of self-reflection, self-rumination, and the need for absolute truth. *The Journal of General Psychology, 140*(1), 29–44. https://doi.org/10.1080/00221309.2012.713407

Slade, A., Aber, J. L., Berger, B., Bresgi, I., & Kaplan, M. (2003). *The parent development interview—revised* [Unpublished manuscript]. Yale Child Study Center, City University of New York.

Smith, J. L., & Bryant, F. B. (2019). Enhancing positive perceptions of aging by savoring life lessons. *Aging & Mental Health, 23*(6), 762–770. https://doi.org/10.1080/13607863.2018.1450840

Smith, J. L., & Hanni, A. A. (2019). Effects of a savoring intervention on resilience and well-being of older adults. *Journal of Applied Gerontology, 38*(1), 137–152. https://doi.org/10.1177/0733464817693375

Smith, J. L., & Hollinger-Smith, L. (2015). Savoring, resilience, and psychological well-being in older adults. *Aging & Mental Health, 19*(3), 192–200. https://doi.org/10.1080/13607863.2014.986647

Smith, J. L., Kim, S., & Bryant, F. B. (2019). Developing savoring interventions for use in multicultural contexts: Bridging the East–West divide. In L. Van Zyl & S. Rothmann Sr. (Eds.), *Positive psychological intervention design and protocols for multi-cultural contexts* (pp. 149–170). Springer. https://doi.org/10.1007/978-3-030-20020-6_7

Spivak, S., Cullen, B., Eaton, W. W., Rodriguez, K., & Mojtabai, R. (2019). Financial hardship among individuals with serious mental illness. *Psychiatry Research, 282*, Article 112632. https://doi.org/10.1016/j.psychres.2019.112632

Srivastava, S., Sharma, H. O., & Mandal, M. K. (2003). Mood induction with facial expressions of emotion in patients with generalized anxiety disorder. *Depression and Anxiety, 18*(3), 144–148. https://doi.org/10.1002/da.10128

Steger, M. F., Frazier, P., Oishi, S., & Kaler, M. (2006). The meaning in life questionnaire: Assessing the presence of and search for meaning in life. *Journal of Counseling Psychology, 53*(1), 80–93. https://doi.org/10.1037/0022-0167.53.1.80

Sternberg, R. M., Nápoles, A. M., Gregorich, S., & Stewart, A. L. (2019). Mentes positivas en acción: Feasibility study of a promotor-delivered cognitive behavioral stress management program for low-income Spanish-speaking Latinas. *Health Equity, 3*(1), 155–161. https://doi.org/10.1089/heq.2019.0012

Straszewski, T., & Siegel, J. T. (2018). Positive emotion infusions: Can savoring increase help-seeking intentions among people with depression? *Applied Psychology. Health and Well-Being, 10*(1), 171–190. https://doi.org/10.1111/aphw.12122

Straszewski, T., & Siegel, J. T. (2020). Differential effects of high- and low-arousal positive emotions on help-seeking for depression. *Applied Psychology. Health and Well-Being, 12*(3), 887–906. https://doi.org/10.1111/aphw.12214

Straszewski, T., & Siegel, J. T. (2021). From writing tasks to a public service announcement: Experimentally assessing savoring as a means of increasing help-seeking for depression. *Social Science & Medicine, 287*, Article 114362. https://doi.org/10.1016/j.socscimed.2021.114362

Suveg, C., Morelen, D., Brewer, G. A., & Thomassin, K. (2010). The emotion dysregulation model of anxiety: A preliminary path analytic examination. *Journal of Anxiety Disorders, 24*(8), 924–930. https://doi.org/10.1016/j.janxdis.2010.06.018

Tackman, A. M., Sbarra, D. A., Carey, A. L., Donnellan, M. B., Horn, A. B., Holtzman, N. S., Edwards, T. S., Pennebaker, J. W., & Mehl, M. R. (2019). Depression, negative emotionality, and self-referential language: A multi-lab, multi-measure, and multi-language-task research synthesis. *Journal of Personality and Social Psychology, 116*(5), 817–834. https://doi.org/10.1037/pspp0000187

Takeuchi, D. T., Alegría, M., Jackson, J. S., & Williams, D. R. (2007). Immigration and mental health: Diverse findings in Asian, Black, and Latino populations. *American Journal of Public Health, 97*(1), 11–12. https://doi.org/10.2105/ajph.2006.103911

Tarbox-Berry, S. I., Perkins, D. O., Woods, S. W., & Addington, J. (2018). Premorbid social adjustment and association with attenuated psychotic symptoms in clinical high-risk and help-seeking youth. *Psychological Medicine, 48*(6), 983–997. https://doi.org/10.1017/s0033291717002343

Tasca, G. A., Ritchie, K., & Balfour, L. (2011). Implications of attachment theory and research for the assessment and treatment of eating disorders. *Psychotherapy: Theory, Research, & Practice, 48*(3), 249–259. https://doi.org/10.1037/a0022423

Taylor, C. T., Lyubomirsky, S., & Stein, M. B. (2017). Upregulating the positive affect system in anxiety and depression: Outcomes of a positive activity intervention. *Depression and Anxiety, 34*(3), 267–280. https://doi.org/10.1002/da.22593

Taylor, C. T., Pearlstein, S. L., Kakaria, S., Lyubomirsky, S., & Stein, M. B. (2020). Enhancing social connectedness in anxiety and depression through amplification of positivity: Preliminary treatment outcomes and process of change.

Cognitive Therapy and Research, 44(4), 788–800. https://doi.org/10.1007/s10608-020-10102-7

Taylor, H. O., Taylor, R. J., Nguyen, A. W., & Chatters, L. (2018). Social isolation, depression, and psychological distress among older adults. *Journal of Aging and Health, 30*(2), 229–246. https://doi.org/10.1177/0898264316673511

Teague, S. J., Gray, K. M., Tonge, B. J., & Newman, L. K. (2017). Attachment in children with autism spectrum disorder: A systematic review. *Research in Autism Spectrum Disorders, 35*, 35–50. https://doi.org/10.1016/j.rasd.2016.12.002

Teague, S. J., Newman, L. K., Tonge, B. J., Gray, K. M., & the MHYPEDD Team. (2020). Attachment and child behaviour and emotional problems in autism spectrum disorder with intellectual disability. *Journal of Applied Research in Intellectual Disabilities, 33*(3), 475–487. https://doi.org/10.1111/jar.12689

Tedeschi, R. G., & Calhoun, L. G. (2004). Posttraumatic growth: Conceptual foundations and empirical evidence. *Psychological Inquiry, 15*(1), 1–18. https://doi.org/10.1207/s15327965pli1501_01

Teplin, L. A. (1984). Criminalizing mental disorder. The comparative arrest rate of the mentally ill. *American Psychologist, 39*(7), 794–803. https://doi.org/10.1037/0003-066x.39.7.794

Tiller, J. M., Sloane, G., Schmidt, U., Troop, N., Power, M., & Treasure, J. L. (1997). Social support in patients with anorexia nervosa and bulimia nervosa. *International Journal of Eating Disorders, 21*(1), 31–38. https://doi.org/10.1002/(sici)1098-108x(199701)21:1%3C31::aid-eat4%3E3.0.co;2-4

Tran, A. N., Ornelas, I. J., Perez, G., Green, M. A., Lyn, M., & Corbie-Smith, G. (2014). Evaluation of Amigas Latinas Motivando el Alma (ALMA): A pilot promotora intervention focused on stress and coping among immigrant Latinas. *Journal of Immigrant and Minority Health, 16*(2), 280–289. https://doi.org/10.1007/s10903-012-9735-y

Treboux, D., Crowell, J. A., & Waters, E. (2004). When "new" meets "old": Configurations of adult attachment representations and their implications for marital functioning. *Developmental Psychology, 40*(2), 295–314. https://doi.org/10.1037/0012-1649.40.2.295

Triandis, H. C. (2001). Individualism–collectivism and personality. *Journal of Personality, 69*(6), 907–924. https://doi.org/10.1111/1467-6494.696169

Tryon, G. S., & Winograd, G. (2011). Goal consensus and collaboration. *Psychotherapy: Theory, Research, & Practice, 48*(1), 50–57. https://doi.org/10.1037/a0022061

Tuck, E. (2009). Suspending damage: A letter to communities. *Harvard Educational Review, 79*(3), 409–428. https://doi.org/10.17763/haer.79.3.n0016675661t3n15

Tugade, M. M., & Fredrickson, B. L. (2004). Resilient individuals use positive emotions to bounce back from negative emotional experiences. *Journal of Personality and Social Psychology, 86*(2), 320–333. https://doi.org/10.1037/0022-3514.86.2.320

Updegraff, K. A., Umaña-Taylor, A. J., Rodríguez De Jesús, S. A., McHale, S. M., Feinberg, M. F., & Kuo, S. I. (2016). Family-focused prevention with Latinos: What about sisters and brothers? *Journal of Family Psychology, 30*(5), 633–640. https://doi.org/10.1037/fam0000200

Uutela, A. (2010). Economic crisis and mental health. *Current Opinion in Psychiatry, 23*(2), 127–130. https://doi.org/10.1097/yco.0b013e328336657d

van IJzendoorn, M. H. (1990). Developments in cross-cultural research on attachment: Some methodological notes. *Human Development, 33*, 3–9. https://doi.org/10.1159/000276498

van IJzendoorn, M. H. (1995). Adult attachment representations, parental responsiveness, and infant attachment: A meta-analysis on the predictive validity of the Adult Attachment Interview. *Psychological Bulletin, 117*(3), 387–403. https://doi.org/10.1037/0033-2909.117.3.387

van IJzendoorn, M. H., & De Wolff, M. S. (1997). In search of the absent father— Meta-analyses of infant–father attachment: A rejoinder to our discussants. *Child Development, 68*(4), 604–609. https://doi.org/10.1111/j.1467-8624.1997.tb04223.x

Veríssimo, M., Santos, A. J., Vaughn, B. E., Torres, N., Monteiro, L., & Santos, O. (2009). Quality of attachment to father and mother and number of reciprocal friends. *Early Child Development and Care, 181*(1), 27–38. https://doi.org/10.1080/03004430903211208

Verona, E., Sprague, J., & Sadeh, N. (2012). Inhibitory control and negative emotional processing in psychopathy and antisocial personality disorder. *Journal of Abnormal Psychology, 121*(2), 498–510. https://doi.org/10.1037/a0025308

Vredeveldt, A., Baddeley, A. D., & Hitch, G. J. (2012). The effects of eye-closure and "ear-closure" on recall of visual and auditory aspects of a criminal event. *Europe's Journal of Psychology, 8*(2), 284–299. https://doi.org/10.5964/ejop.v8i2.472

Waitzkin, H., Getrich, C., Heying, S., Rodríguez, L., Parmar, A., Willging, C., Yager, J., & Santos, R. (2011). Promotoras as mental health practitioners in primary care: A multi-method study of an intervention to address contextual sources of depression. *Journal of Community Health, 36*(2), 316–331. https://doi.org/10.1007/s10900-010-9313-y

Walji, R. (2022). *Connected Parent Journal*. XO Living. https://livingxo.com/connectedparentjournal

Wang, B. A., Bouche, V., Hong, K., Eriksen, D. E., Rice, R., & Borelli, J. L. (2021). Investigating the efficacy of relational savoring among male adolescents in residential treatment. *Residential Treatment for Children & Youth, 38*(3), 307–323. https://doi.org/10.1080/0886571x.2019.1707146

Wang, B. A., Poole, L. Z., & Balderrama-Durbin, C. M. (2022). Effects and mechanisms of a savoring-based single session intervention for partnered individuals. *International Journal of Applied Positive Psychology*, 1–24. https://doi.org/10.1007/s41042-022-00065-3

Waters, E., Crowell, J., Elliott, M., Corcoran, D., & Treboux, D. (2002). Bowlby's secure base theory and the social/personality psychology of attachment styles: Work(s) in progress. *Attachment & Human Development, 4*(2), 230–242. https://doi.org/10.1080/14616730210154216

Watson, D., Clark, L. A., & Tellegen, A. (1988). Development and validation of brief measures of positive and negative affect: The PANAS scales. *Journal of Personality and Social Psychology, 54*(6), 1063–1070. https://doi.org/10.1037/0022-3514.54.6.1063

Watson, D., & Naragon-Gainey, K. (2010). On the specificity of positive emotional dysfunction in psychopathology: Evidence from the mood and anxiety disorders and schizophrenia/schizotypy. *Clinical Psychology Review, 30*(7), 839–848. https://doi.org/10.1016/j.cpr.2009.11.002

Wei, M., Russell, D. W., Mallinckrodt, B., & Zakalik, R. A. (2004). Cultural equivalence of adult attachment across four ethnic groups: Factor structure, structured means, and associations with negative mood. *Journal of Counseling Psychology, 51*(4), 408–417. https://doi.org/10.1037/0022-0167.51.4.408

Whitton, S. W., Weitbrecht, E. M., Kuryluk, A. D., & Bruner, M. R. (2013). Committed dating relationships and mental health among college students. *Journal of American College Health, 61*(3), 176–183. https://doi.org/10.1080/07448481.2013.773903

Williams, D. R., & Williams-Morris, R. (2000). Racism and mental health: The African American experience. *Ethnicity & Health, 5*(3–4), 243–268. https://doi.org/10.1080/713667453

Wilton, R. (2004). Putting policy into practice? Poverty and people with serious mental illness. *Social Science & Medicine, 58*(1), 25–39. https://doi.org/10.1016/s0277-9536(03)00148-5

Wisco, B. E. (2009). Depressive cognition: Self-reference and depth of processing. *Clinical Psychology Review, 29*(4), 382–392. https://doi.org/10.1016/j.cpr.2009.03.003

Woody, S., & Rachman, S. (1994). Generalized anxiety disorder (GAD) as an unsuccessful search for safety. *Clinical Psychology Review, 14*(8), 743–753. https://doi.org/10.1016/0272-7358(94)90040-x

Yap, K., Mogan, C., Moriarty, A., Dowling, N., Blair-West, S., Gelgec, C., & Moulding, R. (2018). Emotion regulation difficulties in obsessive–compulsive disorder. *Journal of Clinical Psychology, 74*(4), 695–709. https://doi.org/10.1002/jclp.22553

Index

A

Absorption, psychological, 156
Abuse, 198–199
Acceptance and commitment therapy, 286
Access to memories, difficulties with, 146–151
Activation, behavioral, 173
Admiration for client, 78
Adult Attachment Interview, 20, 158, 172
Adults
  with eating disorders, 203, 207–212
  interventions with older, 62–67
African American families, 277
Ainsworth, M. D. S., 21, 23, 257, 288
Allen, J. P., 158
Amplification of Positive Activity, 173
Anhedonia, 197
Animals' experiences of being parented, 288
Anorexia nervosa, 207
Anxiety, 152–153, 173, 196, 200
Anxious attachment, 22n2, 44
Arousal, 116
ASD (autism spectrum disorder), 36–37, 202–207
Asian families, 277–279
Asymmetrical relationships, 81, 83
Attachment
  anxious, 22n2, 44
  caregiving/careseeking-related, 72
  dismissing of, 22n1
  insecurity-related, 21–23, 44, 175, 208, 228
  internal working model of, 20, 24–27
  in memories, 80–81
  mental representations of, 25–27
  preoccupied, 22n2
  relationship specificity in, 26
  representations, perspectives, of, 27
  themes of, from positive connectedness memories, 86–91
Attachment avoidance, 55, 56
Attachment models
  cognitive–affective, 20, 25
  internal working, 20, 24–27
  unitary, 26
Attachment needs, 87
Attachment security, 21, 51
Attachment style, 53
Attachment theory, 19–29
Attunement, 21
Autism spectrum disorder (ASD), 36–37, 202–207
Ayduk, O., 159

B

Behavior, help-seeking, 71–73
Behavioral activation, 173
Bereavement, 200. *See also* Grieving
Bidirectional connection, between caregiving and care-receiving, 288–289
Binghamton University, 61
Black families, 277
Borelli, J. L., 260–261
Bowlby, J., 20, 21, 23, 28, 288
Bracho, A., 262

323

Broaden-and-build framework, 29–30, 128
Brown, B., 34, 155
Bryant, F. B., 18, 38
Burkhart, M. L., 56. *See also* Kerr, M. L.
Burnout, 286

C

Calm and reflective stance, 78
Caregivers, 21–24
Caregiving (care-receiving)
  attachment system, 72
  bidirectional connection between, 288–289
  memories, 83
  RS in, 225
Center for Discovery, 261
Centers for Disease Control and Prevention (CDC), 262
Chapman, G. D., 203
Child Attachment Interview, 26
Children
  interventions with, 67–71
  relationships with parents, 81
  with special needs, 202–207
  toddlers, 40–50
Chronic stress, 199
Claremont Graduate University, 72
Client
  selection, 174–181
  therapist's admiration for, 78
Clinical adaptation of RS, 195–217
  adults with eating disorders, 207–212
  and difficulties in savoring, 196–197
  and life stressors, 198–200
  parents of children with special needs, 202–207
  and paucity of positive memories, 197–198
  schizophrenia spectrum disorders, 212–216
Clinical practice, research studies vs., 169–174
Cognitive–affective models, of attachment, 20, 25
Cognitive behavior therapy, 201
Cognitive therapy, 173
Collectivism, individualism vs., 259
Communication savoring, 73
Communities, minoritized, 258–261
Community agencies, 281–283
Community studies, of parents, 50–52
Compassion fatigue, 286
Competence hypothesis, 24

Condensed RS therapy, 264–272
Confía en mí, Confío en ti (therapy), 263
Congruence, cultural, 277–283
Connectedness, 91, 148–149
The Connected Parent Journal (Walji), 190
Control conditions and groups, 35–40, 60–62, 271
Coping Cat, 170
El Corazón de la Comunidad study, 274–277
Costa-Ramalho, S., 52
Couples, 219–256. *See also* Long-distance romantic relationships; Partners; Partners, interventions with
  and insecurity of both partners, 228–256
  and insecurity of one partner, 224–228
COVID-19 pandemic, 286
Craske, M. G., 173
Cultivating the positive, 173
Cultural congruence, 277–283

D

Deactivating emotion regulation strategy, 55
Deployment study, 52–57
Depression, 71–72, 173–174, 196, 200
Difficulties, 145–165
  with access to memories, 146–151
  with elaborate emotional processing, 151–154
  with handling negative emotions, 154–165
  legal, 198
  and resistance, general, 165
  in savoring, 196–197
Discrimination, 199
Dismissing, of attachment, 22n1
Distress, 196–197
Divorce, 198
Domestic violence, 198–199
Duchenne smile, 32
Dyads, 221–224

E

Eating disorders, adults with, 203, 207–212
EFT (emotionally focused therapy), 175
Elaborative emotional processing difficulties, 151–154
Elmo, 87–89
Emotion(s)
  dysregulation of, 200
  negative. *See* Negative emotions
  positive, 29–34, 196–197
  reflection on, 115–125

Emotionally focused therapy (EFT), 175
Emotional resonance, 91–95
Encanto (film), 47
Enhanced Visits Model (EVM), 51–52
Environment, reflective, 151–152
Esposito, G., 37
Evidence base, 35–73
    communication savoring, 73
    community studies, of parents, 50–52
    control condition for, 35–40
    deployment study, 52–57
    Growing Families Study, 40–45
    help-seeking savoring, 71–73
    PARENT Study, 45–50
    Partners Apart Study, 57–61
    Reflections Study, 62–67
    River Stones Study, 67–71
EVM (Enhanced Visits Model), 51–52
Expectation-setting, 78
Experiences in Close Relationships, 68, 172
Extraction of attachment theme, 86–91

F

Facial feedback hypothesis, 31
Familism, 260
Family(-ies). *See also* Couples
    African American, 277
    Asian, 277–279
    systems, 220–224
Females, 279
Fidelity, of intervention, 47
Film-watching study, 31
Financial hardships, 198
Five love languages, 203
Food insecurity, 198
Foster care system, 67, 129
Fraley, R. C., 27
FR behavior, 22–23
Fredrickson, B. L., 29–31
Frightened behavior, 22–23
Functioning, reflective, 50
Future-oriented reflection, 132–139

G

Gaskin, G. E., 37
Goals of therapy, 174, 182–190
Greenberg, Les, 94
Grieving, 201
Growing Families Study, 40–45
Guerra, N., 262

H

Handouts, for brief RS, 265–269
Help-seeking savoring, 71–73
Hesse, E., 22
Heuristics, 20, 28
High-arousal memories, 116
Homework, 191

I

Immediacy, verbal, 158
Immersion, psychological, 158
Individualism, collectivism vs., 259
Individuals, tailoring RS to, 169–193
    client selection for, 174–181
    in research vs. clinical practice, 169–174
    RS between sessions, 190–191
    and therapeutic goals, 182–190
Insecure–ambivalent–resistant attachment, 22
Insecure (insecurity-related) attachment, 21–23, 44, 175, 208, 228
Insecure–avoidant attachment, 21–22, 44
Insecure–disorganized attachment, 22
Insecurity, of partners, 224–256
Internalized attachment response, 23
Internal working model of attachment, 20, 24–27
Intervention(s). *See also* Parents, interventions with; Partners, interventions with
    with children, 67–71
    fidelity of, 47
    with older adults, 62–67
    promotor model of, 50

J

Johnson, S., 175

K

Kaiser Permanente, 190
Kansas Marital Scale, 172
Kansas Parenting Scale, 172
Kendall, P. C., 170
Kerr, M. L., 38, 51. *See also* Burkhart, M. L.
Khatri, V., 52
Kwapil, T. R., 212

L

Lai, J., 213
Latina mothers, 46–47

Latino Health Access (LHA), 261–274
Latinx people, 258–273
Lee, Junh-Ah, 278
Legal difficulties, 198
Levels of Emotional Processing Scale, 94
Levenson, R. W., 31
LHA (Latino Health Access), 50, 261–274
Lieberman, A., 20
Life stressors, 198–200
"Live" RS, 224, 226
Loneliness, 200
Long-distance romantic relationships, 57–62
Love languages, 203
Low-arousal memories, 116
Lower-hanging fruit memories, 85
Lyons-Ruth, K., 23

M

Main, M., 19, 22–23, 158–159
Manualized treatment, 169–170
Martin, E., 213
Maternal care, 21–24
Mayes, L., 20
McAdams, D., 159–160
Meaning-making reflection, 125–132
Memories
    attachment, 80–81
    caregiving, 83
    care-receiving, 83
    connectedness, 80, 148–149
    difficulties with access to, 146–151
    high- vs. low-arousal, 116
    lower-hanging fruit, 85
    role-reversed, 85
    safe haven, 150–151
    secure base, 149–150
Memory reflection, 105–143
    emotion reflection, 115–125
    future-oriented reflection, 132–139
    introduction, to client, 106–108
    meaning-making reflection, 125–132
    nondirective mind-wandering reflection, 139–143
    sensory reflection, 109–115
Memory selection, 77–104, 178–180
    attachment theme extraction, 86–91
    content-based, 81–86
    emotional resonance, 91–95
    introducing RS with the client, 78–79
    memory elicitation, 79–80
    rationale, provided to the client, 95–96
    therapist's approach to, 78
    transcript of a session, 96–104

Mental health populations. *See* Clinical adaptation of RS
Mentalization-based therapy, 256
Miga, A., 158
Military spouses, 52–57
Mindfulness-based cognitive therapy, 173
Mindfulness control condition, 61
Mind-wandering reflection, 139–143
Minoritized communities, 258–261

N

Needs, attachment, 87
Negative emotions
    in clinical populations, 196–197
    common focus on, 18
    in deployment study, 56
    Fredrickson on, 30–32
    in Growing Families Study, 44
    in memory selection/reflection, 160–161
    in mental health populations, 196–197
    in Partners Apart Study, 60–61
    in spoiling, 93–94, 154–165
Nondirective mind-wandering reflection, 139–143
Normativity hypothesis, 23

O

Obsessive–compulsive disorder (OCD), 182, 189, 196
Older adults, interventions with, 62–67

P

Parental care, 21–24
Parent–child relationships, 81, 83
Parent Development Interview, 172
Parenting wellness, 49
Parents
    of children with special needs, 202–207
    relationships with children, 81, 83
    of toddlers, 40–45
Parents, interventions with
    community studies, 50–52
    Growing Families Study, 40–45
    PARENT Study, 45–50
PARENT Study, 45–50
    preliminary outcomes, 47–49
    procedure for, 45–47
    short-term intervention outcomes, 49–50
Partner(s)
    choice of, 28
    as term, 75

Partners, interventions with
  deployment study, 52–57
  Partners Apart Study, 57–61
Pennebaker, J. W., 158–159
Persistent complex bereavement disorder, 200
Personality disorders, 196, 200
Personal savoring, as control condition, 36–38
Perspectives, of attachment representations, 27
Piacentini, J., 182
Pomona College, 262
Pomona Deployment Study, 52–57
Positive affect treatment, 173
Positive and Negative Affect Schedule, 63, 68
Positive connectedness memories, 80
Positive emotion(s), 29–34, 196–197
Positive psychology movement, 18
Positive relational memories, of clinical populations, 197–198
Positivity, 78, 91
Postadoption system, 67, 129
Posttraumatic growth, 156
Preoccupied attachment, 22n2
Pressman, S. D., 32
Promotores de salud, 261–264, 273–274
Prototype perspective, 27
Provision, secure base vs. safe haven, 83
PSAs (public service announcements), 72
Psychological absorption, 156
Psychological immersion, 158
Psychopathology. *See* Clinical adaptation of RS
PTSD (posttraumatic stress disorder), 196, 201
Public service announcements (PSAs), 72

R

Racism, 199
Redemption sequences, 160
Redlands, Calif., 261
Reflections Study, 62–67
Reflective environment, 151–152
Reflective functioning, 50, 51
Relational savoring (RS), 7–11
  at bedtime, 191
  brief, 263–272
  as first-line/second-line approach, 175
  integration into broader treatment plan, 172–173
  mechanisms of, 51

resistance to, 165
between sessions, 190–191
for therapists, 285–289
Relationship(s). *See also* Couples; Family(-ies); Parents; Partner(s)
  current status of, 223
  long-distance, 57–62
  parent–child, 81
  specificity of, in attachment, 26
  symmetrical vs. asymmetrical, 81, 83
Relaxation, 79
Representations, of attachment, 27
Research studies, clinical practice vs., 169–174
Resistance to RS, general, 165
Responsiveness, sensitive, 21–24
Revisionist perspective, 27
River Stones Residential Treatment Facility, 261
River Stones Study, 67–71
Role-reversed memories, 85
Romantic relationships, long-distance, 57–62
RS. *See* Relational savoring
Rumination, 18

S

Safe haven, memories about a, 150–151
Safe haven behavior, 21
Safe haven provision, 83–84, 208
Safe haven receipt, 83–84, 208
Safety, sense of, 200
Samios, C., 52
Santa Ana, Calif., 261
Savoring
  communication, 73
  difficulties in, 196–197
  help-seeking, 71–73
  personal, as control condition, 36–38
  relational, 7–8, 51
  self-distanced, 72
  vicarious, 72
  and well-being, 18–19
Savoring (Bryant), 18
Scaffolding, 153–154
Scales and questionnaires
  Adult Attachment Interview, 20, 158, 172
  Child Attachment Interview, 26
  Experiences in Close Relationships–Relationships Structures Scale, 68
  Experiences in Close Relationships–Revised, 172
  Kansas Marital Scale, 172

Kansas Parenting Scale, 172
Levels of Emotional Processing Scale, 94
Parent Development Interview, 172
Positive and Negative Affect Schedule, 63, 68
Self-Assessment Manikin, 92
Schizophrenia spectrum disorders, 196–197, 212–216
Secure base, memories about a, 149–150
Secure base behavior, 21
Secure base provision, 83, 88, 208
Secure base receipt, 83, 189, 208
Security, attachment, 21, 51
Security priming, 29
Self-Assessment Manikin, 92
Self-distanced savoring, 72
Seligman, M. E. P., 18
Sense of safety, 200
Sensitive responsiveness, 21–24
Sensitivity hypothesis, 23–24
Sensory preferences, 180
Sensory reflection, 109–115
Set points, 26
Siegel, J. T., 72
Simpatía, 259–260
Singapore, 37
Slade, A., 20
Smiles, 32
Social anhedonia, 212–213
Social anxiety, 213
Social connectedness difficulties, 200
Social isolation, 200
Special needs children, 202–207
Specificity, 92–93
Spoiling, 93–94, 154–157, 159–163
Spouses, military, 52–57
Strange Situation Procedure, 24
Straszewski, T., 72
Stream of consciousness, 53–54
Strengths-based approach, 33
Stressors, 198–200
Studies. *See also* Control conditions and groups
   Amplification of Positive Activity, 173
   communication savoring, 73
   community, of parents, 50–52
   El Corazón de la Comunidad, 274–277
   deployment study, 52–57
   film-watching study, 31
   Growing Families Study, 40–45
   help-seeking savoring, 71–73
   PARENT Study, 45–50
   Partners Apart Study, 57–61
   Reflections Study, 62–67
   River Stones Study, 67–71
Substance use disorders, 200
Suchman, N., 20
Symmetrical relationships, 81

T

Theme extraction, attachment, 86–91
Theory of attachment, 19–29
Therapeutic goals, 174, 182–190
Therapy(-ies)
   acceptance and commitment therapy, 286
   cognitive behavior therapy, 201
   cognitive therapy, 173
   Confía en mí, Confío en ti, 263
   emotionally focused therapy, 175
   manualized, 169–170
   mentalizing-based therapy, 256
Toddlers, 40–50. *See also* PARENT Study
Trauma-focused cognitive behavior therapy, 201
Treatment selection guideline, 175, 181
Trust Me, for I Trust You (therapy), 263

U

Uganda, 257
Undoing hypothesis, 31
Unitary model, of attachment, 26
Universality hypothesis, 23
University of California, Irvine, 32, 213, 262
University of California, Los Angeles, 19
University of Wisconsin–Madison, 38, 51

V

Values reflection, 286
van IJzendoorn, M. H., 23
Verbal immediacy, 158
Vicarious savoring, 72

W

Waitlist control groups, 271
Walji, R., 190
Wang, B., 61, 67
Women, 52, 279
Words, emotional depth of, 116

Y

Yale University, 20

About the Author

Jessica L. Borelli, PhD, is a professor of psychological science at the University of California, Irvine. She received her PhD in psychology from Yale University and completed her predoctoral internship at the University of California, Los Angeles Semel Institute for Neuroscience and Human Behavior. Dr. Borelli's work focuses on the intersection of attachment relationships and health, with a particular focus on the impact of relationships on emotion. She has published more than 150 journal articles in her area of interest. In addition to writing journal articles, she enjoys teaching and speaking to the public about the science of relationships. In collaboration with Dr. Stacey Doan, she is the author of a parenting book, *Nature Meets Nurture: Science-Based Strategies for Raising Resilient Kids* (American Psychological Association LifeTools). Alongside her academic work, she is a practicing psychologist specializing in children and families, and is the clinical director of Compass Therapy, a private practice in Newport Beach, California. She lives in Irvine, California, with her husband and three children, with whom she enjoys laughing, singing, and all forms of silliness.